Communications in Computer and Information Science 3085

Series Editors
Gang Li, *School of Information Technology, Deakin University, Burwood, VIC, Australia*
Joaquim Filipe, *Polytechnic Institute of Setúbal, Setúbal, Portugal*
Zhiwei Xu, *Chinese Academy of Sciences, Beijing, China*

Rationale

The CCIS series is devoted to the publication of proceedings of computer science conferences. Its aim is to efficiently disseminate original research results in informatics in printed and electronic form. While the focus is on publication of peer-reviewed full papers presenting mature work, inclusion of reviewed short papers reporting on work in progress is welcome, too. Besides globally relevant meetings with internationally representative program committees guaranteeing a strict peer-reviewing and paper selection process, conferences run by societies or of high regional or national relevance are also considered for publication.

Topics

The topical scope of CCIS spans the entire spectrum of informatics ranging from foundational topics in the theory of computing to information and communications science and technology and a broad variety of interdisciplinary application fields.

Information for Volume Editors and Authors

Publication in CCIS is free of charge. No royalties are paid, however, we offer registered conference participants temporary free access to the online version of the conference proceedings on SpringerLink (http://link.springer.com) by means of an http referrer from the conference website and/or a number of complimentary printed copies, as specified in the official acceptance email of the event.

CCIS proceedings can be published in time for distribution at conferences or as post-proceedings, and delivered in the form of printed books and/or electronically as USBs and/or e-content licenses for accessing proceedings at SpringerLink. Furthermore, CCIS proceedings are included in the CCIS electronic book series hosted in the SpringerLink digital library at http://link.springer.com/bookseries/7899. Conferences publishing in CCIS are allowed to use our online conference service (Meteor) for managing the whole proceedings lifecycle (from submission and reviewing to preparing for publication) free of charge.

Publication process

The language of publication is exclusively English. Authors publishing in CCIS have to sign the Springer CCIS copyright transfer form, however, they are free to use their material published in CCIS for substantially changed, more elaborate subsequent publications elsewhere. For the preparation of the camera-ready papers/files, authors have to strictly adhere to the Springer CCIS Authors' Instructions and are strongly encouraged to use the CCIS LaTeX style files or templates.

Abstracting/Indexing

CCIS is abstracted/indexed in DBLP, Google Scholar, EI-Compendex, Mathematical Reviews, SCImago, Scopus. CCIS volumes are also submitted for the inclusion in ISI Proceedings.

How to start

To start the evaluation of your proposal for inclusion in the CCIS series, please send an e-mail to ccis@springer.com

Raimundas Matulevičius · Tarmo Robal ·
Elena Kornyshova · Anastasija Nikiforova ·
Innar Liiv
Editors

Digital Business and Intelligent Systems

17th International Baltic Conference, Baltic DB&IS
Tartu, Estonia, June 28 – July 1, 2026
Proceedings

Springer

Editors
Raimundas Matulevičius
University of Tartu
Tartu, Estonia

Tarmo Robal
Tallinn University of Technology
Tallinn, Estonia

Elena Kornyshova
Conservatoire National des Arts et Métiers (CNAM)
Paris, France

Anastasija Nikiforova
University of Tartu
Tartu, Estonia

Innar Liiv
Tallinn University of Technology
Tallinn, Estonia

ISSN 1865-0929 ISSN 1865-0937 (electronic)
Communications in Computer and Information Science
ISBN 978-3-032-30862-7 ISBN 978-3-032-30863-4 (eBook)
https://doi.org/10.1007/978-3-032-30863-4

This Springer imprint is published by the registered company Springer Nature Switzerland AG
The registered company address is: Gewerbestrasse 11, 6330 Cham, Switzerland

Preface

We are pleased to welcome you to the proceedings of the 17th edition of the International Baltic Conference on Digital Business and Intelligent Systems (Baltic DB&IS 2026), which took place in Tartu, Estonia, from June 28 – July 1, 2026.

Building on its strong heritage and steadily expanding international reach, Baltic DB&IS provides a vibrant environment for scientists, practitioners, and doctoral students to exchange research findings, discuss emerging trends, and explore transformative ideas shaping modern digital ecosystems. The conference welcomes work spanning conceptual modelling, business process optimisation, intelligent computing, data science, semantic and knowledge technologies, trustworthy and human-centred AI, digital twins, cybersecurity, emerging infrastructures, and other domains where digitalization is reshaping society. Since its first edition in 1994 in Trakai, Lithuania, the conference has been held every second year in one of the three Baltic countries, Lithuania, Latvia, and Estonia. Co-organised by the University of Tartu, Tallinn University of Technology, and Conservatoire National des Arts et Métiers (CNAM), this Baltic DB&IS edition was held at the University of Tartu Delta Center.

The Baltic DB&IS 2026 program included three keynote speeches:

- "From Powerful to Responsible: Rethinking Digital Twin Architectures" by Jelena Zdravkovic, Stockholm University (Sweden),
- "The Enduring Value of Conceptual Modelling - Fundamentally Understanding What We Are Reasoning, Explaining, and Coding About" by Henderik Proper, TU Wien (Austria), and
- "Towards an Era of AI in Data Driven Decision Support - SensusQ's Winning Mind" by Jaan Übi, SensusQ, (Estonia).

In addition, the Doctoral Consortium featured a keynote talk "From Ideas to Impact: Verification, Validation, and Evaluation of Design Artifacts" by Jolita Ralyté from the University of Geneva (Switzerland).

The Baltic DB&IS 2026 conference received 60 submissions, of which 52 were passed to the single-blind peer review process. These were each reviewed by three members of the Program Committee. Twenty papers (an acceptance rate of 38.5%) were selected for presentation at the conference and for inclusion in these proceedings. The papers present original research contributions in the fields of business digitalization and the development of intelligent business systems. Across foundations of information systems engineering, system architectures, and organizational transformation, the contributions examine how digital and intelligent systems are conceived, governed, and evolved in increasingly complex socio-technical environments. They further demonstrate the application of advanced computational methods, from large language models, synthetic data, and computer vision to simulation, digital twins, and predictive analytics, in domains such as education, healthcare, e-government, mobility, and software development. Collectively, the papers highlight a strong emphasis on human-centred design, responsible AI adoption, data quality and privacy, and the integration of intelligent technologies into real-world organizational and societal contexts.

In addition to the main conference, Baltic DB&IS 2026 featured a conference Forum and a Doctoral Consortium. The Baltic DB&IS 2026 Forum provided a platform for researchers and practitioners to present early ideas, ongoing case studies, and exploratory work. The Doctoral Consortium brought together doctoral students working on novel and innovative research into developing reliable, secure, and sustainable systems for digital business and intelligent systems.

The Program Committee of Baltic DB&IS 2026 consisted of 58 members from 23 countries. We are deeply thankful to the Program Committee members for their fair and competent contribution in providing constructive feedback to the authors.

Organizing the conference was a great pleasure, since we had an excellent Organizing Committee. We thank all its members for their time and dedication. Special thanks go to the Baltic DB&IS Steering Committee. Ultimately, we thank all the authors for sharing their research work and all the attendees for their lively participation and fruitful discussions. We hope you will enjoy reading this volume.

May 2026

Raimundas Matulevičius
Tarmo Robal
Elena Kornyshova
Anastasija Nikiforova
Innar Liiv

Organization

General Chairs

Raimundas Matulevičius	University of Tartu, Estonia
Innar Liiv	Tallinn University of Technology, Estonia

Program Committee Chairs

Tarmo Robal	Tallinn University of Technology, Estonia
Anastasija Nikiforova	University of Tartu, Estonia
Elena Kornyshova	Conservatoire National des Arts et Métiers France

Doctoral Consortium Chairs

Mubashar Iqbal	University of Tartu, Estonia
Diana Kalibatienė	Vilnius Gediminas Technical University, Lithuania

Steering Committee

Janis Bubenko (honorary member) (1935-2022)	Royal Institute of Technology and Stockholm University, Sweden
Arne Sølvberg (honorary member)	Norwegian University of Science and Technology, Norway
Guntis Arnicāns	University of Latvia, Latvia
Juris Borzovs	University of Latvia, Latvia
Gintautas Dzemyda	Vilnius University, Lithuania
Jānis Grundspeņķis	Riga Technical University, Latvia
Hele-Mai Haav	Tallinn University of Technology, Estonia
Diana Kalibatienė	Vilnius Gediminas Technical University, Lithuania
Mārīte Kirikova	Riga Technical University, Latvia
Innar Liiv	Tallinn University of Technology, Estonia

Audronė Lupeikienė	Vilnius University, Lithuania
Raimundas Matulevičius	University of Tartu, Estonia
Tarmo Robal	Tallinn University of Technology, Estonia

Program Committee

Lylia Abrouk	University of Burgundy, France
Alla Anohina-Naumeca	Riga Technical University, Latvia
Guntis Arnicāns	University of Latvia, Latvia
Romas Baronas	Vilnius University, Lithuania
Judith Barrios Albornoz	University of the Andes, Venezuela
Justyna Berniak-Woźny	Systems Research Institute, Polish Academy of Sciences, Poland
Zane Bicevska	University of Latvia, Latvia
Stefano Bonnini	University of Ferrara, Italy
Juris Borzovs	University of Latvia, Latvia
Antoine Bossard	Kanagawa University, Japan
Robert Andrei Buchmann	Babeş-Bolyai University of Cluj-Napoca, Romania
Vytautas Čyras	Vilnius University, Lithuania
Rebecca Deneckere	Université de Paris 1 Panthéon-Sorbonne, France
Flavius Frasincar	Erasmus University Rotterdam, the Netherlands
Johann Gamper	Free University of Bozen-Bolzano, Italy
Giovanni Giachetti	Universitat Politècnica de València, Spain
Jānis Grabis	Riga Technical University, Latvia
Jānis Grundspenkis	Riga Technical University, Latvia
Yash Gupta	University of Southern California, USA
Hele-Mai Haav	Tallinn University of Technology, Estonia
Martin Henkel	Stockholm University, Sweden
Jaromír Hrad	Czech Technical University in Prague, Czech Republic
Mirjana Ivanovic	University of Novi Sad, Serbia
Maksims Ivanovs	University of Latvia/ Institute of Electronics and Computer Science, Latvia
Hannu Jaakkola	Tampere University, Finland
Gideon Mekonnen Jonathan	Stockholm University, Sweden
Marcelo Karanik	CETINIA - Rey Juan Carlos University, Spain
Mārīte Kirikova	Riga Technical University, Latvia
Olga Kurasova	Vilnius University, Lithuania
Dejan Lavbič	University of Ljubljana, Slovenia
Martin Lněnička	Univerzita Pardubice, Czech Republic

Audronė Lupeikienė	Vilnius University, Lithuania
José Machado	University of Minho, Portugal
Virginijus Marcinkevičius	Vilnius University, Lithuania
Saulius Maskeliūnas	Vilnius University, Lithuania
Laila Niedrite	University of Latvia, Latvia
Oscar Pastor	Universitat Politècnica de València, Spain
Marinella Petrocchi	IIT-CNR, Italy
Gunnar Piho	Tallinn University of Technology, Estonia
Olivier Pons	CNAM, France
Jolita Ralyté	University of Geneva, Switzerland
Ben Roelens	Open Universiteit/Ghent University, the Netherlands/Belgium
José Raúl Romero	University of Córdoba, Spain
Bruno Rossi	Masaryk University, Czech Republic
Gunter Saake	University of Magdeburg, Germany
Camille Salinesi	Université Paris 1 Panthéon-Sorbonne, France
Kurt Sandkuhl	University of Rostock, Germany
Christoph G. Schuetz	Johannes Kepler University Linz, Austria
Michal Smialek	Warsaw University of Technology, Poland
Luiz Angelo Steffenel	Université de Reims Champagne-Ardenne, France
Janis Stirna	Stockholm University, Sweden
Vjeran Strahonja	University of Zagreb, Croatia
Dimitrios Symeonidis	University of Tartu, Estonia
Marek Szelągowski	Systems Research Institute, Polish Academy of Sciences, Poland
Kuldar Taveter	University of Tartu, Estonia
Bastian Tenbergen	State University of New York at Oswego, USA
Damjan Vavpotič	University of Ljubljana, Slovenia
Robert Wrembel	Poznań University of Technology, Poland

Forum Program Committee

Lylia Abrouk	University of Burgundy, France
Alla Anohina-Naumeca	Riga Technical University, Latvia
Judith Barrios Albornoz	University of the Andes, Venezuela
Justyna Berniak-Woźny	Systems Research Institute, Polish Academy of Sciences, Poland
Zane Bicevska	University of Latvia, Latvia
Jan Bosch	Chalmers University of Technology, Sweden
Lukas Daubner	University of Tartu, Estonia
Olga Fragou	Hellenic Open University, Greece

Hyoil Han	Illinois State University, USA
Hasan Koç	Berlin International University of Applied Sciences, Germany
Ginta Majore	Riga Technical University, Latvia
Jānis Pekša	Riga Technical University, Latvia
Olivier Pons	CNAM, France
Asta Slotkienė	Vilnius University, Lithuania
Luiz Angelo Steffenel	Université de Reims Champagne-Ardenne, France

Doctoral Consortium Mentors

Guntis Arnicāns	University of Latvia, Latvia
Jānis Grabis	Riga Technical University, Latvia
Nikolaj Goranin	Vilnius Gediminas Technical University, Lithuania
Saulius Gudas	Vilnius University, Klaipėda University, Lithuania
Orlenys López-Pintado	University of Tartu, Estonia
Naveed Muhammad	University of Tartu, Estonia
Gunnar Piho	Tallinn University of Technology, Estonia
Kurt Sandkuhl	University of Rostock, Germany
Irina Vinogradova-Zinkevič	Vilnius Gediminas Technical University, Lithuania

Additional Reviewers

Davide Di Pierro
Mubashar Iqbal
Sajad Karim
Maryam Mozaffari
Sana Nadouri
Linda Rosenkron
Eike Schallehn

From Powerful to Responsible: Rethinking Digital Twin Architectures

Jelena Zdravkovic

Stockholm University, Sweden
jelenaz@dsv.su.se

Digital Twins have been promoted as a wonder of digital innovation, promising unique capabilities to observe, predict, and optimise complex real-world systems. By digitally replicating physical entities, processes, and environments, Digital Twins integrate heterogeneous data streams, track system dynamics in real time, explore alternative futures, and support decision-making across various domains such as healthcare, industry, and critical infrastructures. These capabilities depend on intensive data processing and, today, rely on artificial intelligence and machine learning models to generate predictions and recommendations.

As Digital Twins evolve from passive representations to closed-loop systems, they also become actors of the systems they mirror. Through feedback loops, Digital Twins influence decisions and interventions that reshape the physical world, often with direct consequences for human actors. Therefore, optimisation alone is no longer a sufficient design objective. When Digital Twins learn, act, and adapt, questions of responsibility cannot be treated as a post-hoc concern.

This keynote argues that Digital Twin architectures need to be by responsible by design. Many current solutions produce excellent outcomes, but fail to make explicit how those outcomes are derived, who is accountable for them, and how harmful or unintended effects can be anticipated and corrected. A responsible Digital Twin must therefore go beyond accuracy and performance. It must be traceable, explainable, corrective, and preventive—not only accountable for its actions, but designed with foresight, ownership, and ethical self-direction. Grounded on information systems engineering and responsible AI, the keynote proposes architectural principles for Digital Twins that can be trusted not only because they work, but because they can act rightly, be understood, traced, and when necessary - governed.

The Enduring Value of Conceptual Modelling - Fundamentally Understanding What We Are Reasoning, Explaining, and Coding About

Henderik Proper

TU Wien, Austria
henderik.proper@tuwien.ac.at

Conceptual modelling, as a discipline, originated primarily from the field of database design. Its early development was driven by a need to clarify what a database system must "know" about the world, independent of any technology-specific implementation details. We argue, however, that the value of conceptual modelling extends far beyond database design. Conceptual models (including domain ontologies) enable us to explicitly articulate and discuss our understanding of a domain, whether existing, desired, or envisioned, in terms of the involved "things" and their relationships. More specifically, we maintain that, just as logic has given us discipline in how we reason, conceptual modelling can give us more discipline in clarifying and agreeing on what we are reasoning about (and likewise what we are talking, AI-explaining or coding about).

At the same time, within information systems engineering (including database and software engineering), the role of conceptual modelling appears increasingly "under threat". The rise of agile software development, with its emphasis on "coding over documenting over modelling," seems to suggest a reduced need for modelling. Furthermore, large language models are now frequently used to help generate models themselves. This raises an important question: Does conceptual modelling still have a role to play?

We strongly argue that it does. In particular, when it comes to clarifying and aligning our understanding of what we are reasoning about. We will argue the point "ViA RoME". RoME refers to the concept of Return on Modelling Effort. Since creating conceptual models requires effort, it is reasonable to ensure that this effort aligns with the expected benefits. The ViA idea emphasises that models derive value only in action; i.e. when they are created and/or used. Together, these concepts offer a cost-benefit perspective on the creation and use of conceptual models.

Using the ViA RoME perspective as a guiding framework, we illustrate several situations in which conceptual models continue to play a vital role, including:

- *Enabling ownership* - Helping stakeholders take ownership of the concepts and rules embedded in code or in trained sub-symbolic AI systems.
- *Explaining beyond explainable* - Providing meaningful explanations of the behaviour or outputs of AI-driven systems (or any complex software-intensive system) demands

a shared terminology and mutual understanding between the explainer and the explainee.
- *Do you mean interoperability?* - We live in an interconnected world, and both human and digital (including AI-based) actors require a shared (and thus explicit) understanding in order to interoperate effectively.

Towards an Era of AI in Data Driven Decision Support - SensusQ's Winning Mind

Jaan Übi

SensusQ, Estonia
jaan.ubi@ut.ee

The two constraints facing the dual-usage decision support automation agent, when compared to yesterday, have remained unchanged. Firstly, in an adversarial situation, both parties have equal amounts of one resource, namely, time. Secondly, regarding cognitive overload, once data collection is in place, the fact remains that, as we take OSINT (Open Source Intelligence, e.g., X/Twitter or Telegram) clues, for example, in established worst-case situations, critical information has taken approximately two weeks to surface in the public domain. This processing stigmergy, evident in the inverse of information cascades from a distributed collective filtering process, owes a lot to the large number of participants scanning the information. But what if the discovery is even more complex, stemming from the combinations with other, importantly, proprietary "intelligence's" - signals intelligence, human intelligence, image intelligence, geo intelligence, etc.? How to create a data-driven decision support tool for such a purpose?

SensusQ puts forth an AI solution that, having its primary constituents named after the functions in the human brain, solves the problem by addressing the central, top-down, information processing requirements, and by discovering, bottom-up, the "unknown-unknowns" (or things we don't know that we don't know). Winning Mind has fast, slow, memory and executive AI streams that adhere to the constraints and provide the solution.

From Ideas to Impact: Verification, Validation, and Evaluation of Design Artifacts

Jolita Ralyté

University of Geneva, Switzerland
jolita.ralyte@unige.ch

Design-oriented research in digital systems increasingly produces artifacts- methods, models, languages, frameworks, and tools-intended to address real-world problems. Yet, a recurring weakness in doctoral research lies not in the creativity of the proposed artifacts, but in the rigor and clarity of their assessment. Too often, verification, validation, and evaluation are treated as interchangeable terms, reduced to a single "evaluation section", or postponed to the very end of a PhD project.

This talk will argue that every scientific contribution must undergo multiple, distinct levels of assessment, and that verification, validation, and evaluation (VVE) should be explicitly planned as part of a PhD research agenda, not added as an afterthought. Drawing on extensive experience in method engineering and the development of modeling methods, the talk will clarify the meaning, purpose, and complementarity of verification ("am I building the artifact right?"), validation ("am I building the right artifact?"), and evaluation ("is the artifact worthwhile in practice?"). Building on a recent expert-voice article and related work in design science research and quality evaluation frameworks, the talk will illustrate how VVE activities evolve over time, how they align with iterative and incremental research, and how they can be realistically conducted within doctoral constraints. Examples from the development of modeling and method artifacts will be used to highlight common pitfalls, trade-offs, and good practices.

The talk aims to equip PhD students with conceptual clarity, practical guidance, and realistic expectations regarding assessment, empowering them to argue more convincingly for the scientific value and credibility of their research contributions.

Contents

Digitalization and Intelligent Systems for Organisations

Foundations, Methods, and Systems Engineering

Information Systems Engineering: A Journey Through Half a Century of History

Roberto Cortes Morales[1], Carine Souveyet[2], and Rébecca Deneckère[2](✉)

[1] Instituto Technologico de Costa Rica, Cartago, Costa Rica
rcortes@itcr.ac.cr
[2] Centre de Recherche en Informatique, Université Paris 1 Panthéon-Sorbonne, Paris, France
{souveyet,denecker}@univ-paris1.fr

Abstract. Information Systems Engineering (ISE) has evolved over more than five decades at the intersection of database systems, conceptual modeling, and organizational information systems. While many studies examine specific streams such as process management or digital transformation, fewer reconstruct the longitudinal evolution of ISE as an engineering discipline. We present a bibliographic analysis covering 1971–2023, based on a corpus of 24,651 publications authored by 130 contributors identified across major engineering-oriented venues, including DB&IS. Bibliometric mapping and keyword clustering are used to identify structural shifts in dominant research themes. The segmentation into four periods is derived from observable reconfigurations of thematic clusters. The results highlight a progressive transformation of ISE along two dimensions: increasing technical integration depth and expanding organizational-societal scope. The field evolved from data-centered conceptual modeling and database schema design toward semantic interoperability, process-aware and service-oriented architectures, enterprise-wide infrastructures, and AI-driven systems. In parallel, methodological concerns shifted from formal method engineering to adaptive and socio-technical frameworks. By articulating these developments within a two-dimensional interpretative framework, the study clarifies the historical trajectory of ISE and outlines emerging modeling and architectural challenges.

Keywords: Information System Engineering · Literature review · Research agenda

1 Introduction

Over the past five decades, Information Systems Engineering has evolved at the intersection of two closely related but distinct domains: software engineering and information systems management. Software engineering primarily focuses on the technical construction of software artifacts, including programming, architectures, and development processes. In contrast, information systems management addresses the organizational use of information technologies, their alignment with business objectives, and their impact on decision-making and performance. Between these two domains, ISE looks at the

R. Matulevičius et al. (Eds.): DB&IS 2026, CCIS 3085, pp. 3–19, 2026.
https://doi.org/10.1007/978-3-032-30863-4_1

systematic engineering of information systems as socio-technical artifacts, combining technical design with organizational and contextual considerations.

This intermediate position is reflected in the dual understanding of both Information Systems (IS) and Information Systems Engineering. From a narrow perspective, an information system can be viewed as a technical construct composed of interconnected applications and IT resources designed to collect, store, process, and distribute information. Correspondingly, ISE in a narrow sense focuses on software-oriented concerns, such as development processes, modeling languages, and technical architectures. From a broader perspective, however, an information system is conceived as an organizational object embedded in its environment, supporting business processes, involving multiple stakeholders, and contributing to organizational goals. In this broader sense, ISE encloses a wide range of concerns, including requirements engineering, conceptual and enterprise modeling, process engineering, data and knowledge engineering, as well as quality, security, and alignment issues [1, 2]. Alternative perspectives consider information systems as sets of information processes occurring across both natural and artificial environments, sometimes described as cyber-physical-social systems. While this broader view expands the conceptual scope of information systems, the present study focuses on engineered information systems as socio-technical artifacts situated within organizational and societal contexts.

Despite the maturity of the field, the long-term evolution of ISE research remains difficult to apprehend as a whole. Existing surveys and reviews have predominantly focused on specific subdomains, such as conceptual modeling, process management, business intelligence, or digital transformation [3–5]. While these studies provide in-depth insights into particular research streams, they offer only a partial view of how ISE has evolved as an engineering discipline situated between software construction and information systems management. More broadly, the Information Systems field is often described as fragmented, drawing on multiple reference disciplines and research traditions, which further complicates the identification of coherent long-term trends [6].

This paper addresses this gap by proposing a longitudinal analysis of ISE research spanning the period from 1971 to 2023. The study adopts a large-scale bibliographic approach grounded in a systematic selection of major Information Systems conferences and a set of key contributors whose work has had a sustained impact on the field. By analyzing the evolution of dominant research themes across successive periods, the paper aims to characterize how ISE has continuously repositioned itself between software-oriented and organizational concerns, and how its scope has progressively expanded from a primarily technical focus toward broader organizational and societal dimensions. The methodological choices are informed by established practices in historical and bibliographic research in Information Systems [7, 8].

The paper makes three contributions. It provides a structured historical perspective on the evolution of Information Systems Engineering across four major periods, analyzes the shift between narrow and broad perspectives of ISE over time, and discusses emerging research challenges including sustainability, user well-being, ethical concerns, and adaptive systems [9, 10].

By offering a comprehensive and longitudinal view of the field, this study contributes to a clearer understanding of the role of Information Systems Engineering as a central discipline connecting software engineering and information systems management. It aims to support researchers in positioning their work within the evolving landscape of ISE and to identify future research directions.

2 Research Approach

We defined two main research questions: RQ1: How has Information Systems Engineering research evolved over time? RQ2: What emerging engineering and societal challenges currently shape Information Systems Engineering?

This study adopts a longitudinal bibliographic approach to examine the evolution of Information Systems Engineering from 1971 to 2023. The year 2023 was selected as the upper bound to ensure data completeness and bibliographic stability in DBLP indexing. Including more recent years would have introduced partial publication records and unstable citation patterns, potentially affecting the robustness of the longitudinal bibliometric analysis. The corpus construction followed a structured process, summarized in Fig. 1.

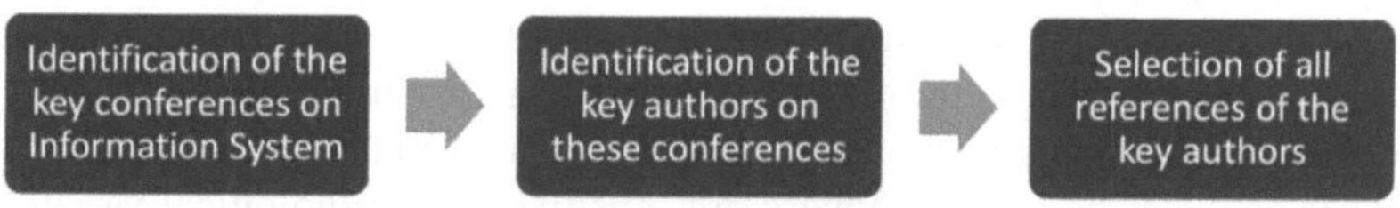

Fig. 1. Corpus Construction Process

We first selected major CORE-ranked A and B conferences that have historically contributed to the development of ISE, including CAiSE, RCIS, and DB&IS (see Appendix A). The objective was to capture research streams representative of the engineering-oriented segment of the IS field rather than the entire IS discipline.

From these venues, authors with at least ten publications were identified, resulting in an initial pool of 285 researchers. A second filtering step retained authors with a cumulative minimum of 25 publications across these venues, ensuring the inclusion of stable and influential contributors while limiting occasional participation. This process led to a final set of 130 authors (see Appendix B).

All publications indexed in DBLP for these authors between 1971 and 2023 were then collected, yielding a corpus of 24,651 records. This approach prioritizes longitudinal coherence over exhaustiveness by focusing on sustained contributors within influential venues. The temporal segmentation into four periods (1971–1999, 2000–2009, 2010–2019, 2020–2023) was derived from observable structural shifts in keyword clusters rather than arbitrary chronological boundaries.

Bibliometric analysis was conducted using VosViewer[1] to identify clusters of co-occurring keywords within each period. The minimum keyword occurrence threshold was adjusted according to publication density, ranging from 2 in earlier periods to 40 in

[1] https://www.vosviewer.com/

more recent ones. Lower thresholds ensured visibility of emerging themes in smaller corpora, while higher thresholds prevented visual saturation in later periods. This calibration preserved interpretability while allowing consistent intra-period comparison.

Cluster evolution was assessed comparatively by examining changes in keyword prominence and inter-term connectivity. The quantitative mapping was complemented by qualitative interpretation grounded in the conceptual foundations of ISE, enabling identification of structural transformations in technical and methodological orientations. The spatial layout of the VOSviewer maps does not correspond to predefined semantic axes. The relative positions of nodes reflect co-occurrence proximity, where shorter distances indicate stronger associations between terms. The orientation of the maps (e.g., north-south or east-west) does not carry intrinsic meaning, while clusters are identified through color coding.

Threats to Validity. A first threat concerns source selection. The study focuses on major IS conferences and on authors with sustained publication activity in these venues. While this ensures that the analysis is grounded in influential research, it may exclude contributions published elsewhere and underrepresent emerging or disruptive topics from newer communities or early-stage researchers. This limitation was mitigated by retrieving the complete publication records of selected authors. Compared with keyword-based corpus construction, the author-centered strategy provides greater longitudinal stability despite favoring structurally stable trends over frontier topics.

A second threat relates to the construction and interpretation of research themes. Bibliometric analyses based on keyword are sensitive to terminological variations and evolving vocabularies over time. Concepts may appear under different labels across periods, which can affect the visibility of certain research streams. To reduce this risk, the quantitative results produced by VosViewer were systematically interpreted in conjunction with qualitative analysis grounded in established concepts of ISE, allowing themes to be consolidated and interpreted at an appropriate level of abstraction.

A third threat concerns the temporal segmentation of the analysis. The definition of time periods inevitably involves subjective choices and may influence the identification of trends and transitions. The periods used in this study were defined based on observed shifts in dominant technologies, methods, and research practices rather than on arbitrary chronological boundaries. Nonetheless, alternative segmentations could lead to different interpretations of the evolution of the field.

Finally, the longitudinal nature of the study favors the identification of dominant and persistent research trends, potentially underrepresenting short-lived or emerging topics that have not yet achieved widespread adoption. While this bias is inherent to retrospective analyses, it is consistent with the objective of characterizing the structural evolution of Information Systems Engineering over several decades.

3 Related Works

The evolution of Information Systems research has been examined from multiple perspectives over the past decades. A major contribution is the fiftieth anniversary survey published in Management Science, which provides a comprehensive overview of IS research themes and intellectual trajectories over five decades [11]. While this work synthesizes the development of IS as a discipline, it primarily emphasizes managerial and organizational perspectives rather than the structural evolution of ISE.

The engineering dimension of IS has been more explicitly developed within specialized venues such as CAiSE, RCIS, and DB&IS. In particular, CAiSE has historically played a foundational role in shaping research on conceptual modeling, method engineering, and enterprise modeling. Early and influential contributions on requirements engineering and method engineering, notably by Colette Rolland and collaborators, established systematic approaches to modeling organizational needs and aligning them with system design [12, 13]. These works significantly contributed to positioning ISE as a discipline concerned not only with technical artifacts but also with structured modeling of organizational intentions and contexts. In parallel, ontological and representation-based analyses of conceptual models [2, 14] reinforced the theoretical foundations of modeling in ISE. Business process management and workflow research, strongly represented within CAiSE and related communities, further expanded the field toward execution, verification, and analysis of processes [4, 15]. Enterprise architecture research [16] consolidated the enterprise-level perspective, bridging data, processes, and organizational structures. RCIS has extended this engineering tradition by addressing research challenges in enterprise information systems, service orientation, and digital transformation, while maintaining a strong emphasis on modeling rigor and business - IT alignment. Similarly, DB&IS has provided a platform for database-centered and modeling-oriented research, including schema evolution, semantic integration, and enterprise information systems engineering.

Importantly, several authors identified as key contributors in our longitudinal corpus (such as Rolland, van der Aalst, Mendling, Reichert, Krogstie, and Guizzardi) have contributed substantially to these venues over extended periods. Their research trajectories illustrate the progressive expansion of ISE from data modeling and method engineering toward process management, enterprise architecture, and digital and data-intensive systems. This continuity across authors and venues supports the relevance of focusing on these communities to analyze the structural evolution of the field.

While numerous surveys have examined individual research streams such as conceptual modeling [2], business process management [4], analytics [3], and digital transformation [5], few studies adopt a longitudinal perspective centered explicitly on ISE as a discipline positioned between software engineering and IS management.

The present study addresses this gap through three complementary contributions. First, it constructs an author-centered longitudinal corpus grounded in sustained scholarly trajectories within key engineering-oriented venues. Second, it derives temporal segmentation from structural shifts in keyword clusters rather than from arbitrary chronological boundaries. Third, it interprets these shifts through a two-dimensional analytical framework capturing both technical integration depth and organizational-societal scope. Together, these elements provide a structured and historically grounded reconstruction of ISE as an evolving engineering discipline.

4 Information System Evolution

The longitudinal distribution of publications indicates a clear expansion of research activity in Information Systems Engineering. As illustrated in Fig. 2, the number of publications grows steadily from the 1970s, with marked acceleration after 2000. This increase coincides with major technological transitions and the emergence of new research themes, suggesting that the quantitative growth of the field is closely linked to structural transformations in its technical and methodological foundations.

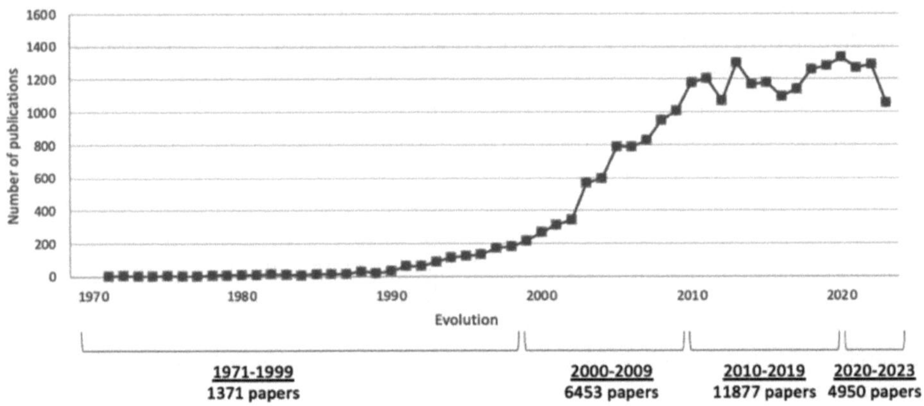

Fig. 2. Publications Evolution

This study contributes not only by describing historical shifts, but by proposing a conceptual framework for understanding ISE evolution along two structural dimensions: technical integration depth and organizational-societal scope.

4.1 1971–1999: From Data-Centered Modeling to Workflow and Method Engineering

The period from 1971 to 1999 corresponds to the foundational stage of Information Systems Engineering. The bibliometric clusters presented in Fig. 3 reveal the dominance of data-centered modeling, database technologies, and the early structuring of development methodologies. This phase established the technical and methodological foundations upon which subsequent transformations would build.

Technical Perspective: Databases, EDI, and Group Support Systems. From a technical standpoint, this period was strongly dominated by database technologies and conceptual data modeling. The Entity–Relationship model [17] and fact-oriented approaches such as NIAM and Object-Role Modeling [18] provided systematic methods for designing semantically grounded database schemas. Research focused on schema design, normalization, integrity constraints, and abstraction mechanisms, reinforcing a narrow, representation-centered view of ISE. Beyond centralized databases, Electronic Data Interchange (EDI) extended data exchange across organizational boundaries, raising challenges of interoperability and standardization. In parallel, Group Support Systems (GSS) addressed collaborative decision-making and shared data environments, introducing concerns related to coordination, concurrency, and human interaction. Together, databases, EDI, and GSS progressively expanded the technical scope of ISE from isolated data structures to distributed and collaborative systems.

Fig. 3. 1971–1999

Methodological Perspective: Data Dimension, Workflow, and Early Method Engineering. This period was characterized by a strong emphasis on the data dimension. There were two main objectives: defining data-centered metamodels and methodologies for schema design, and formalizing knowledge about the real world through structured conceptual models [17, 18]. This reinforced modeling rigor and semantic clarity. As system complexity increased, abstraction management became central. Schema evolution and integration addressed consistency across multiple abstraction layers and heterogeneous models. At the same time, workflow models introduced a dynamic process perspective, complementing static data representations and preparing the ground for later process-oriented research. Early Method Engineering emerged, focusing on the formalization of metamodels and structured development methodologies [12, 13]. This period remained centered on internal system coherence and formal representation, with limited explicit consideration of broader societal implications.

4.2 2000–2009: Semantic Integration and Service-Oriented Architectures

This period marks a transition from isolated data structures toward semantically enriched and service-oriented systems. Ontology modeling, process management, and service composition emerge as central clusters (Fig. 4). It reflects increasing technical integration and a shift toward interoperability and architectural modularity.

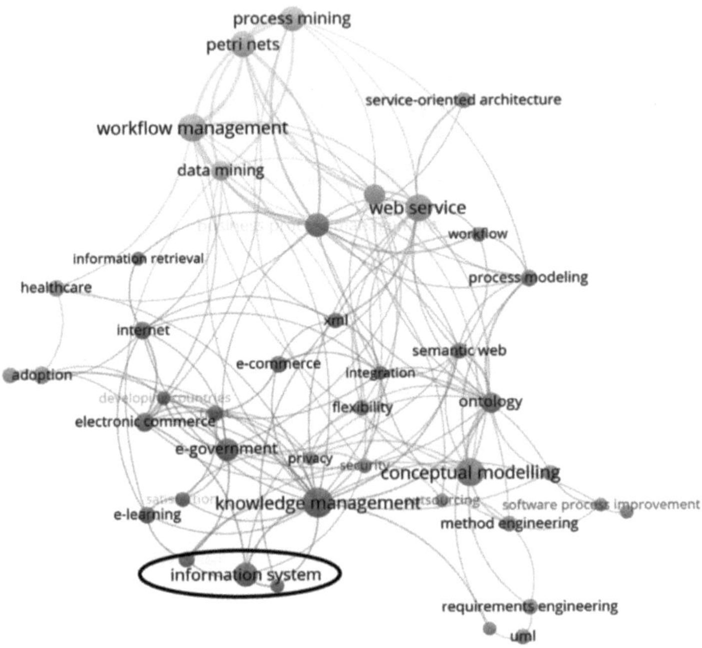

Fig. 4. 2000–2009

Technical Perspective: Semantic Web, Process Mining, and Service Oriented Architectures (SOA). Research extended traditional database models toward semantic integration. The emergence of the Semantic Web introduced ontology-based knowledge representation and machine-interpretable data [19]. Ontologies became key instruments for addressing heterogeneity across distributed systems. At the same time, Business Process Management matured as a research domain. Workflow models were complemented by formal analysis techniques, including Petri Nets, and by data-driven approaches such as process mining, which enabled the discovery and monitoring of real organizational processes from event logs [20]. SOA further transformed system design by promoting loosely coupled service composition instead of monolithic applications [21]. This reconfiguration emphasized interoperability and modular integration within distributed infrastructures.

Methodological Perspective: Adaptation, Requirements, and Agility. This period is characterized by increasing flexibility. Method Engineering evolved toward configuration and customization, allowing development processes to be adapted to project contexts rather than prescribed uniformly [22]. Requirements Engineering gained renewed prominence, particularly goal-oriented approaches that strengthened traceability between organizational objectives and system design [12, 23]. In parallel, agile methodologies introduced iterative and incremental development practices [24], challenging rigid lifecycle models. The methodological focus shifted from formal structuring alone toward adaptability and alignment within dynamic organizational environments. This phase reflects a transition from modeling stability to integration and flexibility. Technical integration depth increased through semantic interoperability and service composition, while organizational scope expanded through stronger alignment between business objectives and system design.

4.3 2010–2019: Enterprise Integration and Data-Intensive Systems

Between 2010 and 2019, Information Systems Engineering expanded toward enterprise-wide infrastructures and data-intensive environments. The clusters displayed in Fig. 5 highlight the prominence of Big Data, cloud computing, IoT, and digital transformation. This period is characterized by architectural intensification and deeper integration across organizational boundaries.

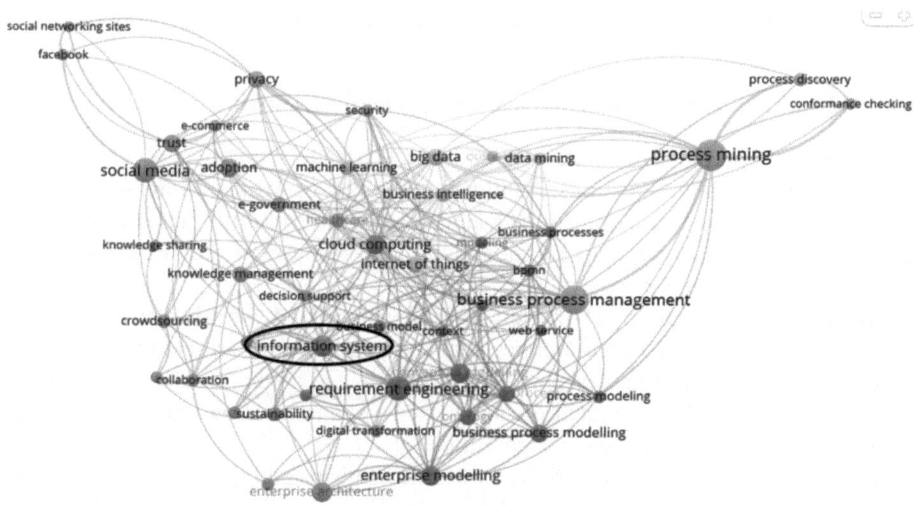

Fig. 5. 2010–2019

Technical Perspective: Big Data, Cloud, IoT, and Intelligent Systems. The rise of Big Data introduced large-scale data processing and advanced analytics as core components of enterprise systems [3]. Machine learning techniques became increasingly integrated into operational architectures, supporting large-scale data analysis and predictive capabilities. These developments marked an early integration of artificial intelligence methods into information systems, preceding their central architectural role in later periods. Cloud computing transformed infrastructure deployment by enabling scalable, distributed platforms [25], while the Internet of Things extended IS into cyber-physical environments [26]. These developments increased architectural complexity and reinforced interoperability and governance challenges. Process mining matured and incorporated predictive capabilities [4], further embedding data-driven insights into process management. Technical integration depth significantly increased during this period. Social media also emerged as a significant cluster, reflecting the growing importance of user-generated data and large-scale interaction platforms in socio-technical ecosystems.

Methodological Perspective: Enterprise Modeling and Digital Transformation. Methodologically, enterprise modeling regained central importance as organizations sought holistic representations of processes, capabilities, and architectures [16, 27]. Information systems were increasingly positioned as enablers of digital transformation and strategic innovation [5, 28].

Development approaches therefore expanded beyond system construction toward enterprise alignment and transformation management. The focus shifted from isolated system design to coordinated, organization-wide engineering frameworks. This period marks a significant intensification of technical integration depth, with data-intensive and cloud-based infrastructures embedding analytics directly into system behavior. In parallel, the scope of ISE broadened toward enterprise-wide transformation, positioning information systems as strategic enablers rather than merely operational supports.

4.4 2020–2023: Artificial Intelligence and Societal-Oriented Systems

The most recent period, from 2020 to 2023, reflects both technological acceleration and expansion of societal implications. As illustrated in Fig. 6, Artificial Intelligence forms dense and central clusters alongside blockchain and sustainability-related themes. This phase signals increasing system autonomy and a broadening of the discipline's scope beyond organizational contexts.

Technical Perspective: AI-Driven and Decentralized Architectures. Artificial Intelligence has become a core architectural component of contemporary information systems, integrating machine learning, deep learning, and predictive analytics into decision processes [29, 30]. Intelligent process systems combine AI with process mining to enable predictive and prescriptive capabilities [4].

Blockchain introduces decentralized trust mechanisms and new governance models [31, 32], further diversifying system architectures. These developments reflect increasing system autonomy and integration across distributed environments.

Methodological Perspective: Ethical, Human-Centered, and Sustainable Engineering. The attention has shifted toward responsible AI, human-centered design, and sustainability. Research addresses algorithmic accountability and ethical implications [33, 34], as the impact of digital systems on user well-being and technostress [9].

IS are increasingly conceptualized as societal infrastructures rather than purely organizational tools. Engineering approaches must therefore integrate ethical, environmental, and governance considerations into system design and lifecycle management. This phase reflects both a further increase in technical integration depth, characterized by

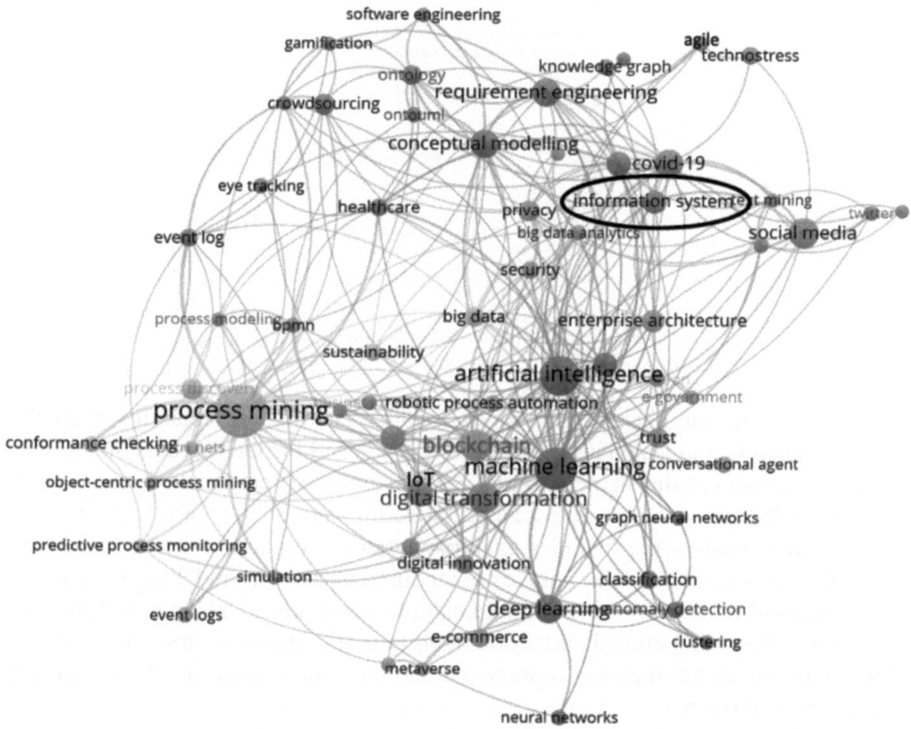

Fig. 6. 2020–2023

AI-driven autonomy and decentralized architectures, and a qualitative shift in organizational–societal scope, as IS are increasingly conceptualized as infrastructures shaping societal practices, public value, and collective well-being.

5 Societal and Engineering Challenges for Information Systems Engineering

The analysis highlights a progressive broadening of the scope of Information Systems Engineering from technical infrastructures to organizational and societal platforms. Figure 7 synthesizes this trajectory by conceptualizing the IS as an IT object, an organizational object, and increasingly a societal object.

This cumulative expansion is consistent with socio-technical perspectives emphasizing the interdependence between technical artifacts and organizational structures [1]. More recent research frames digital infrastructures as institutional and societal platforms shaping collective practices and public value [35].

At the technical level, the integration of Artificial Intelligence into core system architectures represents a major engineering challenge. AI is now embedded in decision processes, automation mechanisms, and predictive systems, increasing both system

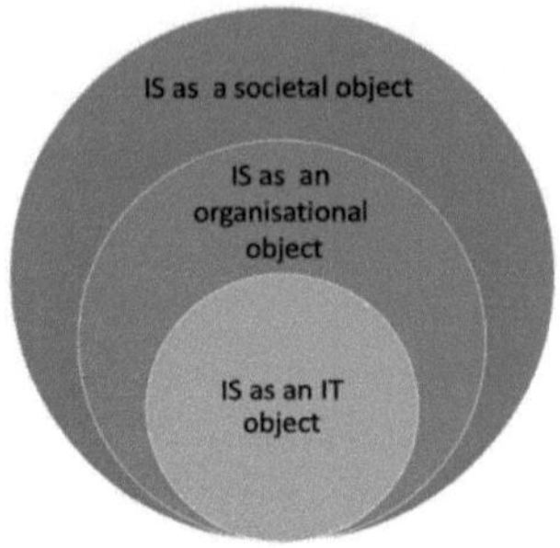

Fig. 7. Evolution of the scope of IS.

autonomy and decision agency. This raises issues related to explainability, traceability, bias mitigation, and accountability [33, 34]. The need for interpretable models and transparent decision chains is increasingly recognized as a prerequisite for trustworthy systems [36]. ISE must therefore extend its modeling and architectural frameworks to incorporate responsible AI principles as intrinsic design dimensions rather than external compliance constraints. This implies extending conceptual modeling languages to represent algorithmic decision logic, explainability constraints, and data provenance. It also requires integrating ethical and accountability requirements as first-class elements within requirements engineering frameworks, rather than treating them as secondary non-functional attributes.

Sustainability constitutes a second structural challenge. Information systems simultaneously consume significant computational resources and enable optimization of organizational processes. Green IS research has highlighted this dual role, emphasizing both environmental impact and transformative potential [37, 38]. For ISE, this implies integrating energy-aware architectures, environmentally informed enterprise models, and sustainability indicators into requirements engineering and evaluation frameworks, including energy-related metrics and traceable sustainability objectives across design and implementation phases.

The increasing autonomy and pervasiveness of digital systems also amplify the need for human-centered and context-aware engineering. Research on technostress and the "dark side" of IT demonstrates that systems affect cognitive load, behavior, and well-being [9, 39]. Human-centered design principles [40] must therefore be embedded into modeling approaches, enabling adaptive interfaces, context-sensitive interactions, and explicit consideration of user agency and psychological sustainability.

Finally, the convergence of AI, cloud infrastructures, IoT, and decentralized technologies transforms information systems into interconnected socio-technical ecosystems. Self-adaptive and autonomic capabilities [41] introduce new challenges related to runtime governance, interoperability, and dynamic reconfiguration. Engineering methods must evolve to manage distributed intelligence and cross-organizational coordination while maintaining architectural coherence.

Taken together, these challenges indicate that the future of Information Systems Engineering depends on its capacity to integrate technical rigor, methodological adaptability, and societal responsibility within coherent engineering frameworks. Rather than replacing earlier concerns, this evolution expands the field's scope, incorporating ethical, environmental, and human-centered dimensions into its structural foundations.

To further structure the challenges identified in response to our second research question, Fig. 8 positions them along the two analytical dimensions developed throughout this study: technical integration depth and organizational-societal scope. This representation emphasizes that emerging challenges do not arise in isolation but result from the combined intensification of system complexity and the expansion of system responsibility. The figure therefore synthesizes how contemporary ISE concerns extend beyond foundational technical properties toward enterprise and societal levels.

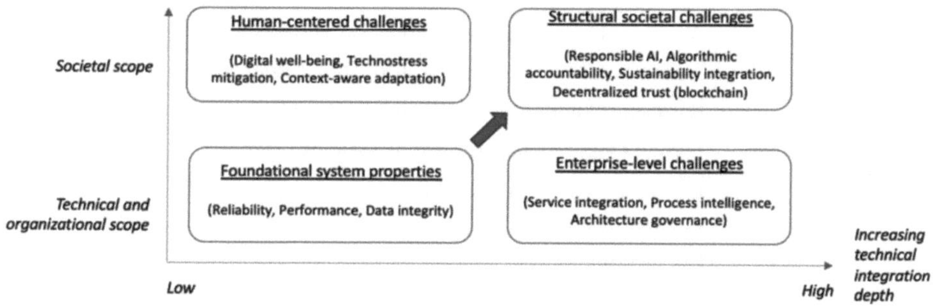

Fig. 8. Two-dimensional positioning of emerging challenges in ISE along technical integration depth and organizational–societal scope.

6 Conclusion

This paper presented a longitudinal analysis of Information Systems Engineering research from 1971 to 2023, based on a large-scale bibliographic corpus covering major conferences and key contributors in the field. By combining bibliometric mapping and qualitative interpretation, the study identified four major evolutionary phases reflecting structural shifts in technical priorities and methodological orientations.

The results show a progressive transformation from data-centered modeling and database systems to semantically enriched, process-aware, and service-oriented architectures, followed by enterprise-wide integration, data-intensive infrastructures, and finally AI-driven and decentralized systems. In parallel, the scope of ISE expanded from IT-centered systems to organizational and societal infrastructures, raising new challenges related to responsible AI integration, sustainability, human-centered design, governance, and adaptive system behavior. These concerns extend earlier engineering foundations toward broader socio-technical responsibilities and reinforce the view of ISE as a discipline positioned between software engineering and IS management. The two-dimensional interpretative framework capturing both technical integration and organizational-societal expansion, this study contributes to clarifying the identity of the field provides an analytical lens for positioning future research contributions according to their impact on technical integration depth and organizational-societal scope.

Future research should further formalize the integration of ethical, environmental, and human-centered considerations into engineering methods, modeling languages, and architectural frameworks. Beyond identifying emerging themes, the two-dimensional interpretative framework proposed in this study offers a positioning tool for future contributions, enabling researchers to situate their work according to its impact on technical integration depth and organizational-societal scope. It not only to historical clarification but also to conceptual structuring of future ISE research.

Appendix A: IS Conferences

Rank	Acronym	Name
A	AMCIS	Americas Conference on Information Systems
A	ACIS	Australasian Conference on Information Systems
A	ECIS	European Conference on Information Systems
A	FOIS	Formal Ontology in Information Systems
A	ISD	Information Systems Development
A	CAiSE	International Conference on Advanced Information Systems Engineering
A	CoopIS	International Conference on Cooperative Information Systems
A	DESRIST	International Conference on Design Science Research in IS and Technology
A	WISE	International Conference on Web Information Systems Engineering
A	PACIS	Pacific Asia Conference on Information Systems
B	CISIS	Computational Intelligence in Security for Information Systems
B	EMCIS	European, Mediterranean and Middle Eastern Conference on Information Systems
B	DB&IS	International Baltic Conference on Database and Information Systems
B	BIS	International Conference on Business Information Systems
B	ICISS	International Conference on Information Systems Security
B	ISTA	International Conference on Information Systems Technology and its Applications

Appendix B: Key Authors

Author	Nb	Author	Nb	Author	Nb
Helmut Krcmar	143	Stefanie Rinderle-Ma	38	Guy G. Gable	30
Jörg Becker	92	H. Raghav Rao	38	J. Leon Zhao	30
Darshana Sedera	84	Alexander Maedche	38	Kieran Conboy	30

(continued)

(*continued*)

Author	Nb	Author	Nb	Author	Nb
Wil M. P. van der Aalst	81	Patrick Finnegan	37	Alexander Benlian	30
Lutz M. Kolbe	75	Sven Laumer	37	Luiz Joia	29
Thomas Hess	75	Yogesh Kumar Dwivedi	36	Sue Newell	29
Björn Niehaves	73	Richard Boateng	36	Michael H. Breitner	29
Sherah Kurnia	55	Ilia Bider	36	Xavier Franch	29
Oscar Pastor	55	Henderik Alex Proper	36	Eric Tze Kuan Lim	29
Heiko Gewald	53	Christy M. K. Cheung	36	José Luís Calvo-Rolle	29
Jan Mendling	52	Kwok Kee Wei	36	Dianne J. Hall	29
Manfred Reichert	51	Steven L. Alter	35	Janis Stirna	29
Boualem Benatallah	51	Falk Uebernickel	35	Hock-Hai Teo	29
Keng Siau	49	Brian J. Corbitt	35	Samir Chatterjee	28
Prashant C. Palvia	48	Lakshmi S. Iyer	35	Quan Z. Sheng	28
Daniel Beimborn	48	Héctor Quintián	35	Qing Li	27
Omar F. El-Gayar	47	Marinos Themistocleous	34	Sjaak Brinkkemper	27
Michael Rosemann	46	Selmin Nurcan	34	Upkar Varshney	27
Jan vom Brocke	46	Philip Powell	34	Paulo Rupino da Cunha	27
Robert M. Davison	44	Robert Winter	34	Pablo García Bringas	27
Tim Weitzel	44	Paul Johannesson	34	Narcyz Roztocki	27
Marite Kirikova	44	Robert D. Galliers	34	Solomon Negash	27
Kurt Sandkuhl	44	John Krogstie	34	Lars Mathiassen	27
Emilio Corchado	43	Kalle Lyytinen	34	Arthur H. M. ter Hofstede	27
Walter Brenner	42	Peter Buxmann	33	Jelena Zdravkovic	27
Yanchun Zhang	42	Starr Roxanne Hiltz	33	Eric W. T. Ngai	27
Chee-Wee Tan	42	Witold Abramowicz	33	Katsumi Tanaka	27
Karlheinz Kautz	42	Heinz-Theo Wagner	33	Geert Poels	27
Claudia Löbbecke	42	Hanna Krasnova	33	Hefu Liu	27
Jan Marco Leimeister	42	Andreas Eckhardt	32	Paolo Giorgini	26
Mathias Weske	41	Gurpreet Dhillon	32	Oliver Thomas	26
Rüdiger Zarnekow	41	Christian Maier	32	Anastasia Papazafeiropoulou	26

(*continued*)

(*continued*)

Author	Nb	Author	Nb	Author	Nb
David Sundaram	41	Dan J. Kim	32	Christoph Rosenkranz	26
Pnina Soffer	40	Stephen Smith	31	Axel Winkelmann	26
Stefan Stieglitz	40	Yongqiang Sun	31	Colette Rolland	26
Álvaro Herrero	40	Raj Sharman	31	Atreyi Kankanhalli	26
Matthias Schumann	39	Johann Eder	31	Yulin Fang	25
Moira C. Norrie	39	Hajo A. Reijers	31	Markus Böhm	25
Shan Ling Pan	39	Dirk Neumann	31	Chih-Ping Wei	25
Eric S. K. Yu	39	Fiona Fui-Hoon Nah	31	Christof Weinhardt	25
John Mylopoulos	39	Hua Wang	31	Iris Reinhartz-Berger	25
Giancarlo Guizzardi	39	Nilmini Wickramasinghe	30	Jan Muntermann	25
Barbara Weber	39	Rahul Singh	30		
Florian Matthes	39	Jung P. Shim	30		

References

1. Hirschheim, R., Klein, H.K., Lyytinen, K.: Information Systems Development and Data Modeling: Conceptual and Philosophical Foundations. Cambridge University Press (1995)
2. Wand, Y., Weber, R.: Research commentary: information systems and conceptual modeling. MIS Q. **26**(4), 363–376 (2002)
3. Chen, M., Chiang, R.H.L., Storey, V.C.: Business intelligence and analytics: from big data to big impact. MIS Q. **36**(4), 1165–1188 (2012)
4. van der Aalst, W.M.P.: Process Mining: Data Science in Action. Springer (2016)
5. Vial, G.: Understanding digital transformation: a review and a research agenda. J. Strat. Inf. Syst. **28**(2), 118–144 (2019)
6. Lyytinen, K., King, J.L.: Nothing at the center? Academic legitimacy in the information systems field. JAIS **5**(6), 220–246 (2004)
7. Mason, R.O., McKenney, J.L., Copeland, D.G.: An historical method for MIS research. MIS Q. **21**(3), 307–320 (1997)
8. vom Brocke, J., Simons, A., Niehaves, B., Riemer, K., Plattfaut, R., Cleven, A.: Literature search in IS research. CAIS **37**(1) (2015)
9. Tarafdar, M., Cooper, C.L., Stich, J.-F.: The technostress trifecta. Inf. Syst. J. **29**(1), 6–42 (2019)
10. Stahl, B.C.: Morality, ethics, and reflection. JAIS **13**(8), 636–656 (2012)
11. Banker, R.D., Karahanna, E., Straub, D.W.: Fifty years of Information Systems research: a review of theoretical foundations and intellectual trajectories. Manage. Sci. **67**(9), 5297–5325 (2021)
12. Rolland, C., Prakash, N.: Bridging the gap between organizational needs and ERP functionality. Requirements Eng. **5**(3), 180–193 (2000)

13. Rolland, C.: A comprehensive view of process engineering. In: CAiSE 1998. LNCS. Springer (1998)
14. Guizzardi, G.: Ontological Foundations for Structural Conceptual Models. CTIT (2005)
15. Dumas, M., La Rosa, M., Mendling, J., Reijers, H.A.: Business Process Management: Concepts, Languages, Architectures, 2nd edn. Springer, Berlin Heidelberg (2018)
16. Winter, R., Fischer, R.: Essential layers of enterprise architecture. J. Enterp. Architect. **2**(2), 7–18 (2006)
17. Chen, P.P.: The entity-relationship model - toward a unified view of data. ACM Trans. Database Syst. **1**(1), 9–36 (1976)
18. Halpin, T.A.: Conceptual Schema and Relational Database Design: A Fact Oriented Approach. Prentice Hall, Englewood Cliffs (1989)
19. Berners-Lee, T., Hendler, J., Lassila, O.: The semantic web. Sci. Am. **284**(5), 34–43 (2001)
20. van der Aalst, W. M. P., Weijters, A., Maruster, L.: Workflow mining. IEEE TKDE **16**(9), 1128–1142 (2004)
21. Papazoglou, M.P., Georgakopoulos, D.: Service-oriented computing. CACM **46**(10), 25–28 (2003)
22. Brinkkemper, S.: Method engineering: engineering of information systems development methods and tools. Inf. Softw. Technol. **38**(4), 275–280 (1996)
23. van Lamsweerde, A.: Goal-oriented requirements engineering. RE (2001)
24. Beck, K., et al.: Manifesto for Agile Software Development. Agile Alliance (2001)
25. Armbrust, M., et al.: A view of cloud computing. Commun. ACM **53**(4), 50–58 (2010)
26. Atzori, L., Iera, A., Morabito, G.: The internet of things: a survey. Comput. Netw. **54**(15), 2787–2805 (2010)
27. Lankhorst, M.: Enterprise Architecture at Work, 4th edn. Springer (2017).
28. Bharadwaj, A., El Sawy, O., Pavlou, P., Venkatraman, N.: Digital business strategy. MIS Q. **37**(2), 471–482 (2013)
29. Jordan, M.I., Mitchell, T.M.: Machine learning. Science **349**(6245), 255–260 (2015)
30. Goodfellow, I., Bengio, Y., Courville, A.: Deep Learning. MIT Press (2016)
31. Nakamoto, S.: Bitcoin: a peer-to-peer electronic cash system (2008)
32. Xu, X., Weber, I., Staples, M.: Architecture for Blockchain Applications. Springer (2019)
33. Floridi, L., et al.: AI4People - an ethical framework for a good AI society: opportunities, risks, principles, and recommendations. Mind. Mach. **28**(4), 689–707 (2018)
34. Mittelstadt, B.D., Allo, P., Taddeo, M., Wachter, S., Floridi, L.: The ethics of algorithms: mapping the debate. Big Data Soc. **3**(2) (2016)
35. Tilson, D., Lyytinen, K., Sørensen, C.: Digital infrastructures: the missing IS research agenda. Inf. Syst. Res. **21**(4), 748–759 (2010)
36. Doshi-Velez, F., Kim, B.: Towards a rigorous science of interpretable machine learning. arXiv preprint arXiv:1702.08608 (2017)
37. Melville, N.P.: Information systems innovation for environmental sustainability. MIS Q. **34**(1), 1–21 (2010)
38. Watson, R.T., Boudreau, M.-C., Chen, A.J.: Information systems and environmentally sustainable development: energy informatics and new directions for the IS community. MIS Q. **34**(1), 23–38 (2010)
39. Salo, M., Pirkkalainen, H., Chua, C.E.H., Koskelainen, T.: Explaining information technology users' ways of mitigating technostress. Inf. Syst. J. **28**(6) (2018)
40. Norman, D.A.: The Design of Everyday Things. Revised and Expanded edn. Basic Books, New York (2013)
41. Kephart, J.O., Chess, D.M.: The vision of autonomic computing. Computer **36**(1) (2003)

When AI Changes the Rules: Managing Resistance in IT Projects Through a Maturity Framework

Teddy Rabarijaona and Rébecca Deneckère(✉)

Centre de Recherche en Informatique, Université Paris 1 Panthéon-Sorbonne, Paris, France
denecker@univ-paris1.fr

Abstract. Resistance to change remains a persistent challenge in IT project management, particularly as digital transformation increasingly involves artificial intelligence based tools. While prior research has identified psychological and organizational sources of resistance, the specific impact of AI mediated systems on resistance dynamics remains underexplored. This exploratory paper examines how resistance manifests in AI-enabled IT projects through a qualitative multi-method approach combining a systematic literature review, semi-structured interviews with IT project managers, and a focus group. The findings show that AI reshapes resistance mechanisms by affecting perceptions of autonomy, transparency, and control. Based on these results, we propose a change management maturity matrix that integrates human centered practices with AI specific socio-technical dimensions. The framework supports the assessment of organizational readiness for AI driven transformation and extends existing change management approaches by conceptualizing artificial intelligence as a mediator of resistance rather than a purely technical factor.

Keywords: Resistance to change · Artificial intelligence · IT project management · Change management · Digital transformation

1 Introduction

Information systems projects are inherently associated with change, as they introduce new technologies, processes, and work practices into organizational environments. In IT projects, resistance to change is therefore a recurrent phenomenon and a major risk factor leading to delays, cost overruns, and reduced system adoption [1, 2]. Despite decades of research, resistance to change remains difficult to anticipate and mitigate, particularly in contexts characterized by rapid technological evolution.

Resistance to change is not inherently negative. Prior studies emphasize that it often emerges from a fundamental human need for stability, control, and psychological balance [3, 4]. When change disrupts established routines or perceived competence, individuals and groups may react through avoidance, passive resistance, or active opposition [5, 6]. In IT projects, these reactions are amplified by organizational constraints, communication issues, and structural rigidity [7, 8]. The challenge becomes even more complex in the

R. Matulevičius et al. (Eds.): DB&IS 2026, CCIS 3085, pp. 20–36, 2026.
https://doi.org/10.1007/978-3-032-30863-4_2

context of digital transformation, where organizations increasingly rely on emerging technologies such as artificial intelligence (AI). AI-based tools introduce new forms of automation, data-driven decision making, and task delegation, which can simultaneously increase efficiency and intensify resistance due to perceived loss of autonomy, lack of transparency, or job related concern [9–11]. While several studies address resistance to change in IT projects, most remain technology agnostic or treat artificial intelligence as a generic contextual factor rather than as a socio-technical mediator of change [4, 5, 8]. This study adopts primarily the perspective of IT project managers and organizational stakeholders involved in the deployment of AI-enabled systems, while also capturing indirect perceptions of end-user resistance through managerial accounts.

Existing research has proposed numerous models and frameworks to manage resistance to change, including Kotter's change model [18], SPI oriented approaches, and technology acceptance theories [1, 7, 19, 20]. However, these models are rarely adapted to explicitly account for AI-enabled systems and their specific impact on user perceptions and organizational dynamics. Moreover, practical tools intended to assess change readiness often remain disconnected from empirical evidence gathered in contemporary IT project environments. This work addresses this gap by examining resistance to change in IT projects involving AI and by proposing a maturity based framework that integrates human, organizational, and AI related dimensions. By combining a systematic literature review with qualitative empirical data collected from IT project managers, this study aims to provide both analytical insights and a structured instrument to support change management in AI-enabled information systems projects.

The remainder is structured as follows. Section 2 presents the research method. Section 3 reviews related work. Section 4 reports the results. Section 5 explains the maturity framework, followed by a discussion and a conclusion in Sect. 6 and 7.

2 Research Method

Research Design. This study adopts an exploratory qualitative research design combining a systematic literature review, semi-structured interviews, and a focus group validation (Fig. 1). The objective was to identify resistance factors and confront them with empirical practices.

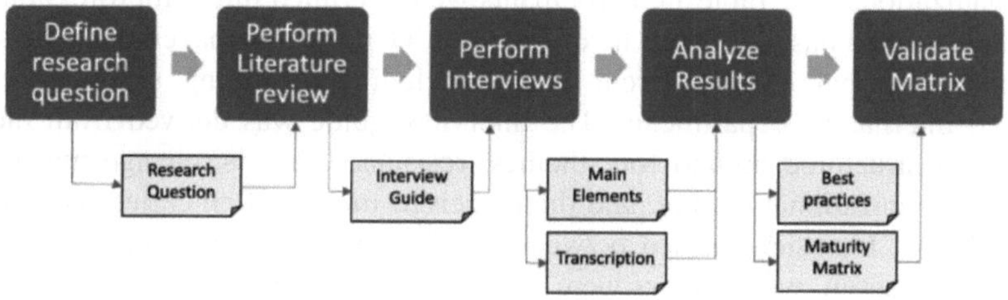

Fig. 1. Research method.

Research Questions. The study was guided by four research questions:

- RQ1. What factors contribute to resistance to change in IT projects?
- RQ2. How does the introduction of emerging technologies, particularly AI, influence resistance to change?
- RQ3. Which change management practices support the adoption of new technologies and reduce resistance?
- RQ4. Which models and frameworks can help prevent or mitigate resistance to change?

These research questions structure both the systematic literature review and the empirical investigation. RQ1 and RQ2 focus on identifying resistance mechanisms, while RQ3 and RQ4 support the development of the proposed maturity matrix.

Systematic Literature Review. The systematic literature review followed the guidelines proposed by Kitchenham and Charters [21]. The objective was to identify primary studies addressing resistance to change in IT-related contexts. The search String was "(TITLE-ABS-KEY("change resistance") OR TITLE-ABS-KEY("change opposition") OR TITLE-ABS-KEY("change reluctance") OR TITLE-ABS-KEY("Change aversion") OR TITLE-ABS-KEY ("Reluctance to adapt") OR TITLE-ABS-KEY ("Adaptation resistance") OR TITLE-ABS-KEY ("Barriers to change")) AND (SUBJAREA ("COMP"))". It was applied to the Scopus database, restricted to the Computer Science subject area, and resulted in 116 papers. This restriction was applied to ensure methodological consistency with software engineering research, although it may have excluded relevant studies from domains such as healthcare or management. As a result, the findings should be interpreted primarily as applying to IT and information systems change contexts rather than to all organizational AI adoption settings. Included studies addressed resistance to change in IT or information systems contexts, were peer-reviewed, and discussed organizational or human factors. Purely technical papers, non-English publications, and studies without full-text access were excluded. The review was restricted to the period 2010–2024. After title/abstract and full-text screening, followed by quality assessment based on relevance, methodological clarity, and theoretical or practical contribution, 12 papers were retained. A forward and backward snowballing process identified five additional relevant studies, resulting in a final corpus of 17 papers (see *SLR references* Section).

Semi-structured Interviews. To complement the literature review, five semi-structured interviews were conducted with project managers from small, medium, and large organizations (see Table 1). Participants were recruited through professional networks and selected based on their involvement in IT project management. The sample includes professionals from different sectors, including consulting, software development, and internal IT departments. The interview guide was derived from the SLR findings and structured around four themes: resistance factors, change management strategies, organizational culture, and the perceived impact of emerging technologies, particularly AI. Interviews lasted between 45 and 75 min. Some were recorded and transcribed verbatim, while others were transcribed during the session. Interview data were thematically analyzed using a coding procedure described in the qualitative data analysis section below.

Table 1. Participants.

Code	Position	Sector	Company Size	AI exposure
[i1]	Cross-functional Project Manager	Consulting	Medium	Yes
[i2]	Cross-functional Project Manager	Software development	Medium	Yes
[i3]	Cross-functional Project Manager	Consulting / internal IT	Medium, Large	Yes
[i4]	Project Manager	Internal IT	Small	No
[i5]	Project Manager	Software services	Small	No

Triangulation and Matrix Development. The maturity matrix was developed through triangulation of three sources: literature findings, interview insights, and theoretical models of change management. The matrix dimensions reflect recurring resistance drivers and mitigation strategies identified across sources. The inclusion of an AI-related dimension emerged from both the SLR gap analysis and empirical observations.

Focus Group Validation. A focus group with four IT project managers was conducted to evaluate the applicability and clarity of the matrix. The session lasted around 90 min and followed a structured protocol. Participants assessed a recent IT project using the proposed maturity levels. Feedback was collected regarding clarity, feasibility, and perceived usefulness. The discussion revealed practical constraints related to time, resources, and organizational priorities.

Threats to Validity. This study presents several methodological limitations. First, the empirical phase is based on a limited number of semi-structured interviews ($n = 5$) and a single focus group ($n = 4$). The objective was exploratory rather than statistically representative, which restricts external validity and prevents generalization. Second, participants were mainly drawn from digitally mature and IT-intensive organizations. This context may shape perceptions of AI adoption and could underrepresent resistance dynamics in less technologically advanced or more hierarchical environments. Although a consistent coding framework was applied, minor variations in detail and interpretative bias cannot be fully excluded. Finally, qualitative coding was conducted iteratively using deductive and inductive strategies. While categories were refined jointly by the authors to ensure analytical coherence, no formal inter-coder reliability metrics were applied, as the study aimed at exploratory conceptual development rather than statistical measurement.

Qualitative Data Analysis and Triangulation. Interview data were analyzed using a structured thematic approach combining deductive and inductive coding. An initial coding framework was derived from the research questions and the categories identified in the systematic literature review, including psychological, organizational, technological, and AI-related dimensions. This ensured alignment between theoretical constructs and empirical material. An inductive phase then allowed the identification of emergent themes not captured by the initial grid. Transcripts were manually coded by associating coherent units of meaning with thematic labels. Coding was conducted iteratively in two cycles, first to identify themes and then to refine category boundaries, particularly regarding AI-related perceptions such as autonomy and job-related concerns. The process continued until no substantially new themes emerged. To enhance internal validity, interview findings were systematically compared with the SLR results. This triangulation confirmed recurrent patterns, identified AI-specific variations, and highlighted discrepancies between theoretical recommendations and field practices. The proposed maturity matrix was subsequently discussed in a reflective focus group with IT professionals, serving as an external validation step and leading to minor refinements.

3 Related Work

Resistance to change has been extensively studied across organizational, information systems, and software engineering research. Early and contemporary studies consistently identify resistance as a multidimensional phenomenon rooted in psychological, organizational, and structural factors [3, 5, 8]. In IT project contexts, resistance is often intensified by the introduction of new tools, methods, and work practices that disrupt established routines and perceived competence [1, 7].

Several works focus on identifying and classifying sources of resistance in software and information systems projects. For instance, [5] provides a structured overview of resistance factors and stakeholder responses in software projects, highlighting escalation mechanisms across individual and organizational levels. Similarly, [8] examines resistance in enterprise architecture adoption, emphasizing the role of organizational structures and strategic misalignment. While these studies offer valuable classifications, they remain largely descriptive and technology agnostic.

Change management models have been proposed to address resistance through structured intervention strategies. Classical frameworks such as Kotter's change model [18] and SPI oriented approaches emphasize leadership, communication, and stakeholder engagement as key levers [7, 12]. Other contributions focus on human and social dimensions in software process improvement, highlighting motivation, participation, and organizational learning [1, 13]. However, these models were largely developed before the widespread adoption of AI driven systems and do not explicitly account for the socio-technical implications of automation and algorithmic decision support. Practitioner-oriented models such as ADKAR emphasize individual readiness and structured change processes, but remain largely technology-agnostic and do not explicitly address AI-related socio-technical dynamics [11].

While these models provide explanatory power at the individual level, they offer limited guidance for managing resistance in complex IT projects involving organizational change and emerging technologies.

More recent studies explore resistance in digital transformation contexts, including education and banking, where AI plays an increasing role [9, 10]. These works highlight concerns related to transparency, loss of control, and trust, but do not propose integrated frameworks to operationalize these insights within IT project management.

This paper positions AI as a socio-technical mediator of resistance and proposes a maturity based framework that integrates human centered change management practices with AI related dimensions. This approach aims to bridge the gap between descriptive analyses of resistance and actionable, empirically grounded tools for managing change in AI-enabled IT projects. However, none of these perspectives explicitly integrate the socio-technical implications of AI-driven systems, which motivates the need for a dedicated analytical framework.

4 Results

This section presents the results of the study structured according to the research questions. The results are interpreted primarily from the perspective of IT project managers involved in organizational change initiatives, with end-user resistance captured indirectly through their accounts. Tables are used as synthesis artefacts that consolidate evidence from the systematic literature review and the empirical investigation. The analysis focuses on patterns, relationships, and dominant mechanisms rather than exhaustive enumeration.

4.1 RQ1: Factors Contributing to Resistance to Change in IT Projects

The analysis identifies three main categories of resistance mechanisms in IT projects: (a) psychological factors, (b) organizational and structural factors, and (c) strategic and vision-related divergences (Table 2). These categories emerge consistently from both the literature review and interview data. Rather than independent drivers, these mechanisms operate across interconnected levels of the socio-technical system.

Psychological Resistance Factors. Psychological resistance originates at the individual level and is primarily associated with cognitive inertia, emotional responses, and perceived competence gaps. Routine preservation and cognitive rigidity are recurrent themes in the literature [1, 2, 7, 18]. Change disrupts cognitive stability and introduces uncertainty, especially when long-standing workflows or tools are modified. Emotional responses such as stress, anxiety, or loss of professional confidence further reinforce resistance. These reactions intensify when new systems are perceived as complex or insufficiently supported. Lack of skills or fear of technological inadequacy amplifies defensive attitudes toward change. It is often a reaction to perceived personal disruption. When individuals anticipate loss of control, status, or expertise, resistance becomes protective rather than ideological.

Organizational and Structural Factors. Organizational resistance is shaped by communication quality, leadership involvement, and available resources. Communication gaps are repeatedly identified as major triggers of resistance [1, 2, 5, 18]. When the purpose of change is unclear, employees often assume hidden risks or costs. Interviews confirm that limited early communication increases suspicion and reduces engagement. Leadership plays a structuring role: visible and consistent managerial support legitimizes the initiative and clarifies priorities, while inaction reinforces uncertainty. Structural constraints such as limited training, time pressure, or insufficient resources increase perceived workload and intensify resistance. In such cases, resistance reflects operational strain rather than disagreement with strategy. Overall, organizational resistance results less from individual reluctance than from a gap between working conditions and change objectives.

Table 2. Factors.

Factors	References
Psychological	
Preference for Routine	[3, 8]
Cognitive Rigidity	[1, 3, 13]
Emotional Reaction to Imposed Change	[3]
Low Motivation	[1, 4]
Lack of Skills & Complexity of New Technologies	[i1, 1, 13]
Threat to Power	[i3, 1, 13]
Organizational and Structural	
Communication Barriers	[1, 7, 8, 13]
Inaction by Leadership	[1, 5, 13]
Resource Allocation	[7, 8]
Political and Cultural Blockages	[1, 7, 8, 13]
Company size	[3, 14, i3, i4, i5]
Organizational culture	[9, 8, i1, i2, i3, i4, i5]
Strategic and vision-related divergences	
Focus on Short-Term Gains	[1, 3, 13]
Trust Issues	[1, 7, 13]
Lack of Clarity on Goals	[1, 7, 13]
Demographic factors	
Age and Experience	[3, 15, i1, i3, i4, i5]
Gender	[i5]
Education level	[15, 2, i5]

Strategic and Vision-Related Divergences. A third category concerns divergences in strategic perception and temporal orientation. Short-term performance pressures often conflict with long-term transformation goals [1, 2, 7]. When employees are evaluated primarily on immediate operational metrics, they may perceive change initiatives as disruptive rather than enabling. Trust deficits also play a decisive role. Resistance increases when employees question the legitimacy or fairness of decision-making processes. Interview evidence highlights that employees are more receptive when they understand the strategic direction and perceive coherence between discourse and action. Finally, lack of clarity regarding the purpose of change fuels skepticism. When expected benefits are abstract or insufficiently articulated, resistance is framed as rational doubt rather than emotional opposition. This category reflects misalignment between strategic intent and operational perception.

Demographic Factors. Demographic characteristics also appear in the data, although their influence is less systematic than psychological or organizational factors. Age and professional experience are the most frequently mentioned variables. Several interviewees observed that older or more experienced employees may be more attached to established routines, especially when they have used the same tools or procedures for many years. However, the empirical data also suggest that age alone does not explain resistance. Organizational culture, previous exposure to change, and perceived support appear to moderate this relationship. Education level may also influence resistance, as employees with stronger technical backgrounds may feel more confident when facing new tools. However, this effect remains context dependent. Gender was mentioned only marginally in the interviews and does not provide sufficient evidence for interpretation. Overall, demographic factors should therefore be treated as secondary and contextual variables rather than primary causes of resistance.

Resistance as a Multi-level Socio-Technical Phenomenon. These findings suggest that resistance in IT projects is not merely the aggregation of isolated psychological reactions. Instead, it emerges from the interaction between individual perceptions, organizational structures, and strategic framing. Resistance intensifies when misalignment occurs simultaneously across these levels. For instance, insufficient communication at the organizational level amplifies individual uncertainty, while short-term strategic pressures legitimize avoidance behaviors at the operational level. This multi-level configuration indicates that resistance should be analyzed as a systemic property of IT-enabled transformation rather than as an individual deficit.

4.2 RQ2: Impact of Artificial Intelligence on Resistance to Change

The findings indicate that AI does not simply introduce new tools, but reshapes resistance mechanisms along three distinct yet interrelated dimensions: (a) efficiency and productivity effects, (b) transformations of work processes, and (c) individual-level impacts. Table 3 synthesizes these dimensions by combining evidence from the literature and empirical observations. The analysis therefore captures common resistance patterns, but does not differentiate systematically between distinct AI paradigms.

Efficiency and Productivity Effects. AI-related technologies generate positive perceptions primarily when they enhance efficiency and task performance. Automation of repetitive activities and data-driven decision support systems reduce operational workload and improve response time [9, 11, i2, i4]. In such cases, resistance decreases because perceived usefulness increases. Users tend to accept AI systems when they are clearly associated with productivity gains and when they enable a shift toward higher value-added tasks. This aligns with classical technology acceptance assumptions, where perceived usefulness acts as a driver of adoption. However, this positive dynamic is conditional. Efficiency gains reduce resistance only when users retain interpretative control over outputs and understand the rationale behind automated decisions.

Transformations of Work Processes. AI systems alter task sequencing, introduce workflow automation, and sometimes redefine role boundaries [9, i2, i3]. Interview data highlight that resistance intensifies when AI reduces perceived autonomy. In roles traditionally associated with expert judgement, algorithmic prioritization was sometimes perceived as narrowing professional discretion. One participant described this shift not

Table 3. Impacts of Emerging Technologies.

Impacts	References
Efficiency and Productivity effects	
Automation of repetitive tasks	[9] [i2] [i3] [i4]
Data-driven decision-making	[9]
Transformations of Work Processes	
Changes in work methods	[9] [i2] [i3]
Reduction of personal control	[i3] [i4]
Employment concerns	[i3]
Trust and Transparency	[7] [4] [14] [10] [i1] [i3]
Individual-level Impacts	
Clarification of benefits	[9] [i1]
Continuous training	[16] [i1] [i2] [i4]
Personalized support	[i1] [i2] [i3] [i4]

as a loss of employment, but as a loss of 'room to decide'. In roles historically characterized by manual decision latitude, algorithmic prioritization is experienced as a reduction of agency. Employment concerns also emerge in this dimension. When AI is associated with task substitution rather than task augmentation, individuals perceive a threat to professional stability [i3, 10]. These concerns are not always linked to actual job loss but to symbolic displacement of expertise. Trust and transparency play a critical mediating role. When algorithmic processes are perceived as opaque, resistance increases [7, 11]. Conversely, transparent communication and explainability mechanisms mitigate negative perceptions.

Individual-Level Impacts. Beyond structural changes, AI adoption produces psychological and cognitive effects at the individual level. Clarification of expected benefits reduces uncertainty and anxiety [9, i1]. Continuous training and personalized support mechanisms significantly moderate resistance by increasing perceived competence and reducing technological anxiety [16, i1, i2, i4]. Interviews indicate that resistance is not solely triggered by the technology itself but by uncertainty regarding personal adaptation capacity. When employees feel supported and accompanied, AI-related change is perceived as progressive rather than disruptive. This dimension confirms that resistance in AI-driven environments remains deeply human-centered, even when the triggering factor is technological.

AI as a Socio-Technical Amplifier. Across these three dimensions, artificial intelligence does not function as a neutral technological variable. Instead, it acts as a socio-technical amplifier of classical resistance factors. It reduces resistance when it enhances usefulness and competence, amplifies resistance when it threatens autonomy, transparency, or professional identity, and shifts resistance from purely organizational concerns toward legitimacy and trust issues. AI does not eliminate traditional resistance mechanisms: in several interviews, participants described reactions that looked like classical concerns about workload or competence, yet these concerns were intensified when decisions were perceived as algorithmically driven. Its impact depends on how efficiency gains, workflow transformations, and individual support mechanisms are balanced within IT projects.

4.3 RQ3: Change Management Practices Supporting Technology Adoption

The analysis identifies several change management practices that contribute to reducing resistance in IT projects. Table 4 provides a synthesis of these practices and illustrates their relative prominence across the literature and the empirical data.

Table 4. Change management methods mentioned for the adoption of new technologies.

Change management methods	Nb	References
Gamification	2	[4, 13]
User-centric design	**7**	[3, 17, i1, i2, i4, i5]
Agile methods	1	[16]
Structured change management practices	6	[16, 15, i1, i2, i3, i4]
Innovation culture	2	[3, i4]

Gamification-based interventions, while context dependent, show potential to enhance motivation and engagement during change initiatives, particularly in software process improvement contexts [1, 13]. Training and continuous support are critical success factors, enabling users to build confidence and reduce anxiety [4, 5, i4]. User centered design and participatory approaches emerge as particularly effective in mitigating resistance by aligning system functionalities with existing work practices and by involving users throughout the change process [3, 23]. Early user involvement fosters a sense of ownership and reduces perceived disruption [i1, i2]. Agile methods support technology adoption by enabling iterative feedback, incremental change, and continuous stakeholder engagement [16, 22]. Although less frequently represented in the literature, agile practices appear effective in identifying early signals of resistance and adapting change strategies accordingly. Leadership engagement and transparent communication cut across all practices and play a central role in legitimizing change initiatives. Visible managerial support contributes to trust building and reinforces commitment to technology adoption [3].

4.4 RQ4: Models and Frameworks for Preventing Resistance to Change

Several structured models have been developed to prevent or mitigate resistance to change in organizational and IT contexts. They provide procedural guidance but were largely conceptualized before the widespread integration of AI-driven systems.

Classical Change Management Models. Among the most influential frameworks, Kotter's eight-step model emphasizes urgency creation, coalition building, vision communication, and institutionalization of change [5, 8]. It conceptualizes change as a structured and sequential process requiring strong leadership and visible sponsorship. Similarly, the ADKAR model developed by Prosci focuses on individual-level transformation through Awareness, Desire, Knowledge, Ability, and Reinforcement [14]. This model is particularly relevant in IT environments where skill acquisition and behavioral adjustment are central to successful adoption. Although not IT-specific, it underpins many contemporary approaches to organizational transformation. [5] further propose structured change frameworks tailored to SPI environments. Across these models, resistance is addressed through structured communication, leadership engagement, training, and incremental implementation. However, these frameworks implicitly assume that change objectives are explainable and stable, technological systems remain largely deterministic, and organizational authority structures remain intact. These assumptions are challenged in AI-mediated environments.

Limits of Classical Models in AI-Driven IT Projects. Algorithmic opacity complicates transparency: while models such as Kotter emphasize communication clarity [5], AI systems may involve complex machine learning mechanisms that are not easily explainable to end users [11]. AI systems redistribute autonomy: automation and intelligent prioritization mechanisms can reduce perceived individual control, a key psychological driver of resistance identified in prior sections [7, 18]. AI integration often follows continuous deployment and iterative retraining cycles, making Lewin's refreeze stage unstable. Organizational equilibrium becomes dynamic rather than fixed as accountability boundaries may blur when decisions are partially delegated to algorithms. This introduces legitimacy concerns not explicitly addressed in classical models [11]. This suggests that AI does not merely introduce technical complexity, but reconfigures socio-technical relationships within IT projects.

These limitations justify the need for a framework that does not replace existing models but complements them with AI-specific socio-technical dimensions. The next section presents such a framework through a maturity matrix designed to assess organizational readiness for managing resistance in AI-enabled IT projects.

5 A Change Management Maturity Matrix

Building on the results presented in Sect. 4, this study proposes a change management maturity matrix designed to assess organizational readiness for managing resistance in AI-enabled IT projects. The matrix is not intended as a prescriptive change method. Rather, it is conceived as a diagnostic and reflective framework that helps project managers identify weaknesses in change preparation, user support, communication, and AI-related governance.

5.1 Rationale and Design Principles

The design of the maturity matrix is grounded in two observations derived from the results. First, resistance to change is shaped by interacting human, organizational, and technological factors rather than isolated causes [1, 3, 5]. Second, AI modifies these interactions by introducing automation, data-driven decision-making, and reduced task discretion, which affect perceptions of control, trust, and legitimacy [9, 10]. Existing change management models provide useful high-level guidance, but they offer limited operational support for assessing readiness in AI-driven contexts [2, 7, 12].

The proposed matrix evaluates whether an organization is able to align strategic intent, organizational structure, technological design, and individual perceptions. In this study, maturity refers to the organization's capacity to anticipate, monitor, and manage resistance across these dimensions. The framework extends prior SPI-oriented approaches [5, 13] by introducing AI-aware evaluation criteria, including transparency, autonomy preservation, trust calibration, and governance clarity in algorithmic decision-making (Fig. 2).

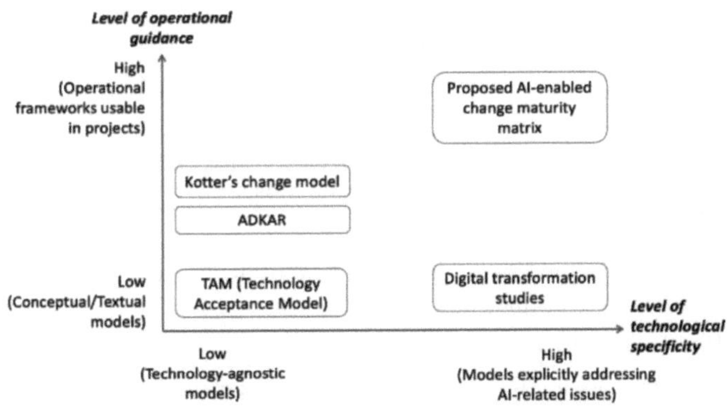

Fig. 2. Positioning of the proposed maturity matrix.

5.2 Structure of the Maturity Matrix

The matrix is structured around six core practices identified through the literature review and empirical analysis: human centered approach, agile integration, training and support, strategic use of AI, innovation oriented culture, and transparent communication with leadership engagement (see Table 5).

The four maturity levels are defined as follows. Level 0 corresponds to the absence of structured practices, where change is handled reactively and AI-related impacts are not explicitly considered. Level 1 represents emerging practices, where some initiatives exist but remain informal, local, or dependent on individual effort. Level 2 reflects managed practices, where change management activities are planned, documented, and partially integrated into project governance. Level 3 corresponds to systematic practices, where change management, AI transparency, user support, and feedback mechanisms are fully embedded in organizational routines and continuously monitored. These levels are applied to each core practice of the matrix, as shown in Fig. 3. These levels explicitly integrate AI-related concerns such as transparency, autonomy, and user understanding.

Table 5. Core practices

Practices / Details
A. Embrace a Human-Centered Approach
• Understand the root causes of resistance: Identify psychological, organizational, and technical drivers of resistance and address employee concerns early
• Leverage participatory methods: Involve employees in the change process through co-creation approaches that strengthen ownership
B. Integrate Agile Methodologies
• Promote flexibility and adaptation: Use short iterative cycles to support gradual adoption and adjustment based on user feedback
• Foster continuous collaboration: Maintain open and ongoing communication among all stakeholders to address concerns and adapt strategies as needs evolve
C. Provide Ongoing Training and Support
• Invest in tailored training: Provide training adapted to different skill levels to reduce anxiety and build confidence
• Offer personalized support: Introduce mentoring or coaching sessions to provide individual support, addressing specific concerns and reducing resistance
D. Strategically Utilize Artificial Intelligence
• Ease technological adoption: Use AI-driven support to simplify tasks, automate workflows, and provide personalized recommendations
E. Foster an Innovation-Oriented Culture
• Encourage experimentation: Treat mistakes as learning opportunities to reduce fear of change and promote adaptability
• Recognize and reward adoption: Establish recognition systems for employees em-bracing new technologies and processes, reinforcing positive attitudes toward change
F. Ensure Transparent Communication and Leader Engagement
• Prioritize transparency: Communicate clearly and frequently about the objectives, benefits, and impacts of change
• Showcase leadership commitment: Visible support from leadership is essential to validate change initiatives. Leaders should act as role models by adopting new technologies themselves and motivating their teams to follow suit

5.3 Empirical Illustration and Validation

The applicability of the matrix was explored through a reflective focus group involving IT project management practitioners. Participants used the matrix to assess a recent project involving a major user interface redesign supported by AI-based features (Fig. 3). The exercise highlighted uneven maturity across practices.

Best Practice	Maturity Level				Comments
	0	1	2	3	
Adopting a human-centered approach				X	The deployed solutions considered user feedback.
Integration of an agile methodology				X	Weekly sprints were organized for the development of each new feature.
Continuous training and support			X		A summary email outlining all the new features was sent out.
Strategic use of artificial intelligence		X			The development of new features did not require AI, but its use is planned for future projects.
Promoting a culture of innovation			X		The change was enforced to prevent adopting another tool that no one would control. The change was driven to avoid experimenting with a new solution and retain control of the existing tool.
Transparent communication and leader engagement			X		Communication about the project was frequently emphasized, often explaining the reasons behind the change and highlighting its expected benefits. However, there is room for improvement.

Fig. 3: Team's maturity level regarding the most recent project involving change management.

This example shows that the matrix can support a differentiated assessment of change management maturity. Instead of producing a single global judgment, it helps identify specific areas where resistance may emerge. In the focus group case, the organization appeared relatively mature in communication and training, but less mature in AI-related transparency. This suggests that the matrix can be used as a practical diagnostic tool before or during AI-enabled IT transformation projects.

5.4 Scope and Limitations

The proposed matrix does not claim universal applicability. Its effectiveness depends on organizational context, project complexity, and the nature of AI integration. Nevertheless, it provides a structured lens through which resistance to change can be analyzed and managed in AI-enabled IT projects, bridging the gap between abstract change management models and situated project practices.

6 Discussion

The findings of this study provide several insights into resistance to change in IT projects and extend existing research by explicitly considering the role of artificial intelligence. This section discusses the results in relation to prior work, highlights theoretical implications, and examines practical and contextual considerations.

The findings largely align with prior research describing resistance as multidimensional and socially embedded. However, the empirical material also suggests that the introduction of AI shifts the balance between these dimensions. In particular, concerns about transparency and delegated decision-making appeared more salient than in earlier IT transformation contexts described in the literature. The empirical findings further suggest that demographic factors such as age or experience play a secondary role when organizational conditions are unfavorable, reinforcing arguments that resistance is largely socially constructed rather than purely individual [2, 15]. The analysis highlights AI as a socio-technical mediator that reshapes existing resistance mechanisms rather than introducing entirely new ones. While previous research has examined resistance in digital transformation contexts [9, 10], this study shows that AI amplifies classical resistance factors by affecting perceptions of autonomy, control, and transparency. In particular, concerns related to algorithmic opacity and loss of decision authority emerge as critical triggers of resistance, extending technology acceptance perspectives that focus primarily on usefulness and ease of use [19, 20]. Figure 5 synthesizes how AI-related characteristics reshape resistance mechanisms and how these mechanisms, in turn, inform change management levers identified in this study.

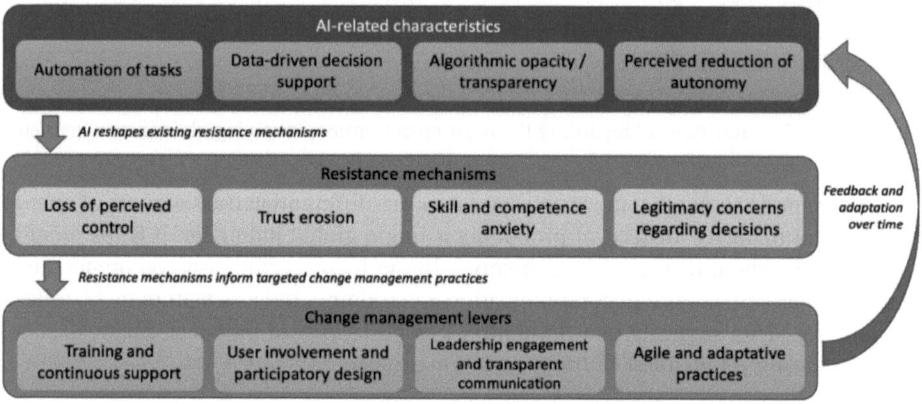

Fig. 5. Synthesis.

The findings call into question the adequacy of existing change management models when applied to AI-enabled IT projects. Classical frameworks such as Kotter's model or SPI oriented approaches provide useful high level guidance but insufficiently account for AI specific dynamics [7, 12]. The proposed matrix addresses this limitation by operationalizing change management practices in a way that explicitly integrates AI related considerations, thereby complementing rather than replacing existing models.

Unlike classical procedural models that prescribe sequences of actions, the proposed maturity matrix operates as a diagnostic and configurational framework. It does not assume that resistance can be mitigated solely through improved communication or training. Instead, it evaluates whether socio-technical conditions are aligned across governance, transparency, autonomy, and skill adaptation dimensions. In AI-enabled environments, where algorithmic opacity and decision delegation introduce structural ambiguity, such alignment becomes a central determinant of change stability. The matrix encourages organizations to examine whether governance structures, training practices, and AI system design are mutually aligned before large-scale deployment. In this sense, it complements procedural models by foregrounding structural preparedness rather than sequential steps.

Although training, user involvement, and transparent communication are widely recognized as effective, empirical evidence suggests that constraints related to time, resources, and organizational priorities often limit their systematic application. This finding aligns with prior observations on the challenges of sustaining change initiatives in practice [1, 13].

Overall, this discussion positions resistance to change in AI-enabled IT projects as a socio-technical challenge requiring integrated analytical frameworks. It also highlights the need for future research to further validate and refine maturity based approaches across diverse organizational contexts. The analysis treats AI as a relatively homogeneous category, although different types of systems may generate distinct resistance dynamics. For instance, decision-support systems may primarily raise issues of trust and transparency, while fully automated systems may more strongly affect perceptions of autonomy and control. Future work should differentiate between AI paradigms to refine the analysis of resistance mechanisms. These findings suggest that resistance in AI-enabled IT projects can be interpreted as a function of perceived autonomy, transparency, and competence alignment, mediated by organizational conditions.

7 Conclusion

This paper contributes to information systems research by reframing resistance to change in AI-enabled IT projects as a socio-technical configuration problem rather than a purely behavioral or managerial issue. This study demonstrates that artificial intelligence reshapes the interaction between autonomy, transparency, and governance structures. By conceptualizing AI as a socio-technical mediator of resistance, the paper extends classical change management and technology acceptance perspectives toward a more integrated analytical framework.

This study proposes a maturity matrix intended to support reflection and structured assessment in AI-enabled IT projects. Rather than introducing a new change doctrine, the framework consolidates existing principles and extends them with AI-specific considerations related to transparency, autonomy, and governance. Unlike existing change management models, the proposed framework explicitly accounts for the impact of automation and data-driven decision making on resistance mechanisms. This matrix provides an analytical tool to assess organizational readiness in AI-enabled IT projects.

Further validation is required to strengthen external validity. In particular, multi-case studies across different sectors and organizational maturity levels would allow assessment of how resistance dynamics and maturity configurations vary depending on context.

References

1. Yilmaz, M., Clarke, P., Messnarz, R., Reiner, M. (eds.): Systems, Software and Services Process Improvement. CCIS, vol. 1442. Springer, Cham (2021). https://doi.org/10.1007/978-3-030-85521-5
2. Abdelhakim, M., Abdeldayem, M.M., Aldulaimi, S.H.: Information technology adoption barriers in public sector. In: 2022 ASU International Conference in Emerging Technologies for Sustainability and Intelligent Systems (ICETSIS), pp. 355–360. IEEE (2022)
3. Enders, T., Martin, D., Sehgal, G.G., Schüritz, R.: Igniting the spark: overcoming organizational change resistance to advance innovation adoption – the case of data-driven services. In: Nóvoa, H., Drăgoicea, M., Kühl, N. (eds.) Exploring Service Science. Lecture Notes in Business Information Processing, vol. 377. Springer, Cham (2020)
4. Gasca-Hurtado, G.P., Gómez-Álvarez, M.P., Herrera, S.: Resistance in software process improvement: a classification proposal of causes, resistance models and gamification. In: 14th Iberian Conference on Information Systems and Technologies (CISTI), pp. 1–6 (2019)

5. Vrhovec, S.L.R.: Responding to stakeholders' resistance to change in software projects – a literature review. In: 39th International Convention on Information and Communication Technology, Electronics and Microelectronics (MIPRO), pp. 1157–1161. IEEE (2016)
6. Moitra, D.: Managing change for software process improvement initiatives: a practical experience-based approach. Software Process Improvement Pract. **4**(4) (1998)
7. Narciso, H., Allison, I.: Overcoming structural resistance in SPI with change management. In: 9th International Conference on the Quality of Information and Communications Technology (QUATIC), pp. 8–17. IEEE (2014)
8. Cordeiro, J., Hammoudi, S., Maciaszek, L., Camp, O., Filipe, J. (eds.): Enterprise Information Systems. LNBIP, vol. 227. Springer, Cham (2015). https://doi.org/10.1007/978-3-319-22348-3
9. Cheng, E.C.K., Wang, T.: Leading digital transformation and eliminating barriers for teachers to incorporate artificial intelligence in basic education in Hong Kong. Comput. Educ. Artif. Intell. **5**, 100171 (2023)
10. Diener, F., Špaček, M.: Digital transformation in banking: a managerial perspective on barriers to change. Sustainability **13**(4), 2032 (2021)
11. Prosci Inc.: The Prosci ADKAR® Model Book Bundle. Prosci Inc. (2018)
12. Mathiassen, L., Ngwenyama, O.K., Aaen, I.: Managing change in software process improvement. IEEE Softw. **22**(6), 84–91 (2005)
13. Gasca-Hurtado, G.P., Gómez-Álvarez, M.C., Herrera, S., et al.: Design of a gamification strategy to intervene in social and human factors associated with software process improvement change resistance. IET Software **15**(6), 428–442 (2021)
14. McCaffery, F., O'Connor, R.V., Messnarz, R. (eds.): Systems, Software and Services Process Improvement. CCIS, vol. 364. Springer, Heidelberg (2013). https://doi.org/10.1007/978-3-642-39179-8
15. Wasilah, Nugroho, L.E., Santosa, P.I.: IT-based change resistance in higher education. Int. J. Eng. Technol. **7**(4.40), 98–103 (2018)
16. Hanslo, R., Vahed, A., Mnkandla, E.: Quantitative analysis of the Scrum framework. In: Przybyłek, A., Morales-Trujillo, M. (eds.) Advances in Agile and User-Centred Software Engineering. LNBIP, vol. 376. Springer (2020)
17. Sedley, A., Müller, H.: Minimizing change aversion for the Google Drive launch. In: CHI '13 Extended Abstracts on Human Factors in Computing Systems. ACM, New York (2013)
18. Kotter, J.P.: Leading Change. Harvard Business School Press, Boston (1996)
19. Davis, F.D.: Perceived usefulness, perceived ease of use, and user acceptance of information technology. MIS Q. **13**(3), 319–340 (1989)
20. Venkatesh, V., Morris, M.G., Davis, G.B., Davis, F.D.: User acceptance of information technology: toward a unified view. MIS Q. **27**(3), 425–478 (2003)
21. Kitchenham, B., Charters, S.: Guidelines for performing systematic literature reviews in software engineering. Version 2.0 (2007)
22. Conboy, K.: Agility from first principles: Reconstructing the concept of agility in information systems development. Inf. Syst. Res. **20**(3), 329–354 (2009)
23. Nebie, E., Elmoukhtar, T.: Organizational change resistance in public sector governance: Best practices for successful transformation. Revue de Manag. Cult. **7**(2) (2022)

Towards a Fractal-Based System Architecture for LLM-Based Multiagent Systems

Aritha Kumarasinghe(✉) and Marite Kirikova

Institute of Applied Computer Systems, Riga Technical University, 6A Kipsalas Street, Riga 1048, Latvia
{balasuriyage-aritha-dewnith.kumarasinghe, marite.kirikova}@rtu.lv

Abstract. Fractals are geometric patterns that exhibit a recurring structure across different scales. This concept, when applied to systems, considers them to be self-similar, goal-oriented, self-organizing, and dynamic. This work applies fractal principles when developing an LLM-based Multiagent System (LMAS) and proposes a fractal-based system architecture for LMAS (FSA4LMAS). The proposed architecture is implemented and applied in curriculum engineering for evolving curricula (represented as a knowledge graph) based on user queries. The results from two separate cases demonstrate how using the knowledge gained from self-organizing fractal units that have the same structure can be propagated to improve the performance of weaker agents, thereby improving the overall performance across the system (in terms of the mean output quality for all fractal units) by approximately 25%. While these results are specific to certain tasks performed within the context of curriculum engineering, further research can consider the generalizability of the benefits gained from using FSA4LMAS.

Keywords: Large Language Models · Multi-agent systems · LLM-based Multi-agent systems · Knowledge Graph Augmented LLM agents · Fractal Information Systems

1 Introduction

Multi-agent systems (MASs) are composed of multiple autonomous agents that are capable of independently perceiving their environment, making decisions, and collaborating together in order to perform a specific task, resulting in increased adaptability and efficiency (when compared to single-agent systems) [1]. Large Language Model (LLM) based MASs (LMASs) leverage an LLM's ability to understand natural language, reason, and plan to solve complex tasks [1]. A systematic literature review conducted in 2024 [1] identified how LMASs have been utilized in domains such as software development, industrial engineering, and societal simulation. The review defined a unified framework for an LLM-based MA system, which consists of five functional modules. The first module is responsible for 'generating' specialized LLM-based agents that are suited for executing subtasks by defining specific profiles that include information about the role

R. Matulevičius et al. (Eds.): DB&IS 2026, CCIS 3085, pp. 37–51, 2026.
https://doi.org/10.1007/978-3-032-30863-4_3

that the agent is supposed to fulfil. In order to 'perceive' the environment that the agent is in, the perception module captures relevant information about the environment that is used by the agent during the decision-making process. The self-action module integrates different kinds of knowledge (e.g., historical knowledge, perceived information, and external knowledge) to make decisions. Enabling collaboration between agents, the mutual interaction module facilitates the transfer of messages between different agents. Finally, there is the evolution module, where changes are made based on self-reflection and feedback from various sources (e.g., the environment, agent interaction, and human feedback) through methods such as feedback learning and prompt engineering. While progress has been made within LMAS, the systematic review [1] identifies that creating an LMAS that can adapt to a dynamically evolving environment in terms of changing external conditions and task demands is still a challenge. Another review article published in 2026 [2] indicates that this remains an open area of research. In addition, [1] identifies the need for collective intelligence in multi-agent systems, which could potentially be realized through agents being able to periodically update their knowledge base independently while periodically sharing insights with other agents.

In order to further explore the topic of the LMAS, this work seeks to approach the problem by adopting a fractal perspective. Fractals and the underlying fractal theory have their roots in geometry, focusing on shapes that have patterns or structures that repeat themselves across different scales [3]. The key underlying concept of fractals is self-similarity, where parts of a system are simply scaled-down copies of the whole [3]. Fractals as a lens through which to analyze a system have been used for analysis of organizations in industries such as manufacturing to define system architectures that are capable of self-evolution in order to continuously adapt to an ever-changing environment [4]. The development of systems based on the principles of fractal systems, such as self-similarity, self-organizing, goal-orientation, and dynamism, has been previously applied when developing information systems, with the results demonstrating how it can lead to improved collaboration between users [5, 6]. The application of a fractal perspective when developing LMAS could, potentially, result in an architecture that is capable of adapting to changes in the environment as well as the tasks it must complete. This is the precise subject that this work seeks to address by defining a fractal-based software systems architecture that would implement an LMAS architecture capable of adapting to an evolving environment and changing tasks. By doing so, this work seeks to explore how fractal design principles can be applied from a conceptual level when defining an LMAS architecture. Based on this subject, the research question we seek to answer is: "*How can fractal design principles be used to develop a system architecture for LMAS that supports self-organization, change-propagation, and performance improvement across agents*?

To explore this topic, we consider curriculum engineering as an application case, since the design and redesign of curricula within a higher education institution (university) represents a process that requires the consideration of several ever-evolving factors, such as industrial knowledge and skill requirements, scientific knowledge, and legal obligations [7]. The proposed software architecture is implemented in order to demonstrate how it can be used for redesigning curricula across study courses and study program levels based on the tasks defined by the user. This hierarchical structure of the curricula, where programs are composed of several courses and courses are composed of topics, is represented as a hierarchical knowledge graph, thereby creating a full or partial representation (depending on the assigned task) of the environment in and with which the LLM-based agents must interact.

The remainder of this paper is organized as follows. Section 2 provides a background on several concepts that are used in this work. This is followed by Sect. 3, which proposes the fractal-based system architecture for an LMAS. Section 4 presents the demonstration and preliminary evaluation of the proposed system architecture within the context of curriculum engineering. Section 5 discusses the results in relation to previous research and the limitations of the proposed solution. Finally, Sect. 6 concludes the paper.

2 Background

This section discusses several concepts based on existing research relating to the topic of this paper. The first subsection introduces LLM-based Multiagent Systems, and the second subsection introduces Fractal Systems.

2.1 LLM-Based Multiagent Systems

The natural language processing/understanding capabilities of LLMs have made them one of the key areas of research within the domain of agentic Artificial Intelligence (AI) [1, 2]. In order to go beyond the capabilities of LLM-based single-agent systems and to make them more suitable for complex environments, LLM-based multi-agent systems (LMASs) have been introduced, which utilize several specialized agents, each with a specific role and task, collaborating to solve complex problems. The results of two systematic literature reviews (one conducted in 2024 [1] and another in 2025 [2]) present an overarching framework of how LMAS architectures are developed, with [1] defining a profile module, perception module, self-action module, mutual interaction module, and the evolution module. Similarly, [2] defines a basic architecture of LLM-based agents being composed of profiling, memory, planning, and action execution, with a multi-agent system having the additional communication structure, adaptive learning through feedback, and a dynamic agent's role. Based on these results, a multiagent system shall be able to do the following:

1. Perceive the environment in which the system operates.
2. Make decisions on how to change the environment in which it operates.
3. Interact with the (changing) environment in which it operates.
4. Communicate with other agents that are present in the system.
5. Evolve the manner in which it operates, based on feedback from previous steps.

When discussing specific LMAS architectures, Talk Structurally, Act Hierarchically (TalkHier), [9] proposes a formal communication protocol between agents where each agent is considered as a combination of Role (assignment of generator, evaluator, or revisor based on the task), Plugin (the external tool that relates to the specific task), Memory (a memory that stores and retrieves information that relates to the task), and Type (whether the agent is supervising or responsible for executing a specific task). The system is comprised of several teams (composed of a generator, evaluator, and revisor) which are organized hierarchically with the main supervisor agent sending the response to evaluation supervisors, which facilitates the execution of the evaluation using other agents that carry out the evaluation, each based on different criteria, which the evaluation supervisor then aggregates in order for the main supervisor to check if overall results are sufficient. If the results are not sufficient, the result revisor regenerates the answer based on the generated feedback. The evaluation results demonstrate how implementing such a hierarchical communication approach, where evaluation is based on the works of several agents, enables improvements in the final result. The authors of [9] also emphasize the importance of each agent having an individual memory that is only accessible by a single agent and not by a pool, which allows the agent to carry out reasoning based on past interactions.

This theme of agents having memory was further explored in a systematic review on Graph-Augmented LLM Agents, which provides an overview of how graphs have been utilized in LLM-agent systems [10]. Given the utility of graphs in the tasks carried out by the LLM, representing the environment, and acting as memory for the agents, we seek to adapt them for both the representation of the environment and as a memory for the LLM, where previous results that are generated by the agent can be stored within the nodes related to each agent, and therefore can also be used for communication since other agents are allowed to access the nodes in order to change the manner in which the LLM agents are structured and used. Creating an architecture that dynamically evolves with the tasks that must be carried out by the agents is explicitly identified as a direction for future research in the review presented in [10].

In terms of the applications of LMAS in education, several works have demonstrated how they can be used to either recommend existing learning materials or generate new materials, and how knowledge graphs can be used to guide curriculum towards trustworthy knowledge sources [8]. However, the applications have been focused on content generation and not on design, development, and maintenance of curricula.

2.2 Fractal Systems

A fractal is an idea rooted in geometry, with the core concept being self-similarity, where the smaller parts of a system are a reduced-scale copy of the whole [3]. Given its geometric roots, the fractal is used mostly as a mathematical concept, which has been applied in fields such as electrical, mechanical, and biomedical [3]. However, fractals as a concept have also been applied in other fields, including manufacturing, with a 2020 systematic review on fractal manufacturing systems being used as the key theory forming research that is referenced [4].

The review identifies the design principle of fractal systems as being *self-similar*, which translates to a system where a global objective is divided into smaller self-similar units (characterized by the same configuration and structure) that work autonomously while also interacting with other units [4]. These autonomous units that are independently carrying out functions to achieve their individual goal (leading to *goal-oriented* being the second principle of fractal systems) initially take the structure of a Basic Fractal Unit (BFU), which in turn can be restructured in order to best carry out their functions; therefore, each fractal unit is *self-organizing*, which is the third principle of fractal systems [4]. This approach to organizing a fractal unit based on the given goal, combined with the same starting structure (BFU) results in fractal units being both flexible and scalable where if higher levels of output are needed more fractal units can be deployed and, if there is a change in the environment or the assigned task, the system is free to change the structure of the agents [4]. The goal-oriented nature additionally supports the evolution of the fractal unit based on how well they perform a given task, with each fractal unit having the ability to self-assess, co-evolve based on the environment and other fractal units, manage short-term actions, and explore (manage long-term actions). This results in the final principle of fractal systems, which is *dynamism* [4].

In terms of the actual structure of a fractal manufacturing system, an agent-based fractal architecture is proposed in [11], which defines five modules that comprise a BFU. The observer module is responsible for monitoring the state of the fractal unit and receiving messages from other fractal units [11]. The analyzer checks job profiles and decides the best course of action. The resolver is responsible for generating job profiles, goal formation, and decision making, and sends the configuration of sub fractals to the analyzer [11]. The organizer ensures the restructuring of the fractal in order to optimize the production process [11]. Based on the outputs generated by the resolver and organizer, the reporter module provides command actions to actuators that influence the system environment [11]. Each of the modules consists of several agents that are responsible for achieving the functions of the module [11].

Several works have also considered the application of a fractal approach to information systems, one of which is a thesis that adopts a fractal approach to developing health information systems and demonstrates how it can be used to improve cooperation among health care workers [5]. The basic fractal unit proposed in this work is similar to the BFU presented in [11], and is composed of a controller, analyzer and planner, an executor, and the knowledge and data base. The controller is responsible for checking if there are any new activities (within the fractal unit to which it belongs and in other fractal units). If there are new activities within the fractal, then the analyzer and planner identify which data within the database is related to the new activity, after which the executor extracts this data and adds it to the knowledge base, and then sends announcements to the other fractals of the new activity, making the implementation of the next activity easier.

Other works that have adopted a fractal approach to information systems do so by explicitly considering the context of a higher educational institution [12–15]. While [12–14] focus on different aspects of a fractal information system, [15] discusses how best practices (processes) can be propagated within a fractal enterprise where each fractal unit can evolve independently with the identified best practices, then propagated to other fractal units, which can easily implement them due to the self-similar structure. A blueprint for a framework of an educational ecosystem-oriented knowledge management system is proposed in [14], which defines a fractal-based architecture for a knowledge management system across course, program, department, and university levels (meaning that the knowledge management systems related to each level have the same structure/components). From the other two works, [13] presents an information architecture that can be utilized by a fractal information system and provides an argument on how a fractal information architecture enables more flexibility when compared to centralized IS solutions and facilitates the propagation of changes made in a fractal unit to other fractal units. The work in [12] presents an information architecture for a fractal information system and demonstrates how it enables improved change propagation.

Overall, these works discuss how the principles of the fractal systems can be applied to improve the flexibility of an information system and the underlying systems that it supports. Our research applies those principles when developing an LMAS capable of adapting to new tasks and to changes in the environment.

3 Fractal-Based System Architecture for LLM-Based Multiagent Systems

This section presents the fractal-based system architecture for LMAS by first defining the underlying BFU, which will be used to form the proposed LMAS (Subsect. 3.1). This is followed by a definition of how fractal units are instantiated and how change propagation occurs (Subsect. 3.2).

3.1 Basic Fractal Unit for the Fractal-Based System Architecture for LLM-Based Multiagent Systems

The basic fractal unit for the FSA4LMAS was defined based on the framework LMAS proposed in [1, 2] and based on how knowledge graphs can be used to augment [10] such systems. Therefore, the architecture proposed in this paper was influenced by the structure of the curriculum knowledge graph, which is structured hierarchically according to the study programs (which are composed of several study courses) and study courses (which are composed of several topics). The intention is that each fractal unit handles a single node that represents a single curriculum element (either a study program, a course, or a topic). Therefore, the following components were defined for each fractal unit:

1. *Orchestrator*: Which serves the role of the 'defining profile' module identified in [10], which defines a plan for fulfilling the user's request by specifying the LLM model to be used, the prompt (assigning a profile), and the evaluation criteria for the response.
2. *Generator*: Which is responsible for executing the prompt generated by the *orchestrator*.
3. *Evaluator*: Which is responsible for evaluating the response that is generated by the *generator* based on the evaluation metrics defined by the *orchestrator*.
4. *Reporter*: Is responsible for defining knowledge queries to alter the knowledge graph reflecting the response defined by the LLM, as well as metadata relating to what model was used, what the output generated by the model was, and the data evaluation results. This is done to ensure communication among the agents and facilitate change propagation.

An overview of the proposed solution is represented in Fig. 1.

The BFU enables self-similarity, given that the fractal units at higher levels (e.g., fractal units responsible for study programs) also have the same structure as fractal units at lower levels. Additionally, self-organization is ensured by the *orchestrator* since, for each prompt, an LLM (the *orchestrator*) selects a specific type of LLM (*generator*) as

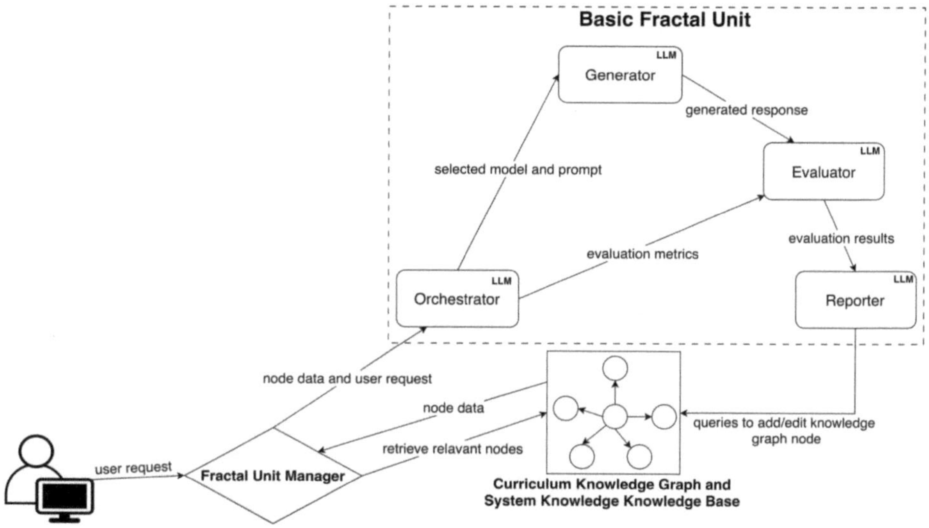

Fig. 1. Model of the BFU representing the basic fractal unit constituting the FSA4LMAS.

well as a specialized prompt that will be used to generate a response to the user's query. Each fractal unit is also goal-oriented since the goal of the fractal unit is based on the user's query, and the data contained in the node that the fractal unit is responsible for.

3.2 Change Propagation Mechanism Within Fractal-Based System Architecture for LLM-Based Multiagent System

Within a fractal system it is not sufficient to only define a BFU; it is also necessary to define how fractal units will be instantiated and how change propagation will occur, since dynamism is one of the principles of fractal systems. Given the hierarchical nature of the curriculum knowledge graph, whether the request made by the user requires a certain level and is related to a specific curriculum element must be considered. To do this, an LLM-based fractal manager is utilized to decide (based on the user's query) which curriculum level (all, program, course, topic) the query relates to and whether it relates to a specific curriculum element within a given level. Based on the response defined by the fractal unit manager, fractal units are defined iteratively, ensuring that one fractal unit is responsible for a single curriculum element.

In order to address change management, we define for each hierarchical level a Fractal Level Manager that is responsible for managing the performance of fractals at a lower level (Fig. 2). The Fractal Level Manager is responsible for evaluating how all the fractals at a given level performed, based on the evaluation results that are stored in their respective nodes. For LLMs that did poorly on the evaluation, a new structure (the specific LLM and prompt) is defined based on the structure of the fractal units that performed better. This defined structure is used by the poorly performing fractal units to define new responses, which are then recorded in the curriculum nodes.

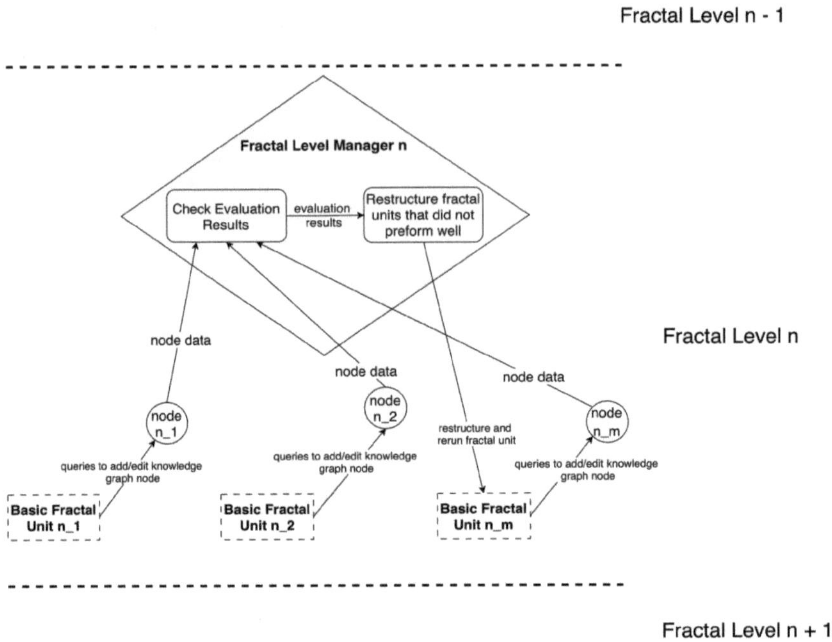

Fig. 2. Change propagation mechanism within FSA4LMAS.

The expected benefits of the FSA4LMAS are that each fractal unit is capable of independently defining its structure, more specifically, the structure of the *generator* and the *evaluator* in terms of the specific task that must be carried out by the system. Additionally, the change propagation mechanism enables the FSA4LMAS to improve the performance across fractal units based on evaluation results. Through this mechanism, the knowledge (relating to LLM selection, prompts, and evaluation metrics selection) from better-performing fractal units for a given task is propagated to the fractal units with comparatively weaker evaluation results. This change propagation mechanism enables collective intelligence (integration of diverse perspectives and decision-making through collaboration among agents [1]) to be achieved within the FSA4LMAS by leveraging its fractal features [15].

It should also be noted that while the FSA4LMAS is described in relation to its application for curriculum engineering, it can be implemented in other use cases that can be represented by a hierarchical knowledge graph.

4 Demonstration and Preliminary Evaluation of FSA4LMAS for Supporting Curriculum Engineering

To demonstrate the applicability of the proposed approach, we consider the case of supporting curriculum engineering of several study programs at Riga Technical University (RTU). Additionally, to evaluate the performance of the proposed FSA4LMAS, the LLM-based *evaluator* component is used to implement the 'LMM as an evaluator/judge' approach [16]. This approach utilizes an LLM to evaluate natural language generation and is suitable for contexts where access to benchmarking data is not available [16]. In the implementation discussed in this section, the outputs generated by the *generator* component are evaluated by a separate LLM-instance (*evaluator*) based on metrics defined by the *orchestrator* component.

To demonstrate and evaluate the FSA4LMAS, we first extracted and aggregated the data from relevant university documents to construct a hierarchical knowledge graph that represents three study programs and five individual study courses from each of the study programs. The resulting knowledge graph is shown in Fig. 3, where 'composedOf' relationships are defined from the study field nodes and the study program nodes, from the study program nodes to the study course nodes, and from the study course elements to the topic nodes.

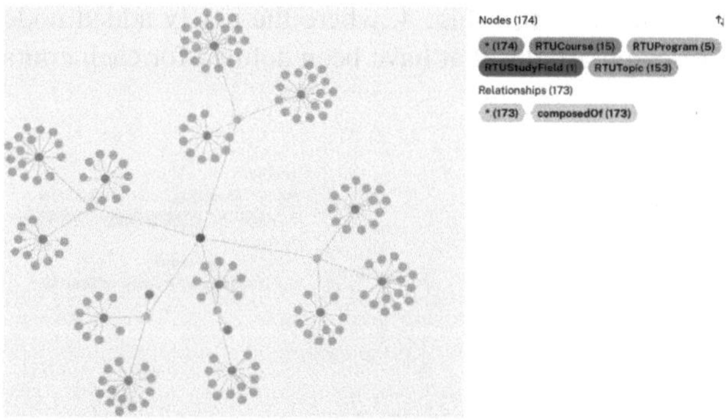

Fig. 3. Curriculum knowledge graph utilized to demonstrate the FSA4LMAS implementation.

To implement the FSA4LMAS, a Python script was created, which utilizes the OpenAI API library and the Neo4j API to access the required knowledge graph and LLMs in order to respond to a user query. Additionally, the Python script creates fractal units and their execution in a sequential manner where first the Fractal Unit Manager (which utilizes GPT-5.2, temperature = 0.2) defines which fractal level the query relates to and then based on the graph nodes within that level instantiates a BFU (according to the structure shown in Fig. 1). Then each BFU generates an output which is realized by editing the data of the node to which the fractal unit relates or by defining new nodes, depending on the user's query. Within the implementation, the *orchestrator* for all fractal units is based on GPT-5.2 with temperature = 0.2. Once all the fractal units relating to the fractal level (e.g., All, Study Field, Program, Course, and Topic) have finished executing their functions, the Fractal Level Manager (implemented using GPT-5.2 with temperature = 0.2) is prompted to analyze the results of the prompts that are stored in the AgentLog property of each of the nodes that a fractal unit interacted with. Based on this analysis, the manager component defines (playing the role of an *orchestrator*) a prompt, the specific LLM (e.g., GTP-4o), and evaluation criteria that must be utilized by the fractal units that performed weakly (based on the results of the evaluation generated by the evaluator of each node) so that they can be used during the next iteration. The full Python script that implements the proposed FSA4LMAS is available on GitHub [17].

To demonstrate the implementation of the FSA4LMAS, the authors use a hypothetical scenario where the university decides that every course must include a selected set of research articles that a student is recommended to read, in order to ensure that they are aware of existing knowledge for a specific domain. To utilize the FSA4LMAS implementation, the prompt *"For each course define one or more research articles that a student must read. The articles should be relevant to the course annotation and aim to deepen students' understanding of the course topics. Add the nodes (of type 'ResearchArticle') to the knowledge graph to represent these articles in a manner that includes their titles, citation, and source URLs with a 'HAS_RECOMMENDED_READING_MATERIAL' relationship to the course nodes."* is used with the expected outcome being that, for each course node, a fractal agent defines one or more articles that relate to the course. To do this, the *generator* must select an LLM for the executor that is capable of searching the web for relevant scientific literature. The results from the first run (without any change propagation) are shown in Fig. 4, where the newly added nodes (compared to Fig. 3) represent research articles that have been defined for each course by the fractal unit.

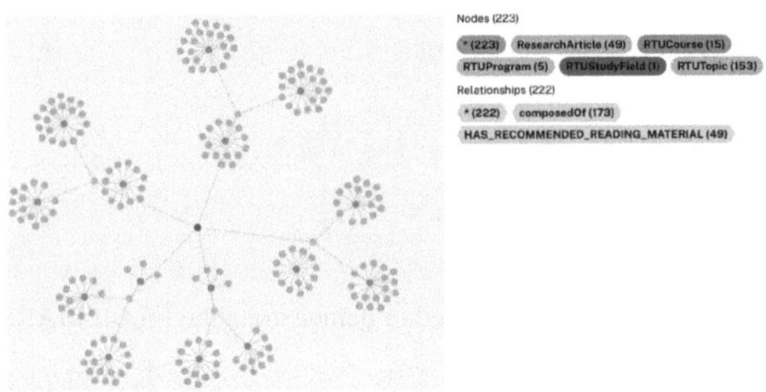

Fig. 4. The resulting knowledge graph of the first iteration (iteration without change propagation) of the fractal agents defining research articles (represented as pink nodes).

In terms of the variation between the structure of different fractal units, two different LLMs have been used (GPT-4o and GPT-4.1), different evaluation metrics were defined (e.g., conformance with the JSON schema, conformance with the knowledge graph structure, reliability of research article data, etc.), and different evaluation scores were achieved. A few examples of the evaluation data are presented in Table 1 (some of the Evaluation Metrics Defined are summarized for readability).

In the case of the first two rows, an example where a fractal was updated through change propagation is presented, where initially the GPT-4o model was utilized, but then GPT-4.1 was used with an updated profile of a 'Generator agent producing graph mutations ONLY in the canonical_graph_mutations_v1 JSON format'. The same pattern (identical generation prompts, model, and evaluation metrics) was seen in the other fractal units that were altered based on change propagation. In the case of the Business Sociology course, an improvement of 0.20 was observed, which corresponded to an improvement in the research articles that were not hallucinated, increasing from 1 out of

3 to 2 out of 3, with one of the research article nodes defined in the first iteration (before propagation) being replaced.

Table 1. Example results from the definition of research articles for courses (the full set of results is available on GitHub [17]).

Courses Related to Fractals	Model Used	Generator Role Assigned	Evaluation Metrics Defined	Evaluation Score	Propagation Status
Business Sociology	gpt-4o	*Generator* agent for a curriculum knowledge-graph enrichment task	Relevance; Scholarly quality; Factual accuracy; URL reliability; Schema compliance; Output format	0.25	Pre
Business Sociology	gpt-4.1	*Generator* agent producing graph mutations ONLY in the canonical_graph_mutations_v1 JSON format	Strict schema compliance; Node property compliance; Relationship compliance; Scholarly type compliance; Verifiability; Internal consistency	0.45	Post
Microwave Telecommunications Systems	gpt-4.1	*Generator* agent producing graph mutations in the fixed system-wide format canonical_graph_mutations_v1	outputs strictly conform to canonical_graph_mutations_v1; Only Research Article nodes are created; Research article node properties; Connection to course node; Quality of research article; Citations and Source URLs are accurate and non-hallucinated; Articles are non-duplicative and collectively cover key aspects; Answer text quality	0.62	Fractal Unit was not updated

Across the 15 courses, the mean evaluation score achieved was 0.315, with the evaluation results after back propagation being 0.398, which represents an approximately 26% gain. When focusing on the fractal units that were rerun using the structure defined by the fractal level manager, across the five fractal units that were rerun, there was a mean increase in score of 0.24.

To test the adaptability of the proposed architecture when the task changes, the aforementioned Python script was run with an updated query that relates to identifying competencies that are taught by each of the programs and courses. The query used was *"For each of the courses in the curriculum, define competencies which the students are expected to achieve. Define them as competency nodes (with a unique label, and id) connected to the respective course nodes by a relationship of type 'defines_competency'. Focus on defining competencies that are relevant for guiding students towards selecting and engaging with research articles. Prioritize defining competencies that can be directly linked to research articles as learning resources. If relevant, also add relationships from competencies to research articles with a relationship type like 'can_be_learned_by' or 'is_demonstrated_by'."* with the intention being to define competencies based on the courses and trying to relate them to the research articles, thereby presenting the relationship between the competencies and the results shown in research.

The newly defined knowledge graph after change propagation (for the second prompt) is shown in Fig. 5, with the graph now being composed of red nodes that represent the competencies taught by each study program and study course.

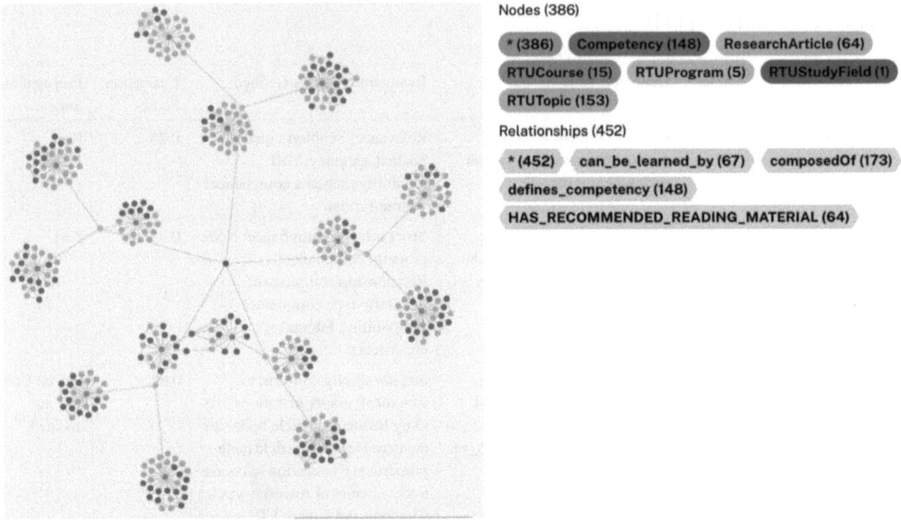

Fig. 5. The resulting knowledge graph representing the competencies defined for each study course and how they relate to the defined research articles.

In this case, 8 of the course nodes went through change propagation, and the resulting increase in performance was similar to the first scenario, with the mean evaluation score across the 15 courses being 0.65 (pre propagation) and 0.80 (post propagation), representing a similar 25% increase in performance. The detailed evaluation results for each course are available on GitHub [17].

Overall, the results of the demonstration indicated how the proposed FSA4LMAS is capable of adapting to different user queries and defining (fractal) units of agents, which initially self-organize through the selection of specific LLMs and the assignment of different agentic roles. The knowledge gained from all the fractal units at a given level (in terms of the prompts, agent profiles, LLMs used, and how evaluation takes place) is then propagated in a manner where the poorly performing fractal units can adopt in order to improve performance.

5 Discussion and Limitations

This work demonstrates how fractal design principles can be applied to LMASs and the potential benefits of doing so. Previous works [5, 13] have demonstrated how a fractal approach to information systems can support the fractal structure that is present in organizations. For instance, [5] demonstrates how the fractal features of healthcare centers can be used to improve the cooperation among healthcare professionals by supporting the transfer of knowledge relating to the activities carried out in distributed healthcare centers. However, to the best of the authors' knowledge, the approach proposed in this paper is the first work that applies fractal design principles to LLM-agents-based systems, resulting in the IS and its components being self-similar, self-organizing, goal-oriented and being able to evolve based on changing environment or tasks (dynamism). Fractal organization enables the LLM-based fractal units within the FSA4LMAS to carry out the same task (based on user queries) with different knowledge (which in this context is curriculum) elements that belong to the same knowledge organization level independently. The knowledge (relating to LLM selection, prompts, and evaluation metrics selection) gained by a fractal unit completing a given task is then propagated across fractal units through the fractal level manager, resulting in improved performance of fractal units with comparatively worse evaluation results.

This ability of LLM-based agents to perform a task independently with the knowledge gained then being propagated to other agents is a key characteristic of the proposed solution that is enabled by the self-similar structure of fractal units. While previous work on collaborative intelligence [18] and information propagation [19] within LMASs demonstrates how the exchange of information across agents can lead to increased coordination [18] and reduced error propagation [19], the exchanged information relates to intentions, intermediate outputs, and decision signals rather than the propagation of knowledge relating to the execution of tasks.

While the initial LLM-based evaluation results for two curriculum engineering tasks demonstrate the benefits of enabling change propagation by applying fractal design principles when developing LMAs, the generalizability of these results is limited. Therefore, further experimentation is required to provide conclusive evidence of the benefits of the FSA4LMAS.

6 Conclusions and Future Work

This work proposes a fractal-based system architecture for LLM-based multi-agent system (FSA4LMAS), with the core principles of fractal systems being adopted to create a system architecture that has the flexibility to adapt to the requests made by a user, in addition to evolving based on the results of similar agent units (fractal units). In this work, the recurring structure of each fractal unit is composed of an *orchestrator*, *generator*, *evaluator*, and *reporter*. This basic fractal unit is instantiated by a Fractal Unit Manager based on the structure of the knowledge graph, which represents the environment and the query defined by the user.

Additionally, a fractal-level manager is present within the architecture to facilitate change propagation after the self-organization of each fractal unit. The fractal level manager (which in this case is another LLM) uses the evaluation results of all the fractal units belonging to a specific fractal level to define (based on AgentLog information stored in each node which a given fractal unit is responsible for) a common structure (in terms of the LLM used, evaluation criteria used, and the *generator* agent role used) that the fractal units that did not perform well during self-organization adopt. Doing so ensures that the knowledge gained for each fractal unit is utilized for change propagation.

To demonstrate how the proposed architecture operates, we considered the case of curriculum engineering, where the hierarchical knowledge organization structure (with the levels: study field, study program, course, and topic) is represented as a knowledge graph, and a Python script that implements the FSA4LMAS is used to alter this knowledge graph based on user queries. The two scenarios of defining research articles for each course, followed by defining competencies that represent each course and relating them to the previously defined research articles, demonstrate how the architecture adapts based on the user's query by selecting different agent profiles and LLMs, leading to the definition of new nodes in the knowledge graph. Additionally, within these scenarios, one iteration of change propagation improved the evaluation results across the fractal units by 25%, demonstrating how the knowledge generated from independently evolving fractal units can be used to improve performance across the whole system.

While this demonstration serves as initial evidence of the applicability of the FSA4LMAS, future work should systematically evaluate the generalizability of these results to more curriculum engineering tasks and other contexts.

References

1. Li, X., Wang, S., Zeng, S., Wu, Y., Yang, Y.: A survey on LLM-based multi-agent systems: workflow, infrastructure, and challenges. Vicinagearth **1**, 9 (2024)
2. Chowa, S.S., et al.: From language to action: a review of large language models as autonomous agents and tool users. Artif. Intell. Rev. **59**(2), 71 (2026)
3. Frischer, R., Singh, M.P., Porcaro, C., Namazi, H.: Fractal theory: a comprehensive review of applications across engineering disciplines. Fractals **33**(7), 1–18 (2025)
4. Peralta, M.E., Soltero, V.M.: Analysis of fractal manufacturing systems framework towards Industry 4.0. J. Manufact. Syst. **57**, 46–60 (2020)
5. Ahmed, N.S.: A fractal-based model to improve cooperation among physicians in distributed healthcare information systems. PhD thesis, University of Malaya, Kuala Lumpur (2013)
6. Poenaru, C.E., Dobrescu, R.: Fractal techniques in health information systems management: can they be used? In: 2019 22nd International Conference on Control Systems and Computer Science (CSCS), pp. 592–597. IEEE, Piscataway (2019)
7. Kok, D.L., Xu, M., Trumble, S., Matthews, K., Wright, C.: Categorising drivers of curriculum renewal in entry-to-practice health professional education: a scoping review. Med. Educ. **59**(8), 812–822 (2025)
8. Chu, Z., et al.: LLM agents for education: advances and applications. arXiv preprint arXiv:2503.11733 (2025)
9. Wang, Z., Moriyama, S., Wang, W.Y., Gangopadhyay, B., Takamatsu, S.: Talk structurally, act hierarchically: a collaborative framework for LLM multi-agent systems. arXiv preprint arXiv:2502.11098 (2025)
10. Liu, Y., Zhang, G., Wang, K., Li, S., Pan, S.: Graph-augmented large language model agents: current progress and future prospects. IEEE Intell. Syst. **41**(2), 45–55 (2026)
11. Ryu, K., Jung, M.: Agent-based fractal architecture and modelling for developing distributed manufacturing systems. Int. J. Prod. Res. **41**(17), 4233–4255 (2003)
12. Kirikova, M.: Towards flexible information architecture for fractal information systems. In: 2009 International Conference on Information, Process, and Knowledge Management (eKNOW 2009), pp. 135–140. IEEE, Piscataway (2009)
13. Grabis, J., Kirikova, M., Vanags, J.: Information architecture of fractal information systems. In: Proceedings of the 11th International Conference on Enterprise Information Systems (ICEIS 2009), vol. ISAS, pp. 150–155. SCITEPRESS, Setúbal (2009)

14. Kirikova, M., Grundspenkis, J., Sukovskis, U.: Educational "ecosystem" for information systems engineering. In: Horváth, I., Rusák, Z. (eds.) Proceedings of the Seventh International Symposium on Tools and Methods of Competitive Engineering, vol. 2, pp. 769–783. Delft University of Technology, Delft (2008)
15. Stecjuka, J., Makna, J., Kirikova, M.: Best practices oriented business process operation and design. In: Proceedings of the BPMDS 2008 Workshop: Business Process Life-Cycle: Design, Deployment, Operation & Evaluation, pp. 171–184. CEUR-WS.org (2008)
16. Gao, M., Hu, X., Yin, X., Ruan, J., Pu, X., Wan, X.: LLM-based NLG evaluation: current status and challenges. Comput. Linguist. **51**(2), 661–687 (2025)
17. FSA-LMAS GitHub repository. https://github.com/ArithaRTU/FSA-LMAS. Accessed 1 May 2026
18. Qiu, X., et al.: Towards collaborative intelligence: propagating intentions and reasoning for multi-agent coordination with large language models. arXiv preprint arXiv:2407.12532 (2024)
19. Shen, X., et al.: Understanding the information propagation effects of communication topologies in LLM-based multi-agent systems. In: Proceedings of the 2025 Conference on Empirical Methods in Natural Language Processing, pp. 12347–12361. Association for Computational Linguistics, Suzhou (2025)

Applications of Intelligent Systems

Towards Fully Synthetic Schema-Based Tabular Test Data Generation in Estonian E-Government Settings

Maj-Annika Tammisto[1(✉)], Dietmar Pfahl[1], Faiz Ali Shah[1], and Daniel Rodriguez[2]

[1] Institute of Computer Science, University of Tartu, Tartu, Estonia
maj-annika.tammisto@ut.ee
[2] Department of Computer Science, University of Alcala, Madrid, Spain

Abstract. Testing of e-government services relies on privacy-preserving synthetic test data that are as similar as possible to actual real-life raw data, but also satisfy the requirements of the test cases. Obtaining such test data in Estonian e-government settings is a resource-intensive and largely manual process. This work addresses the challenges of the current process and suggests a novel synthetic test data generation approach that is largely automated, does not require access to real-life raw data, and generates realistic synthetic test data for Estonian e-government settings. We validate the Proof of Concept of our novel synthetic test data generation approach in real-life-like settings. We conclude that the approach can already generate synthetic data for simpler test cases, but needs additional work to cover more complex test cases that require synthetic test data to be compatible across different data services.

Keywords: Synthetic Test Data · Data Synthesis · Synthetic Data Generation · Rule-based Generation · Schema-based Generation · Tabular Data

1 Introduction

Digital government services, also referred to as e-government services, have been a conventional part of Estonian citizens' and residents' lives since the early 2000s [1]. For Estonian citizens and residents, it is taken for granted that they can submit pre-filled annual tax reports online with just a few clicks, drive without carrying a physical driving license, and even complete divorce proceedings over the internet without needing to be physically present with their spouse.

The e-government services rely on secure data exchange that seamlessly runs in the background and aggregates information from various government institutions. This enables, for example, the automatic inclusion of relevant data in tax reports, real-time access to driver information for law enforcement, and the efficient processing of online divorce proceedings by family officials. The framework

R. Matulevičius et al. (Eds.): DB&IS 2026, CCIS 3085, pp. 55–71, 2026.
https://doi.org/10.1007/978-3-032-30863-4_4

used for secure data exchange in Estonian e-government settings uses a local implementation of the X-Road®[1] technology, called the X-tee[2]. Each member of this framework can act as a data service client requesting data, a data service provider providing data, or both. Data services that are used for requesting and providing data over the X-tee data exchange framework are, in nature, web services that use Simple Object Access Protocol (SOAP) and Representational State Transfer Protocol (REST) interaction style. The scope of data that a data service client can request from a data service provider is limited by the structure and description of data services that the data service provider provides.

Every e-government service is developed and tested before it is made available for citizens and residents. An e-government service that relies on input data received from data services when made available to citizens and residents also requires input data while it is tested, with the exception that actual, real-life raw data can't be accessed and used for testing for data privacy reasons. Therefore, there is a constant need for realistic synthetic test data that is consistent between different data services. The synthetic test data often needs to be created ad hoc so that development teams can meet their deadlines. As we have demonstrated in [2], generating synthetic test data upon request is currently a largely manual and lengthy process. The challenges that users of the current synthetic test data generation process face can be mitigated by partly automating the process and, therefore, reducing the time and resources needed for ad hoc synthetic test data generation.

In [3], we identified and classified existing approaches that can be used to generate synthetic test data without direct access to actual real-life raw data. Existing approaches that can be used to generate complex tabular synthetic data without requiring real-life raw data as input can be classified as either specification-based or rule-based synthetic data generation approaches. However, formal specifications are usually not available, and the limitation of rule-based synthetic data generation approaches preventing their wider implementation in e-government settings is that they rely on extensive manual work and substantial domain knowledge in the rule definition phase. This makes existing rule-based synthetic data generation approaches inefficient and expensive to use in e-government settings. The solution is, therefore, to develop and validate a novel rule-based synthetic data generation approach where not only the synthetic data generation itself, but also the prior definition of rules (and constraints, if needed) requires as little manual work from humans as possible.

Our contribution includes the Proof of Concept (PoC) of a novel rule-based synthetic data generation approach for data services that use the SOAP interaction style. We use Large Language Models (LLMs) to derive rules and constraints from data service descriptions and relevant documents, and to generate synthetic test data for the respective data services with minimal intervention by humans. We validate the PoC by generating synthetic test data for a playground where

[1] https://x-road.global/.
[2] https://x-tee.ee/en/home.

an application uses input from data services that are provided in the Estonian e-government settings by different government entities.

The rest of this paper is structured as follows: Sect. 2 gives an overview of previous work related to ours. Section 3 describes the steps and activities of our novel synthetic test data generation approach. Section 4 explains the validation process and defines our Research Question (RQ) that guides the validation. Section 5 describes the validation results and answers the RQ. Section 6 discusses the results, explains the limitations of the PoC of our approach, and provides insight into future work. Finally, Sect. 7 concludes this paper.

2 Related Work

Creating synthetic test data automatically from code or descriptions is not a new idea. Automating unit test generation by exploring the input space and producing effective test cases for given programs has been studied for decades [4,5]. Approaches for test case generation from WSDL definitions [6], OpenAPI specifications [7], or both [8] have also been suggested for many years. Still, the complexity and variety of data generated with these methods have always been too limited for high-level test cases. The vast development of LLMs has only recently allowed us to reuse the idea and, for the first time, to create complex, versatile, and realistic synthetic test data without accessing the real-life raw data and using it as training data.

The potential of using LLMs to extract business rules that are defined in natural language and to use them for test case and test data generation has also not gone unnoticed. Recent contributions are aiming to automate test case generation from business rules and requirements that are defined in natural language [9,10]. Nevertheless, we have not been able to identify an existing approach that combines both a web service specification and unstructured business rules as input, considers the need to generate consistent synthetic data for more than one web service, and does not need to access real-life raw data.

3 Approach

In Fig. 1, we show a high-level overview of our PoC. In the first step, we generate the schema that contains the structure, rules, and constraints for synthetic data generation for a specific data service, as discussed in Sect. 3.1. The second step is to generate the synthetic data based on the previously generated schema, by doing the activities described in Sect. 3.2.

3.1 Schema Generation

This Subsection describes the necessary inputs for the schema generation step of our PoC, as well as the activities and outputs of each activity of the *schema generation* step.

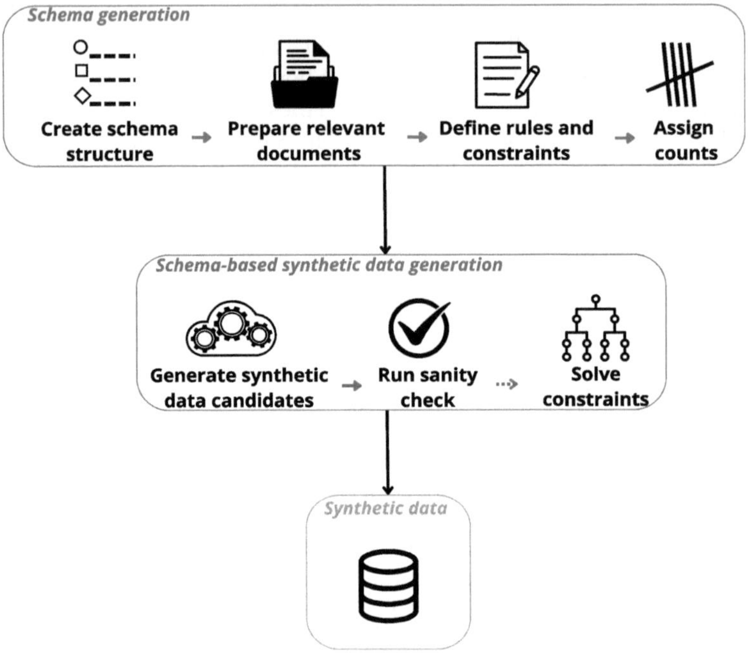

Fig. 1. Overview of the PoC.

Create Schema Structure. The *Create schema structure* activity is currently designed for data services that use the SOAP interaction style, as this interaction style is currently mostly used in Estonian e-government settings. The activity has two input variables where the values need to be specified by the user:

- WSDL description location: the location of the WSDL description that contains the description of the operation (data service) of interest. All WSDL descriptions for data services that are used in the Estonian e-government settings are publicly available in the Catalogue of all X-tee subsystems with methods and WSDL descriptions[3]. The value of the WSDL description location variable can therefore be either the location of the WSDL in the Catalogue or the location of a locally stored WSDL description file.
- Operation name: the name of our data service of interest that would, in the previous manual synthetic data generation process, be forwarded to the data service provider as reference.

Defining the two input values is the only manual contribution that is required from the user of the synthetic data generation approach. After adding the input, the schema structure will be automatically created by a Python program.

[3] https://x-tee.ee/catalogue/EE.

The Python program uses the Python Zeep SOAP Client[4] to parse the WSDL description and extract all elements that belong to the defined operation, together with the required data types of their values in the data service. A JSON schema is composed of the extracted elements and data types, following the sequence of elements in the data service. The element names are listed as property names with the extracted data type specified as the type of each respective property in the JSON schema. The JSON schema, which contains the data service structure, element names of the data service as property names, and allowed data types as property types, is hereinafter referred to as the schema structure and as the output of the *Create Schema Structure* activity.

The *Create Schema Structure* activity can be summarized as follows:

```
#Create schema structure
SET wsdl_url to {WSDL location}
SET operation_name to {name of the data service}
    FOR each element in the WSDL
        IF element belongs to the data service
            ADD element name in the schema structure as
            property name
            ADD element data type in the schema structure
            as type
        ELSE
            SKIP
        END IF
    END FOR
RETURN schema structure
```

Prepare Relevant Documents. In Estonia, all government institutions that act as data service providers must describe their information systems as well as the data that they gather and process in the catalogue of interoperability resources (RIHA)[5]. The RIHA catalogue, therefore, contains unstructured data that includes descriptions of systems, components, services, data models, semantic assets, and more. The RIHA catalogue provides a REST API interface that can be used to query the data related to a specific data service provider. In our context, the data related to the data service provider who provides our data service of interest are the relevant documents.

The *Prepare relevant documents* activity requires the name of the data service provider to be entered manually as input. The remainder of the activity is done automatically: the REST API interface provided by the RIHA catalogue is queried for all relevant data. All documents of different types (.txt, .pdf, .csv, etc.) are downloaded, converted to text, and saved as .txt files in UTF-8 encoding.

[4] https://docs.python-zeep.org/en/master/.
[5] https://www.riha.ee/Avaleht.

The .txt files are then split into chunks. We use the RecursiveCharacterTextSplitter by LangChain[6] with chunk size 200 and no overlap to split the documents, as this chunking method has been proven to perform well for later retrieval of information from the chunks [11]. We then create a collection for the data service of interest in a vector database. Since we use only publicly available documents, we have currently chosen the Chroma Cloud[7] vector database to reduce the technical overhead. The cloud-based database can nevertheless be easily replaced with a local vector database.

To create embeddings, or in other words, the vector representations, from each chunk, we use OpenAI's[8] text-embedding-3-large embedding model. We then add the embeddings, chunk text, and metadata (source and name of each document) to the created collection in the vector database. The output of the *Prepare relevant documents* is the collection in the vector database together with embeddings, chunk text, and metadata.

The *Prepare relevant documents* activity can be summarized as follows:

```
#Prepare relevant documents
SET document_endpoint to {document catalogue API base URL}
+{name of the data service provider}
GET all document URLs from document_endpoint
    FOR each document URL
        IF URL starts with "file://"
            EXTRACT document_id from URL
            JOIN {API base URL}+"files"+document_id
           SAVE document
           EXTRACT text from document
           SAVE text as .txt
       ELSE
           SAVE document
           EXTRACT text from document
           SAVE text as .txt
       END IF
    END FOR
```

Define Rules and Constraints. The *Define rules and constraints* activity is a chain of five primitive LLM operations (LLM POs), as illustrated in Fig. 2. Each LLM PO is designed to perform a specific task of a certain type and with default data and prompting structure [12].

PO1 takes the output of the *Create schema structure* activity as input. Each subsequent PO takes the output of the previous PO as input. In addition to that, factual queries PO2, PO3, and PO4 use the output of the *Prepare relevant documents* activity to find the k nearest neighbours to the data service name,

[6] https://www.langchain.com/.
[7] https://www.trychroma.com/cloud.
[8] https://openai.com/.

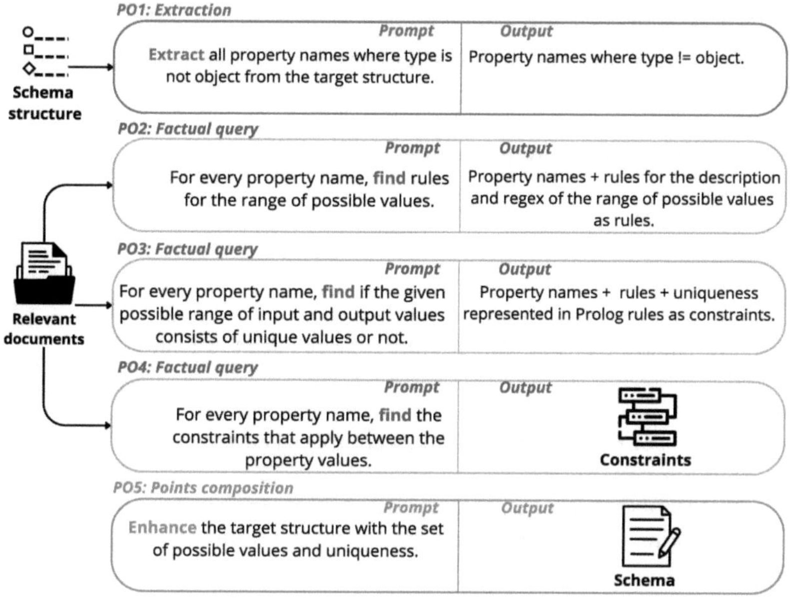

Fig. 2. The chain of LLM POs.

as well as every property name in the schema structure, to provide context and improve the LLM output with Retrieval-Augmented Generation (RAG) [13].

We use the gpt-4.1 LLM from OpenAI, which is a non-reasoning model, in all LLM POs. While PO1 and PO5 are simple extraction and points composition tasks, PO2, PO3, and PO4 can be viewed as operations that also require some reasoning. Especially if the answer can't be explicitly found in the context or in the data that has been used to teach the model. With this consideration, we have also evaluated the family or OpenAI's gpt-5 reasoning models for PO2, PO3, and PO4. We did not notice a significant advantage in using a slower and more expensive reasoning model for PO2, PO3 and PO4. Non-reasoning and reasoning models both show inconsistencies in the rules and constraints for properties where they can't be explicitly derived from the context. Surprisingly, we did see a 15 percent increase in inconsistencies in rules and constraints when running PO2, PO3, and PO4 repeatedly for the same data service and with the same context with the reasoning model, compared to running PO2, PO3, and PO4 repeatedly for the same data service and with the same context with the non-reasoning model. Based on these results, we concluded that the gpt-4.1 non-reasoning model is currently more suitable for our LLM POs than a reasoning model.

The first output of the *Define rules and constraints* activity is the schema structure that is enhanced with rules for the value of every property in the schema. The second output of this activity is a separate file with constraints.

The *Define rules and constraints* activity can be summarized as follows:

```
#Define rules and constraints
SET path to {name of the schema structure file}
    FOR each property in schema structure
        IF property type is object
            EXTRACT property name
        ELSE
            SKIP
        END IF
    END FOR
RETURN list of property names
SET path to {name of the directory where .txt files
are stored}
    FOR each .txt file
        SPLIT .txt file to chunks(chunk_size=x,
        chunk_overlap=y)
        CREATE embeddings(number_of_dimensions=z)
        ADD chunks and embeddings to vector database
    END FOR
QUERY vector database for {name of the data service provider}+
{name of the data service}+
every property name in the list of property names
RETURN results
FIND the set of possible values
    FOR the list of property names+results+
    {name of the data service provider}+
    {name of the data service} as context
        PROMPT LLM
    END FOR
RETURN the set of possible values
FIND the uniqueness of values
    FOR the set of possible values+results+
    {name of the data service provider}+
    {name of the data service} as context
        PROMPT LLM
    END FOR
RETURN the set of possible values + uniqueness as rules
FIND constraints
    FOR rules+results+{name of the data service provider}+
    {name of the data service} as context
        PROMPT LLM
    END FOR
RETURN constraints
ENHANCE schema structure file
    FOR each property in schema structure
        IF property type is object
```

```
            ADD rules as description of the property
        ELSE
            SKIP
        END IF
    END FOR
RETURN properties with rules
```

Assign Counts. From the output of the *Define rules and constraints* activity, synthetic test data can be generated by randomly specifying the size of the population only. This allows for generating a required number of sets of synthetic values from the schema where all values are within the allowed value ranges of each property, and then solving the constraints between property values within every set of synthetic values. Nevertheless, test cases often require a more specific distribution of values, e.g., specific types of tax records, certain pre-defined vehicle data, or synthetic test persons of age groups defined by the test cases.

To allow synthetic data generation based on a specific pre-defined distribution of values within the ranges of all possible values of certain properties, we split the rules for these properties into equivalence classes. Every equivalence class represents a certain tax record, a vehicle data class, an age group, or any other attribute where the value is directly associated with a test case or another requirement of the user. We use conditional logic and pre-defined "helper values" and we define in the schema to which of the equivalence classes a synthetic data value that is generated for a specific property must belong. The creation of equivalence classes is currently a manual process, with the perspective of automating it in the future.

The output of the *Assign counts* activity is the schema with rules and counts.

The *Assign counts* activity can be summarized as follows:

```
#Assign counts
SET path to {properties with rules}
    FOR each property in properties with rules
        IF property type is object
            SPLIT description to equivalence classes
            ADD helper_id to every equivalence class
            ASSIGN count for every equivalence class as
            helper_id value
        ELSE
            SKIP
        END IF
    END FOR
RETURN schema
```

3.2 Schema-Based Synthetic Data Generation

This Subsection describes the necessary inputs for the schema-based synthetic data generation step of our approach, as well as the activities and outputs of each activity of the schema-based synthetic data generation step.

Generate Synthetic Data Candidates. The *Generate synthetic data candidates* activity aims to generate a population of candidate sets, with synthetic values for every required property in the schema. The generated synthetic values comply with the rules defined for respective properties as well as with the counts within every equivalence class of the rule for one property, if the equivalence classes and counts are defined. The *Generate synthetic data candidates* activity requires the user to manually enter the size of the population. It then takes the schema as input and uses a LLM-based synthetic data generator to generate the requested amount of synthetic data candidate sets. The gpt-4.1 from OpenAI is used to generate the synthetic data candidates. The value of the model temperature parameter is set to 0 to minimize the creativity of the model and to force it to explicitly follow the schema.

The output of the *Generate synthetic data candidates* activity is a JSON file that includes the generated synthetic data candidates.

Run Sanity Check. The *Run sanity check* activity takes the JSON file with generated synthetic data candidates as input and validates it against the schema. The goal is this activity is to check that all required values exist. In other words, this activity mostly checks the performance of the LLM and identifies its failure to generate all requested synthetic data values.

The sanity check is performed automatically by a dedicated Python program. If no errors are found by the program, no manual intervention is necessary from the user. Should the sanity check identify errors in the generated data candidates, the user will receive the error report, which then needs to be investigated manually.

The output of the *Run sanity check* activity is the sanity check report, together with the error report, if applicable.

Solve Constraints. The *Solve constraints* activity aims to identify which candidate values are not allowed across properties and to correct these values. It takes the JSON file with the generated synthetic data candidates and the file with constraints as input and uses the gpt-4.1 from OpenAI as the constraint solver.

In addition to an LLM-based constraint solver, we have previously experimented with the Z3 solver from Microsoft Research[9]. While the Z3 showed more consistent results in 2024, the results of the Z3 and the gpt-4.1 were already

[9] https://www.microsoft.com/en-us/research/project/z3-3/.

similar in our context by the second half of 2025. Considering the vast and continuous advancement of LLMs and the complexity of setting up the Z3 solver correctly for every individual set of data candidates and constraints, a LLM-based constraint solver is better suited for our context.

The output of the *Solve constraints* activity is either a statement "No incompliances found", or a JSON file where the generated synthetic data candidates with values that were identified as not compliant with the constraints are corrected. If the constraint solver outputs corrected synthetic data candidates, the respective candidates are replaced in the JSON file that includes all generated synthetic data candidates. This creates a final JSON file including the generated synthetic data as output of the Schema-based synthetic data generation step.

4 Validation

This Section describes the validation process of our PoC, defines the RQ, and validation metrics for answering the RQ.

To validate the PoC, we set up a playground with an application that uses data from three different Estonian e-government data services as input. The application served as our System Under Test (SUT). To emulate the real-life test data ordering process described in [2], we wrote test cases based on the functional requirements of our SUT, as well as synthetic test data ordering requests for all three data service providers to enable the execution of our test cases. We used the PoC to generate the requested synthetic test data.

Figure 3 shows the architecture of the playground. MySQL[10] was used to build the Synthetic Data Digital Twin (SDDT). The generated synthetic test data was inserted into the MySQL database. For each of the three data services, a mapping view was created to combine data from different tables into one dataset that matches the structure of the respective data service. MySQL REST Service (MRS)[11] was used to create the REST services that mimicked the request- and response structures of the three actual data services. We built the API with FastAPI[12], using the uvicorn[13] web server. The SUT was an executable Java application.

To explore some variations that are likely to occur in real-life-like settings, we designed three slightly different experiments.

Ex1: The SUT uses data from three different data services. The generated synthetic test data does not have to be consistent between the three data services.

Ex2: The SUT uses data from three different data services. One set of the generated synthetic test data has to be consistent between two of the three data services.

[10] https://www.mysql.com/.
[11] https://dev.mysql.com/doc/dev/mysql-rest-service/latest.
[12] https://fastapi.tiangolo.com/.
[13] https://uvicorn.dev/.

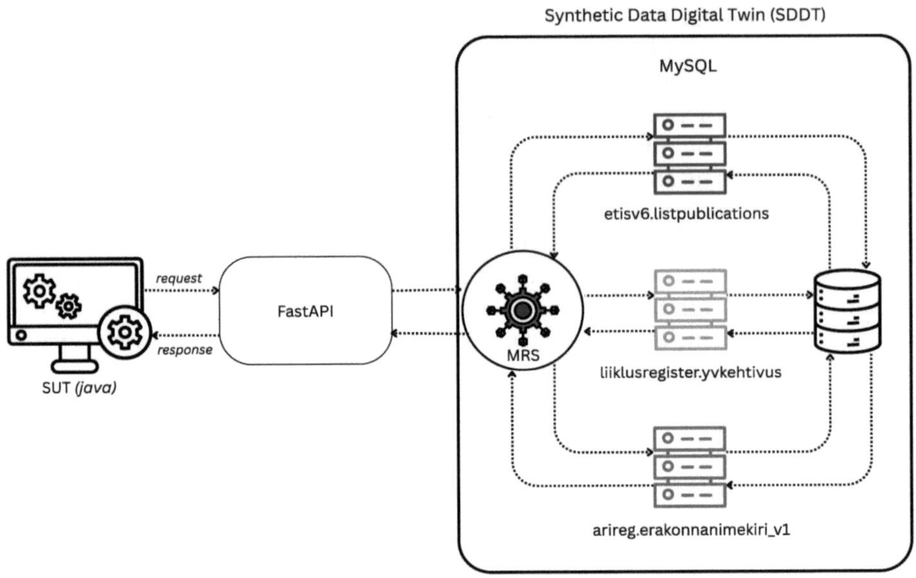

Fig. 3. Architecture of the playground.

Ex3: The SUT uses data from three different data services. One set of the generated synthetic test data has to be consistent between two of the three data services. The PoC can use only LLMs that store data in the EU.

We have defined the following RQ to be answered based on experiment results:

Does the suggested synthetic data generation approach support the ad hoc generation of synthetic test data in real-life-like settings?

4.1 Validation Metrics

We have defined the following binary metrics to answer our RQ:

M1: Every requested synthetic test data is generated.

M2: The quality of generated synthetic test data enables the execution of all test cases on the SUT.

M3: Changing the LLM in the PoC does not affect the results of M1 or M2.

5 Results

This Section describes the validation results of our PoC and provides the answer to our RQ.

5.1 Results of Ex1

Every test case required a response with synthetic test data from all three data services. We were able to generate all the requested synthetic test data with our PoC. The generated synthetic test data did not cause any false negatives while executing the test cases.

5.2 Results of Ex2

Every test case required a response with synthetic test data from all three data services. One test case required that the value of an element in one data service would be the same as the value of an element in another data service. With our PoC, we were not able to generate test data for one test case, where the synthetic test data needed to be consistent between two of the three data services. We were able to generate all other requested synthetic test data. The generated synthetic test data did not cause any false negatives while executing the test cases.

5.3 Results of Ex3

Every test case required a response with synthetic test data from all three data services. One test case required that the value of an element in one data service would be the same as the value of an element in another data service. The mistral-embed embedding model and mistral-medium-latest from Mistral AI[14] were used instead of OpenAI's text-embedding-3-large embedding model and gpt-4.1. With our PoC, we were not able to generate test data for one test case, where the synthetic test data needed to be consistent between two of the three data services. We were able to generate all other requested synthetic test data. The generated synthetic test data did not cause any false negatives while executing the test cases.

Answer to the RQ: The suggested synthetic data generation approach supports the ad hoc generation of synthetic test data in real-life-like settings for simpler requests that don't require data consistency between different data services.

Table 1 summarizes the experiment results by stating where a validation metric was achieved ("Yes"), where a validation metric was not achieved ("No"), and where a metric was not applicable ("N/A"). We publicly share the experiment reports with the PoC code and the generated synthetic test data.[15]

[14] https://mistral.ai/.

[15] Data availability: https://doi.org/10.6084/m9.figshare.31699558.

Table 1. Validation results

Validation metric	Ex1	Ex2	Ex3
M1 - test data complete	Yes	No	No
M2 - test data correct	Yes	Yes	Yes
M3 - LLM effect	N/A	N/A	Yes

6 Discussion

This study provides the first validation results for the PoC of a novel synthetic data generation approach that not only generates data but also aims to automate the underlying rule and constraint definition without accessing real-life raw data. The results of Ex1 demonstrate that the approach can effectively generate synthetic test data for test cases where no consistency between synthetic data received from different data services is required. This shows that the approach can potentially already be a useful alternative to the currently used manual test data ordering process, as described in [2].

The results of Ex2 point out that our approach has difficulties with preserving relations between different data services. More specifically, the LLMs struggle with some of the conditional logic used in the *Assign counts* activity, which is described in Sect. 3. Despite our investigation into this matter, which included the revision of the execution logs of OpenAI, searching for relevant literature, and consulting the LLMs themselves, we were not able to fully identify why conditional logic structured in the same way was ignored for one property, and followed for another property. We conclude that although LLMs are already great at reading JSON, it is not sufficient to simply include conditional logic in the schema. Although in our experiments, it prevented us from generating synthetic test data that is consistent between two data services, an unexpected failure to understand the conditional logic in a Schema may also cause failures in generating synthetic test data that meets the requirements within one data service.

For Ex3, we replaced the embedding model and LLM from the OpenAI product family with the embedding model and LLM of the EU-based Mistral AI. Changing the embedding model and LLM did not affect achieving the metrics: both LLMs were able to generate synthetic test data for most test cases, and both LLMs struggled with conditional logic in the Schema, when generating synthetic test data where consistency between data from two data services had to be achieved. This shows that the approach is generally robust enough that it can be operated with different embedding models and LLMs. Moreover, the POs that are described in Sect. 3 are designed to be so small and simple that they do not necessarily require very large or expensive LLMs.

There are, nevertheless, important limitations that need to be addressed in our future work. As the current PoC still requires human intervention in several activities, we will continue with automating the approach. We will implement a chain of additional POs for the LLM to automatically extract client input from test data queries and translate those into data taxonomies and ontologies. These will be used respectively in the generation of synthetic data candidates and in solving constraints with the aim of increasing the alignment of the generated synthetic data with real-world patterns. Since we learned from this study that using conditional logic in the Schema is not a reliable solution, we will add the data generation instructions that were previously captured in conditional logic to property descriptions instead. We will also find an alternative for the Python Zeep SOAP Client that sometimes fails to parse WSDL documents due to namespace issues and requires WSDL documents to be patched manually. When developing the alternative, we will aim for a solution that can be used with WSDL, as well as OpenAPI descriptions. The improved approach requires evaluation in actual real-life settings, where e-government services are tested.

7 Conclusion

Testing of e-government services that rely on realistic synthetic test data that can be used as input from data received from data services. We developed the PoC of a rule-based synthetic data generation approach that, in addition to generating the synthetic data itself, also creates the rules and constraints that are the basis for synthetic data generation. Our approach does not require direct access to real-life raw data. We validated the PoC of our approach in a playground that simulated a real-life-like situation with an SUT requesting test data from three different data services. We found that although our approach has potential and could theoretically already be used in simpler cases, the PoC struggles with generating synthetic test data that is compatible across different data services. Our future work focuses on removing the identified limitations and evaluating the improved approach in actual real-life settings.

Acknowledgments. The research reported in this paper has been partly funded by BMIMI, BMWET, and the State of Upper Austria in the frame of the SCCH competence center INTEGRATE (FFG grant no. 892418), in the COMET (Competence Centers for Excellent Technologies) Programme managed by Austrian Research Promotion Agency FFG. Daniel Rodriguez is supported by JCLM project SBPLY/24/180225/000143 and TSI-100920-2023-1.

Disclosure of Interests. The authors have no competing interests to declare that are relevant to the content of this article.

References

1. Anthes, G.: Estonia: a model for e-government. Commun. ACM **58**(6), 18–20 (2015). https://doi.org/10.1145/2754951
2. Tammisto, M.A., Ramler, R., Shah, F.A., Pfahl, D.: Obtaining test data in the Estonian e-government system: challenges and improvement potential. In: Scanniello, G., Lenarduzzi, V., Romano, S., Vegas, S., Francese, R. (eds) Product-Focused Software Process Improvement. Industry, Doctoral-Symposium, Tutorial, and Workshop Papers. PROFES 2025. Lecture Notes in Computer Science, vol. 16362. Springer, Cham (2026). https://doi.org/10.1007/978-3-032-12092-2_1
3. Tammisto, M.A., Ali Shah, F., Rodriguez, D., Pfahl, D.: The challenge of generating and evolving real-life like synthetic test data without accessing real-world raw data—a systematic review. Expert Syst. **42**(12) (2025). https://doi.org/10.1111/exsy.70164
4. Baresi, L. and Miraz, M.: TestFul: automatic unit-test generation for Java classes. In Proceedings of the 32nd ACM/IEEE International Conference on Software Engineering - Volume 2 (ICSE '10). Association for Computing Machinery, New York, NY, USA, 281–284 (2010). https://doi.org/10.1145/1810295.1810353
5. Wang, S., Shrestha, N., Kucheri Subburaman, A., Wang, J., Wei, M., Nagappan, N.: Automatic unit test generation for machine learning libraries: how far are we? In: 2021 IEEE/ACM 43rd International Conference on Software Engineering (ICSE), pp. 1548–1560. IEEE (2021)
6. Bartolini, C., Bertolino, A., Marchetti, E., Polini, A.: WS-TAXI: a WSDL-Based testing tool for web services. In: 2009 International Conference on Software Testing Verification and Validation, Denver, CO, USA, pp. 326–335 (2009). https://doi.org/10.1109/ICST.2009.28
7. Ed-douibi, H., Cánovas Izquierdo, J. L., Cabot, J.: Automatic generation of test cases for REST APIs: a specification-based approach. In: IEEE 22nd International Enterprise Distributed Object Computing Conference (EDOC), Stockholm, Sweden, 2018, pp. 181–190 (2018). https://doi.org/10.1109/EDOC.2018.00031.
8. Fuchs, A., Kuchen, H.: Test-case generation for web-service clients. In: Proceedings of the 33rd Annual ACM Symposium on Applied Computing (SAC '18), pp. 1518–1527. Association for Computing Machinery, New York, NY, USA (2018). https://doi.org/10.1145/3167132.3167294
9. Xue, Z., et al.: LLM4Fin: fully automating LLM-Powered test case generation for FinTech software acceptance testing. In Proceedings of the 33rd ACM SIGSOFT International Symposium on Software Testing and Analysis (ISSTA 2024). Association for Computing Machinery, New York, NY, USA, 1643–1655 (2024). https://doi.org/10.1145/3650212.3680388
10. Korraprolu, B.R., Pinninti, P., Reddy, R.Y.: Test case generation for requirements in natural language - an LLM comparison study. In: Proceedings of the 18th Innovations in Software Engineering Conference (ISEC '25), vol. 9, pp. 1–5. Association for Computing Machinery, New York, NY, USA (2025). https://doi.org/10.1145/3717383.3717389
11. Smith, B., Troynikov, A.: Evaluating chunking strategies for retrieval. Chroma Technical Report, Chroma (2024). https://research.trychroma.com/evaluating-chunking
12. Wu, T., Terry, M., Jun Cai, C.: AI Chains: transparent and controllable human-AI interaction by chaining large language model prompts. In: Proceedings of the 2022 CHI Conference on Human Factors in Computing Systems (CHI '22), vol. 385, pp.

1–22. Association for Computing Machinery, New York, NY, USA (2022). https://doi.org/10.1145/3491102.3517582
13. Arabzadeh, N., et al.: IR-RAG @SIGIR25: the second edition of the workshop on information retrieval's role in RAG systems. In: Proceedings of the 48th International ACM SIGIR Conference on Research and Development in Information Retrieval (SIGIR '25), pp. 4168–4171. Association for Computing Machinery, New York, NY, USA (2025). https://doi.org/10.1145/3726302.3730362

Phase-Based Safety Analysis of Automated Driving System Using Simulations

Fauzia Khan(✉), Ali Ihsan Güllü, Hina Anwar, and Dietmar Pfahl

University of Tartu, Narva mnt 18, 51009 Tartu, Estonia
{fauzia.khan,ali.ihsan.gullu,hina.anwar,dietmar.pfahl}@ut.ee

Abstract. Simulation-based safety testing (SBST) is a cost-effective method for assessing the safety of Automated Driving Systems (ADS). However, the systematic execution of SBST that will identify the safe driving boundaries (SDB) of an ADS remains a major challenge. In this paper, we present a phase-based analysis of ADS safety behavior in a safety-critical follow-lead-vehicle interaction scenario. Using simulation, we evaluate system performance under varying conditions with safety metrics including Time-to-Collision (TTC), Responsibility-Sensitive Safety (RSS), and jerk. We decompose the ego vehicle's behavior into distinct driving phases and analyze phase-wise safety violations and metric distributions. Our analysis reveals that across different phases, the ego vehicle behaves safely and exhibits stable performance at lower speeds; however, at higher speeds, increased violations of safety metrics and pronounced oscillatory behavior are observed. These findings highlight the importance of phase-aware evaluation in understanding ADS behavior. We further derive insights that inform improvements to both ADS control strategies and simulation-based testing practices, providing a structured, interpretable approach to safety analysis.

Keywords: Automated Driving Systems (ADS) · Simulation-based Testing · Scenario Selection · Follow Lead Vehicle Scenario

1 Introduction

Automated Driving Systems (ADS) require rigorous safety testing before deployment in the real world. Simulation-based safety testing provides a cost-effective and scalable approach to assessing ADS safety. It accelerates the testing process while significantly reducing effort and resources required [2,10,12]. Safety-critical events such as collisions or near misses often arise under specific dynamic conditions, making them difficult to anticipate and systematically evaluate. By varying scenario parameters, simulation can generate extensive data on safety behavior under different conditions. However, while simulation provides detailed information about when safety violations occur, it often does not offer direct insights into how and why they occur. Careful analysis of simulation logs is needed to interpret those periods during the simulation that result in safety alerts. A structured

R. Matulevičius et al. (Eds.): DB&IS 2026, CCIS 3085, pp. 72–87, 2026.
https://doi.org/10.1007/978-3-032-30863-4_5

analysis approach can help address this challenge by providing a better understanding of why safety violations occurred. In addition, a structured analysis has more power to disclose issues related to the setup of the simulation environment, which might point to a potential simulation-to-reality gap and, thus, help avoid an incorrect transfer of observed behavior in the simulator to reality.

In this paper, we propose a structured approach that relies on a phase-based analysis of safety metrics. We illustrate our approach with the help of an example scenario, i.e., the follow-lead-vehicle scenario combined with an emergency braking of the lead vehicle, and an example ADS software stack, i.e., the software stack developed for the UT-ADS[1], and experimental ADS developed at the University of Tartu (UT).

We decompose the ego vehicle's driving behaviour into distinct phases (acceleration, overshoot, settling, cruising, and deceleration) and analyze how safety metrics evolve across these phases. This representation enables a more interpretable understanding of safety behavior and supports comparison of safety performance under different dynamic conditions. In particular, the analysis enables localization of safety violations in time and their relation to specific dynamic conditions, such as relative speed and inter-vehicle distance, thereby improving the interpretability of simulation results.

This study serves as a representative analysis demonstrating how a structured, phase-based interpretation can be applied to simulation results. While the analysis focuses on a specific scenario, the approach can be extended to other scenarios and metrics to support systematic interpretation of safety behavior in simulation-based evaluation.

Our results reveal distinct phase-dependent patterns, with safety violations occurring mainly during phases involving rapid speed changes and reduced distance between the ego and lead vehicle. These findings provide insights that can support improvements in ego vehicle control behavior and guide more informed use of simulation in safety evaluation.

The main contributions of this paper are as follows:

- A phase-based analysis of the ego vehicle safety behavior in a follow-lead-vehicle driving scenario.
- A systematic evaluation of safety metrics (Time-to-Collision (TTC), Responsibility Sensitive Safety (RSS), and jerk) across different driving phases.
- Identification of phase-dependent risk patterns and conditions that lead to safety violations.
- Insights that inform improvements to both the ego vehicle software stack and the simulation environment.

The rest of this paper is organized as follows. Section 2 presents the background. Section 3 presents related work. Section 4 describes the methodology, while Sect. 5 presents the results. Section 6 presents the discussion, Sect. 7 presents the limitations and future work, and Sect. 8 presents the conclusion.

[1] UT-ADS: An automated vehicle developed at the University of Tartu, Estonia.

2 Background

In this section, we provide a definition of scenario and give a brief overview of the SafeBound toolchain used in our analysis.

2.1 Scenario

In the context of ADS, a scenario is an informal, temporal description of a traffic situation, including the actions and interactions between various traffic participants (e.g., vehicles, pedestrians) and their environment over a specific time sequence. Scenarios are foundational for the development, testing, and validation of ADS, helping to evaluate how safely a vehicle acts in both routine and rare, complex environments [4,18].

2.2 SafeBound Toolchain

Scenario-based simulation is widely used to systematically evaluate the safety of ADS. In this work, we utilize the SafeBound[2], an automated simulation tool chain designed to support scenario-based safety analysis of ADS. The toolchain operates across several stages, including scenario selection, scenario implementation and configuration, simulator and ADS integration, simulation execution, and subsequent data processing and visualization. Given a set of input scenarios, the tool chain prioritizes, selects, instantiates, and configures them in a simulation environment, runs multiple simulations with the ADS under test, and records system behavior. The resulting simulation data is processed to calculate safety-relevant metrics, which are then aggregated and visualized to facilitate systematic analysis of ADS performance across diverse conditions. For this study, UT-ADS is integrated into SafeBound and evaluated in a high-prioritized follow-lead-vehicle interaction scenario. Figure 1 shows the stages of the SafeBound toolchain and their relationships.

3 Related Work

This section highlights a focused set of representative studies on simulation-based safety testing of ADS. Tang et al. [17] proposed Causal-Fuzzer that models relationships between scenarios, actions, and violations using causal graphs and evaluated it on the Apollo ADS with the LGSVL simulator. Their method improves testing coverage and efficiently identifies diverse and critical safety violations. Peshin et al. [16] analyzed different Generative Adversarial Networks (GANs) architectures for producing realistic synthetic data that captures both spatial and temporal driving conditions. They highlighted the importance of synthetic scenarios in improving testing under rare and complex situations where real-world data is limited. Phaiboon et al. [9] evaluated Autoware with AWSIM-Labs for scenario-based safety analysis. Their study shows that simulation is

[2] SafeBound source code.

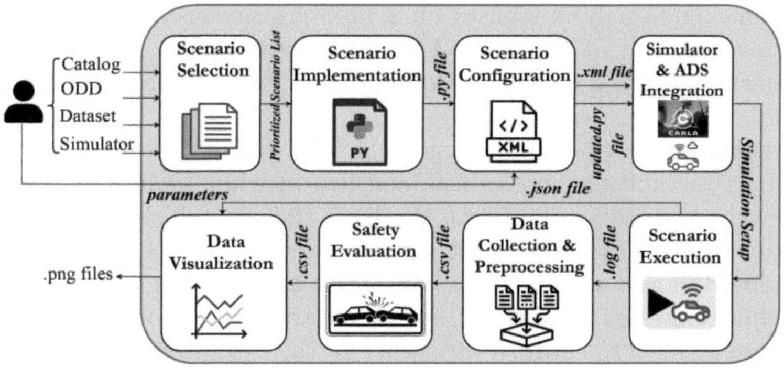

Fig. 1. Overview of the SafeBound Toolchain.

feasible but reveals gaps between safety analysis and simulation results, highlighting challenges for future improvement. Li et al. [13] proposed AV-FUZZER, which utilizes genetic algorithms to identify safety violations in Baidu Apollo within urban driving environments. Garcia et al. [3] conducted a systematic analysis of bugs in Apollo and Autoware by examining their GitHub repositories. Goyal et al. [5] proposed the VIVAS framework, combining formal methods, symbolic models, and simulation to test ADS. They used CARLA to generate diverse scenarios and systematically evaluate ADS safety. Hu et al. [7] proposed MetaDrive and ScenarioNet, which integrate real-world driving and accident data to generate realistic scenarios. They introduced a scenario-scoring mechanism to prioritize safety-critical test cases and to include real-world scenarios for evaluation. Matthew et al. [15] proposed a scalable simulation framework using adaptive sampling to test ADS, particularly those incorporating deep learning-based perception and control. Unlike the above studies, which primarily focus on generating test scenarios, identifying failures, or assessing ADS robustness, our work takes a different perspective by analyzing ADS behavior at a finer granularity. We focus on a phase-based analysis of the follow-lead-vehicle scenario, allowing us to deeply understand the ADS behavior across different driving phases.

4 Methodology

In this section, we present the experimental design and the safety metrics used, along with phase-based behavior analysis.

4.1 Experimental Design

The objective of this study is to analyze the safety behavior of an ego vehicle in a follow-lead-vehicle interaction scenario and to derive insights that inform improvements to both the ego vehicle autonomous stack and the simulation environment. The analysis focuses on a high-priority scenario in which a lead vehicle travels ahead of the ego vehicle at a lower speed and abruptly stops. This scenario is selected using SafeBound due to its relevance as a safety-critical scenario.

To systematically evaluate the ego vehicle's response, we vary the lead vehicle speed across multiple levels (3, 6, and 9 m/s) while maintaining a fixed initial inter-vehicle distance d_i of 5 m. We limit the ego vehicle's maximum speed to 13.89 m/s (50 km/h), consistent with the speed limit of the test road. The selected speed range also captures low-speed traffic, with 2.78 m/s (10 km/h) representing congested conditions. For each parameter configuration, the simulation is run 3 times to capture variability in the ego vehicle behavior.

Safety is assessed using three metrics: Time-to-Collision (TTC), Responsibility-Sensitive Safety (RSS), and jerk, capturing collision risk, rule-based safety violations, and ride comfort, respectively.

To enable a structured analysis, the ego vehicle's behavior is examined across five distinct driving phases: acceleration, overshooting, settling, cruising, and deceleration. For each phase, we quantify safety performance using TTC, RSS Safety Margin, and jerk, enabling us to analyze how risk evolves under different dynamic conditions. The analysis is further guided by phase-based hypotheses H1 to H15 on the expected behavior of safety metrics across the driving phases.

Safety Metrics. To evaluate the ego vehicle's safety behavior, we analyze the following three safety metrics extracted using SafeBound.

1. Time-to-Collision (TTC): TTC is the remaining time before the ego vehicle would collide with the lead vehicle if both continue moving at their current velocities along the same trajectory.

$$TTC = \frac{d}{v_{ego} - v_{lead}} \tag{1}$$

where d is the distance between the ego and lead vehicle, v_{ego} is the velocity of the ego vehicle, and v_{lead} is the velocity of the lead vehicle. TTC values below 3 s are considered unsafe [1].

2. Responsibility-Sensitive Safety (RSS) Safety Margin: The RSS safety margin is derived from the RSS model proposed by Mobileye [11,14]. It defines a formal condition under which a following (ego) vehicle maintains a safe longitudinal distance from the leading vehicle. The RSS framework assumes worst-case conditions by considering the ego vehicle response time, acceleration, and braking limits. The minimum RSS safe distance is given by:

$$d_{\min} = \max\left(0,\ v_{ego}\rho + \frac{1}{2}a_{\max,\text{accel}}\rho^2 + \frac{(v_{ego} + \rho a_{\max,\text{accel}})^2}{2a_{\min,\text{brake}}} - \frac{v_{lead}^2}{2a_{\max,\text{brake}}}\right) \tag{2}$$

where v_{ego} and v_{lead} are the longitudinal velocities of the ego and lead vehicles, respectively; ρ is the response time; $a_{\max,\text{accel}}$ and $a_{\min,\text{brake}}$ are the maximum acceleration and minimum braking capabilities of the ego vehicle; and $a_{\mathsf{max,brake}}$ is the maximum braking capability of the lead vehicle. The RSS safety margin is defined as the difference between the actual distance and the minimum required safe distance:

$$RSS_{margin} = d_{actual} - d_{safe} \tag{3}$$

where d_{actual} is the distance between the ego and lead vehicle, and d_{safe} is the RSS minimum safe distance. RSS safety margin values below 0 are considered unsafe.

3. **Jerk:** This metric evaluates the smoothness of the ego vehicle longitudinal motion, quantified as the time derivative of acceleration. High jerk values indicate rapid changes in acceleration, which can cause passenger discomfort and raise concerns about driving quality. Jerk is computed as:

$$J(t) = \frac{|\boldsymbol{a}(t)| - |\boldsymbol{a}(t-1)|}{\Delta t} \tag{4}$$

where $|\boldsymbol{a}(t)|$ is the magnitude of acceleration at time t, and Δt is the sampling interval. Jerk values exceeding $\pm 2.94\,\mathrm{m/s^3}$ are considered unsafe [6,8].

4.2 Phase-Based Behavior Analysis

The driving behavior of the ego vehicle is analyzed by decomposing its motion into distinct driving phases. These phases represent different stages of the ego vehicle's response to the lead vehicle. The phase-based analysis provides a structured way to interpret safety behavior. While raw time-series data show how safety metrics change over time, they do not clearly capture the underlying driving behavior. By decomposing the ego vehicle's motion into distinct phases, we can identify when and why safety issues occur and better understand the ego vehicle's behavior. The driving behavior of the ego vehicle is divided into five phases: (i)acceleration, (ii) overshooting, (iii) settling, (iv) cruising, and (v) deceleration.

The driving phases are identified by observing changes in the ego vehicle's speed relative to the lead vehicle over time. For example, when the lead vehicle is assigned a constant speed of $3\,\mathrm{m/s}$, the phases are defined as follows: In the acceleration phase, the ego vehicle increases its speed to reach the lead vehicle's speed. In the overshooting phase, the ego vehicle exceeds the lead vehicle's speed. In the settling phase, the ego vehicle reduces its speed to match the lead vehicle. In the cruising phase, both vehicles maintain approximately the same speed. Finally, in the deceleration phase, the ego vehicle reduces its speed in response to the lead vehicle slowing down. Phase boundaries are determined through manual inspection of the ego and lead vehicle speed profiles over time.

Phase-wise Metric Computation. For each identified phase, we extract the corresponding time segments from the simulation logs, including the positions, speeds, relative distances, and accelerations of both the ego and lead vehicles.

These data are used to compute safety metrics, i.e., TTC, RSS safety margin, and jerk at each time step throughout the simulations.

Safety metrics are evaluated using predefined thresholds to distinguish between safe and unsafe conditions. Specifically, TTC values below 3 s are considered unsafe, RSS safety margin values below 0 indicate unsafe behavior, and jerk values exceeding $\pm 2.94\,\mathrm{m/s^3}$ are classified as unsafe or uncomfortable.

For the Time-to-Collision (TTC) metric, TTC is computed at each time step, and values below the predefined threshold are considered unsafe.

For the RSS safety margin metric, the minimum safe distance is computed at each time step using the RSS model, and the margin is defined as the difference between the actual distance and the minimum safe distance. Values below zero are considered unsafe.

For the jerk metric, the magnitude of jerk is computed at each time step, and values exceeding the predefined threshold are considered unsafe.

For each phase, the computed metrics are aggregated to obtain phase-wise distributions. The minimum TTC, minimum RSS safety margin, and maximum absolute jerk are computed to capture the most critical conditions in each phase. These metrics are then analyzed across phases and with respect to relative speed and inter-vehicle distance to identify when safety-critical events are more likely to occur. The analysis enables phase-wise comparisons of safety metrics and identifies patterns in ego vehicle behavior.

Phase 1: Acceleration

- **H1:** TTC values remain above the safety threshold (TTC > 3 s) during acceleration phase.
  This is expected, as both vehicles accelerate from rest at low relative speed, reducing the risk of collision.
- **H2:** RSS Safety Margin remains non-negative (RSS ≥ 0) during acceleration phase.
  This is expected as the initial inter-vehicle distance is sufficient and the relative speed remains small while both vehicles accelerate.
- **H3:** Jerk increases and may exceed the unsafe threshold ($|jerk| > 2.94\ \mathrm{m/s^3}$) during the acceleration phase.
  This is expected due to rapid changes in acceleration as the ego vehicle accelerates from rest.

Phase 2: Overshooting

- **H4:** TTC values decreases and may reach critical levels (TTC < 3 s) during the overshoot phase.
  This is expected as the ego vehicle exceeds the lead vehicle speed, resulting in increased relative velocity and rapid gap closure.
- **H5:** RSS Safety Margin decreases and may become unsafe (RSS < 0) during the overshoot phase .
  This is expected due to reduced headway and increased closing speed.

- **H6:** Jerk may be high and may exceed the unsafe threshold ($|jerk| > 2.94\ \mathrm{m/s^3}$) during the overshoot phase.
  This is expected as the ego vehicle transitions from acceleration to corrective deceleration.

Phase 3: Settling

- **H7:** TTC remains stable and within safe limits (TTC $> 3\,\mathrm{s}$) during the settling phase.
  This is expected as the ego vehicle reduces its speed and converges toward the lead vehicle speed, decreasing relative velocity and maintaining the inter-vehicle distance.
- **H8:** RSS Safety Margin recovers toward safe values (RSS ≥ 0) during the settling phase.
  This is expected as the ego vehicle reduces its speed and restores a safe following distance.
- **H9:** Jerk remains low and within safe limits ($|jerk| > 2.94\ \mathrm{m/s^3}$) during the settling phase.
  This is expected, as the ego vehicle stabilizes its motion and converges on the lead vehicle's speed.

Phase 4: Cruising

- **H10:** TTC remains stable and within safe limits (TTC $> 3\,\mathrm{s}$) during the cruising phase.
  This is expected as both vehicles travel at approximately equal speeds, resulting in negligible relative velocity and a nearly constant inter-vehicle distance.
- **H11:** RSS Safety Margin remains near safe limits, although it may become marginal when the inter-vehicle distance is small during the cruising phase.
  This is expected, as both vehicles travel at stable speeds, although small inter-vehicle distances may still leave marginal safety margins.
- **H12:** Jerk remains low and within safe limits ($|jerk| > 2.94\ \mathrm{m/s^3}$) during the cruising phase.
  This is expected as the motion is slow with minimal changes in acceleration.

Phase 5: Deceleration

- **H13:** TTC decreasesand may reach critical levels (TTC $< 3\,\mathrm{s}$) during the deceleration phase.
  This is expected as the lead vehicle reduces its speed while the ego vehicle reacts with a delay, resulting in a high risk of collision.
- **H14:** RSS Safety Margin decreases and may become unsafe (RSS < 0) during the deceleration phase.
  This is expected as the lead vehicle brakes while the ego vehicle reacts, resulting in rapid inter-vehicle distance reduction.
- **H15:** Jerk may high and may exceed the unsafe threshold ($|jerk| > 2.94\ \mathrm{m/s^3}$) during the deceleration phase.
  This is expected due to braking and the corresponding change in acceleration as the ego vehicle reacts.

5 Results

In this section, we present the results of phase-based analysis of the ego vehicle behavior. Figure 2 shows the ego and lead vehicle speeds with phase annotations, and the relative inter-vehicle distance. Figure 2 is organized row-wise, where each row corresponds to a specific target speed of the lead vehicle. The left sub-figures (a, c, and e) show the ego vehicle speed profiles at 3, 6, and 9 m/s, while the corresponding right sub-figures (b, d, and f) present the relative distance profiles. The colored regions denote the different driving phases: acceleration, overshoot, settling, cruising, and deceleration. The ego vehicle initially undergoes an acceleration phase with a brief overshoot, then stabilizes at the desired cruising speed during the settling phase. Increasing target speed induces greater speed overshoot in the ego vehicle. For the case with the highest target speed (9 m/s), the ego vehicle has much larger fluctuations before stabilization.

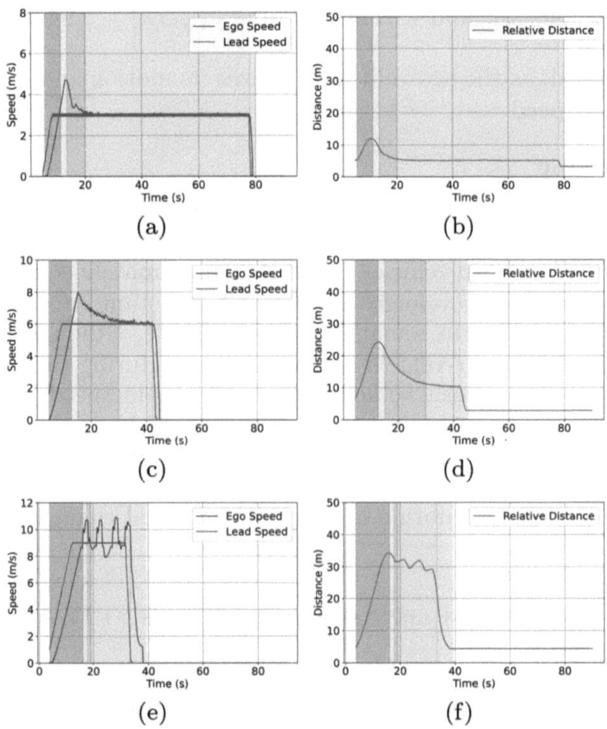

Fig. 2. Time-series plot for ego–lead vehicle speeds with phase annotations, and relative inter-vehicle distance. Colored regions indicate driving phases: acceleration (pink), overshooting (grey), settling (green), cruising (blue), and deceleration (orange). (Color figure online)

Phase-wise quantitative results, including minimum TTC, RSS safety margin, and jerk, are presented in Sects. 5.1, 5.2, 5.3, 5.4 and 5.5 Within each subsection, values indicating unsafe conditions are highlighted in red. Finally, an additional time-series plot is added at the end for TTC, RSS safety margin, and jerk profiles of the ego vehicle for varying lead vehicle speeds across driving phases.

As consistent behavior was observed across runs, one representative run is presented in both the tables and figures for clarity, while the results from the remaining runs are provided online[3].

5.1 Results for Phase 1: Acceleration

Table 1 summarizes the minimum TTC, RSS safety margin, and jerk values observed for the ego vehicle at varying lead vehicle speeds during the acceleration phase. For all speeds, TTC remains above the safety threshold, and the RSS safety margin is positive. However, jerk exceeds the acceptable threshold at 9 m/s (4.95 m/s^3). Overall, the ego vehicle maintains safety at lower speeds, while at higher speeds, it violates the jerk safety during acceleration. Accordingly, H1 and H2 are accepted, while H3 is partially rejected.

Table 1. Safety Metrics in the Acceleration Phase ($d_i = 5\,\text{m}$)

Lead Speed (m/s)	Min TTC	RSS	Jerk (m/s^3)
3	1000	5.25	2.33578
6	1000	5.79	1.20229
9	1000	4.95	4.94676

5.2 Result for Phase 2: Overshooting

Table 2 summarizes the minimum TTC, RSS safety margin, and jerk values observed for the ego vehicle at varying lead vehicle speeds during the overshooting phase. For each speed, the minimum TTC values remain above the safety threshold, and RSS safety margins are positive. However, Jerk remains within acceptable limits for 3 m/s and 6 m/s but exceeds the threshold at 9 m/s (17.62 m/s^3). Overall, the ego vehicle maintains safety at lower speeds, while at higher speeds, it violates the jerk safety threshold during the overshooting phase. Accordingly, H4 and H5 are rejected, while H6 is accepted.

[3] Results For Each Iterations.

Table 2. Safety Metrics in the Overshooting Phase ($d_i = 5\,\text{m}$)

Lead Speed (m/s)	Min TTC	RSS Safe Margin	Jerk (m/s^3)
3	5.78731	2.01833	0.27076
6	11.5220	2.70519	1.07114
9	19.0642	2.25583	17.6172

5.3 Result for Phase 3: Settling

Table 3 summarizes the minimum TTC, RSS safety margin, and jerk values observed in the ego vehicle for different lead vehicle speeds during the settling phase. For each speed, the minimum TTC values remain above the safety threshold, and RSS margins are positive. However, jerk exceeds the acceptable limits at 6 m/s and 9 m/s, with significantly higher values at higher speeds. Overall, the ego vehicle maintains safety at lower speeds, while at higher speeds, it violates the jerk limit during the settling phase. Therefore, H7 and H8 are accepted, while H9 is rejected.

Table 3. Safety Metrics in the Settling Phase ($d_i = 5\,\text{m}$)

Lead Speed (m/s)	Min TTC	RSS Safe Margin	Jerk (m/s^3)
3	5.28151	1.09755	2.06473
6	10.9711	1.98464	4.54494
9	18.5402	1.81332	18.8784

5.4 Result for Phase 4: Cruising

Table 4 summarizes the minimum TTC, RSS safety margin, and jerk values observed in the ego vehicle for different lead vehicle speeds during the cruising phase. The minimum TTC value and RSS safety margin remain within safe limits. At 9 m/s, the minimum TTC drops below the safety threshold (2.46 s) and the RSS safety margin becomes negative (−30.39). Jerk also exceeds acceptable limits at higher speeds. Overall, the ego vehicle is safe at lower speeds, while at higher speeds, it exhibits unsafe behavior during the cruising phase. Therefore, H10 and H11 are partially rejected, while H12 is rejected.

5.5 Result for Phase 5: Deceleration

Table 5 summarizes the minimum TTC, RSS safety margin, and jerk values observed in the ego vehicle for different lead vehicle speeds during the deceleration phase. The minimum TTC values fall below the safety threshold for all

Table 4. Safety Metrics in the Cruising Phase ($d_i = 5\,\text{m}$)

Ego Speed (m/s)	Min TTC	RSS Safe Margin	Jerk (m/s^3)
3	22.0296	3.20238	2.67025
6	38.1804	2.85646	4.55155
9	2.45848	-30.3885	21.6693

speeds. RSS margins become negative for 6 m/s and 9 m/s. However, at 3 m/s, RSS is slightly above zero but remains close to the safety limit. Jerk exceeds the threshold across all speeds. Overall, the ego vehicle shows unsafe behavior across all speeds, with consistent violations in TTC and jerk, and additional RSS safety violations at higher speeds during the deceleration phase. Therefore, H13, H14, and H15 are accepted.

Table 5. Safety Metrics in the Deceleration Phase ($d_i = 5\,\text{m}$)

Ego Speed (m/s)	Min TTC	RSS Safe Margin	Jerk (m/s^3)
3	1.68380	0.85069	17.0763
6	1.25375	-6.87313	10.0259
9	1.99432	-32.5901	20.8087

Overall, we observed no collisions across the evaluated scenarios, suggesting that the ego vehicle maintains a baseline level of safety under the tested conditions. Overall, the phase-wise evaluation indicates that during the acceleration and settling phases, the ego vehicle behaves as expected, with TTC and RSS safety margins (H1, H2, H7, H8) remaining within safe limits. However, in the case of jerk, the ego vehicle does not behave as expected at higher speeds (H3 and H9). During the overshooting phase, the ego vehicle does not behave as expected with respect to TTC and RSS (H4 and H5), while jerk behaves as expected (H6). During the cruising phase, the ego vehicle does not behave as expected with respect to TTC and RSS (H10 and H11) at higher speeds, while jerk does not behave as expected (H12). During deceleration, the ego vehicle behaves as expected with respect to TTC, RSS, and jerk (H12, H13, H14).

Figure 3, TTC, RSS safety margin, and jerk profiles of the ego vehicle for lead vehicle speeds of 3, 6, and 9 m/s, with an initial distance of $d_i = 5$ m. The figure is organized row-wise by target speed, with each row presenting the corresponding TTC, RSS safety margin, and jerk profiles for that speed. In each sub-figure, the red dotted lines indicate the safety thresholds:

6 Discussion

The results indicate that the ego vehicle's deviations from expected behavior become more pronounced as its speed increases, and jerk is the most consis-

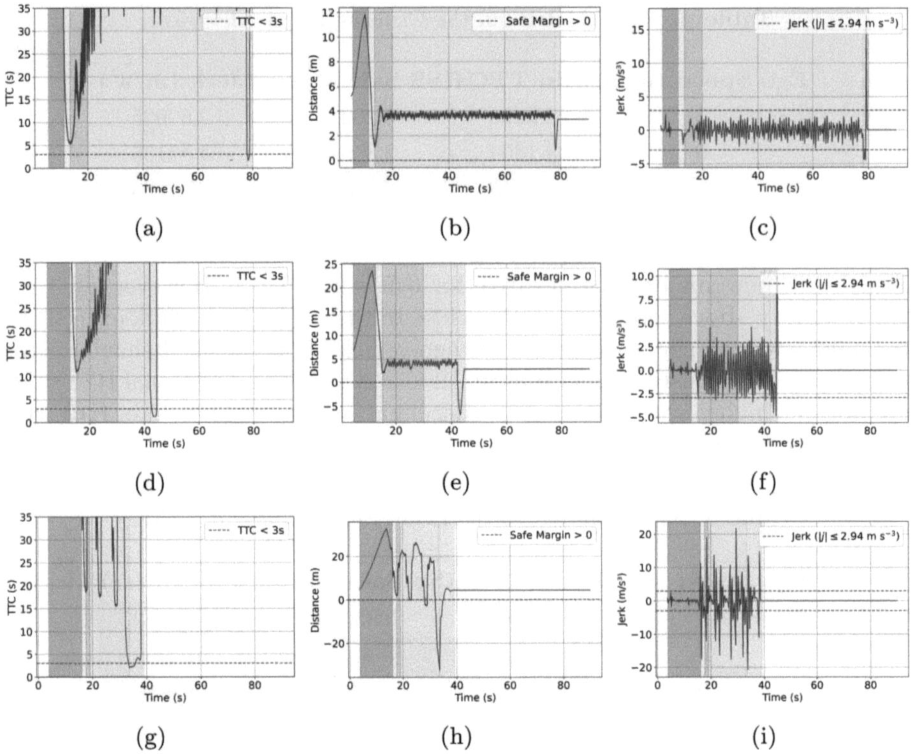

Fig. 3. Time-series plots presenting TTC, RSS safety margin, and jerk. Colored regions indicate driving phases: acceleration (pink), overshooting (grey), settling (green), cruising (blue), and deceleration (orange). (Color figure online)

tently violated safety metric, even when TTC and RSS remain within acceptable bounds. A violation of safety metrics right after the emergency braking of the lead vehicle started is understandable, but the oscillating behavior of jerk during the cruising phase requires further investigation as to its root cause.

Figure 4 shows that jerk exhibits increasing oscillatory behavior with increasing speed. Our further investigation identified the longitudinal PID controller as the primary source of these oscillations. A PID controller regulates speed using:

- Proportional (K_p),
- Integral (K_i),
- Derivative (K_d),

If the PID controller is improperly tuned, these gains can lead to oscillations, overshoot, and instability. Since the PID controller is part of the simulation environment, if the target speed sent to the PID controller from the UT-ADS software stack was smooth, then the UT-ADS software stack cannot be responsible for the observed behavior. Based on the results and observations, we provided the following feedback to the developers of the ego vehicle:

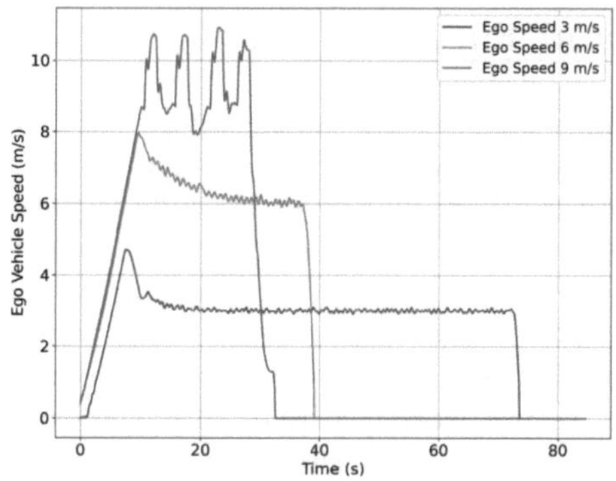

Fig. 4. Ego vehicle speed profiles across different lead vehicle speeds.

Positive Aspects:

- The ego vehicle faces no collisions across the evaluated scenarios, indicating that baseline safety is maintained under the tested conditions.
- The ego vehicle demonstrates stable and consistent behavior at lower speeds (3 m/s and 6 m/s), with clear convergence to the desired speed.
- The ego vehicle operates within acceptable safety limits even without explicit implementation of RSS constraints in the UT-ADS software stack.

Potential Areas For Improvement:

- The ego vehicle shows increased violation of the RSS safety metric at higher speeds.
- The ego vehicle shows consistent jerk violations due to oscillatory behavior, indicating that the current PID controller parameters are not optimally tuned and require re-tuning, particularly for higher-speed scenarios.

In the 3 m/s and 6 m/s cases, the ego vehicle exhibits consistent, expected behavior, with clearly distinguishable driving phases and stable convergence to the target speed. However, at a higher speed of 9 m/s, the behavior changes significantly. While the initial acceleration and overshoot phases are still observable, the system fails to reach a stable settling phase. Instead of converging smoothly, the ego vehicle shows sustained oscillations (See Fig. 4).

Due to these inconsistencies, we did not proceed with the initially planned higher-speed simulations (12 and 15 m/s). We were unsure whether they accurately reflected the ego vehicle's behavior. We were unclear whether this behavior originates solely from the ego vehicle's software stack or is influenced by limitations in the simulation environment. Since the ego vehicle operates within a closed-loop architecture involving the environment, sensor simulation, and ego vehicle modules, the observed deviations may result from interactions between these components. Therefore, we require further investigation to accurately determine the root cause of this behavior.

7 Limitations and Future Work

The analysis is based on a limited number of simulation runs, and the evaluation is conducted on a single follow-lead-vehicle scenario, limiting the applicability of the findings to more complex and diverse traffic situations. In addition, the phase identification is currently performed manually based on observed vehicle behavior, which may introduce subjectivity. However, we believe that subdividing driving scenarios into phases based on steering (straight, left, right) and acceleration (zero, positive, negative) patterns is easily transferable across all types of scenarios. As future work, we plan to extend our analysis to higher-speed scenarios with more simulation runs and additional driving conditions to further evaluate the ADS behavior. We also aim to develop automated, data-driven phase segmentation methods to improve objectivity and reproducibility. Furthermore, we will investigate the impact of re-tuning the PID controller on system stability and passenger comfort.

8 Conclusion

In this paper, we perform a phase-based analysis of an ADS in a follow-lead-vehicle scenario using simulation. We proposed a phase-based analysis method to systematically evaluate the ego vehicle response by decomposing its behavior into five distinct phases: acceleration, overshoot, settling, cruising, and deceleration. For each phase, we assessed three safety metrics: TTC, RSS safety margin, and jerk. Overall, no collisions are observed. However, unsafe behavior is identified in certain phases, with the 'jerk' metric being the most frequently violated.

Acknowledgment. Thanks for the support of the Autonomous Driving Lab (ADL) and the University of Tartu, Estonia. The research reported in this article has been partly funded by BMIMI, BMWET, and the State of Upper Austria in the frame of the SCCH competence center INTEGRATE (FFG grant no. 892418), part of the FFG COMET Competence Centers for Excellent Technologies Programme.

References

1. Deveaux, D., Higuchi, T., Uçar, S., Wang, C.H., Härri, J., Altintas, O.: Extraction of risk knowledge from time to collision variation in roundabouts. In: 2021 IEEE International Intelligent Transportation Systems Conference (ITSC), pp. 3665–3672. IEEE (2021)
2. Fremont, D.J., et al.: Formal scenario-based testing of autonomous vehicles: from simulation to the real world. In: 2020 IEEE 23rd International Conference on Intelligent Transportation Systems (ITSC), pp. 1–8. IEEE (2020)
3. Garcia, J., Feng, Y., Shen, J., Almanee, S., Xia, Y., Chen, Q.A.: A comprehensive study of autonomous vehicle bugs. In: Proceedings of the ACM/IEEE 42nd International Conference on Software Engineering, pp. 385–396 (2020)
4. de Gelder, E., den Camp, O.O., de Boer, N.: Scenario categories for the assessment of automated vehicles. CETRAN, Singapore, Version **1** (2020)

5. Goyal, S., Griggio, A., Tonetta, S.: System-level simulation-based verification of autonomous driving systems with the vivas framework and carla simulator. Sci. Comput. Program. **242**, 103253 (2025)
6. Hoberock, L.L.: A survey of longitudinal acceleration comfort studies in ground transportation vehicles. Tech. rep, Council for Advanced Transportation Studies, USA (1976)
7. Hu, Y., Zhao, D.: A simulation-based testing framework for autonomous driving: ensuring realism and priority of test scenarios. J. Intell. Trans. Syst. **29**(6), 654–673 (2025)
8. Hubbard, G.A., Youcef-Toumi, K.: System level control of a hybrid-electric vehicle drivetrain. In: Proceedings of the 1997 American Control Conference (Cat. No. 97CH36041), vol. 1, pp. 641–645. IEEE (1997)
9. Jaradnaparatana, P., et al.: Bridging gaps between scenario-based safety analysis and simulation-based testing for autonomous driving systems. In: 2024 IEEE 29th Pacific Rim International Symposium on Dependable Computing (PRDC), pp. 216–219. IEEE (2024)
10. Kalra, N., Paddock, S.M.: Driving to safety: how many miles of driving would it take to demonstrate autonomous vehicle reliability? Trans. Res. part A policy pract. **94**, 182–193 (2016)
11. Koopman, P., Osyk, B., Weast, J.: Autonomous vehicles meet the physical world: RSS, variability, uncertainty, and proving safety. In: International Conference on Computer Safety, Reliability, and security, pp. 245–253. Springer (2019)
12. Koopman, P., Wagner, M.: Challenges in autonomous vehicle testing and validation. SAE Int. J. Trans. Saf. **4**(1), 15–24 (2016)
13. Li, G., et al.: Av-fuzzer: finding safety violations in autonomous driving systems. In: 2020 IEEE 31st International Symposium on Software Reliability Engineering (ISSRE), pp. 25–36. IEEE (2020)
14. Mobileye: RSS explained: the five rules for autonomous vehicle safety (2019). https://www.mobileye.com/blog/rss-explained-the-five-rules-for-autonomous-vehicle-safety/. Accessed 07 July 2024
15. O'Kelly, M., Sinha, A., Namkoong, H., Tedrake, R., Duchi, J.C.: Scalable end-to-end autonomous vehicle testing via rare-event simulation. Adv. neural Inf. process. syst., **31** (2018)
16. Peshin, C., Doshi, U., Ramesh, A., Kunnanath, J., Kansal, M., Penumaka, A.: Generating critical driving scenarios through generative adversarial networks: a review. In: 2025 International Conference on Advanced Machine Learning and Data Science (AMLDS), pp. 212–220. IEEE (2025)
17. Tang, W., et al.: Causality-aware safety testing for autonomous driving systems. IEEE Trans. Softw. Eng. (2026)
18. Ulbrich, S., Menzel, T., Reschka, A., Schuldt, F., Maurer, M.: Defining and substantiating the terms scene, situation, and scenario for automated driving. In: 2015 18th IEEE ITSC, pp. 982–988. IEEE (2015)

A Dual-Stage Cascade Deep Learning Framework for Automated Road Defect Detection and Severity Assessment

Lauma Jokste[1(✉)], Viesturs Pavlovs[1], Edijs Ilvess[1], Martins Gailis[2], and Janis Vempers[2]

[1] Riga Technical University, Riga, Latvia
lauma.jokste@rtu.lv
[2] Dativa Ltd., Riga, Latvia

Abstract. Road infrastructure defects pose a significant threat to traffic safety, leading to vehicle damage, traffic accidents and substantial economic losses each year. Ensuring timely identification and prioritization of such defects is essential for maintaining safe driving conditions. Traditional inspection practices are predominantly manual and reactive, limiting their ability to support large-scale, continuous, and data driven road monitoring. This substantiates the need of scalable automated solutions that enable proactive, safety-oriented road maintenance strategies. This paper presents a dual-stage cascade deep learning framework for automated road defect detection and severity assessment within an intelligent road maintenance platform. In the first stage, a unified object detection model based on YOLO11m is employed to identify road defects. In the second stage, task-specific refinement modules are applied depending on the road defect class. The proposed cascade architecture enables joint detection and contextual assessment within a single processing pipeline while maintaining computational efficiency suitable for edge deployment. The framework was evaluated on real-world road defect imagery collected from different sources. In addition to quantitative performance metrics, an expert-based evaluation approach was applied, where domain specialists independently assessed defect severity and compared their judgments with the model-generated severity scores. The framework enables data-driven prioritization of maintenance actions and provides a foundation for proactive, all-season road infrastructure management in Latvian municipalities.

Keywords: Intelligent road maintenance · road defect severity assessment · machine learning · deep learning · YOLO11

1 Introduction

Road infrastructure conditions have a direct impact on traffic safety, vehicle operating costs, and the long-term sustainability of transport networks. Road defects such as potholes, cracks, and surface deformation can rapidly deteriorate if not detected at an early stage, increasing repair costs and elevating accident risks. Timely identification and prioritization of such defects is therefore an essential component of effective road maintenance management.

R. Matulevičius et al. (Eds.): DB&IS 2026, CCIS 3085, pp. 88–103, 2026.
https://doi.org/10.1007/978-3-032-30863-4_6

In many countries, road condition monitoring is still based on periodic manual inspections or reports submitted by road users. These procedures require substantial human effort and often provide incomplete spatial coverage of the road network. Defects are frequently identified only after they have developed into more serious damage. Studies on road maintenance practices indicate that reactive inspection strategies may delay interventions and increase the scope of required repairs, while data-driven monitoring approaches can improve both efficiency and safety [1, 2].

Recent advances in computer vision have enabled automated approaches for road condition monitoring using visual data. Deep learning models have demonstrated strong performance in detecting and classifying road defects in complex road environments [3, 4]. The increasing availability of low-cost sensing devices, including smartphones and vehicle-mounted cameras, enables scalable data collection for large road networks. Previous studies have also shown the feasibility of smartphone-based pothole detection using machine learning techniques [5], while drone-based inspection is increasingly investigated as a method for expanding spatial coverage of infrastructure monitoring [6].

Existing research has primarily focused on detecting the presence of road defects. In practical road maintenance workflows, the severity of the detected damage is equally important, as it determines the urgency of maintenance interventions and prioritization of repair actions. Reliable assessment of defect severity therefore remains an important challenge for automated road monitoring systems.

This paper presents a dual-stage cascade framework for automated road defect detection and severity assessment within an intelligent road maintenance support platform. A unified object detection model based on YOLO11m is used to identify the type and location of road infrastructure defects, while severity assessment is performed in a separate stage using defect specific processing pipelines. This design is based on initial experiments with direct end to end severity prediction, which produced unstable and inconsistent results.

The proposed approach separates detection from severity estimation to improve robustness and interpretability in real world conditions. It is intended for integration into continuous road monitoring workflows using vehicle mounted or mobile sensing devices and supports data driven maintenance prioritization. The current validated implementation focuses on two defect categories, potholes and partially occluded road signs, which are used to demonstrate the feasibility of the approach in practical scenarios.

The remainder of the paper is organized as follows: Sect. 2 reviews related work on automated road defect detection methods. Section 3 presents the conceptual overview of the proposed intelligent road maintenance support system. Section 4 describes the dataset construction and annotation process. Section 5 discusses the deep learning model development and comparative evaluation. Section 6 introduces the proposed dual-stage cascade architecture and defect-specific assessment pipelines. Section 7 presents the initial experimental validation of the proposed approach. Section 8 concludes discussions and directions for future work.

2 Related Work

Research on automated road condition monitoring has developed rapidly with the advancement of computer vision and machine learning technologies. Early studies focused on detecting road defects using image processing techniques such as edge detection and texture analysis. These approaches enabled identification of cracks and potholes in controlled environments but showed limited robustness in complex road scenes with varying lighting conditions and background elements [7]. Later work introduced machine learning methods for road surface inspection, demonstrating, that data-driven models can significantly improve defect detection performance and reliability in real-world environments [8].

The introduction of deep learning significantly expanded the capabilities of automated road and pavement inspection systems. Convolutional neural networks have been widely applied for detecting road defects such as cracks, potholes, and surface deterioration directly from road imagery [9]. Subsequent studies confirmed that deep learning models can outperform traditional image processing methods and achieve high detection accuracy in complex road environments [3, 4]. Modern object detection architectures are particularly suitable for this task because they allow simultaneous localization and classification of multiple defect types within a single image [10].

Large, annotated datasets have played an important role in enabling the development and evaluation of automated road monitoring algorithms. Public datasets containing labelled images of road defects allow researchers to train and benchmark machine learning models under standardized conditions. Several datasets have been proposed for this purpose, including collections of road images captured from smartphones or vehicle-mounted cameras and annotated with multiple pavement damage categories [10, 11]. These datasets support the evaluation of detection algorithms using widely adopted metrics such as precision, recall and mean average precision.

In addition to algorithm development, several studies describe automated road monitoring systems deployed in real inspection environments. Vision-based inspection platforms equipped with vehicle-mounted cameras can continuously collect road imagery during normal traffic operation and detect pavement damage automatically [12]. Such systems reduce the need for manual inspection and enable large-scale monitoring of road networks. Research on intelligent road monitoring also explores the integration of machine learning with sensor-based measurements to improve pavement condition assessment and maintenance planning [13]. Similar approaches have been investigated in smart infrastructure monitoring frameworks, where distributed sensing technologies and data analytics support continuous road condition monitoring [14].

Alternative data acquisition platforms have also been explored to improve spatial coverage of road inspections. Smartphone-based sensing systems combine camera data with motion sensors to detect pavement anomalies under real-world conditions [5]. Aerial inspection using unmanned aerial vehicles has also been proposed for monitoring road infrastructure and capturing high-resolution imagery of pavement defects [6]. These approaches demonstrate the potential of combining computer vision with mobile sensing platforms to enable scalable road monitoring solutions.

Existing research primarily focuses on detecting and classifying road defects. Road maintenance practice also requires information about the severity and potential impact of the detected damage. Several studies therefore investigate methods that combine defect detection with segmentation or geometric analysis to estimate defect size or structural impact [15, 16]. While these approaches demonstrate the importance of integrating detection and condition assessment, they are often limited to specific defect types or rely on tightly coupled pipelines that reduce flexibility and interpretability. Approaches that attempt to jointly predict defect type and severity in a single model may lead to unstable performance, particularly in heterogeneous real-world datasets. These limitations highlight the need for a structured approach that separates defect detection from severity assessment while maintaining compatibility with practical road monitoring workflows.

3 Conceptual Overview of the Intelligent Road Maintenance Support System – IRoM

Road maintenance activities in many countries, including Latvia, are still predominantly reactive. Infrastructure defects are typically identified through periodic inspections or through reports submitted by road users. Such an approach requires municipal personnel to conduct field inspections of road sections and manual documentation of the detected defects. These procedures involve a considerable amount of manual work and generate substantial operational costs, particularly in large road networks. The time interval between the appearance of a defect and its identification may also be significant, which can delay maintenance actions and increase risks for road users.

The proposed intelligent road maintenance support system (IRoM) aims to support a more systematic and data-driven approach to road condition monitoring and maintenance planning. Instead of relying solely on periodic manual inspections, the proposed approach utilizes a mobile application capable of recording video of road segments during normal vehicle operation. The application can be used by municipal service providers whose vehicles already circulate daily within the road network, including public transport vehicles, waste collection trucks, and postal delivery services. Therefore, road condition data can be collected continuously without the need for dedicated inspection trips. The use of vehicles that are already part of routine municipal operations reduces inspection costs and contributes to lowering associated CO_2 emissions.

The conceptual workflow of the system is illustrated in Fig. 1. Road video streams captured by the mobile application are analyzed using machine learning models that detect road infrastructure defects and determine their type. The detected defects are associated with geographic coordinates and visualized on an interactive map, providing road maintenance operators with an overview of the current condition of the road network. The severity level of each detected defect is estimated by the dual-stage cascade approach analysis described in the following sections. Based on the identified defect type and its estimated severity, a rule-based recommendation component generates maintenance actions according to applicable road maintenance regulations and established operational practices.

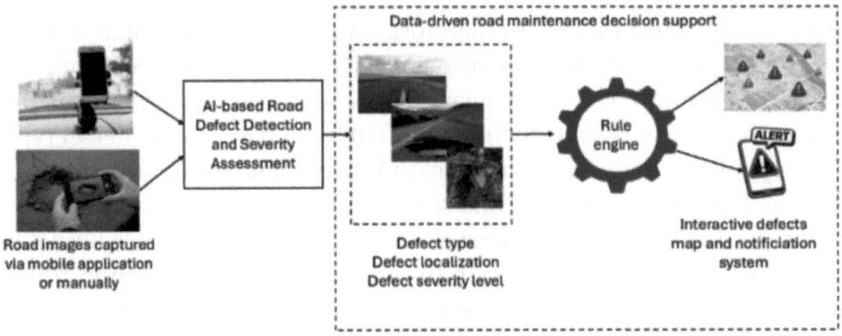

Fig. 1. Conceptual overview of the IRoM road maintenance support system.

4 Data Acquisition and Dataset Construction

The development of reliable machine learning models for automated road defect detection requires a representative and well-annotated training dataset. The quality, diversity, and size of the dataset directly influence the performance and generalization capability of deep learning models. This section describes the process used to construct the dataset employed in this study, including the data sources, annotation strategy, and the overall composition of the dataset used for model training and evaluation.

4.1 Data Sources and Collection Protocol

The initial objective of the project was to obtain training images directly from Latvian municipalities and road maintenance organizations. Such data would provide the most representative examples of road infrastructure defects encountered in the Latvian road network. However, due to administrative and legal constraints related to data sharing, the datasets obtained during the early stages of the project contained only a few hundred images. This volume of data was insufficient for training reliable machine learning models for road defect detection.

A public campaign was also organized and announced through national media channels inviting residents to submit photographs of road defects observed in their local areas. The aim of this initiative was to expand the dataset with real-world examples of infrastructure damage recorded across different regions. While the campaign collected additional data, the total number of images collected remained limited to a few hundred samples and therefore did not provide a sufficiently large dataset for training deep learning models.

The amount of training data required for reliable visual recognition depends on the complexity of the classification task. Studies on machine learning data set preparation indicate that multi-class image recognition problems typically require several hundred or even thousands of images per class to capture the variability present in real-world environments. [17] report that approximately 500–1000 images per class may be required for stable model performance in multi-class image classification tasks. Transfer learning approaches can reduce the required dataset size by adapting models pre-trained on large image datasets to a specific domain [18].

The datasets obtained from municipalities and the public campaign were therefore insufficient for training deep learning models. To increase the size and diversity of the training data, additional images were collected from publicly available road defect datasets. These datasets contain images of typical road infrastructure defects, including potholes, road surface cracks, and partially occluded traffic signs. Among the sources used were several widely adopted road damage datasets, including datasets dedicated to pothole detection and large-scale road damage datasets such as RDD2020 and RDD2022 [8, 10, 11].

The collected images were reviewed and filtered to ensure their suitability for the intended application. Images of insufficient quality, containing irrelevant content, or not clearly depicting road infrastructure elements were excluded. As the datasets originate from different geographic regions, additional filtering was applied to ensure compatibility with the Latvian road environment specifics. For instance, traffic sign images were reviewed to retain only sign types used in Latvia, while images containing infrastructure elements significantly different from those present in the Latvian road network were removed. Although the dataset includes images from multiple public sources, this filtering process ensures consistency with Latvian road infrastructure characteristics. The resulting collection of filtered images formed the basis for the dataset used in subsequent stages of the research, including defect class definition and image annotation for machine learning model training.

4.2 Dataset Annotation and Preparation

Image annotation was performed using the Label Studio platform. The annotation format was dependent on the defect type. Objects with clearly defined boundaries, such as traffic signs and obstacles on the roadway, were annotated using bounding boxes, while pavement defects such as potholes and cracks were initially annotated using semantic segmentation masks to capture the damaged pavement area more precisely. The defined defect classes include potholes, pavement cracks, partially occluded traffic signs, worn road markings, roadside vegetation affecting visibility, and obstacles on the roadway. Annotators followed predefined labeling guidelines specifying how defect boundaries and object extents should be marked.

The annotated images were reviewed to ensure data quality and labeling consistency. Images with insufficient visual quality and duplicate samples were removed. Annotations were also verified by domain experts from the road maintenance sector, who corrected labeling errors and refined annotations where necessary. The dataset was further refined iteratively during the initial stages of machine learning model development. Early model outputs helped identify underrepresented classes and ambiguous samples, guiding additional annotation and dataset improvements. Data augmentation was applied during model training, including geometric transformations such as rotation, scaling, translation, and horizontal flipping, as well as photometric adjustments and mosaic augmentation to increase the variability of training samples.

Although multiple defect categories were initially annotated, the availability of sufficiently large and consistent datasets varied across classes. Reliable training of deep learning models requires a substantial number of annotated examples for each defect type. At the current stage of the research, sufficient data were available only for two categories: potholes and partially occluded traffic signs.

The resulting dataset contains approximately 5200 annotated images representing these two classes, with roughly equal numbers of samples for both categories and including images where both defect types appear in the same scene. About 80% of the data were used for training, while the remaining 20% were used for validation and testing, including a subset of 250 images for validation. Care was taken to ensure that similar images from the same source were not distributed across different subsets. As additional high-quality annotated data become available, the IRoM system will progressively extend to support additional defect categories.

5 Deep Learning Model Development and Comparative Evaluation

Automatic detection of road infrastructure defects requires machine learning models capable of reliably identifying different types of damage in heterogeneous road imagery. In recent years, deep learning–based object detection architectures have become the dominant approach for such tasks because they combine accurate localization with efficient inference performance. Models from the YOLO family are widely used in road damage detection studies and have demonstrated strong performance on large-scale image datasets containing different categories of road defects and infrastructure elements [9]. Later benchmark studies confirmed that YOLO-based architectures provide stable detection results across diverse road environments and imaging conditions, while similar convolutional models have also been applied in infrastructure inspection tasks where object localization forms the basis for further condition assessment [10].

Road maintenance planning and the urgency of intervention depend directly on the severity of detected defects. Minor defects may require monitoring, whereas larger defects may require immediate repair because of the higher risk they pose to traffic safety. The initial modelling strategy therefore aimed to determine defect severity directly during the detection stage. Training images were annotated using predefined severity classes, and YOLO11m model was trained to predict these classes directly from the input images.

The results of this formulation were not satisfactory. The model produced unstable predictions across severity categories and showed limited ability to distinguish between defects that differed mainly in geometric characteristics such as size or depth. The experiments indicated that direct prediction of severity in a single detection stage introduced excessive complexity into the learning task and reduced the reliability of the results.

The training strategy was revised, and the system architecture was reorganized as a dual-stage cascade, where the first stage detects the type and location of the infrastructure defect, while the second stage performs defect-specific severity assessment. This separation simplifies the learning problem and allows the severity estimation stage to incorporate additional geometric and contextual information.

Once the cascade architecture was defined, the main objective of the first stage became the selection of the most reliable detection model. Several deep learning architectures were therefore evaluated for defect detection. Experiments were conducted using three object detection models from the YOLO family: YOLO11m, YOLO12m, and YOLO26m. Model training and evaluation were performed using a dataset containing approximately 5200 annotated images, including road scenes with potholes, partially occluded traffic signs or both.

The model training process was carried out iteratively. Multiple training cycles were performed while refining the dataset and adjusting training parameters. Dataset preparation included filtering incorrectly annotated images, removing visually ambiguous samples, and improving annotation consistency. Data augmentation techniques were applied to increase robustness to variations in illumination, camera viewpoint, and road surface appearance.

Different model configurations were evaluated during the development phase; however, in the final framework a unified object detection approach based on a YOLO11m model was adopted for detecting both potholes and traffic signs. Segmentation for pothole analysis was performed using a separate SAM2-based pipeline applied to the detected regions of interest, while traffic sign detection relied on bounding box annotations. The model was initialized using pretrained weights and trained using a transfer learning approach for up to 150 epochs with a batch size of 6, applying early stopping based on validation performance. Data augmentation included geometric transformations such as rotation, scaling, translation, and horizontal flipping, as well as photometric adjustments and mosaic augmentation.

The comparative performance of the evaluated YOLO architectures is summarized in Table 1. Among the tested models, YOLO11m achieved the best overall detection performance. The model produced the highest accuracy while maintaining stable results across defect classes. Larger model variants did not provide sufficient improvement in detection quality to justify their higher computational cost, particularly given the dataset size and variability constraints.

Table 1. Comparative performance of evaluated YOLO models.

Model	Precision	Recall	mAP50	mAP50-95
YOLO11m	0.92	0.87	0.92	0.74
YOLO12m	0.87	0.81	0.88	0.68
YOLO26m	0.86	0.82	0.88	0.67

All models were trained using the same experimental configuration to ensure a fair comparison. The training process was performed for 300 epochs using the same dataset and training parameters for each evaluated architecture. In addition to achieving the best detection performance, YOLO11m also demonstrated significantly faster training time, requiring approximately half the training time of the other evaluated models. Based on these results, YOLO11m model was selected as the primary detection model for the first stage of the proposed framework. The model performs defect localization and classification, while the detected regions of interest are subsequently processed by the defect-specific assessment pipelines described in the following section.

6 Dual-Stage Cascade Architecture

Reliable road maintenance decision-making requires not only accurate defect localization, but also consistent and interpretable severity estimation. For instance, a small pothole may not pose an immediate risk to traffic safety. However, continuous monitoring is necessary to track its progression and enable timely interventions if its condition deteriorates. Large or structurally deep potholes have a direct impact on safe driving conditions and require an immediate corrective action.

Direct end-to-end severity prediction did not provide sufficient accuracy, as discussed in the previous section. Therefore, defect recognition and severity evaluation were separated into two stages. In the first stage, a unified object detection model based on a YOLO11m model identifies the defect type and localizes it within the image. In the second stage, class-specific refinement pipelines are activated depending on the defect category. The Dual-stage framework for road defect detection and severity assessment is illustrated in Fig. 2.

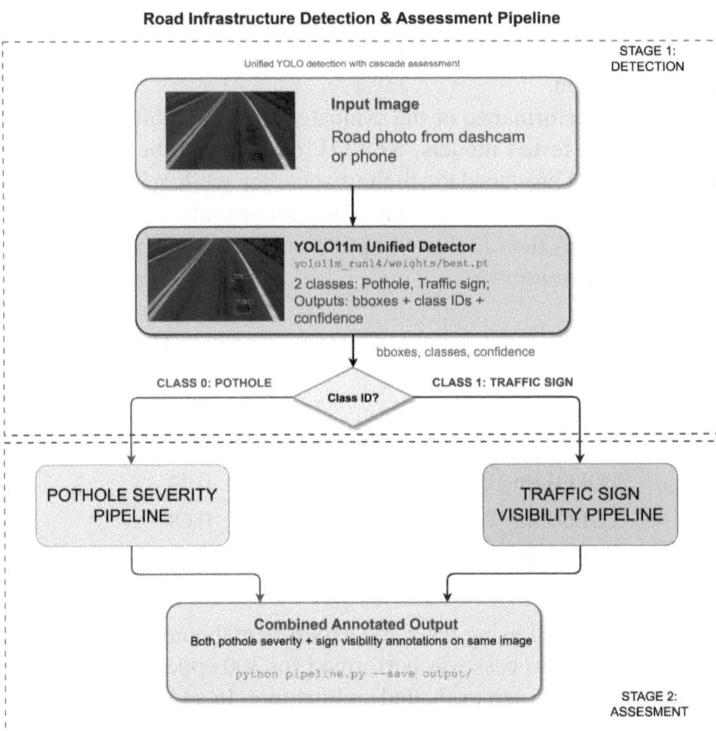

Fig. 2. Dual-stage cascade architecture for road defect detection and severity assessment.

The current implementation of the proposed framework includes dedicated processing pipelines for two defect types: potholes and partially occluded traffic signs. The selection of these categories was primarily driven by data availability, as sufficiently large and representative datasets were available to ensure reliable model training and evaluation. For other defect types, detection is supported at the initial stage, while the development of full severity estimation pipelines will be incorporated progressively as additional annotated datasets become sufficient.

6.1 Pothole Severity Estimation Pipeline

Methods for detecting road defects increasingly combine object detection with additional processing stages that estimate geometric characteristics of the defect. Segmentation-based approaches allow the damaged region to be delineated and enable extraction of features such as defect area and shape [15]. Other studies apply depth estimation or three-dimensional reconstruction techniques to approximate pothole depth from monocular images or fused sensor data [19, 20]. Such information can support automated assessment of road condition and prioritization of maintenance actions [16]. In the proposed framework, pothole severity is estimated through a dedicated processing pipeline activated after pothole class detection in the first stage of the cascade (see Fig. 3).

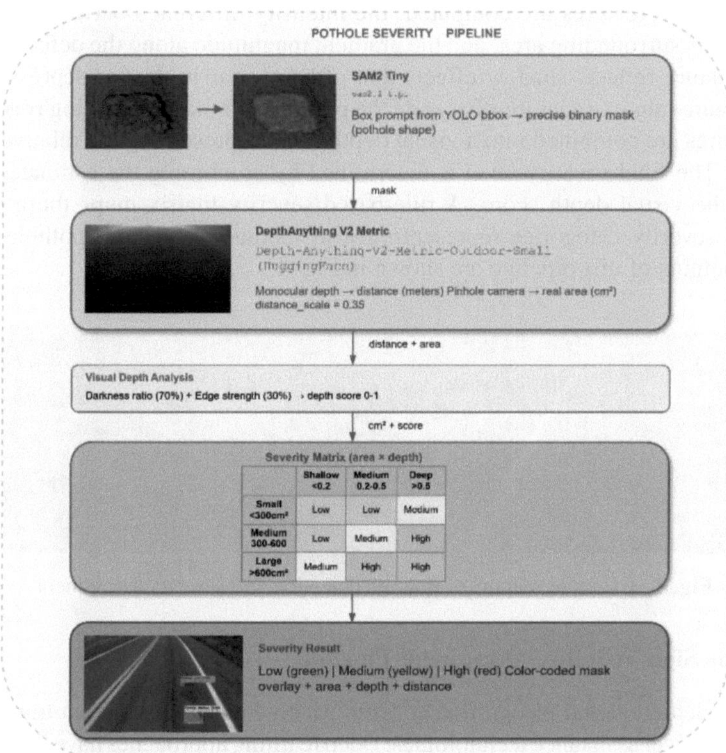

Fig. 3. A processing pipeline for pothole severity estimation.

The processing begins by using the bounding box predicted by the detection model to define the region of interest. This region is processed by the SAM2 Tiny segmentation model [21], which generates a binary mask corresponding to the pothole shape.

The segmentation mask provides a more precise representation of the defect than the bounding box and enables further geometric analysis.

Monocular depth estimation is also applied to the region of interest to approximate the relative depth of the detected pothole. A pre-trained monocular depth estimation model, Depth Anything V2 (Metric, Outdoor Small configuration) [22], is used to estimate the depth of the detected pothole. The median depth value within the segmented region provides an estimate of the distance between the camera and the pothole. The depth estimates are used as relative indicators and are not calibrated against ground-truth measurements. Calibration is planned as part of future validation in municipal pilot deployments.

The mask is used to compute the pixel area of the defect. A depth map is then generated using a monocular depth estimation model. The median depth value within the segmented region provides an estimate of the distance between the camera and the pothole. Using a pinhole camera projection model, the pixel area is converted into an approximate real-world area.

Depth-related visual cues are extracted from the image region corresponding to the pothole. Two features are computed: the intensity difference between the pothole interior and its surrounding area, and the gradient magnitude along the defect boundary. The first feature reflects shadow effects that often appear in deeper depressions. The second captures sharp transitions between the pothole and the surrounding road surface. These features are combined into a visual depth score representing the relative depth of the defect. The final severity level is determined by combining the estimated pothole area with the visual depth score. A rule-based severity matrix maps these values to predefined severity categories representing low, medium, and high pothole severity. Example outputs of this pipeline are shown in Fig. 4.

Fig. 4. Example outputs of pothole detection and severity assessment.

6.2 Traffic Sign Visibility Assessment Pipeline

Traffic sign detection and recognition constitute a core task in intelligent transportation systems and driver assistance technologies. Deep learning approaches have demonstrated high performance in detecting and classifying traffic signs in complex road environments [23]. Modern object detection frameworks such as YOLO-based models enable reliable localization of traffic signs in real-world driving scenarios [24]. Comparative evaluations of deep neural network architectures confirm that these models achieve high detection accuracy even in challenging conditions such as varying illumination, cluttered backgrounds, and partial occlusions [23]. While most studies focus on identifying the sign category, infrastructure monitoring tasks require additional evaluation of the sign's visibility and functional condition.

The proposed system estimates traffic sign visibility using a dedicated processing pipeline activated after the detection stage of the cascade. The bounding box produced by the detection model defines the region of interest for further analysis (Fig. 5). The corresponding image region is extracted from the original frame and clipped to valid image boundaries. The cropped image is converted to RGB format, resized to 224 × 224 pixels, and normalized prior to inference.

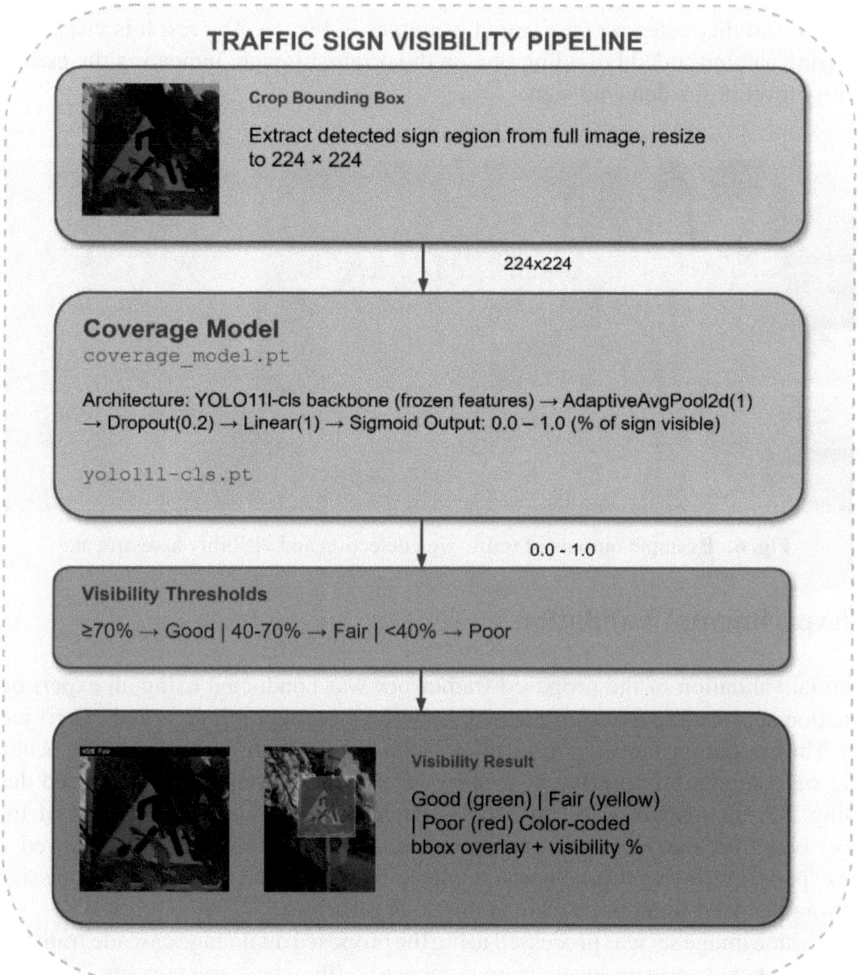

Fig. 5. A processing pipeline for traffic signs visibility estimation.

Visibility estimation is performed by a regression model derived from a YOLO11m classification backbone. The original classification head is replaced with a regression layer producing a continuous visibility score in the range *[0,1]*. The output value represents the estimated proportion of the visible sign surface within the detected region.

The continuous visibility score is converted into discrete visibility categories using predefined thresholds. Scores above 0.7 indicate fully visible signs, values between 0.4 and 0.7 correspond to partially visible signs, and values below 0.4 indicate poor visibility caused by occlusion or other environmental factors. These thresholds provide an interpretable representation of traffic sign conditions that can support infrastructure inspection and maintenance prioritization. The threshold values were determined empirically based on exploration analysis of the dataset and preliminary experiments.

The final output of the pipeline includes the detected sign location together with the predicted visibility category (see output examples in Fig. 6). The result is visualized by overlaying a color-coded bounding box on the original image, indicating the estimated visibility level of the detected sign.

Fig. 6. Example outputs of traffic sign detection and visibility assessment.

7 Experimental Validation

An initial validation of the proposed framework was conducted using an expert-based evaluation approach to assess agreement between system predictions and expert judgement. The evaluation data set consisted of 250 images of potholes and partially occluded traffic signs representing different severity levels. These images were not used during training. Severity labels were initially assigned by a domain expert involved in the project based on standard road maintenance criteria and subsequently reviewed with other experts. Following this review, a small number of borderline cases were reassigned, reflecting the need for consensus in ambiguous situations.

The same image set was processed using the proposed dual-stage cascade framework, and the predicted severity levels were compared with expert assessments. The system achieved 94% agreement for high-severity potholes, with 30 out of 32 cases classified consistently. Lower agreement was observed in less critical categories, with pothole classification accuracy of 62% for low severity and 82% for medium severity. For traffic signs, agreement ranged from 42% for fully visible signs to 91% for poorly visible signs, depending on the level of occlusion.

The observed variability indicates that severity assessment is not always unambiguous and may be interpreted differently even among experts, particularly in borderline cases. This was also evident during the review process, where some images required discussion before a final classification was agreed upon. From a practical perspective, reliable identification of critical defects is the primary requirement for maintenance planning, and in this respect the proposed approach provides sufficiently consistent results. The presented evaluation represents an initial validation, and further assessment will be carried out in municipal pilot deployments under real operating conditions using larger and more diverse datasets.

8 Discussion and Future Work

The development of automated road defect detection systems presents several practical challenges. Road defects must be detected under varying viewing angles, distances, and lighting conditions, which significantly affect visual appearance and detection reliability. In real deployments, images are collected during normal vehicle movement using mobile devices, introducing additional variability related to motion, camera orientation, and environmental factors. These conditions increase the complexity of reliable defect detection and require robust models capable of handling heterogeneous data. The proposed framework is intended for use within an all-season road maintenance platform, where data may originate not only from vehicle-mounted systems but also from manually submitted images provided by residents. This further increases variability in image quality and capture conditions, reinforcing the need for models that generalize well across different acquisition scenarios.

Another limitation is the availability of sufficiently large and well-annotated training datasets. Although the current study focuses on defect types with adequate data, such as potholes and partially occluded traffic signs, other defect types could be included in future versions of the system. Training reliable models requires several thousand labelled images per class to capture the diversity present in real-world environments. In the context of the proposed platform, this limitation is particularly relevant, as expanding system functionality to additional defect categories will depend on the availability of high-quality annotated data. As the platform is deployed and used in practice, it is expected that additional data can be collected and incorporated into the training process, gradually improving model performance and supporting the extension of the framework to a broader range of infrastructure defects.

The experiments also showed that direct prediction of defect severity using a single model produces unstable results. Severity depends on geometric and contextual characteristics such as size, visibility, and spatial context, which are not always captured reliably by image-based classification alone. The results indicate that combining machine learning with additional analytical procedures provides a more reliable and interpretable approach. This is particularly important in the context of road maintenance applications, where severity estimates are directly linked to maintenance prioritization and decision-making processes. The dual-stage cascade architecture therefore provides a practical balance between detection accuracy and the ability to incorporate domain-specific criteria into severity assessment.

Future work will focus on pilot deployments of the system in selected municipalities, where the proposed framework will be integrated into the all-season road maintenance platform and evaluated under real operating conditions. These deployments will provide additional data for validating model robustness, improving generalization across diverse environments, and further refining severity estimation methods. The collected data will also support iterative improvements of the framework, including the extension to additional defect types and the enhancement of existing processing pipelines.

Acknowledgments. The research leading to these results has received funding from the project "Competence Centre of Information and Communication Technologies for Research" of the Recovery and Resilience Facility, contract No. 5.1.1.2.i.0/2/24/A/CFLA/007 signed between IT Competence Centre and Central Finance and Contracts Agency, Research No. 1.3 "Development of a New Intelligent All-Season Road Maintenance Support Information System for Improving Maintenance Process Efficiency (IRoM)".

References

1. Ali, R., Cha, Y.: Deep Learning Based Pothole Monocular Depth Estimation and Segmentation Using 3D Scanner-derived Depth Maps, March 2023. https://doi.org/10.12783/shm2023/37016
2. Arya, D., Maeda, H., Ghosh, S.K., Toshniwal, D., Sekimoto, Y.: RDD2020: an annotated image dataset for automatic road damage detection using deep learning. Data Brief **36** (2021). https://doi.org/10.1016/j.dib.2021.107133
3. Askarzadeh, T., Bridgelall, R., Tolliver, D.D.: Drones for road condition monitoring: applications and benefits. J. Transp. Eng. Part B Pavements **151**(1) (2025)
4. Baroudi, U., Bahamid, A., Elalfy, Y., Al Alami, Z.: Enhancing pothole detection and characterization: integrated segmentation and depth estimation in road anomaly systems (2025)
5. Benmhahe, B., Chentoufi, J.A.: Automated pavement distress detection, classification and measurement: a review. Int. J. Adv. Comput. Sci. Appl. **12**(8), 708–718 (2021)
6. Dilek, E., Dener, M.: Computer vision applications in intelligent transportation systems: a survey. Sensors **23**(6) (2023)
7. Fan, R., Ai, X., Dahnoun, N.: Pothole-600: a dataset for pothole detection (2018)
8. Hong, K., Zhou, Y., Han, H.: The pipelines of deep learning-based plant image processing. In: Quantitative Plant Biology, vol. 6. Cambridge University Press (2025)
9. Huang, L.L., Lin, J.D., Huang, W.H., Kuo, C.H., Huang, M.Y.: Application of automated pavement inspection technology in provincial highway pavement maintenance decision-making. Appl. Sci. (Switzerland) **14**(15) (2024)
10. Li, J., Zhang, S., Wang, X.: Data-driven multi-objective optimization of road maintenance using XGBoost and NSGA-II. Autom. Constr. **168**, 105750 (2024)
11. Ma, Y., Wang, M., Feng, Q., He, Z., Tian, M.: Current non-contact road surface condition detection schemes and technical challenges. Sensors **22**(24) (2022). https://doi.org/10.3390/s22249583
12. Maeda, H., Sekimoto, Y., Seto, T., Kashiyama, T., Omata, H.: Road Damage Detection Using Deep Neural Networks with Images Captured Through a Smartphone (2018). https://doi.org/10.1111/mice.12387
13. Malihi, S., et al.: Review of multimodal data and their applications for road maintenance. Smart Constr. (2024)

14. Passos, B.T., Cassaniga, M.J., Fernandes, A.M.R., Medeiros, K., Comunello, E.: Cracks and Potholes in Road Images (2020)
15. Quintana, M., Torres, J., Menéndez, J.M.: A Simplified computer vision system for road surface inspection and maintenance. IEEE Trans. Intell. Transp. Syst. **17**(3), 608–619 (2016)
16. Ranyal, E., Sadhu, A., Jain, K.: Road condition monitoring using smart sensing and artificial intelligence: a review. Sensors **22**(8) (2022). https://doi.org/10.3390/s22083044
17. Wang, G., Jin, P., Qi, Z., Li, X.: Traffic sign detection method based on improved YOLOv8. Sci. Rep. **15**(1) (2025)
18. Wu, C., et al.: An automated machine-learning approach for road pothole detection using smartphone sensor data. Sens. (Switzerland) **20**(19), 1–23 (2020)
19. Yang, G., Xiang, X., Rui, W., Yu, S., Fei, L.: Pothole road detection and identification based on improved DeepLab V3+. In: Highlights in Science, Engineering and Technology ICMCE, vol. 2024 (2024)
20. Zhong, J., Kong, D., Wei, Y., Pan, B.: YOLOv8 and point cloud fusion for enhanced road pothole detection and quantification. Sci. Rep. **15** (2025)
21. Zhu, W., Braun, B., Chiang, L.H., Romagnoli, J.A.: Investigation of transfer learning for image classification and impact on training sample size. Chemometrics Intell. Lab. Syst. **211** (2021). (Article no: 104269)
22. Zhu, Y., Yan, W.Q.: Traffic sign recognition based on deep learning. Multimedia Tools Appl. **81**(13), 17779–17791 (2022)

Human-Centric Intelligent Systems

Digital and Physical Educational Games: Children's Engagement and Problem-Solving Strategies in Early Childhood Education

Ljubov Jaanuska(✉), Lidia Feklistova, and Linda Koobas

University of Tartu, 51009 Tartu, Estonia
{ljubov.jaanuska,lidia.feklistova,linda.koobas}@ut.ee

Abstract. The rapid integration of digital tools in early childhood education necessitates a deeper understanding of their impact on cognitive development compared to traditional tools. This is particularly important in relation to foundational STEM competencies such as spatial reasoning, logical thinking, problem-solving, and computational thinking skills. This study compares children's engagement, problem-solving strategies, and time spent on tasks when interacting with educational games in digital and physical formats. Using a pre-experimental counterbalanced within-subject design with a non-probability sample, a comparative observational study was conducted with 20 preschool children (aged 6-7) in a kindergarten setting. Two types of puzzles were used: a grid-based connection game focusing on algorithmic thinking and a hexagonal spatial-visual puzzle. The results indicated that digital format of the games facilitated faster, more consistent solutions and encouraged independent trial-and-error strategy through immediate feedback of the medium. Conversely, physical paper-based format required more strategic planning, deeper concentration, fine motor skills, and supported social interaction. Digital format of the games promoted autonomy, while the physical format demanded greater cognitive persistence. These findings indicate that a balanced integration of both media is crucial in early childhood education to support development of foundational cognitive and learning skills alongside digital competence.

Keywords: early childhood education · digitalisation of education · STEM · computational thinking · puzzle-type educational games · engagement

1 Introduction

Early childhood represents a critical developmental period during which cognitive control, social interaction, and fine motor skills are rapidly formed and consolidated [1,2]. Traditionally, these competencies have been nurtured through

R. Matulevičius et al. (Eds.): DB&IS 2026, CCIS 3085, pp. 107–121, 2026.
https://doi.org/10.1007/978-3-032-30863-4_7

physical games and embodied play experiences that stimulate hands-on exploration and communication. Such activities provide rich sensory, social, and cognitive stimulation that supports early learning [3]. They also contribute to the gradual development of structured thinking and problem-solving strategies, as well as early aspects of computational thinking (CT). These include decomposition (breaking problems into manageable parts), pattern recognition (identifying regularities), abstraction (focusing on relevant elements while filtering out distractions), and algorithmic thinking (constructing structured, step-by-step solutions) [4].

In recent years, digital technology has been increasingly integrated alongside traditional methods, providing new ways to engage children and expand learning opportunities. Digital tools allow personalised instruction [2, 5–7], interactive and visually stimulating content captures young learners' attention, supports engagement with scientific concepts, problem solving, critical thinking, and CT [8]. The appeal of digital educational games lies particularly in their variety of choices and affordability. According to Plass et al. [9], digital learning games can function as effective instructional tools because they are capable of automatically adjusting task difficulty according to the learner's level, thereby providing personalised learning experiences. In addition, digital games frequently incorporate motivational strategies designed to make learning more engaging and goal-oriented, such as point systems, rewards, and leaderboards. Importantly, failure in digital learning environments is typically framed not as a negative outcome but as a natural and necessary part of the learning process [9]. Hoffman and Nadelson [10] argue that such an approach encourages learners to take risks, experiment with different solution strategies, and learn from mistakes within a safe environment.

Recognizing the development and potential of digital technologies, many European countries reinforce the digital shift at the political level [11–14]. For instance, the latest Estonian national kindergarten curriculum [14] emphasises the development of digital competence from an early age. By the age of seven, children are expected to use technology and the Internet safely and creatively, recognise potential risks in digital environments, and program simple robotics devices. According to the curriculum, preschool learners are also encouraged to create digital content, combining technical skills with creativity and problem-solving. Such expectations position early childhood education not merely as preparation for school, but also as an opportunity to gradually introduce children to the skills and attitudes needed to navigate in increasingly digital everyday environment.

Despite the increasing integration of digital tools in early childhood education, their pedagogical value remains a subject of ongoing debate. Many digital educational games claim to enhance academic readiness; yet their specific effects on algorithmic thinking, planning behaviour, and problem-solving strategies (core components of CT) are less understood compared to traditional physical learning tools [15–19]. Empirical research directly comparing digital and physical game-based learning in authentic early childhood settings remains limited.

Beyond questions of measurable learning outcomes, important qualitative differences between digital and physical learning environments have also to be considered. Fang et al. [20] explored why virtual board games have not fully replaced physical ones by examining user satisfaction, emotional responses, and social interaction across physical, computer, and tablet formats. Their findings revealed that physical games were preferred at multiple levels. At the sensory level, participants valued tactile and visual engagement, which enhanced overall satisfaction. At the behavioral level, physical board games were perceived as more intuitive and user-friendly, providing a smoother and more comfortable experience. At the reflective level, physical games fostered stronger feelings of self-esteem, empathy, and social engagement - dimensions that digital formats did not replicate to the same degree.

Previous findings suggest that embodied and socially mediated aspects of learning may be reduced in digital environments. Such aspects are important for the development of collaborative problem-solving and CT skills. This limitation carries particular weight in early childhood STEM (Science, Technology, Engineering, and Mathematics) education, which traditionally relies on teacher-guided instruction, collaborative activities, and hands-on materials that support exploration through direct manipulation and communication [21,22]. Furthermore, competencies developed within digital environments may not transfer automatically to real-world contexts, as such environments may insufficiently replicate the full complexity of physical interaction and embodied social experience [18].

In the absence of a clearly established framework for balancing traditional and digital pedagogical approaches, early childhood educators continue to face conceptual and practical challenges [23]. Without adequate pedagogical training and intentional instructional design, digital games risk functioning primarily as entertainment rather than as structured learning tools that support meaningful problem-solving, CT, and early STEM learning [18,24]. Additionally, excessive screen time can negatively impact children's health and well-being, so the use of digital games should be balanced with other age-appropriate activities [25].

The listed limitations and considerations underscore the need for systematic, evidence-based investigation into the cognitive, social, and developmental implications of digital tools in early childhood education in comparison to traditional (physical) ones. Puzzle-based learning offers a particularly suitable research tool for such comparison. Puzzles are widely recognised as powerful tools for developing visual-spatial intelligence, a key predictor of later achievement in STEM domains [1,26]. Engaging with puzzles requires children to manipulate shapes, mentally rotate elements and anticipate spatial relationships. Furthermore, solving puzzles allows children to practice CT through passing the stages of the problem-solving process: defining the problem, choosing an appropriate solution, and implementing it [27]. These activities foster patience, strategic thinking, and structured reasoning [28]. Thus, puzzle-type games serve as an appropriate context for investigating how digital and physical formats may differentially contribute to the development of CT skills and STEM.

Against this background, the present study aims to examine how children's engagement and problem-solving strategies differ when interacting with digital and paper-based puzzle-type educational games. Specifically, the current study poses the following research questions.

1. How do preschool children's engagement patterns differ when interacting with digital and paper-based puzzle-type games?
2. Which advantages and challenges do children perceive in digital and paper-based puzzle-type games?

To the best of the authors' knowledge, similar observational comparisons focusing on children's engagement and preferences in digital and physical STEM learning environments in early childhood education settings have not previously been reported.

By comparing children's engagement and preferences across digital and physical learning environments, this study provides context-specific insights based on one Estonian kindergarten group. Although the results are not generalisable due to a small cohort, they may contribute to pedagogical considerations related to the integration of digital tools in early STEM education and the development of children's CT skills.

The remainder of this paper is organised as follows. Section 2 describes the research methodology, including the artefacts used and the study procedure. Section 3 presents the results of the study, which are subsequently discussed in Sect. 4. Section 5 outlines the limitations of the study and proposes directions for future research. Finally, Sect. 6 concludes the paper by summarising its main contributions.

2 Methodology

2.1 Artifacts

The research involved two distinct types of educational puzzle-type games, each presented in a digital and a physical (paper-based) format.

- Game 1: Grid Connection (Fig. 1*a*). This game requires children to connect identical pairs of shapes within a 5×5 grid using lines that do not cross or block each other. Games 1.1 – 1.3 included four pairs of shapes, whereas games 2.1 – 2.3 increased the complexity by presenting five pairs.
  From STEM perspective, the game supports early mathematical thinking through spatial reasoning, pattern recognition, and understanding of rows and columns. The task also promotes engineering-related problem-solving skills, as children test hypotheses, adjust strategies, and refine solutions based on constraints.
  From CT perspective [29,30], the game involves decomposition through identifying shapes, determining their positions within the grid, and analysing relationships between the pairs of shapes. The task solution requires algorithmic thinking through developing a systematic procedure: selecting a pair

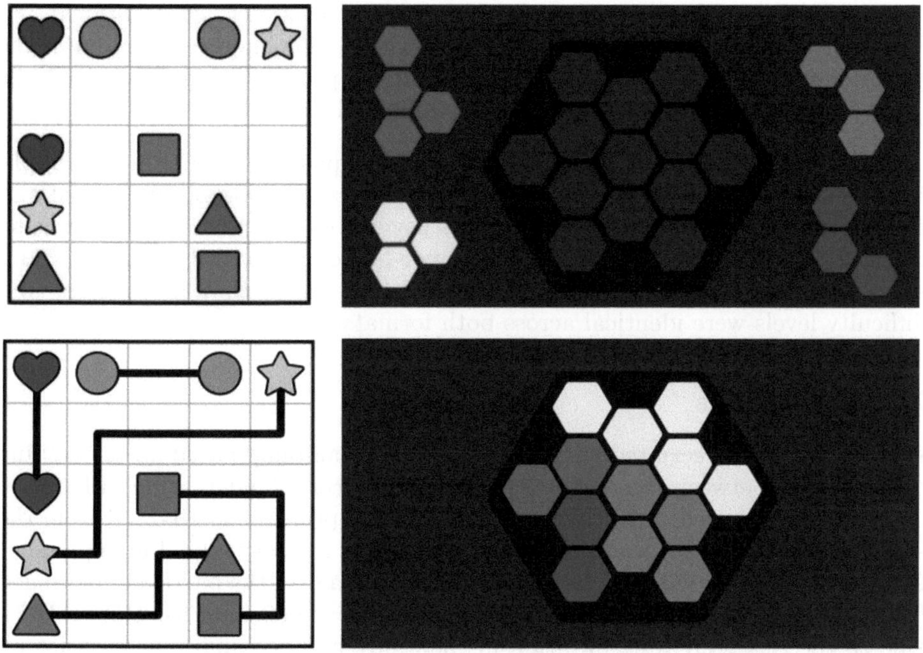

(a) Game 1: Grid Connection. (b) Game 2: Hexagonal Puzzle.

Fig. 1. Puzzle-type educational games and solutions.

of shapes, analyzing their positions, checking for patterns or constraints, and applying the same process consistently across the grid. A clear sequence of steps ensures that all possible pairs or positions are considered logically and efficiently, leading to a complete and organized solution.

- Game 2: Hexagonal Puzzle (Fig. 1*b*). This game challenges children to arrange hexagonal pieces into a larger honeycomb grid. The first set (games $1.1 - 1.3$) involved three pieces of the puzzle, while the second set (games $2.1 - 2.3$) introduced a fourth piece, making the task more challenging.
From STEM perspective, the puzzle strengthens geometric reasoning, awareness of symmetry, and understanding of tessellation concepts commonly explored in mathematics and engineering. Children must experiment with rotations (available in the paper-based format), predict how pieces fit into the honeycomb, and revise the approach when gaps or overlaps occur, promoting iterative problem solving.
From CT perspective [29,30], the task can be broken down into identifying the central hexagonal grid and separate colored shape clusters around it. Each cluster is treated as a unit of smaller hexagonal elements. While color helps distinguish clusters, successful placement relies on geometric and spatial properties. The problem is approached by examining one cluster at a time, recognizing structural patterns such as the number of hexagons, their connec-

tivity, and how the cluster might fit within the central grid. Rotational and symmetrical similarities must also be considered. Solving the task requires CT through a systematic strategy: decomposition, pattern recognition, analysis, and verification of fit without overlap, repeated for each piece.

The digital versions of both games were developed by the ALPA Kids application [31], who created its games through close collaboration with school and preschool teachers, speech therapists, child psychologists, and leading researchers in child development. The traditional paper-based versions of the games consisted of printed versions of the digital tasks to ensure that the content and difficulty levels were identical across both formats.

2.2 Participants

Participants were recruited through convenience sampling based on an existing collaboration between the university and a public rural kindergarten in Estonia. The sample consisted of 20 children (coded in the protocol as $L1$-$L20$) from the same preschool group who were preparing to enter primary school in September 2025. The group included 12 boys and 8 girls. The age of the participants ranged from 6 years 7 months to 7 years 7 months (M = 84.8 months, SD = 3.17). Due to the relatively long duration of the study and seasonal illnesses, not all participants were able to complete every version of the games.

Ethical standards were upheld throughout the current study. Informed consent was obtained from children's parents via the institutional information system prior to participation. The anonymity of all participants was ensured, maintained and regulated by the kindergarten at every stage of the research process.

2.3 Procedure

The study was conducted in a quiet kindergarten setting familiar to the participants in order to minimise distractions and ensure children's well-being. Before the main data collection, a pilot study was conducted with one child to refine the interview questions and task difficulty. The actual observation period took place between March 19 and April 10, 2025.

The pre-experiment interview revealed that only one child had previously engaged with the ALPA Kids application. This limited prior exposure reduces the likelihood that the application and its task familiarity acted as a confounding factor in comparisons between digital and physical formats.

The observation procedure was conducted individually with each child. The participants solved two different games, each comprising six puzzles, in both digital and paper-based formats. The digital version was presented on a smartphone, while the paper-based version was solved using a pencil and eraser, or physical pieces of the puzzle. To prevent fatigue and maintain attention, children solved only one format of one game per week. The alternate format of the same game was presented a week later, while the second game was introduced in subsequent weeks following the same procedure.

To control for potential order effects, the presentation of digital and paper-based formats was counterbalanced across participants, with half of the children starting with the paper-based version and the other half with the digital version.

2.4 Data Analysis

The present research used a mixed-methods approach (qualitative and quantitative data collection) to examine how the format of educational games relates to preschool children's CT, visual-spatial skills, problem-solving strategies, and engagement.

The quantitative data analysis focused on examining children's time spent on tasks across digital and paper-based versions of the games. Time was recorded in seconds. Descriptive statistics, such as means and standard deviations, were calculated to summarize the distribution of time spent on each task.

Due to the small sample size and non-normal distribution of the data, non-parametric data analysis methods were applied. The ShapiroâĂŞWilk test indicated significant deviations from normality for the majority of the variables ($p < 0.05$), with only four variables meeting the assumption of normal distribution.

The Wilcoxon signed-rank test was applied to compare time differences between the digital and physical versions of the same tasks. The analyses were conducted separately for each game based. Although data were collected from 20 children, not all participants completed both versions of the games. Therefore, only complete paired observations were included in the Wilcoxon signed-rank analyses, resulting in 12 matched pairs for Game 1 and 16 matched pairs for Game 2. Missing data were handled using listwise deletion, and no imputation was performed. As a result, the sample size varied across the tasks.

All quantitative analyses were conducted using IBM SPSS Statistics (v 30).

The qualitative data collection relied on systematic observations of solving process and semi-structured interviews to capture children's preferences, emotional reactions, subjective experiences, and strategic approaches within different educational contexts. Through a total of ten hours of observation, subtle differences were identified in how children perceived tasks and implemented solutions. The qualitative observations also allowed the researchers to track non-verbal cues, such as body language and frustration, which could not be captured through quantitative time-tracking alone.

3 Results and Analysis

3.1 How Do Preschool Children's Engagement Patterns Differ When Interacting with Digital and Paper-Based Puzzle-Type Games? (RQ1)

To address this research question, the followings aspects were analyzed.

Table 1. Task completion times and Wilcoxon signed-rank test results for digital and paper-based versions of Game 1 and Game 2.

		Game 1					Game 2				
Level	Format	Children	Mean time	*Std. Dev.*	*Z*-value	*p*-value	Children	Mean time	*Std. Dev.*	*Z*-value	*p*-value
1.1	paper	13	44.9	27.115			17	29.5	28.829		
	digital	16	42.5	59.046	−0.471	0.638	18	19.3	17.779	−1.655	0.098
1.2	paper	12	29.3	20.374			17	36.1	31.925		
	digital	16	27.6	33.593	−1.245	0.213	18	20.7	10.682	−2.276	**0.023**
1.3	paper	12	34.0	27.383			17	46.7	40.749		
	digital	16	25.9	26.331	−2.403	**0.016**	18	13.1	5.631	−3.105	**0.002**
2.1	paper	12	55.8	25.107			17	113.4	111.154		
	digital	16	45.3	35.232	−0.059	0.953	17	39.7	33.893	−2.785	**0.005**
2.2	paper	12	68.5	75.335			16	121.3	138.380		
	digital	16	32.5	25.576	−1.364	0.173	17	56.0	65.809	−3.181	**0.001**
2.3	paper	12	95.08	64.308			16	86.6	70.702		
	digital	16	37.2	31.049	−2.578	**0.010**	17	41.6	36.158	−2.556	**0.011**

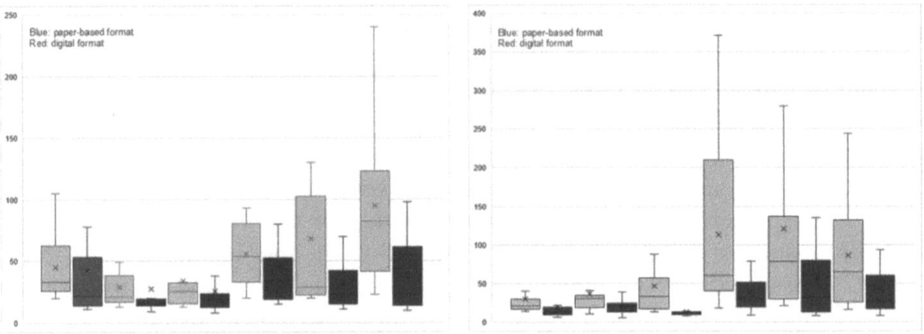

(a) Game 1 (b) Game 2

Fig. 2. Time spent on each task of Game 1 and Game 2 ("-" represents the median; "×" indicates the mean).

- *Time per task.* Overall, task completion in the digital format was faster and more consistent than in traditional, paper-based, format. The distribution of time spent on each game is presented in the Table 1 and Fig. 2.
  For Game 1, the Wilcoxon signed-rank test revealed that the game's more complex levels (1.3 and 2.3) were solved significantly faster on a smartphone than on paper. No statistically significant differences were observed in the time spent solving the digital and paper-based versions at the simplest levels (1.1, 1.2; 2.1, 2.2): in both cases, all $p > 0.05$.
  For Game 2, differences in solution time were statistically significant in all levels (except 1.1), consistently favoring the digital version.
- *Error Tolerance.* In the digital version of Game 2, puzzle pieces were sometimes dragged and released without a clear placement strategy. When a piece was released near its correct location, the application accepted it and pro-

vided immediate positive feedback. A similar effect was observed in the Grid Connection game, where near-correct connections were acknowledged. This feature reduced the "cost" of minor errors and maintained engagement without penalizing accidental solutions. In contrast, in the paper-based version, minor errors were not recognized, and participants received no guidance or feedback.

- *Trial-and-Error Practice.* The digital format of both games encouraged a trial-and-error approach, as the application provided immediate feedback, acknowledged accidental solutions and allowed participants to retry immediately without needing to learn from mistakes. In the paper-based format, participants engaged in more deliberate planning because correcting errors required additional effort, such as erasing lines or reorganizing puzzle pieces.
- *Assistance Requests.* Overall, the participants completed the tasks independently. During the observations, requests for help or confirmation appeared more common in the paper-based format than in the digital format. In the digital format, children generally relied on the interface and its immediate visual feedback when evaluating their actions.
- *Persistence.* For the digital version of Game 1, all tasks were completed correctly. For the paper-based version of Game 1, children solved on average 5.3 out of 6 tasks correctly due to perceived complexity, despite the tasks being identical across formats. For Game 2, all tasks were solved correctly in both the digital and paper-based formats.
- *Spatial Interaction and Physical Manipulation.* In the paper-based format, the participants frequently adjusted their hand positions (Game 1) or rotated the puzzle piece (Game 2) to better understand spatial relationships - a form of interaction not present in the digital version. Furthermore, correcting mistakes often required physically erasing lines (Game 1) or rearranging pieces (Game 2), which added an additional layer of manual manipulation and encouraged more deliberate planning and reflection before committing to a solution.
- *Emotional Engagement.* Observations of body language and facial expressions indicated stronger emotional reactions during the digital version. Digital tasks elicited higher levels of excitement, and occasionally frustration, fueled by the application's sound and visual rewards. Instances of frustration also occurred when the device did not respond as expected. In contrast, the paper-based format offered lower emotional intensity but greater feelings of satisfaction and pride when the participants successfully completed tasks independently.

3.2 Which Advantages and Challenges Do Children Perceive in Digital and Paper-Based Puzzle-Type Games? (RQ2)

In the semi-structured interviews, the participants provided verbal feedback regarding their experiences with and preferences for the digital and paper-based versions of the puzzle-type educational games.

For Game 1, Grid Connection, the preferences reported after completing the game in both formats indicated that four children (30.8% of the participants who gave feedback) preferred to solve similar tasks in paper-based format, whereas eight children (61.5%) expressed their preference for the digital format; one child remained neutral. Children who preferred the paper-based version emphasized that drawing lines was more enjoyable and allowed creativity. In contrast, those favoring the digital version highlighted the ease of erasing lines and completing tasks more quickly. These children also said that the digital format enabled them to "play more" and provided a more engaging overall experience. These results highlight the important role of immediate feedback, clear visual layout, and audiovisual cues in supporting engagement and perceived ease of use.

For Game 2, Hexagonal Puzzle, preferences reported after completing the game in both formats showed that six children (37.5%) preferred the paper-based version, while nine children (56.3%) favored the digital format; one child remained neutral. Participants who preferred the digital version highlighted faster positive experience, simpler task navigation, and automated feedback. The children also noted that digital format enabled them to work through the tasks without interruption. In contrast, the paper-based version required greater spatial reasoning, manual manipulation, and creative problem-solving, which some participants perceived as challenging. Nevertheless, children who favored the paper-based format stated that it supported "better thinking" and provided a more comfortable problem-solving experience.

Overall, the findings suggest that digital formats enhance perceived ease of use and engagement, whereas paper-based formats may encourage deeper spatial reasoning and more deliberate problem-solving processes.

4 Discussion

The findings of this study provide insights into how digital and paper-based learning environments shape children's cognitive processes, behavioural strategies, and engagement patterns in early childhood education. While both formats, digital and paper-based, supported successful task completion, differences emerged in the approaches children used to solve problems, suggesting that the formats relate to the problem-solving strategies more than overall performance.

One of the most striking differences between formats was the acceleration effect observed in the digital environment. Children completed the digital versions of the games faster than the paper-based versions. This finding aligns with the results of Robinson and Brewer [32], who also reported that the computerized version of the Tower of Hanoi game was solved more quickly than the traditional physical version. Additionally, the variability in tasks' completion time, as indicated by the standard deviation, was lower for the digital versions than for the paper-based versions studied in the present research. These results suggest that interactive interfaces may function as structured cognitive scaffolds [33]. The system's visual boundaries, automatic alignment of elements, and immediate feedback reduced uncertainty and lowered the cognitive load associated with error detection. As a result, children were able to focus on progressing through the task rather than evaluating whether intermediate steps were valid.

Nevertheless, efficiency does not necessarily imply deeper cognitive engagement. In the paper-based format, children often paused before drawing connections or placing puzzle pieces. The physical "cost" of error correction, such as erasing lines or repositioning pieces, introduced friction into the task. This friction seemed to encourage anticipatory thinking. Children were more likely to visually scan the entire grid, trace potential paths with their finger before committing to a line, or rotate the paper to reorient spatial perception. These behaviours indicate a more deliberate problem-solving approach, which in turn reflects the application of CT. The requirement to manually undo mistakes created a natural checkpoint for reflection, which may support the development of strategic reasoning and executive control processes.

In contrast, the digital format encouraged more iterative and exploratory behaviour. Because undoing an action required minimal effort, children engaged more freely in trial-and-error strategies. This does not imply superficial processing; rather, it reflects a different mode of interaction. The digital system externalised certain regulatory functions and absorbed part of the metacognitive burden.

The relation between task complexity and format further supports this interpretation. Differences between digital and paper-based versions became more pronounced as tasks increased in difficulty. In simpler tasks, time differences were minimal, suggesting that when cognitive demands are low, format plays a smaller role. As complexity rises, the structuring effect of digital systems becomes more influential. This indicates that digital scaffolding may be particularly impactful in higher-level problem-solving contexts.

As such, an important implication concerns the balance between cognitive support and cognitive challenge. Digital environments may reduce unnecessary mechanical difficulty, thereby allowing children to access tasks that might otherwise exceed their current motor skills. At the same time, reducing friction may unintentionally reduce opportunities for strategic forethought. In contrast, physical, paper-based or hands-on tools, while often slower and more demanding, appear to promote planning, spatial reasoning, and physical manipulation in ways that digital interfaces partially streamline. These observations align with Feng et al. [2], who highlighted that tactile and physically interactive learning contexts foster deeper cognitive engagement. Therefore, while digital environments can enhance speed and immediate engagement, their use should be pedagogically balanced to ensure that children continue to develop planning skills, spatial reasoning, and self-regulation [34].

Emotional responses further highlighted the divergence between environments. The digital version of the game elicited stronger visible reactions - excitement, vocal expressions, and occasionally frustration when the touchscreen did not respond as expected. The audiovisual feedback appeared to amplify engagement intensity. The immediacy of reinforcement likely contributed to sustained attention and motivation. In comparison, the physical paper-based format generated calmer but more stable emotional states. Children often displayed quiet concentration and visible pride after independently completing a game.

5 Limitations and Future Research

Several limitations should be considered when interpreting the findings of the present pre-experimental study. First, the sample size was small, which limits the generalizability of the results. Nevertheless, small-scale studies like this can still play an exploratory role to identify trends, refine research questions, and inform the design of larger, more comprehensive investigations.

Second, the study was conducted within a single institutional setting in Estonia, meaning that contextual factors such as pedagogical culture, prior digital exposure and experience with puzzle-type educational games as well as classroom routines may have influenced the outcomes.

Third, the data were based on short-term observations, which capture immediate responses and preferences. However, this approach does not provide insight into longer-term cognitive or developmental effects.

Fourth, it should also be acknowledged that the digital version of the games was implemented by the ALPA Kids application. As a commercially developed educational platform, its design includes specific interaction features, such as tolerance for near-correct placements and immediate corrective feedback, which may not be present in other digital learning environments. These platform-specific characteristics may have influenced children's performance, particularly in terms of speed and error correction strategies. As such, the findings should be interpreted in relation to the affordances of this specific application and may not be fully generalisable to other types of digital educational tools.

Future research should address these limitations by employing larger and more diverse samples across multiple educational contexts. Longitudinal studies would be particularly valuable in examining how sustained exposure to digital and physical puzzle-type activities influences cognitive development, engagement patterns, and CT skills over time. Additionally, further investigation into adaptive learning systems based on artificial intelligence (AI) could provide insight into how personalized feedback and dynamic task adjustment affect children's learning processes. Comparative analyses using data-logging and learning analytics could also deepen understanding of strategy use and problem-solving efficiency across formats.

6 Conclusion

This study adopted a pre-experimental counterbalanced within-subject design with a non-probability sample to investigate preschool children's responses to puzzle-type educational games delivered in paper-based and digital formats. The dual-format design facilitated direct comparison of problem-solving strategies, engagement behaviors, and modality preferences across the same participant cohort, effectively controlling for individual differences that would otherwise confound between-group analyses.

The results suggest that digital and physical (paper-based) educational games do not simply represent two versions of the same pedagogical tool. They create quantitatively and qualitatively different learning experiences. Digital environments promote time efficiency, responsiveness, and engagement intensity. Physical environments stand for deliberation, tactile reasoning, and embodied spatial processing. Rather than framing these as competing approaches, the findings support a complementary model. A hybrid pedagogical strategy that intentionally alternates between digital acceleration and physical reflection may provide the most developmentally balanced learning experience.

Disclosure of Interests. The authors have no competing interests to declare that are relevant to the content of this article.

References

1. Pratiwi, R.D., Andriati, R., Indah, F.P.S.: The positive effect of educative game tools (puzzle) on cognitive levels of pre-school children (4–5 years). Malays. J. Nurs. (MJN) **11**(3), 35–41 (2020). https://doi.org/10.31674/mjn.2020.v11i03.006
2. Feng, Y.: The effectiveness of online vs. traditional STEM education methods for preschool children aged 5–6 years in China. J. Educ. Educ. Res. **10**(2) (2024)
3. Anggraini, K.: Integrating traditional games to enhance creativity and social skills in early childhood education institutions. Int. J. Sci. Rev. **2**(2), 95–103 (2025). https://doi.org/10.71364/ijfsr.v2i2.18
4. Wing, J.M.: Computational thinking. Commun. ACM **49**(3), 33–35 (2006). https://doi.org/10.1145/1118178.1118215
5. González, Y.A.C., Muñoz-Repiso, A.G.V.: Educational robotics for the formation of programming skills and computational thinking in childish. In: Proceedings of the 2017 International Symposium on Computers in Education (SIIE), pp. 1–5 (2017). https://doi.org/10.1109/SIIE.2017.8259652
6. Sulistyaningtyas, R., Fauziah, P.: The implementation of traditional games for early childhood education. Adv. Soc. Sci. Educ. Humanit. Res. **326**, 431–435 (2019). https://doi.org/10.2991/iccie-18.2019.75
7. Herlina, U.N.M.: Adapting early childhood curriculum to technology: insights from South Sulawesi, Indonesia. Southeast. Philippines J. Res. De. **30**(2), 1–23 (2025). https://doi.org/10.53899/spjrd.v30i2.974
8. Lamrani, R., Abdelwahed, E.H.: Game-based learning and gamification to improve skills in early years education. Comput. Sci. Inf. Syst. **17**(1), 339–356 (2020). https://doi.org/10.2298/CSIS190511043L
9. Plass, J.L., Homer, B.D., Kinzer, C.K.: Foundations of game-based learning. Educ. Psychol. **50**(4), 258–283 (2015). https://doi.org/10.1080/00461520.2015.1122533
10. Hoffman, B., Nadelson, L.: Motivational engagement and video gaming: a mixed methods study. Educ. Tech. Res. Dev. **58**, 245–270 (2010). https://doi.org/10.1007/s11423-009-9134-9
11. Critten, V., Hagon, H., Messer, D.: Can pre-school children learn programming and coding through guided play activities? A case study in computational thinking. Early Childhood Educ. J. **50**, 969–981 (2022). https://doi.org/10.1007/s10643-021-01236-8

12. Otterborn, A., Schönborn, K.J., Hultén, M.: Investigating preschool educators' implementation of computer programming in their teaching practice. Early Childhood Educ. J. **48**(3), 253–262 (2019). https://doi.org/10.1007/s10643-019-00976-y
13. Stupurienå, G., Lucas, M., Bem-Haja, P.: Teachers' perceptions of the barriers and drivers for the integration of informatics in primary education. Comput. Educ. **208**, 104939 (2024). https://doi.org/10.1016/j.compedu.2023.104939
14. Minister of education and research. National Curriculum For Early Childhood Education (2025). https://www.riigiteataja.ee/en/eli/501122025007/consolide
15. Vandewater, E.A., et al.: Digital childhood: electronic media and technology use among infants, toddlers, and preschoolers. Pediatrics **119**(5), e1006–e1015 (2007). https://doi.org/10.1542/peds.2006-1804
16. Garrison, M.M., Christakis, D.A.: A teacher in the living room?: Educational media for babies, toddlers and preschoolers: a background report prepared for Kaiser Family Foundation. Tech. rep. Kaiser Family Foundation (2005)
17. Wartella, E., Lee, J.H., Caplovitz, A.G.: Children and interactive media: an updated research compendium (2002)
18. Alotaibi, M.S.: Game-based learning in early childhood education: a systematic review and meta-analysis. Front. Psychol. **15** (2024). https://doi.org/10.3389/fpsyg.2024.1307881
19. Domoff, S.E., et al.: Development and validation of the problematic media use measure: a parent report measure of screen media "addiction" in children. Psychol. Pop. Media Cult. **8**(1), 2–11 (2019). https://doi.org/10.1037/ppm0000163
20. Fang, Y.M., Chen, K.M., Huang, Y.J.: Emotional reactions of different interface formats: comparing digital and traditional board games. Adv. Mech. Eng. **8**(3), 1–8 (2016). https://doi.org/10.1177/1687814016641902
21. Wan, Z.H., Jiang, Y., Zhan, Y.: STEM education in early childhood: a review of empirical studies. Early Educ. Dev. **32**(7), 940–962 (2021). https://doi.org/10.1080/10409289.2020.1814986
22. Sydon, T., Phuntsho, S.: Highlighting the importance of STEM education in early childhood through play-based learning: a literature review. RABSEL **22**(1), (2022). https://doi.org/10.17102/rabsel.22.1.3
23. Sosa-Alonso, J.J., Hernåndez Rivero, V.M., Sanabria Mesa, A.L., Bethencourt Aguilar, A.: Adoption of digital educational resources by early childhood education teachers: a fad or a conviction? Comput. Educ. **238**, 105396 (2025). https://doi.org/10.1016/j.compedu.2025.105396
24. All, A., Castellar, E.N.P., Van Looy, J.: Digital game-based learning effectiveness assessment: reflections on study design. Comput. Educ. **167**, 104160 (2021). https://doi.org/10.1016/j.compedu.2021.104160
25. Przybylski, A.K., Weinstein, N.: Digital screen time limits and young children's psychological well-being: evidence from a population-based study. Child Dev. **90**(1), e56–e65 (2019). https://doi.org/10.1111/cdev.13007
26. Levine, S.C., Ratliff, K.R., Huttenlocher, J., Cannon, J.: Early puzzle play: a predictor of preschoolers' spatial transformation skill. Dev. Psychol. **48**(2), 530–542 (2012). https://doi.org/10.1037/a0025913
27. Choi, J., Lee, Y., Lee, E.: Puzzle based algorithm learning for cultivating computational thinking. Wireless Pers. Commun. **93**(1), 131–145 (2016). https://doi.org/10.1007/s11277-016-3679-9
28. Yusnita, N.C.: The effectiveness of puzzle games in stimulating problem solving ability in early childhood. Jurnal Scientia **12**(01), 788–793 (2023)

29. Bilbao, J., et al.: Categorization of computational thinking. In: ICERI2024 Proceedings of the 17th Annual International Conference of Education, Research and Innovation. IATE, pp. 7466–7473 (2024). https://doi.org/10.21125/iceri.2024.1802
30. Dagienå, V., Sentance, S., Stupurienå, G.: Developing a two-dimensional categorization system for educational tasks in informatics. Informatica **28**(1), 23–44 (2017). https://doi.org/10.15388/Informatica.2017.119
31. ALPA Kids. Alpa kids (2024). https://alpakids.com/et/
32. Robinson, S.J., Brewer, G.: Performance on the traditional and the touch screen, tablet versions of the CORSI Block and the Tower of Hanoi tasks. Comput. Hum. Behav. **60**, 29–34 (2016). https://doi.org/10.1016/j.chb.2016.02.047. https://www.sciencedirect.com/science/article/pii/S0747563216300991
33. Plass, J.L., Homer, B.D., Kinzer, C.K.: Foundations of game-based learning. Educ. Psychol. **50**(4), 258–283 (2015). https://doi.org/10.1080/00461520.2015.1122533
34. Öngören, S.: Teachers' use of ICT in the preschool period: a mixed research method. Educ. Inf. Technol. **27**, 11115–11136 (2022). https://doi.org/10.1007/s10639-022-11066-9

A Modular System for VR-Based Upper-limb Rehabilitation: Adaptive Visual Feedback and Structured Kinematic Data Pipeline

Théo Combe, Lucie Deplaude, Tony Hu, Olivier Pons, Thomas Roig, and Eulalie Verhulst(✉)

CEDRIC Laboratory, Conservatoire National des Arts et Métiers (Cnam), Paris, France
{theo.combe,lucie.deplaude,tony.hu,olivier.pons,thomas.roig, eulalie.verhulst}@lecnam.net

Abstract. The digitalization of rehabilitation processes requires software systems capable of delivering adaptive visuomotor feedback while collecting structured kinematic data for longitudinal monitoring and analysis. We present a modular software framework for Virtual Reality-based Mirror Therapy (VR-MT) targeting upper-limb motor rehabilitation in clinical populations. The proposed architecture addresses three limitations commonly observed in existing VR rehabilitation systems: fixed mirroring strategies, ad hoc visual correction mechanisms, and software designs that limit reproducibility and data reuse. To address these challenges, the framework introduces four independently extensible components. First, a configurable hand mirroring model that explicitly separates global wrist pose from local finger articulation, enabling three mapping strategies (full, global, and local). Second, a blending-based visual error modulation model applicable at both global and joint levels, initialised through a personalised data-driven calibration procedure that automatically estimates the user's residual motor capabilities. Third, a structured kinematic logging pipeline exporting full 26-joint hand skeleton data and task events in JSON, providing a reusable data infrastructure for performance monitoring and future data-driven decision-support components. Fourth, a task layer decoupled from the transformation engine, facilitating the development of reusable therapeutic activities. The framework is implemented in Unity and OpenXR using markerless hand tracking on commercial VR head-mounted displays. Two therapeutic tasks—a range-of-motion assessment and a gesture-based serious game—illustrate the architecture. Preliminary feasibility sessions confirm stable operation and the practical utility of structured logs, motivating further evaluation in paediatric rehabilitation contexts, notably for children with cerebral palsy.

Authors are listed in alphabetical order.

R. Matulevičius et al. (Eds.): DB&IS 2026, CCIS 3085, pp. 122–136, 2026.
https://doi.org/10.1007/978-3-032-30863-4_8

Keywords: Intelligent Rehabilitation System · Virtual Reality · Mirror Therapy · Kinematic Data Pipeline · Digitalization of Healthcare

1 Introduction

The digitalization of healthcare is increasingly calling for intelligent, data-capable systems that support clinical workflows with structured, reusable data and adaptive feedback mechanisms. Motor rehabilitation of the upper limb is a domain where such systems are particularly needed: recovery from neurological disorders such as stroke or cerebral palsy (CP, a group of permanent motor disorders caused by non-progressive brain injury during development) requires intensive, repetitive practice over prolonged periods, and the ability to monitor progress objectively, adapt difficulty dynamically, and sustain patient motivation are all critical factors for therapeutic success.

Mirror Therapy (MT) is a widely used approach to upper-limb motor rehabilitation [2]. It exploits a visual illusion in which movements performed with the unaffected limb are reflected by a physical mirror, creating the impression that the affected limb is moving normally. This *visuomotor* illusion - the coupling between visual perception of movement and motor execution - has been shown to facilitate motor network activation and to support functional recovery [13]. Virtual Reality-based Mirror Therapy (VR-MT) extends this approach by replacing the physical mirror with a virtual hand representation rendered in a VR head-mounted display (HMD), a device worn on the head that immerses the user in a computer-generated environment. The use of VR-MT could help overcome some of the limitations of conventional MT [16]. Indeed, VR-MT systems have demonstrated potential to improve upper limb function during stroke [6] and CP [18] rehabilitation. This enables flexible task design, precise control over visual feedback, and-critically-automatic recording of structured kinematic data (positions and orientations of hand joints over time) that can feed clinical decision-support tools.

Despite these advantages, existing VR-MT systems suffer from three recurring limitations that hinder their integration into digital rehabilitation pathways. First, they typically implement a single, fixed mirroring strategy, without explicitly distinguishing between global hand pose (wrist position and orientation) and local joints. Second, mechanisms for adaptive visual correction, such as error attenuation to compensate for motor deficits, or error augmentation to drive motor adaptation-remain largely ad hoc, tightly coupled to specific tasks, and rarely formalised as reusable components. Third, the software architectures of published systems are rarely described in sufficient detail to support replication, comparison, or extension to new clinical contexts, limiting their potential as a foundation for intelligent monitoring or decision-support systems.

These gaps are particularly significant in paediatric rehabilitation where systems may use generic processes to provide adaptable and personalized sessions. For instance, in children with CP, upper-limb motor deficits frequently affect fine finger movements, grasping, and forearm rotation, and rehabilitation extends over years. Intelligent systems capable of adapting feedback to residual motor capabilities, logging longitudinal data systematically, and engaging patients through gamified interaction are therefore strongly needed, yet remain largely underdeveloped.

This paper presents a modular VR-MT framework that addresses these limitations. The main contributions are:

- A **modular software architecture** implemented in Unity 2022.3 and OpenXR, with independent and reusable tracking, transformation, modulation, and logging components;
- A **configurable hand mirroring model** that explicitly separates global hand pose and local finger articulation, supporting three mirror mapping strategies (full, global, local);
- A **blending-based visual error modulation model** supporting both error attenuation and error augmentation at the joint level, initialised through a personalised, data-driven calibration procedure;
- A **structured kinematic data logging pipeline** exporting full hand skeleton data and task events in JSON format, constituting a data infrastructure for performance monitoring, session comparison, and future intelligent clinical components;
- **Two therapeutic tasks**-a range-of-motion assessment and a gesture-based serious game-designed under markerless tracking constraints in consultation with healthcare professionals.

The remainder of this paper is organised as follows. Section 2 reviews related work. Section 3 describes the modular architecture. Section 4 presents the mirror mapping model. Section 5 details the adaptive visual modulation model. Section 6 presents the therapeutic tasks. Section 7 describes the data logging pipeline. Section 8 reports preliminary experiments, and Sect. 9 concludes.

2 Related Work

2.1 Gesture Recognition in VR Rehabilitation Systems

Real-time gesture recognition is a core component of VR rehabilitation systems based on markerless hand tracking. Our system relies on the rule-based shape and pose detection API provided by the Unity XRHands package, which exploits the skeleton estimated by the Meta Quest's algorithm and onboard cameras. This design choice prioritises deployment simplicity and real-time stability over recognition flexibility. We do not require additionnal hardwares and custom gestures classification algorithm which can complicate system comparison and the capacity of professionnal to get access to the system.

The limitation of this approach is that it constrains the gesture vocabulary to postures that are reliably supported by the SDK. Compound movements such as forearm pronation and supination are particularly challenging, as they involve wrist orientation changes that can cause tracking instability [7]. In our framework, we have developed specific heuristics on top of the XRHands API to detect these movements robustly, combining joint angle thresholds with temporal filtering. For these specific gestures, the detection does not rely on a single static hand pose. Instead, we implemented a step-based recognition in which a complex movement is validated only if a predefined sequence of hand configurations and orientation changes is observed within a fixed temporal window. For instance, pronation and supination are detected by monitoring successive wrist-orientation states while ensuring that the hand remains in an expected posture pattern at both key frame. Such compound gesture validation is not directly provided by the standardOpenXR hand-tracking API and therefore required an additional heuristic layer on top of the SDK-provided shape and pose detection mechanisms. The gesture set was defined iteratively in consultation with healthcare professionals, and gestures with insufficient recognition rates were excluded. This is a deliberate design constraint: favouring feedback stability over an exhaustive gesture repertoire is essential to maintain a coherent visuomotor experience in a rehabilitation context.

2.2 VR Mirror Therapy Systems

Virtual Reality-based Mirror Therapy (VR-MT) is a rehabilitation approach in which a virtual representation of the user's hands replaces the physical mirror of conventional mirror therapy. The user's hand movements are tracked and mapped onto virtual hands, and the mirror effect is implemented through a software transformation that maps the healthy hand's motion to the virtual representation of the impaired hand.

Several VR-MT systems have been developed, primarily targeting adult post-stroke populations. Early systems relied on external optical sensors such as the Leap Motion controller - a dedicated hand-tracking device placed in front of the user - to track hand and finger movements in real time [8,10,13–15]. More recent systems exploit markerless hand tracking integrated directly in commercial HMDs: the HMD's onboard cameras continuously reconstruct a skeletal model of the user's hands without any external device or physical markers, enabling controller-free deployment [4,9,17]. Recent validation studies confirm that this HMD-integrated tracking provides a viable and cost-effective alternative to traditional marker-based motion capture for upper-limb kinematic analysis [3,5].

Table 1 summarises the key characteristics of existing systems. Most implement a single, fixed full-hand mirror mapping and focus on a limited set of tasks. Visual error modulation is rarely formalised: only Curiel et al. [4] explicitly integrate an error augmentation mechanism. Data recording capabilities vary widely, and implementation details are often insufficiently described to support replication or systematic comparison - which limits the potential of these systems as components of broader digital clinical workflows.

Table 1. Summary of existing VR mirror therapy systems. ROM: Range of Motion; ADL: Activities of Daily Living.

System	Tracking	Mirror	Tasks	Data
MNVR-Rehab [14,15]	Leap Motion	Full	Grasp & release	Time, score
VRMT [10,13]	Leap Motion	Full	Range of motion	-
BeST-ART [8]	Leap Motion	Full	Range of motion	-
VR Mirrored-Hand [9]	Markerless	Full	ADL simulation	Time, score
VRSelfCo [4]	Markerless	Full + aug.	Classification	Time, score
VR-MT [17]	Markerless	Full	Classification, ADL, game	-
Ours	Markerless	Full/Global/Local	ROM + serious game	Full skeleton

2.3 Adaptive Visual Feedback and Motor Learning

Error augmentation consists in exaggerating the perceived deviation from an ideal movement to facilitate motor adaptation [11,19]. Conversely, error attenuation visually reduces the perceived error to support task engagement when the motor deficit is severe. Shum et al. [18] applied visual error augmentation in reaching tasks with adolescents with CP. In our framework, both mechanisms are unified in a single blending-based model applicable at both the global (wrist) and local (finger) level, and initialised through a data-driven calibration procedure - making it a reusable, configurable component independent of any specific therapeutic task.

2.4 Markerless Hand Tracking Performance

The accuracy of HMD-integrated markerless hand tracking directly conditions the fidelity of the visuomotor feedback. Two key metrics characterise tracking quality: *position error* (the average distance between the real and tracked hand position) and *jitter* (frame-to-frame instability of the tracked position at rest, i.e. measurement noise). The Meta Quest 2 exhibits a position error of approximately 1.1 cm with ∼45 ms end-to-end latency (the delay between a physical movement and its visual display) [1]. The Meta Quest 3 reports lower jitter (1.11 cm) but higher position error (1.73 cm), with both devices showing wide latency ranges in practice depending on operating conditions [7]. Tracking quality also degrades when hands move to the periphery of the sensor field of view [1,7]. These constraints directly inform our task design strategy (Sect. 6).

3 Modular Software Architecture

The framework is implemented in Unity 2022.3.20f1 using OpenXR [12] (an open standard that provides a unified API for VR/AR hardware across vendors) and the Unity XRHands package (v1.5) to access a 26-joint articulated hand skeleton estimated by the HMD. It has been validated in two execution modes: *standalone* (the application runs directly on the Android-based HMD, without a PC) and *PCVR* (the HMD is connected to a Windows PC that handles rendering). Tests were conducted on Meta Quest 2 and Meta Quest 3. The reproducibility configuration is summarised in Table 2.

Table 2. Reproducibility configuration of the VR-MT framework.

Component	Specification
Unity	2022.3.20f1
XR Runtime	OpenXR 1.14.3 [12]
Hand Tracking	XRHands package v1.5 (26-joint skeleton)
HMDs tested	Meta Quest 2, Meta Quest 3
Execution modes	Standalone (Android), PCVR (Windows 10/11)
Output format	JSON (timestamps, joint poses, task events)

The architecture follows a component-based design that decouples four functional layers, each independently extensible:

Tracking Module. Acquires raw joint poses from the XR runtime at each frame. Gesture recognition uses the shape and pose detection API of XRHands and is constrained to the *foveal zone* of the HMD, the central region of the visual field where the onboard cameras provide the highest hand tracking reliability [1,7].

Transformation Engine. Implements the global and local mirror mapping strategies (Sect. 4) and the blending-based visual modulation (Sect. 5). This component is entirely decoupled from the task layer.

Task Layer. Defines therapeutic exercises and game mechanics. Tasks access the transformation engine through a configuration interface, allowing the mirror strategy, modulation parameter, and gesture set to be specified without modifying the core pipeline.

Logging Module. Records the full kinematic state and task events at each frame (Sect. 7), independently of task logic.

This separation ensures that new therapeutic tasks can be integrated without modifying the visuomotor transformation or data recording pipelines, and that the same modulation mechanisms can be systematically evaluated across different tasks. The system operates within the standard Unity update loop so that tracking, transformation, rendering, and logging occur within a single frame cycle, minimising additional *motion-to-photon latency* (the total delay between a physical hand movement and its appearance on the display).

4 Mirror Mapping Model

4.1 Hand Representation and Symmetry Plane

For each frame, the pose of each of the 26 tracked joints is expressed in the HMD reference frame and then transformed into the local coordinate system of the virtual avatar. A *sagittal symmetry plane* - the vertical plane dividing the body into left and right halves - is used to compute the geometrically mirrored pose of the reference (healthy) hand. The system supports both *unimanual* configurations - where only the healthy hand is physically moved and the impaired hand is fully replaced by its virtual mirror image - and *bimanual* configurations - where both hands are tracked and visual feedback is selectively modulated on the impaired side while the user engages both limbs.

Fig. 1. Illustration of full mirror mapping strategies where the right hand position is fully mirror mapped to the left hand model.

4.2 Three Mirror Mapping Strategies

Our framework explicitly separates the *global* component of the hand pose (wrist position and orientation) from the *local* component (finger joint rotations). This distinction enables three configurable mapping strategies:

Full Mirror Mapping. The complete pose of the reference hand is mirrored and mapped to the virtual impaired hand, reproducing the classical VR-MT paradigm [9,13]. Primarily used in unimanual configurations.

Global Mirror Mapping. Only the wrist position and orientation are mirrored; finger joint rotations are taken from the tracked impaired hand. This preserves fine motor engagement of the impaired hand while correcting its global spatial positioning.

Local Mirror Mapping. Only the finger joint rotations are mirrored; the wrist pose is taken from the tracked impaired hand. This maintains the user's spatial self-consistency while selectively correcting fine motor articulation - particularly relevant in bimanual configurations where the impaired hand retains residual mobility.

By exposing this global/local distinction as a configurable parameter, the framework enables systematic comparison of strategies and their combination with the visual modulation model. The Fig. 1 illustrates mirror mapping strategies.

5 Adaptive Visual Error Modulation

5.1 Blending Model

Visual error modulation is implemented by the `HandOffsetManager`, which compares the finger joints of the impaired hand (source) to those of a target hand and applies a joint-specific angular correction. Two types of correction are distinguished: *vertical offset* (flexion–extension), applied to the metacarpal, proximal, and distal articulations of each finger; and *spread offset* (abduction–adduction), applied to the metacarpal articulation only.

Let $\theta_o^{(j)}$ and $\theta_r^{(j)}$ denote the angle of articulation j in the source and target hand respectively. The displayed angle is:

$$\theta_d^{(j)} = \theta_o^{(j)} + \alpha^{(j)} \left(\theta_r^{(j)} - \theta_o^{(j)}\right), \quad \alpha^{(j)} \in [0, 1],$$

where $\alpha^{(j)}$ is the correction coefficient for articulation j, configurable independently for each joint via a dictionary editable from the Unity inspector. This displaces joint j a fraction $\alpha^{(j)}$ of the angular distance toward the target posture.

The target hand can be set to either the *original* hand (the pre-mirroring state of the impaired hand, saved by the `HandMirroringPreProcessor`) or the *opposite* hand (the healthy hand at the time the processor runs). In the mirror therapy context, using the original hand as target allows modulating the degree of full mirroring: rather than imposing complete symmetry, the system applies only a fraction of the correction at each articulation—from a subtle visual bias to a complete substitution of the impaired hand's motion by its healthy counterpart.

The primary therapeutic strategy implemented is **error attenuation** ($\alpha^{(j)} > 0$): the visual representation of each joint is progressively shifted toward the target, reducing the perceived motor error. Another classic rehabilitation strategy is **error augmentation**, which operates in the opposite direction: the perceived deviation is amplified beyond the actual motor error, encouraging the patient to overcorrect and thereby driving motor adaptation [11,18,19]. Although this approach has been explored in the literature, it remains peripheral to the present work, which focuses on mirror therapy as its primary therapeutic strategy. While the technical components are in place, error augmentation has not yet been fully implemented or experimentally validated.

The correction can be applied consistently with the mirror mapping strategies of Sect. 4: to the global component (root pose), to the local component (finger articulations), or to both.

5.2 Personalised Data-Driven Calibration

A key feature of the framework as an intelligent system is that the correction coefficients $\alpha^{(j)}$ are not set manually but estimated automatically through a short calibration phase prior to each session:

1. The user attempts to reach a target posture (e.g., full hand closure) with the impaired hand;

2. For each articulation j, the angular deviation $\Delta\theta^{(j)} = \theta_r^{(j)} - \theta_o^{(j)}$ between the observed posture and the target is measured;
3. The system evaluates whether, for the corrected posture, a predefined functional threshold is reached (e.g., 90% of the target closure angle);
4. If the threshold is not reached, $\alpha^{(j)}$ is incrementally increased for the articulations that have not yet met the criterion, until the threshold is satisfied - defining a personalised correction profile $\boldsymbol{\alpha} = (\alpha^{(j)})_j$ for the session.

This data-driven initialisation automatically scales the visual correction at each articulation to the user's actual residual range of motion, without manual parameter tuning by the therapist. The resulting profile $\boldsymbol{\alpha}$ is logged at the start of each session and can be tracked over time, constituting a quantitative indicator of motor performance per articulation. It represents a first step toward fully data-driven adaptation of therapeutic feedback within the intelligent system architecture.

5.3 Design Considerations

High correction values ($\alpha^{(j)} \to 1$) for some articulations may introduce perceptual inconsistencies when the displayed joint angle deviates substantially from the *proprioceptive* information (the internal bodily sense of limb position and movement) associated with the actual movement. Such discrepancies may alter the user's *sense of agency*, the feeling of being in control of one's own actions, which is a critical factor for motor rehabilitation.

This risk is particularly relevant in bimanual configurations, where the impaired hand is physically present and actively tracked: large angular corrections on certain articulations may create a visible mismatch between the felt and displayed hand posture. The joint-specific nature of the correction profile $\boldsymbol{\alpha}$ offers a practical mitigation: articulations with preserved mobility can be assigned low or zero correction, limiting the visuoproprioceptive conflict to only those joints where the motor deficit is significant.

The framework thus provides a controlled basis to systematically investigate, in future clinical studies, which correction profiles are therapeutically effective while remaining perceptually acceptable.

6 Therapeutic Tasks

Task design is explicitly driven by the constraints of markerless hand tracking: all interactions are confined to the foveal zone of the HMD (see Sect. 3), gesture validation relies on temporal windows rather than single-frame detections, and interaction pacing is deliberately slowed to accommodate reduced execution speed and improve recognition stability [7]. The gesture set was defined through iterative testing and consultation with healthcare professionals, retaining only robustly recognised gestures: *flexion–extension* (opening and closing the hand or fingers), *pronation–supination* (rotation of the forearm so the palm faces downward or upward respectively), and *grasp–release* (closing the hand around an object and releasing it).

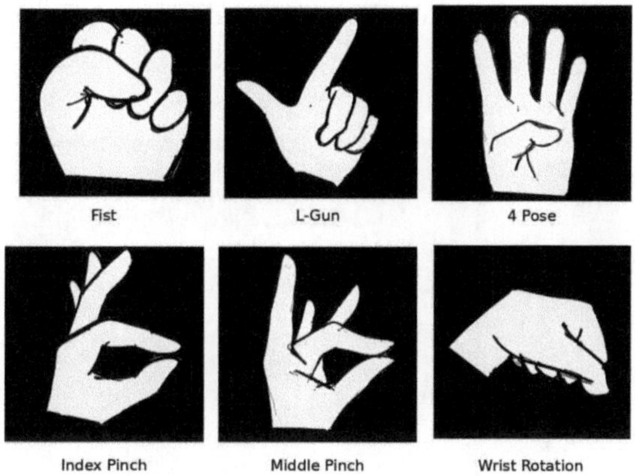

Fig. 2. The six target hand gestures considered in the experiment: Fist, L-Gun, 4 Pose, Index Pinch, Middle Pinch, and Wrist Rotation.

6.1 Range-of-Motion Assessment Task

Range of motion (ROM) refers to the extent of movement achievable at a joint; its measurement is a standard clinical assessment of upper-limb motor function. In this task, the user performs a predefined sequence of gestures specified by the experimenter. The hands are placed on a virtual table; a 3D animation and the name of the target gesture are displayed. Two modes are supported: (1) a *speed mode*, where the user reproduces the gesture as quickly as possible, and (2) a *hold mode*, where the user maintains the posture for a configurable duration. This task is designed for systematic evaluation-probing gesture recognition, response time, and spatial accuracy for each gesture and each hand-and directly feeds the data logging pipeline described in Sect. 7.

6.2 Mage Motion: A Gesture-Based Serious Game

Mage Motion is a fixed-shooter serious game in which the user performs hand gestures to defeat enemies approaching a tower (Fig. 3). Each enemy type is associated with a specific gesture (Fig. 2), which must be performed in the foveal zone so that the user observes their own movements. The game begins with a short tutorial delivered by a wizard character. Dynamics are deliberately paced to accommodate reduced motor speed in users with impairments.

The serious game format was chosen to support motivation during the repetitive practice required in upper-limb rehabilitation-a particular concern in paediatric populations (e.g., children with CP), where prolonged rehabilitation and the adolescent period can reduce adherence to conventional exercise protocols. Feedback from preliminary sessions led to a simplification of the gesture set and a reduction in game speed to better match the motor capabilities of participants with impairments. The game component further illustrates how the modular architecture supports the development of distinct interactive experiences-assessment and training-on top of the same underlying transformation and logging pipeline.

Fig. 3. Tutorial screen of the Mage Motion serious game. The blue circle indicates the foveal zone where gestures must be performed. (Color figure online)

7 Kinematic Data Logging Pipeline

The data logging pipeline is central to the framework's role as a digital health infrastructure component. At each frame, the positions and quaternion orientations of all 26 tracked joints of both hands are recorded with high-precision timestamps. Task-specific events-gesture detection, target acquisition, task transitions-are logged synchronously in the same data stream. All data are exported in a structured JSON format, enabling:

- **Offline Kinematic Replay**: full reconstruction of hand motion sequences for debugging and visual inspection;
- **Performance Metric Computation**: movement timing, spatial deviation from target gestures, and joint angle trajectories are derived from raw data computed *before* visual correction is applied, so that recorded data reflect the user's actual motor output, not the displayed feedback;
- **Technical Validation**: identification of tracking failures, gesture recognition errors, or skeleton instabilities - a use case demonstrated in our preliminary experiments; (Fig. 4).
- **Clinical Indicator Extraction**: longitudinal evolution of range of motion, reaction times, and asymmetry indices across sessions are candidate variables for future correlation with standardised upper-limb clinical scales, and for driving intelligent monitoring or dynamic difficulty adjustment components.

The decision to log the full skeleton rather than derived summaries deliberately preserves maximum information for future analyses, and avoids premature commitment to specific clinical metrics. The calibration parameter α is also logged at the start of each session, providing a simple but quantitative proxy for motor evolution over time. This design reflects the dual role of the pipeline: serving immediate technical validation needs while building a data infrastructure compatible with future intelligent clinical decision-support components.

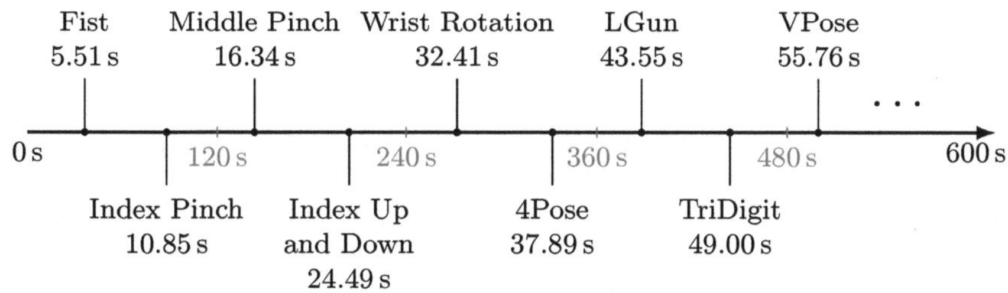

Fig. 4. Illustrative timeline of gesture-event timestamps extracted from a logged run. The full session spans 600 s (10 min); selected gesture occurrences are shown here schematically for readability and are not placed to scale.

8 Preliminary Experiments

Prior to any formal clinical study - which requires dedicated ethics approval given the involvement of persons with disabilities, and in particular children - exploratory feasibility sessions were conducted to assess technical operability and identify issues requiring correction.

Experiments involved a convenience sample of healthy adults (students and colleagues) and one volunteer adolescent with *hemiparesis* (partial weakness affecting one side of the body, here the upper limb). Sessions used both the range-of-motion task and the Mage Motion game Meta Quest 3 in both standalone mode for range motion and PCVR for range motion. The following observations emerged:

- The system operated stably on both devices throughout all sessions, confirming the cross-device portability of the OpenXR-based architecture;
- Several gesture recognition errors were identified and corrected via the logging pipeline, particularly for pronation and supination movements, confirming the practical utility of structured JSON logs for iterative system refinement.
- The calibration procedure successfully produced stable personalised values of α for both the participant with motor deficit and the healthy participants, confirming its practical feasibility.
- Qualitative feedback from Mage Motion sessions led to a simplification of required gestures, a reduction in game speed, modification of the spawn area and UI placement, improving compatibility with the motor capabilities of the participant with hemiparesis.

- The participant with hemiparesis completed the full session without discomfort and reported the Mage Motion game as engaging, providing an initial positive signal regarding acceptability in the target population.

These preliminary results confirm the global feasibility of the experimental setup and demonstrate the concrete utility of the logging pipeline for system refinement.

9 Conclusion

This paper presents a modular intelligent system for VR-based upper-limb mirror therapy, addressing three recurring limitations of existing approaches: fixed mirroring strategies, lack of reusable adaptive visual correction mechanisms, and insufficient architectural transparency. The main contributions are (1) a configurable hand mirroring model explicitly separating global and local hand components, (2) a blending-based visual error modulation model with personalised data-driven calibration, (3) a structured kinematic data logging pipeline, and (4) a modular component architecture decoupling visuomotor transformations from therapeutic tasks.

From a digital and intelligent systems perspective, the framework constitutes a data-capable rehabilitation platform: it generates structured kinematic datasets suitable for performance monitoring, session comparison, and future integration of intelligent components such as dynamic difficulty adjustment, automated gesture quality assessment, or clinical decision-support tools. The serious game component addresses the motivational dimension critical in paediatric populations. The personalised calibration procedure provides a first step toward fully data-driven adaptive feedback, and its logged output constitutes a quantitative proxy for motor progress over time. Currently the system lack of empirical data and need proper evaluation on validity, usability and of quantitative evaluation of motor performance improvements.

Future work will focus on providing empirical validation of the system and its components. It is plan to conduct (1) a formal usability study in a paediatric rehabilitation department, (2) evaluation of the perceptual effects of mirror mapping strategies and modulation parameters on motor performance, (3) integration of session-level performance indicators derived from logged data, and (4) investigation of intelligent dynamic difficulty adaptation based on real-time kinematic features extracted from the logging pipeline. These developments and experiments will support the transition from a technically operational prototype toward a valid and usable rehabilitation system.

Acknowledgments. The authors thank the CEDRIC Laboratory for funding this work as part of an exploratory research project, the healthcare professionals who provided clinical advice throughout the design process, and all participants in the preliminary sessions.

Disclosure of Interests. The authors have no competing interests to declare that are relevant to the content of this article.

References

1. Abdlkarim, D., et al.: A methodological framework to assess the accuracy of virtual reality hand-tracking systems: a case study with the meta quest 2. Behav. Res. Methods **56**(2), 1052–1063 (2024). https://doi.org/10.3758/s13428-022-02051-8
2. Cantero-Tellez, R., Naughton, N., Algar, L., Valdes, K.: Outcome measurement of hand function following mirror therapy for stroke rehabilitation: a systematic review. J. Hand Ther. **32**(2), 277–291 (2019)
3. Casile, A., et al.: Quantitative comparison of hand kinematics measured with a markerless commercial head-mounted display and a marker-based motion capture system in stroke survivors. Sensors **23**(18), 7906 (2023). https://doi.org/10.3390/s23187906
4. Curiel, M., Gutierrez-Maldonado, J., Garcia-Palacios, A., Cipresso, P.: Virtual reality self co-embodiment with error augmentation for upper limb rehabilitation. IEEE Trans. Neural Syst. Rehabil. Eng. **32**, 1125–1134 (2024). https://doi.org/10.1109/TNSRE.2024.3361427
5. De Pasquale, P., Bonanno, M., Mojdehdehbaher, S., Quartarone, A., Calabrò, R.S.: The use of head-mounted display systems for upper limb kinematic analysis in post-stroke patients: a perspective review on benefits, challenges and other solutions. Bioengineering **11**(6), 559 (2024). https://doi.org/10.3390/bioengineering11060559
6. Gebreheat, G., Antonopoulos, N., Porter-Armstrong, A.: Application of immersive virtual reality mirror therapy for upper limb rehabilitation after stroke: a scoping review. Neurol. Sci. **45**(9), 4173–4184 (2024)
7. Godden, E., Steedman, W., Pan, M.K.: Robotic characterization of markerless hand-tracking on meta quest pro and quest 3 virtual reality headsets. IEEE Trans. Visual Comput. Graphics **31**(5), 3025–3034 (2025). https://doi.org/10.1109/TVCG.2025.3549182
8. Heinrich, C., Zahn, M., Bhatt, T., Bhatt, N.: Feasibility of a head-mounted display-based immersive virtual reality-powered mirror therapy system for upper limb rehabilitation: Best-art. Front. Neurol. **13**, 828204 (2022). https://doi.org/10.3389/fneur.2022.828204
9. Hsieh, Y.W., et al.: Design and evaluation of a bimanual virtual reality mirror therapy system for upper limb rehabilitation in patients with stroke. J. Neuroeng. Rehabil. **22**(1), 10 (2025). https://doi.org/10.1186/s12984-025-01536-3
10. Hsu, C.Y., Hu, Y.C., Lin, B.S., Chou, C.W., Chen, J.J.J.: Effects of virtual reality-enhanced mirror therapy for upper extremity rehabilitation in stroke patients. Neuropsychol. Rehabil. **32**(10), 2509–2527 (2022). https://doi.org/10.1080/09602011.2021.1967960
11. Israely, S., Carmeli, E.: Error augmentation as a possible technique for improving upper extremity motor performance after a stroke - a systematic review. Top. Stroke Rehabil. **23**(2), 116–125 (2016). https://doi.org/10.1179/1945511915Y.0000000007
12. Khronos Group: OpenXR specification (2020). https://www.khronos.org/openxr/
13. Lin, B.S., Chen, J.J.J., Hsu, H.Y.: Novel application of a mobile-device-based virtual reality system to facilitate mirror therapy for upper limb rehabilitation in patients with stroke. J. Neuroeng. Rehabil. **18**(1), 34 (2021). https://doi.org/10.1186/s12984-021-00821-9
14. Mekbib, D.B., et al.: Proactive motor functional recovery through mirror visual feedback-based virtual reality rehabilitation in stroke patients. Ann. N. Y. Acad. Sci. **1464**(1), 5–18 (2020). https://doi.org/10.1111/nyas.14251

15. Mekbib, D.B., et al.: A novel fully immersive virtual reality paradigm for upper limb rehabilitation in patients with stroke. J. Visualized Exp. (168), e62146 (2021). https://doi.org/10.3791/62146
16. Norris, T.A., Augenstein, T.E., Rodriguez, K.M., Claflin, E.S., Krishnan, C.: Shaping corticospinal pathways in virtual reality: effects of task complexity and sensory feedback during mirror therapy in neurologically intact individuals. J. Neuroeng. Rehabil. **21**(1), 154 (2024)
17. Quintana, L., Santos, B.S., Dias, P., Morais, P.: Limitations and solutions of low cost virtual reality mirror therapy for post-stroke patients. Sci. Rep. **13**, 14554 (2023). https://doi.org/10.1038/s41598-023-40546-2
18. Shum, L.C., Valdes, B.A., Hodges, N.J., Van der Loos, H.F.M.: Error augmentation in immersive virtual reality for bimanual upper-limb rehabilitation in individuals with and without hemiplegic cerebral palsy. IEEE Trans. Neural Syst. Rehabil. Eng. **28**(1), 541–549 (2020). https://doi.org/10.1109/TNSRE.2019.2953602
19. Wei, Y., Bajaj, P., Scheidt, R., Patton, J.L.: Visual error augmentation for enhancing motor learning and rehabilitative relearning. In: Proceedings of the IEEE 9th International Conference on Rehabilitation Robotics (ICORR), pp. 505–510. (2005). https://doi.org/10.1109/ICORR.2005.1501152

A Predictive Anthropometric Data Infrastructure for 3D Body Modeling

Andrejs Neimanis[1], Zane Bicevska[1(✉)], and Janis Bicevskis[2]

[1] DIVI Grupa Ltd., Fridriha Candera Str. 1, Riga LV-1046, Latvia
{Andrejs.Neimanis,Zane.Bicevska}@di.lv
[2] University of Latvia, Raina Blvd. 19, Riga LV-1586, Latvia
Janis.Bicevskis@lu.lv

Abstract. Reliable anthropometric data underpin garment construction, virtual fitting, and digital body modeling, yet the integration of validated measurement collection with measurement-conditioned 3D geometry generation remains insufficiently addressed. This paper presents AntrDB, a predictive anthropometric infrastructure combining hybrid manual-digital data collection, statistical completion of partial measurement vectors, and conditional 3D avatar generation under explicit measurement preservation. In contrast to traditional parametric body models, where body shape is controlled by latent shape parameters, anthropometric measurements serve as the primary conditioning variables and are geometrically verified during generation. AntrDB is modular, supports incremental retraining as the dataset grows, and targets garment engineering workflows.

Keywords: Anthropometric data infrastructure · body measurement value completion · measurement-conditioned 3D generation · 3D body scanning · predictive anthropometry

1 Introduction

Anthropometric measurement data – such as chest circumference, waist height, and inseam length – underpin garment construction, ergonomics, and product design. While national sizing surveys provide statistical reference data and parametric 3D models enable compact body representations, these two strands remain insufficiently integrated: parametric models are shape-driven and do not guarantee that specific body measurements are met with defined accuracy. For garment engineering, where individual measurements are construction-critical parameters, this gap is significant.

The AntrDB project addresses it through an architecture resting on three pillars:

- A hybrid manual-digital measurement infrastructure with an explicit landmark basis.
- Statistical completion of incomplete measurement vectors.
- Topology-consistent 3D avatar generation under an explicit measurement preservation criterion.

R. Matulevičius et al. (Eds.): DB&IS 2026, CCIS 3085, pp. 137–151, 2026.
https://doi.org/10.1007/978-3-032-30863-4_9

A key architectural principle is the separation between measurement-space modeling and geometry modeling, implemented as independent yet combinable components, enabling modular validation, incremental retraining, and flexible adaptation to different measurement schemas. The paper describes the conceptual foundations, infrastructural implementation, and current development status, and discusses remaining methodological challenges.

This paper makes the following contributions:

- A measurement-centered architecture that treats anthropometric measurements as primary conditioning variables rather than latent shape parameters.
- An integrated infrastructure combining validated data acquisition, statistical measurement completion, and measurement-conditioned 3D avatar generation.
- A modular, versioned system design enabling independent retraining, validation, and deployment of predictive components.
- A system-level approach to ensuring geometric consistency through explicit measurement preservation and post-generation verification.

2 Related Work

2.1 National Anthropometric Studies

Large-scale anthropometric studies have historically formed the empirical basis for garment sizing systems. They are also used in ergonomic design and population modeling. Notable studies include: SizeUSA [1], SizeUK [2], SizeGERMANY [3], Size Thailand [4], as well as studies of military personnel such as ANSUR II [5].

These studies combine structured measurements with demographic metadata (e.g., age, sex), enabling stratified statistical analyses with typical sample sizes in the five-digit range. While sampling strategies aim to approximate national distributions, detailed documentation of statistical representativeness is not uniformly available. In more recent studies, 3D avatars are commonly created from anatomically defined landmarks, but standardized landmark coordinates in topology-consistent, machine-readable form are not consistently provided. While landmark definitions are typically specified, the practical procedures used to determine landmark positions (e.g., physical marking, manual annotation on scans, or automated detection algorithms) are often only partially documented in publicly available reports—limiting reproducibility and integration into generative modeling frameworks. Suitability for generative modeling is further limited by significant underrepresentation of individuals at body size extremes, particularly high-BMI and plus-size ranges [6, 7].

2.2 3D Anthropometric Datasets

Several public or semi-public 3D datasets are available, including CESAR [8], DINED [9], WEAR [10], and various commercial sizing study databases. These resources provide 3D scans, derived anthropometric measurements, and population statistics.

Their objectives, however, differ from those of predictive modeling infrastructures. Typical limitations include:

- licensed or controlled access to high-resolution raw meshes,
- scan meshes lack a shared anatomical correspondence structure, requiring additional preprocessing before modeling,
- inconsistent availability of explicit 3D landmark coordinates and limited documentation of landmark derivation,
- lack of standardized programmatic interfaces for direct integration into generative or inference pipelines.

Most existing scan databases were designed primarily for descriptive statistics and the definition of sizing systems. They therefore do not inherently contain prediction methods for 3D avatars, parametric modeling frameworks, topology-consistent shape spaces, or real-time conditional generation capabilities.

2.3 Predictive Anthropometry

Predictive anthropometry uses multivariate dependencies between body measurements to estimate missing or validate existing dimensions, traditionally via regression methods and principal component analysis, with more recent approaches employing regularized and nonlinear models. In earlier work by the AntrDB project team [11], regression-based validation and correction of anthropometric datasets was demonstrated, confirming stable linear dependencies for structured inference.

2.4 Measurement-Driven 3D Avatar Generation

Parametric 3D body models such as SMPL [12] and its extensions (e.g., STAR [13]) represent body shape in low-dimensional, PCA-based parameter spaces learned from large scan datasets. These template-based models enable efficient decoupling of pose and shape but rely on globally entangled shape coefficients. Precise adherence to multiple local anthropometric constraints is therefore inherently difficult, as changes to individual parameters induce correlated non-local deformations.

For stronger measurement control, several works combine statistical models with optimization methods. Earlier approaches deform PCA-based models using nonlinear optimization [14], while more recent methods learn regression mappings from measurements to SMPL(-X) shape parameters (e.g., A2B [15]). However, such approaches remain limited by the expressiveness and entanglement of the underlying low-dimensional shape space.

Qualitative evaluation of SMPL-X tooling (Blender add-on, Meshcapade) confirms these limits: PCA parameters and vertex groups do not map to anthropometric attributes, local edits (e.g. ankle girth) cause distant deformations, and out-of-range inputs yield non-plausible shapes—motivating measurement-primary conditioning.

Deep generative models, in particular Variational Autoencoders (VAEs), allow more flexible nonlinear shape representations. Methods such as DHNN [16] and Semantic-Human [17] focus on latent space structure[1] and disentanglement to enable more intuitive

[1] The internal low-dimensional representation learned by the generative model capturing shape variability.

local editing and metric control. However, these models are typically optimized for reconstruction quality or attribute editing, not for strict adherence to high-dimensional explicit anthropometric measurement vectors.

More recent work directly conditions 3D body generation on anthropometric measurement vectors. AnthroNet [18] presents a generative body model trained end-to-end on synthetic data that takes a full schema of anthropometric measurements as input and produces body meshes with accurate anthropometry. Despite this significant advance, AnthroNet relies on synthetically generated training data and does not include explicit post-generation geometric verification of measurements as a training objective.

Overall, existing approaches operate either in globally entangled parametric shape spaces, with optimization methods of poor scalability at high constraint dimensionality, or with a focus on visual plausibility rather than verified geometric measurement preservation. A generative framework that combines real-world measurement data collection, topology-consistent mesh generation, and explicit post-generation geometric measurement verification as a training objective remains, to our knowledge, unreported.

2.5 Identified Methodological Gaps

The literature and publicly available solutions thus reveal four persistent limitations:

1. Anthropometric measurements are rarely treated as primary conditioning variables with explicit geometric consistency enforcement.
2. Extreme body configurations are underrepresented.
3. Measurement completion and 3D avatar generation are typically addressed separately.
4. Configurable measurement schemas and standardized B2B interfaces are frequently absent.

2.6 Positioning of the AntrDB Framework

The AntrDB framework addresses these limitations through an architecture that integrates hybrid measurement data collection, topology-consistent mesh standardization, modular measurement completion, and geometry generation under explicit measurement preservation conditions—combining data collection, validation, statistical inference, and constrained 3D avatar generation into a coherent predictive infrastructure with standardized interfaces.

3 System Architecture Overview

3.1 Core Architectural Principles and Processing Pipeline

The AntrDB framework is an integrated predictive anthropometric system that combines validated data collection, statistical measurement modeling, and measurement-conditioned 3D avatar generation. It supports two prediction tasks:

- Completion of anthropometric measurement vectors from partial inputs.
- Generation of metrically consistent 3D avatars conditioned on these measurements.

These capabilities are intended to improve workflows in the garment industry, particularly in virtual fitting.

The processing pipeline from raw data to deployable prediction models proceeds through the following stages: manual body measurement collection and validation; multi-view photography and Gaussian Splatting[2]-based 3D avatar generation; uniform positioning and scaling of avatars; landmark identification and verification; digital measurement extraction from landmarked avatars; reconciliation and validation of the combined measurement dataset; training of the measurement completion model; mesh standardization; and training of the 3D avatar prediction model on the final measurement datasets and standardized meshes.

3.2 Layered Architecture

The framework is organized into five logically independent layers, each communicating via defined interfaces:

1. Collection—manual measurement and multi-view 3D reconstruction.
2. Harmonization—validation and consistency management between manual and digital measurements.
3. Measurement completion—statistical reconstruction of full measurement vectors from partial inputs.
4. 3D avatar prediction—conditional generative modeling on topology-consistent meshes under explicit measurement constraints.
5. Integration—provision of predictive functions for external systems.

From an information systems perspective, the architecture emphasizes separation between versioned data storage and independently deployable model artifacts. The integration layer exposes REST endpoints for measurement completion and avatar generation, accepting JSON-formatted measurement vectors conforming to a configurable schema and returning validated predictions; authentication and versioning follow standard B2B API conventions. This design supports controlled model updates, reproducibility, and interoperability with heterogeneous stakeholders.

4 Acquiring Body Measurement Data

4.1 Selection of Anthropometric Measurements and Landmarks to Be Used

The measurements and landmarks used in AntrDB were drawn from a consolidated catalog of 491 anthropometric and garment-relevant measurements and 146 anatomical landmarks, derived from ISO standards, established anthropometric studies, and pattern construction systems, all stored in a database with unique identifiers and anatomical descriptions. A project-specific subset was defined based on predictive relevance and commercial applicability, comprising **42 physically attachable landmarks**, **51 manually collected measurements**, and **117 digitally extractable measurements**. Valid

---

[2] A radiance-field technique that reconstructs dense 3D geometry from multi-view photographs.

value ranges and collection methods are recorded in the database, ensuring semantic traceability[3] and pipeline consistency.

4.2 Use of Landmarks for Anatomical Referencing

To ensure anatomical correspondence between manual and digital measurements, physical landmarks are applied to participants prior to scanning using palpation-based identification of skeletal reference points, marked with self-adhesive Topcodes [19] that allow digital detection. A subset of 42 landmarks was selected from the full catalog of 146, serving as reference points for digital measurements, orientation points during manual measurement, correspondence points in mesh processing (Sect. 5.5), and reference points for virtual fitting evaluation (Sect. 10). Anatomical descriptions and collection instructions are stored in the database, ensuring that digital and manual measurements follow identical anatomical definitions.

4.3 Participant Strategy

The long-term goal is to cover the broadest possible range of adult body configurations, deliberately including body types underrepresented in existing datasets. Participants are segmented along sex, age groups, and chest circumference—not to mirror population distributions, but to ensure strong representation of both central and extreme body types. Target dataset size is approximately 500 women and 500 men, a figure based on Meyer et al. [20], who found that regression models for body measurement prediction stabilize at around 500 samples per sex.

Targeted recruitment activities for rarer body types are planned. Should any segment be overrepresented, the training subset is selected by maximizing the total Mahalanobis distance [21] among members within each segment—prioritizing internal diversity over quantity.

4.4 Participant Consent and Data Protection

Data collection follows strict data protection and consent procedures. Participants are informed prior to collection about data scope, purpose, storage policy, and withdrawal rights, and sign a consent declaration. Each participant receives a unique identifying code linking their records in the AntrDB database and image processing software; identifying personal data (name, email) exist only on paper and are not stored electronically. Participation is voluntary and open to people aged 18 and over. Participants may optionally request a body measurement report with sizing recommendations and/or a 3D avatar generated from their photographs.

[3] The ability to map each measurement to a uniquely defined anatomical landmark and definition stored in the database.

4.5 Body Measurement Data Collection Procedure

The participant undresses to underwear. Trained staff apply landmarks in teams of two (lead and assistant), typically within 10–15 min, followed by photography (Sect. 5.1) in three poses. Manual measurements are taken by the lead while the assistant enters values into the measurement management system; an audio input option is available for solo operation. The process takes 15–20 min. All values are checked against stored bounds, and the statistical validation procedure (Sect. 6) is applied before the participant is released, allowing re-measurement of any flagged values.

4.6 Digital Measurement Extraction

Digital body measurements are obtained from 3D avatars of the participant (for the provision of avatars, see Sect. 5). The digital measurements are essentially based on the landmarks physically attached to the participant, which are made available as specially marked vertices in the 3D avatars (Sect. 5.4).

Digital measurement is carried out by a set of Python programs that process the .obj files with the specially marked vertices. These programs use four geometric methods to determine distances in three-dimensional space:

- Geodesic distance (follows the surface).
- Tape measure-like distance (follows the surface in concave areas, takes the shortcut through the air in convex areas).
- Axis-parallel projections onto the surface (follows the surface in accordance with a fictitiously performed cross-section).
- Euclidean distance.

These four metrics are applied or combined in a measurement-specific manner; in many cases, the identified landmarks are supplemented by algorithmically determined imaginary landmarks.

All body measurements calculated digitally in this way are also stored in the database; this enables not only harmonized data management, but also direct comparison and validation using both body measurement datasets.

4.7 Harmonization of the Manual-Digital Dataset

For each participating individual, both the manually collected and the digitally extracted body measurements are stored. The immediate validation of the manually collected dataset can thus be complemented at a later stage by a validation of the complete body measurement dataset.

Deviations are treated as diagnostic signals for algorithm refinement, not as implicit equivalence assumptions. A fully formalized deterministic validation protocol for digital measurements is under development; the current framework enables structured comparison processes and controlled release of datasets for the modeling workflow.

Only after validation of the measurement is completed are the vectors released for downstream statistical analysis and model training.

As a final safeguard in the prediction workflow, the measurement data management system allows the specification of an alternative value to be used as input for prediction algorithms. Under normal operation, all predictions use the validated measured values stored in the database. If the post-measurement validation process indicates a measurement error with high probability, a corrected value can be defined specifically for prediction input. This mechanism does not modify the original measurement records; the originally acquired values remain unchanged and preserved in the database, ensuring full traceability of the acquisition data.

4.8 Database Architecture

The schema organizes data around three primary entities: participants (identified only by anonymous code), measurement records (linking values to their catalog definitions, collection method, and operator), and landmark assignments (mapping physical marker positions to anatomical definitions). The event-log approach—recording every write with operator, timestamp, and operation type rather than overwriting in place—preserves the full provenance chain from raw collection to model-ready vectors. GitLab-versioned SQL scripts are the sole permitted mechanism for schema and data modification, ensuring that any historical database state can be reconstructed. Predictive model artifacts are versioned independently of the database layer, enabling side-by-side comparison of model generations without modifying source data.

This design ensures that any combination of dataset snapshot and model artifact version can be exactly reconstructed, making experimental results independently reproducible and enabling controlled longitudinal evaluation as the dataset grows.

5 Photo Data Acquisition and the 3D Avatar Creation Pipeline

5.1 Multi-camera Capture Studio

Anthropometric 3D data are acquired in a dedicated circular capture studio (2.6 m diameter) equipped with 96 synchronized cameras arranged in 16 vertical columns. Uniform diffuse lighting ensures stable surface conditions, while near-simultaneous image capture minimizes motion artifacts and soft tissue deformation. This configuration enables full 360° coverage and supports accurate geometric reconstruction.

5.2 IT Architecture of the Multi-camera Capture Studio

The capture system is implemented as a dedicated client–server architecture. A central server coordinates the 96 Raspberry Pi Zero W-based cameras over a dedicated Wi-Fi network, handling time synchronization via NTP, synchronized trigger dispatch, acoustic start signals, and image upload management. A web-based client interface manages session control, participant registration, camera status monitoring, and image transfer to the project's server environment. The solution was implemented in C# (.NET/Blazor), Rust, and Python.

5.3 3D Reconstruction Using Gaussian Splatting

3D reconstruction is performed from multi-view images using a Gaussian Splatting [22]–based radiance field pipeline, comprising camera pose estimation, radiance field optimization, and mesh extraction. The resulting meshes are scaled and aligned to a common coordinate system, ensuring consistent spatial positioning across all subjects.

5.4 Landmark Identification and Processing

Landmark identification is performed using a semi-automatic pipeline combining image-based detection, manual verification, and projection onto the reconstructed 3D mesh. Identified landmarks are encoded as dedicated vertices and linked to their anthropometric definitions. This ensures consistent anatomical correspondence between manual measurements and digital representations and provides the basis for subsequent measurement extraction and modeling.

5.5 Mesh Standardization and Topological Harmonization

To enable predictive modeling, reconstructed meshes are transformed into a topology-consistent representation with fixed vertex indexing while preserving global geometry and landmark positions. This standardization ensures uniform input dimensionality, supports vertex-wise comparison, and enables stable conditioning within the generative modeling framework.

6 Validation and Completion of Body Measurement Data

In many application areas, only a subset of the anthropometric measurements recommended for 3D avatar prediction is available. The measurement completion component provided by the AntrDB project can close this gap. It allows a complete measurement vector to be estimated from partial inputs, with the observed values being exactly preserved.

Let $x \in R^n$ denote the complete measurement vector and $x_{obs} \subset x$ the observed subset; the goal is to estimate the missing components under the conditions that.

- observed measurements remain unchanged, and
- predicted values are statistically consistent with the learned multivariate dependencies between anthropometric variables.

The statistical foundations of this approach—including regression-based modeling and quality control mechanisms—were described in earlier work by the AntrDB project team [11, 23]. In the AntrDB project, these methods are applied to the collected dataset and implemented in a modular, schema-configurable software architecture.

Predictive models are trained on the accumulated anthropometric dataset using the defined measurement schema.

The prediction system supports externally defined measurement schemas and allows retraining with alternative measurement sets as well as domain-specific configurations.

Trained models are serialized independently of the database layer, enabling controlled versioning and deployment.

For each completed vector, the prediction solution will provide uncertainty indicators and global consistency metrics. The method can thus also be used to validate individual measurement values, as for example in the AntrDB project itself (Sect. 4.5). The software architecture supports incremental retraining as the dataset grows.

7 Measurement-Conditioned 3D Avatar Prediction

7.1 Problem Formulation

As described in Sect. 5.5, all subject meshes are transformed into a topology-consistent standardized representation with fixed vertex indexing; let M denote this space. Let the distance mapping d: $M \rightarrow Rn$ be the distance mapping yielding anthropometric vector $x$full $\in Rn$, representing the digital measurement programs described in Sect. 4.6. The model learns a mapping f: $Rn \rightarrow M$ under the constraint that the generated mesh meets the conditioning measurements within predefined tolerances. After mesh generation, digital measurements are re-extracted and a consistency loss function enforces g(M) $\approx x$full within tolerances comparable to professional manual measurement variability, as part of a composite objective that also includes latent distribution regularization, geometric reconstruction, and surface consistency terms.

This explicit supervision distinguishes AntrDB from image-driven or unconstrained generative body models.

7.2 Conditional Generative Architecture

The generative component is a Conditional Variational Autoencoder (CVAE). The encoder learns a latent representation of standardized meshes conditioned on measurement vectors; these inputs are projected using Fourier features to capture high-frequency geometric details more effectively. The decoder reconstructs meshes conditioned on measurements and latent variables. The latent space captures residual geometric variability not uniquely determined by anthropometric measurements, for example variations in body surface shape resulting from differences in soft-tissue distribution. The model architecture allows retraining as additional data become available. Uncertainty indicators from measurement completion can optionally guide latent sampling for uncertainty-aware generation. After generation, digital measurements are re-extracted and compared with conditioning values to verify tolerance compliance, closing the predictive loop.

7.3 Architectural Classification

In contrast to global parametric body models, which encode anthropometric variation in low-dimensional shape coefficients, the proposed architecture treats anthropometric measurements as primary conditioning variables and separates statistical measurement modeling from geometric variability.

The 3D avatar prediction layer constitutes the geometric endpoint of the predictive pipeline. Its purpose is not merely visual reconstruction, but the generation of metrically validated geometry suitable for virtual fitting within garment engineering applications.

8 Current Status and Open Challenges

8.1 Data Collection

The data collection component of the AntrDB project was initially validated with individuals from the acquaintance circle of the executing project team. The collection and data management infrastructure is operational and has been used for more than 150 participants to date. The measurement team consists of 6 trained female staff members; operation of the 96-camera multi-view capture system is handled by 4 members of the project team. Manual landmark placement, manual measurement data collection, and the validation procedure for manual measurements are functioning as specified.

The 96-camera multi-view capture system can process approximately 4 participants per hour including loading time. The capacity of the rendering process is approximately 25 persons per day but could be expanded through additionally provided hardware.

8.2 Recruiting Participants

Beyond general research participation willingness, a primary recruitment incentive is the offer of a personalized 3D avatar—for most participants their first encounter with a realistic avatar of themselves. Early avatar deliveries suffered from poor facial texture quality due to multi-view image compositing artifacts; this has since been resolved and avatars are now usually delivered by email the day after the session. The project has been publicly promoted [24] since December 2025. The principal bottleneck for data growth is the stationary nature of the capture system, which requires all participants to be photographed on site.

8.3 Pipeline Completion Status

At the time of writing, the software team is focused on closing two gaps in the pipeline described in Sect. 3.1: reconciliation and validation of the complete body measurement dataset, and automated landmark identification on 3D avatars. All other pipeline components are at minimum unit-tested. Once these gaps are closed, the focus will shift to full pipeline integration and automation.

8.4 Prediction Methods for Body Measurements

The prediction method for body measurements is implemented and is being used in the AntrDB project for validating manually collected data (Sect. 4.5). Within the AntrDB project, a reference implementation in an end-user application is currently being prepared: in an online sales platform for individualized garments, entered body measurements can both be validated and missing ones estimated. It is also still planned to implement the component in a B2B reference application.

The prediction component is designed to support periodic retraining as new data becomes available. Since the available dataset is continuously growing, the validation and prediction component is retrained on a regular basis.

8.5 Prediction Methods for 3D Avatars

The 3D avatar prediction model is currently being trained on an alternative dataset due to the still limited volume of standardized AntrDB meshes. For a transition to training on the native AntrDB dataset, it is necessary to close the remaining gaps in the processing pipeline (Sect. 8.3).

The geometric accuracy of the acquisition pipeline has been evaluated using controlled mannequin experiments. The mean point-to-surface (P2S) distance between independently reconstructed meshes is 0.50 mm, with 95% of surface deviations below 1.4 mm. Landmark consistency across reconstructions shows typical deviations in the range of 0.2–1.7 mm for physically attached markers, with higher variance for manually inferred points.

Complementary results from a companion study within the same project [25], focusing on measurement-conditioned 3D reconstruction, indicate that dense anthropometric conditioning enables high predictive precision. Using a comparable dataset size (~400 samples per group), a deterministic regression model achieves approximately 2 mm mean measurement error, with worst-case deviations remaining within a single clothing size gradation step. The companion study compares the same regressor against OLS (Ordinary Least Squares) and a CVAE: OLS reaches ~1 mm in-distribution error but collapses into non-human geometry on out-of-distribution measurements; the CVAE is non-repeatable and exceeds 2 cm worst-case on most samples. The deterministic dense-conditioned regressor stays within one clothing size step while preserving surface plausibility.

Taken together, these results confirm that both the measurement data quality and the reconstruction pipeline meet the tolerances required for garment engineering workflows. The remaining step is to close the processing pipeline—automated landmark identification and dataset reconciliation (Sect. 8.3)—so that native AntrDB mesh-measurement pairs can be used directly for generative model training.

The separation between stored measurement data and versioned model artifacts enables controlled model updates, comparative evaluation of model generations, and incremental improvement of predictive robustness with increasing dataset coverage.

8.6 Preliminary Evaluation

A limited quantitative assessment was conducted to characterize the accuracy of key pipeline components. For the acquisition and reconstruction stage, controlled repeated captures yield a mean point-to-surface deviation of 0.50 mm, with 95% of deviations below 1.4 mm; landmark localization accuracy is in the range of 0.2–1.7 mm. These values are within typical manual measurement tolerances and indicate reliable geometric input for downstream processing.

For the predictive components, preliminary validation was performed using partial masking of measurement vectors and re-extraction of measurements from generated meshes. Measurement completion shows stable reconstruction of missing values, while measurement-conditioned mesh generation produces deviations typically within a few millimeters for major garment-relevant dimensions. Although a full end-to-end evaluation on the native AntrDB dataset is still pending, these results indicate that the current system operates within accuracy ranges suitable for garment engineering applications.

In comparison, OLS fails under out-of-distribution inputs, while CVAE-based generation is non-deterministic with larger deviations (>2 cm); the proposed approach maintains deterministic predictions within a clothing size step, supporting its use where robustness and multiple constraints are required.

9 Discussion

AntrDB's core contribution lies not in any single algorithm but in treating anthropometric measurements as primary, controllable variables throughout—bridging data collection, statistical inference, and geometry generation under explicit consistency conditions.

The proposed approach is advantageous in applications where multiple independent anthropometric constraints must be satisfied simultaneously. In contrast to parametric models, where shape parameters are globally entangled, measurement-conditioned generation enables direct control over garment-relevant dimensions, making it suitable for engineering-oriented use cases such as pattern construction and virtual fitting.

The added effort is justified where multiple local measurement constraints, deterministic repeatability, and OOD (Out-of-distribution) stability are required (pattern construction, B2B fitting APIs); for purely visual use cases, standard parametric models remain lighter. End-to-end validation on native AntrDB topology is pending, so quantitative claims currently rest on the SMPL-topology results in [25].

At the same time, challenges remain. The mapping of a measurement vector to a complete body geometry is not unique; different soft tissue distributions can exhibit identical circumference or length measurements. Modeling this residual variability requires a careful balance between latent flexibility and explicit measurement constraints.

A further methodological focus lies in the harmonization of manual and digitally extracted measurements. Despite standardized landmarks and validation mechanisms, systematic deviations can occur, for example due to geometry approximation or soft tissue deformation during capture. The ongoing statistical analysis of these differences is crucial for the long-term calibration of the system.

A further open challenge concerns the absence of formal quantitative evaluation of the 3D avatar prediction component on AntrDB's native dataset. Although geometric quality on the current training data is high, systematic evaluation of measurement preservation precision and reconstruction accuracy on real AntrDB meshes remains pending. This limits how far claims about the system's predictive robustness can currently be substantiated and represents a primary target for the next development phase.

Overall, it is evident that measurement-based generation is only reliable when data collection, modeling, and validation are understood as an integrated overall system.

The development of the system revealed several practical insights. Landmark placement and visibility constitute a dominant source of measurement uncertainty. Geometric reconstruction accuracy alone does not ensure measurement accuracy and therefore requires explicit validation loops. Dense measurement conditioning significantly reduces ambiguity in 3D reconstruction. Finally, dataset diversity has a stronger impact on predictive robustness than dataset size in early stages.

10 Conclusion and Future Work

This paper presented AntrDB, an integrated anthropometric infrastructure that combines hybrid measurement data collection, measurement completion, and measurement-conditioned 3D avatar generation in a modular architecture. The central feature is the explicit anchoring of geometry generation in the anthropometric measurement space and the enforcement of a measurement preservation criterion.

The system is in an operational implementation phase: collection infrastructure and data management are in productive use, prediction components are prototypically implemented, and mesh standardization enables consistent training of generative models.

The central remaining challenge is not algorithmic but infrastructural: closing the processing pipeline so that AntrDB's own scan data can serve as training input for the generative model. The two open steps identified in Sect. 8.3—automated landmark identification on reconstructed avatars and reconciliation of the complete manual-digital measurement dataset—are prerequisites for generating the topology-consistent, landmarked meshes with verified measurement vectors that the CVAE requires as training pairs. Once these steps are complete, the system possesses all necessary components: validated measurement data of sufficient quality, high-fidelity reconstructed avatars confirmed to be within garment-engineering tolerances, and a generative architecture designed for explicit measurement preservation. The transition from a partially proxy-trained system to one trained and validated on native AntrDB data represents the concrete next development phase.

In the long term, the project aims to establish a reliable bridge between anthropometric data processing and geometry-based garment development, enabling virtual fitting of new garment models across a wide range of body types without physical prototyping.

Acknowledgments. The research leading to these results has received funding from the project "Competence Centre of Information and Communication Technologies for Digitalization" of the Recovery and Resilience Facility, contract No. 2.2.1.3.i.0/1/24/A/CFLA/006 signed between IT Competence Centre and Central Finance and Contracts Agency, Research No. 1.2 "Anthropometric Database for the Digitalization of the Apparel Industry".

References

1. Size USA Homepage. https://www.tc2.com/size-usa.html. Accessed 15 Feb 2026
2. SizeUK Homepage. https://www.size.org/. Accessed 15 Feb 2026
3. SizeGERMANY Homepage. https://www.avalution.net/de/news-events/blog/sizegermany.html. Accessed 15 Feb 2026
4. Size Thailand. https://www.nstda.or.th/archives/size-thailand/. Accessed 15 Feb 2026
5. ANSUR II Homepage. https://www.openlab.psu.edu/ansur2/. Accessed 15 Feb 2026
6. Wiggermann, N., Bradtmiller, B., Bunnell, S., et al. Anthropometric dimensions of individuals with high body mass index. Hum. Fact. **61**(8), 1277–1296 (2019). https://doi.org/10.1177/0018720819839809
7. Morlock, S., Schenk, A., Klepser, A., Schmidt, A.: XL Plus Men – New Data on Garment Sizes (2016). https://doi.org/10.15221/16.255
8. CESAR Database Homepage. https://www.caesar-database.com/. Accessed 15 Feb 2026

9. DINED Homepage. https://dined.io.tudelft.nl/en. Accessed 15 Feb 2026
10. WEAR. https://bodysizeshape.com/. Accessed 15 Feb 2026
11. Bicevskis, J., Bicevska, Z., Diebelis, E., Purina, L.: Quality control of body measurement data using linear regression methods. In: Annals of Computer Science and Information Systems (ACSIS), pp. 289–300 (2024). https://www.researchgate.net/publication/385188106_Quality_Control_of_Body_Measurement_Data_Using_Linear_Regression_Methods
12. Loper, M., et al.: SMPL: a skinned multi-person linear model. ACM Trans. Graph. (TOG) **34**(6) (2015). https://dl.acm.org/doi/10.1145/2816795.2818013
13. Osman, A.A., Bolkart, T., Black, M.J.: STAR: a sparse trained articulated human body regressor (2020). https://link.springer.com/chapter/10.1007/978-3-030-58539-6_36
14. Wuhrer, S., Shu, C.: Estimating 3D human shapes from measurements. Mach. Vis. Appl. **24**(6), 1133–1147 (2012). https://link.springer.com/article/10.1007/s00138-012-0472-y
15. Ludwig, T., Bhatnagar, B.L., Pons-Moll, G.: Leveraging anthropometric measurements to improve human mesh estimation and ensure consistent body shapes (2024). arXiv:2409.17671. https://doi.org/10.48550/arXiv.2409.17671
16. Jiang, B., et al.: Disentangled human body embedding based on deep hierarchical neural network. IEEE TVCG (2020). https://ieeexplore.ieee.org/document/9072593
17. Sun, X., et al.: Learning semantic-aware disentangled representation for flexible 3D human body editing. In: IEEE/CVF Conference on Computer Vision and Pattern Recognition (CVPR) (2023). https://ieeexplore.ieee.org/document/10204534
18. Picetti, F., et al.: AnthroNet: Conditional Generation of Humans via Anthropometrics (2023). https://www.researchgate.net/publication/373753954_AnthroNet_Conditional_Generation_of_Humans_via_Anthropometrics
19. Topcodes Homepage. https://users.eecs.northwestern.edu/~mhorn/topcodes/. Accessed 15 Feb 2026
20. Meyer, P., Birregah, B., Beauseroy, P., et al.: Missing body measurements prediction in fashion industry: a comparative approach. Fash Text **10**, 37 (2023). https://doi.org/10.1186/s40691-023-00357-5
21. Wikipedia Homepage. https://en.wikipedia.org/wiki/Mahalanobis_distance. Accessed 15 Feb 2026
22. Kerbl, B., Kopanas, G., Leimkühler, T., Drettakis, G.: 3D gaussian splatting for real-time radiance field rendering, arXiv e-prints, Art. no. arXiv:2308.04079 (2023). https://doi.org/10.48550/arXiv.2308.04079
23. Neimanis, A., Purina, L., Bicevska, Z., Diebelis, E., Bicevskis, J.: Application of statistical methods in the product development of customized clothing. In: Ziemba, E.W., Chmielarz, W., Wątróbski, J. (eds) Information Technology for Management: Intelligent Alignment of IT with Business and Society. FedCSIS-ITBS ISM 2024. LNBIP, vol. 555. Springer, Cham (2026). https://doi.org/10.1007/978-3-031-93580-0_5
24. AntrDB Project Homepage. https://antrdb.di.lv/. Accessed 15 Feb 2026
25. Barbina, O., Bicevska, Z.: Deterministic Measurement-Conditioned 3D Body Reconstruction for Precision Digital Fitting (2026, under review)

Socio-Technical Systems

Quality Characteristics of Cyber-Physical-Social Systems: A Systematic Literature Review

Audronė Lupeikienė, Jolanta Miliauskaitė(✉), Asta Slotkienė, Laima Paliulionienė, Saulius Maskeliūnas, and Darius Sabaliauskas

Institute of Data Science and Digital Technologies, Vilnius University, Akademijos G. 4, 06412 Vilnius, Lithuania
{audrone.lupeikiene,jolanta.miliauskaite,asta.slotkiene, laima.paliulioniene,saulius.maskeliunas, darius.sabaliauskas}@mif.vu.lt

Abstract. Cyber-physical-social systems (CPSS) are a research topic receiving increasing attention due to the set of domains covered, the nature of the relationships between these domains and, therefore, the features of the emergent whole. There are many published surveys on the quality of CPSS constituents; however, the quality of the whole CPSS is still an open question. The purpose of this work is to identify the specific and most common quality characteristics of CPSS and to analyse their coverage by ISO/IEC 25010 and ISO/IEC 25019 standards. A systematic literature review was carried out to answer the research questions. The results of analysis showed that 1) CPSS quality characteristics are broadly aligned with established software quality standards, although this consistency is often implicit; 2) the socio-economic aspect and quality-in-use are reflected in quality characteristics to a very minimal extent; 3) CPSS qualities, which are compositions of quality characteristics describing different domains of CPSS, are an essential issue for further research.

Keywords: Cyber-Physical-Social System · Quality Characteristic · ISO/IEC 25010 · ISO/IEC 25019 · Metric

1 Introduction

The concept of an information processing system has changed significantly over its relatively short history. Nowadays, various systems, in other words, different sets of interconnected components that transform data from input to output by means of computation, have evolved into so-called cyber-physical-social systems. That is, different systems converge and configure hybrid forms of CPSS – from a unified whole to collectives.

The quality of systems is their essential feature, as it determines the choice among systems with the same functionality. There are many published studies on the quality of CPSS constituents (such as cyber-physical-systems or social IoT). A number of works examine the quality characteristics of CPSS, related to design aspects. This means that the descriptive theory of CPSS is incomplete, and the quality of CPSS is an open

R. Matulevičius et al. (Eds.): DB&IS 2026, CCIS 3085, pp. 155–168, 2026.
https://doi.org/10.1007/978-3-032-30863-4_10

question. The purpose of this work is to identify the specific and most common quality characteristics of CPSS and to analyse their coverage by ISO/IEC 25010 and ISO/IEC 25019 standards.

A literature review was carried out to answer the main research question "*How is quality conceptualized and evaluated in scientific research on cyber-physical-social systems (CPSS)?*". In this systematic literature review, we found 99 papers written over the past 14 years that were analysed in detail. The contribution to the descriptive theory of CPSS is threefold. First, the results provided a comprehensive picture of the quality characteristics of the computational/communicative aspect of CPSS. This is obtained from the fact that all the highest-level quality characteristics from ISO/IEC 25010 have been covered. Second, the literature analysis allows us to conclude that the socio-economic aspect, which is the most important impact of CPSS on business, and quality-in-use are reflected in quality characteristics to a very minimal extent. Third, the literature analysis revealed that CPSS qualities, which are compositions of quality characteristics describing different aspects (domains) of CPSS, are essential questions for further research.

This paper is structured as follows. Section 2 clarifies the main concepts. Section 3 describes the research methodology. Section 4 presents the results and discusses the findings. Finally, the last section concludes the paper and highlights further research.

2 Background

2.1 Cyber-Physical-Social Systems

Complex systems are nowadays increasingly referred to as Cyber-Physical-Social Systems (CPSS). These systems, by definitions from different sources (e.g., [1, 2]), integrate three interconnected domains: cyber – computational/communicational, physical – real-world, and social – humans and organizations. The cyber constituent includes computing infrastructures, data processing, communication infrastructures, information processing, intelligent (active, proactive, able to learn, etc.) components. The physical constituent comprises sensors, actuators, real-world environments, IoT devices, embedded systems. The social constituent encompasses humans, their behaviours, interactions, social networks, collective decision-making processes, as well as cultural, ethical, and societal factors.

It should be noted that cyber-physical-social system is a multi-sided concept. It is defined quite differently in different contexts and by different authors. Those who emphasize the computing aspect see the origins of CPSS in embedded systems, which were developed into cyber-physical systems (CPS): "Cyber-Physical-Social Systems is the new name for CPS" [3]. For authors, who emphasize the information processing aspect and understand modern information systems as essential components of any enterprise system, that will lead to an epoch of intelligent enterprises, cyber-physical-social systems is the new name for information systems. [4] emphasizes that cyber-physical systems are considered as future infrastructures that will host next-generation information systems, i.e., they play the role of a deployment environment.

In this paper, we consider CPSS primarily as a system. According to [5], a human-made technology-based system is an integrated set of elements, subsystems and assemblies. These elements include products (including software), processes, people, information, techniques, facilities, services, and other support elements. CPSS as a rule are complex systems, so they can be conceptualized as a system of systems. As stated in [6], the fundamental difference between a "system" and a "system-of-systems" is related to the nature of its composition and therefore to the nature of the emergent whole. One example of such composition might be a group of independently motivated agents that maximize the performance of the system by pursuing their own goals. Finally, we understand the system as a next generation information system that is composed of a set of constituents for providing information, knowledge, and digital products. In summary, it is required to deeply understand and describe the essence of this complex and complicated phenomenon.

2.2 ISO/IEC 25010 and ISO/IEC 25019 Standards

There are a number of published surveys on the quality of CPSS subsystems (in other words, of domains). Such surveys are dedicated to social IoT [7, 8], data in IoT [9], etc. Quite a few studies examine quality characteristics in the con-text of CPSS design solutions or development paradigms. For example, survey [9] analyses the role of quality attributes during the design of service-based systems. However, there is also a need to focus on the quality characteristics of CPSS as a whole.

For the systematic literature review, we used the ISO/IEC 25010:2023 and ISO/IEC 25019:2023 standards, which are complementary within the SQuaRE framework and address quality from the perspectives of software product properties and end-user outcomes, respectively [10]. The quality characteristics specified in ISO/IEC 25010:2023 can be interpreted as an extension of the quality-in-use outcomes captured by ISO/IEC 25019:2023 in a context of use.

The ISO/IEC 25010:2023 standard defines a product quality model comprising characteristics – functional suitability, performance efficiency, compatibility, interaction capability, reliability, security, maintainability, flexibility, and safety – along with their corresponding sub-characteristics, which have been widely adopted as a frame-work for evaluating the quality of software systems. The 2023 version introduced the safety and scalability (as a sub-characteristic of flexibility) quality characteristics, thereby partially addressing gaps previously identified in cyber-physical systems research [11, 12].

The ISO/IEC 25019:2023 standard specifies a quality-in-use model structured around three characteristics – beneficialness, freedom from risk, and acceptability – which shift the evaluation perspective from the system itself to the stakeholder's experience within a particular context of use [13].

Ogawa et al. [14] identified that mapping of non-functional characteristics, such as safety and others, to quality-in-use characteristics, provides different evaluation results for each stakeholder, and it implies that both standards are complementary.

3 Research Methodology

This systematic literature review was conducted in accordance with the guidelines and recommendations proposed by Kitchenham et al. [15, 16]. The PRISMA[1] guidelines provided a consistent framework for each stage of the review (see Fig. 1).

As shown in Fig. 1, the research process consists of the identification, screening, and inclusion steps. At each step of the research, the results are presented in brackets. A detailed description of each step of the research is provided below.

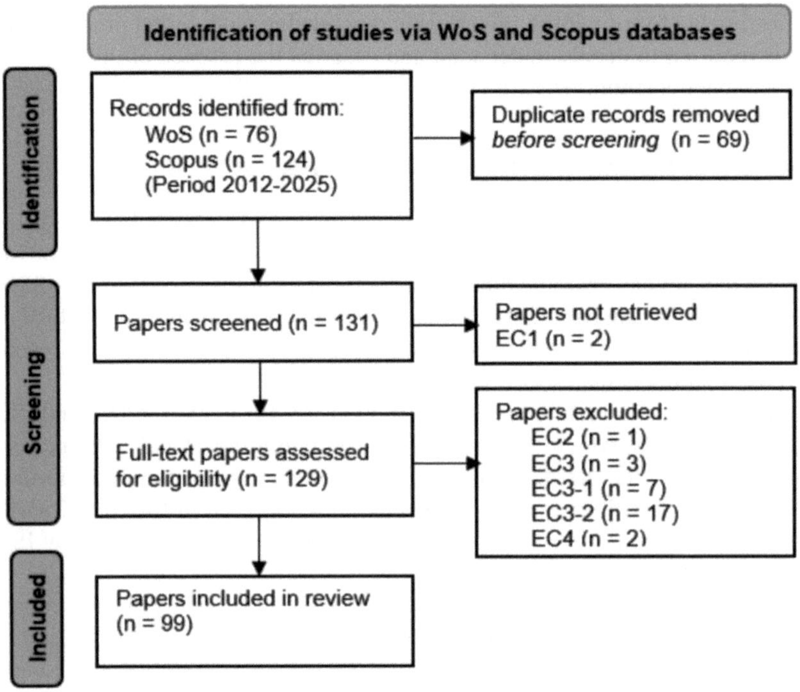

Fig. 1. PRISMA flow diagram for the review.

3.1 Identification of Records

Defining Research Questions. In this step, the main research question (MRQ), "*How is quality conceptualized and evaluated in scientific research on cyber-physical-social systems (CPSS)?*", and the arising research questions (RQs) were identified as follows:

RQ1: Which product quality characteristics are investigated for CPSS?

RQ2: How many of the identified CPSS quality characteristics are covered by the ISO/IEC 25010:2023 and ISO/IEC 25019:2023 standards?

[1] https://www.prisma-statement.org/prisma-2020.

RQ3: What measurement approaches or metrics are proposed or used to assess the identified CPSS quality characteristics?

RQ4: How has the emphasis on quality characteristics evolved over the analysed period (2012–2025)?

This review was conducted from December 2025 to March 2026.

Defining Research Scope. The scope of this research includes all scientific papers on cyber-physical-social systems.

Defining Inclusion Criteria (IC) and Exclusion Criteria (EC). According to guidelines [17], the inclusion and exclusion criteria for relevance and quality of the reviewed sources were predefined as follows:

IC1: The papers are available to download.

IC2: The paper presents relevant research on quality characteristics in cyber-physical-social systems.

EC1: The full text of the paper is not available.

EC2: The paper is not written in English.

EC3: The paper analyses generic topics.

EC3–1: The paper contains relevant keywords, but quality characteristics and metrics are not the main topic of the paper (e.g., review papers).

EC3–2: The paper contains relevant keywords, but examines methods, algorithms, frameworks, or models that are not related to CPSS.

EC4: The paper is shorter than 6 pages.

Defining Search Sources. Clarivate's Web of Science (WoS) and Elsevier's Scopus databases were selected for this research, based on the rationale described in [18].

Defining Search String. The identification of keywords and the formulation of the search string based on the research questions were performed using PICOC (Population, Intervention, Comparison, Outcomes, Context) criteria [15]. Based on the research scope, the search string was defined according to the context, with its individual parts connected by the logical operator "AND" (Table 1).

Table 1. The search string in Web of Science (WoS) and Scopus

Context		Parts of the Search String (connected with AND)
Type of the System		("Cyber?Physical?Social System$" OR "Social?Cyber?Physical System$" OR "Human?Cyber?Physical System$" OR "Human?Centric?Cyber?Physical System$" OR "Cognitive?Cyber?Physical System$" OR "Social Internet of Things" OR "SIoT")
Quality	Quality & Standards	("quality" OR "non?functional$" OR "ISO*" OR "IEC*")
	Quality evaluation	("metric$" OR "characteristic$" OR "attribute*" OR "measur*" OR "assess*" OR "evaluat*")

Searching Using the Search String. In this step, the predefined search string was used to search the WoS and Scopus databases. Additional filters were applied for language (English) and document type (Article, Proceeding Paper, Early Access). As a result, a primary set of papers was identified.

3.2 Screening of Papers

To obtain relevant papers on the research topic, the predefined inclusion and exclusion criteria (IC and EC) were applied to the primary set of papers, and the eligibility of the full-text papers was assessed, resulting in the secondary set of papers (see https://github.com/KSIG-VU/Baltic-DB-IS, Appendix A).

3.3 Inclusion of Papers

From the secondary set of papers, quality characteristics and quality metrics in CPSS were extracted and tabulated. Using the extracted data, the research questions were analysed, and conclusions were drawn (see Results section).

The trend of the research topic is illustrated in Fig. 2. As can be seen, the number of papers on quality characteristics in CPSS has increased. This suggests that technological development stimulates interest in these systems, their qualitative characteristics, and their application across various domains.

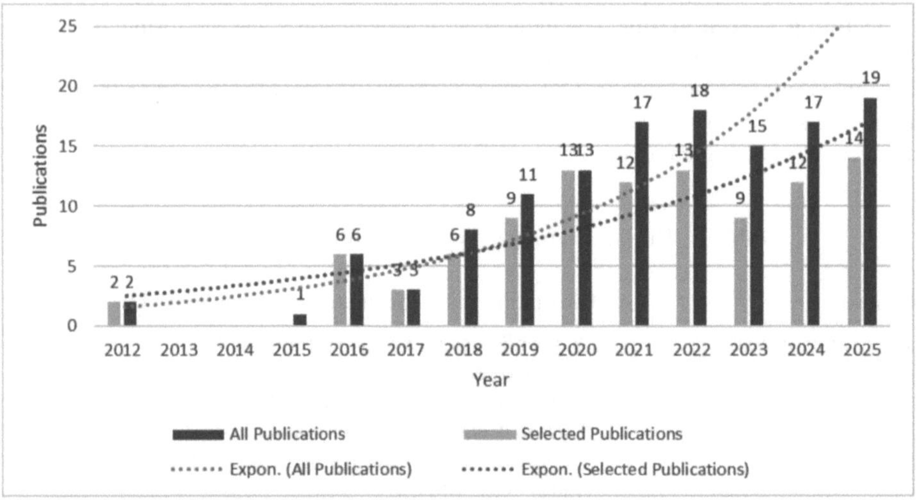

Fig. 2. Number of selected papers before and after applying IC/EC.

3.4 Threats to Validity

There are several threats to the validity of this review. The first threat relates to the coverage of all relevant literature that could potentially answer the above-mentioned research questions. The search was conducted in the two most influential bibliographic databases – WoS and Scopus. Such a choice creates the prerequisites for the completeness of the relevant contributions, as WoS is one of the key sources of scientific information and Scopus is one of the world's largest abstract and citation databases. Scholarly literature included in these databases are selected, and the selection is made from peer-reviewed publications. In addition, these databases ensure a variety of articles – they store literature from academic journals, books, conference proceedings, and other documents (for example, technical papers).

The second threat concerns the choice of the publication time interval of the scholarly literature. It was decided to examine the choice of the time interval as a separate question, the answer to which would lead to the final choice of the period under consideration. The results of examining this question are further supported by the data presented in Fig. 2.

The third threat is related to the understanding and interpretation of the content of the articles under review, more specifically, the quality characteristics under examination. This was avoided in two ways.

First, quality characteristics are not only listed in the standards but also defined, including their role, in detail and unambiguously. Therefore, it was possible to unambiguously identify such characteristics in the reviewed literature, even in cases where, for example, a quality characteristic and a metric share the same name.

Second, naming quality characteristics not covered by standards is more sensitive to different terminology, since such characteristics may be described by different authors using different concepts and terms, and defined according to different conceptual assumptions. In order to reduce this threat, reference conceptual models of such quality characteristics, including sets of sub-characteristics, were developed. Each identified quality characteristic was compared with the corresponding reference model by qualitatively juxtaposing them.

4 Results

For the analysis of the research questions, each selected paper served as the unit of analysis. From each paper, explicitly named quality characteristics and sub-characteristics were extracted, excluding the Related Works section.

To address RQ1, the quality characteristics mentioned across the 99 selected papers were systematically extracted and aggregated, yielding 53 distinct characteristics encompassing 116 individual mentions. The frequency distribution of the quality characteristics is visualized as a radial graph in Fig. 3, where node size is proportional to the number of mentions of each quality characteristic.

As shown in Fig. 3, reliability, security, performance, robustness, and safety are the most frequently investigated quality characteristics, suggesting that CPSS research is predominantly oriented toward dependability and operational integrity rather than usability or maintainability concerns. As observed, trust-related characteristics, including trustworthiness, trust, and trust/trustworthiness variants, emerge as a distinct quality characteristic.

The answer to RQ2 was obtained as follows: each identified quality characteristic was mapped to the product quality characteristics or sub-characteristics defined in the

ISO/IEC 25010:2023 product quality model and the ISO/IEC 25019:2023 quality-in-use model, along with their measurement metrics. If the name of the quality characteristic mentioned in the paper did not match the analysed standards, we analysed the context and associated metrics, and assigned the characteristic to one of the nine defined characteristics. As a result, all nine characteristics were recognized, meaning that all quality characteristics defined in the standards were covered in the analysed papers. In addition, ten sub-characteristics corresponding to the ISO/IEC 25010:2023 standard and five sub-characteristics (honesty, selfishness, sensitive, efficiency, energy efficiency) corresponding to the ISO/IEC 25019:2023 standard were recognized. For five quality characteristics, additional analysis was performed, because their names differed from those used in the standards.

The relationships among the identified quality characteristics and sub-characteristics, such as between performance efficiency and security, or between reliability and safety, were not systematically analysed, as the majority of the reviewed papers address quality characteristics in isolation rather than as interrelated or mutually impacting.

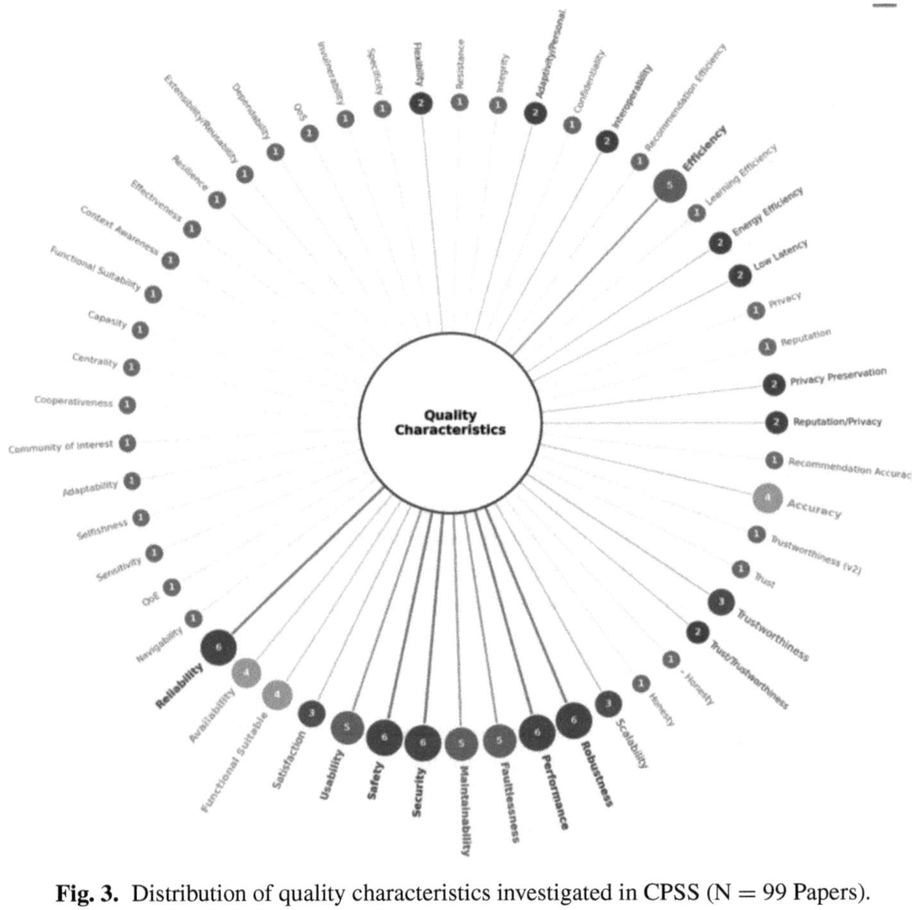

Fig. 3. Distribution of quality characteristics investigated in CPSS (N = 99 Papers).

Table 2, Table 3 and Fig. 4 indicate that CPSS quality research focuses primarily on performance efficiency, security, reliability, and trustworthiness. This finding confirms that quality characteristics with direct system-level measurement metrics or tools (such as latency, throughput, uptime, resource use, incident counts) tend to dominate quality evaluation. The trustworthiness and suitability quality characteristics are frequently mentioned because user acceptance and trust in the system's functionality are significantly important from a social perspective and have a huge impact on the system's quality in use.

Regarding the ISO/IEC 25019:2023 quality-in-use model, the mapping revealed an imbalance. Only three sub-characteristics (Table 3) of this standard were identified, and none were accompanied by measurement metrics. This indicates that the quality-in-use perspective, which represents stakeholders' experience, is not substantially discussed or measured in CPSS applications and research compared to product quality in ISO/IEC 25010:2023.

Regarding RQ3, performance efficiency is consistently mentioned as a significant quality dimension across the analysed papers, and as a quantifiable metric in CPSS evaluation. Of the 99 articles, 54 only mention this quality characteristic, while 31 propose how it should be measured.

Table 2. Quality characteristics distribution based on the ISO/IEC 25010:2023 standard

Quality characteristics (ISO/IEC 25010:2023 standard)	Distribution (%)
Functional suitable	3.03
Performance efficiency	77.78
Compatibility	6.06
Interaction capability (usability)	7.07
Reliability	23.23
Security	39.39
Maintainability	18.18
Flexibility	17.17
Safety	2.02

Table 3. Quality sub-characteristics distribution based on the ISO/IEC 25019:2023 standard

Quality sub-characteristics (ISO/IEC 25019:2023 standard)	Distribution (%)
Usability	10.91
Suitability	32.73
Trustworthiness	56.36

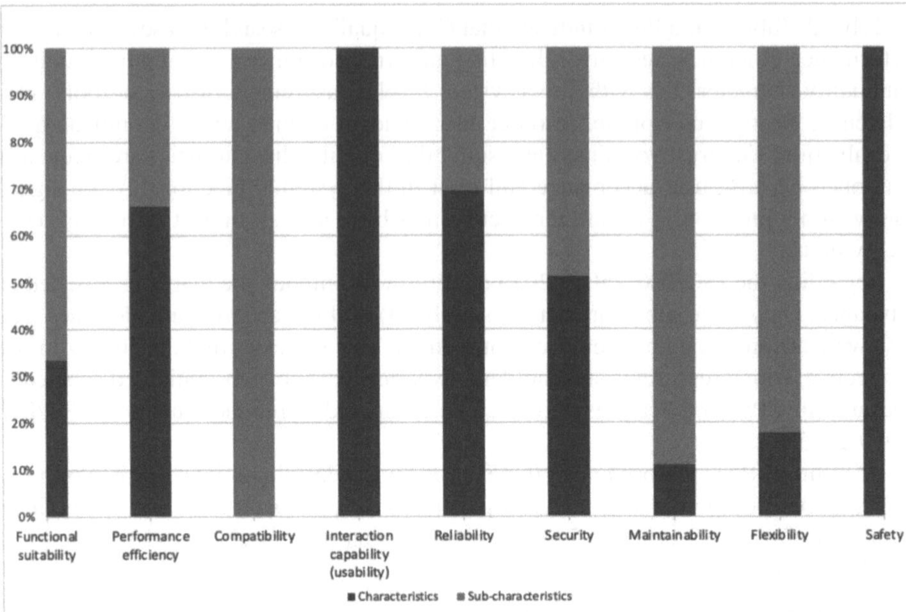

Fig. 4. Quality characteristics and sub-characteristics distributions based on ISO/IEC 25010:2023 standard

As shown in Table 4, energy consumption and throughput are the most widely applied metrics, followed by response time, indicating that resource utilization and communication efficiency are the prevailing concerns in the analysed papers.

RQ4 examines how the emphasis on product quality characteristics has evolved over the analysed period. Figure 5 presents the annual distribution of articles across nine ISO/IEC 25010-aligned quality characteristic categories from 2012 to 2025, enabling the identification of temporal trends and shifts in research prioritization within CPSS.

The annual distribution reveals an intensification of research activity from 2019 onwards, with the annual number of relevant publications increasing substantially compared to preceding years. The quality characteristic Performance Efficiency consistently emerges as the most frequently investigated characteristic throughout the analysed period, reaching peaks in 2022 and 2025. This suggests that performance efficiency and computational resource management remain persistent research challenges within CPSS applications. From the diagram, the quality characteristic Security has received increased attention since 2020, while Reliability, Maintainability, and Functional Suitability exhibit a gradual but steady growth in recent years, indicating a broadening of quality evaluation within the CPSS scope.

Our systematic literature review's observations for RQ4 demonstrate that research emphasis on quality characteristics for CPSS has evolved from a focus on computational performance (2012–2018) to an increasingly diversified quality evaluation landscape in recent years (2019–2025). Of the 99 articles, 23 distinct metrics were identified. These metrics were subsequently grouped into three measurement categories – Energy, Time and Latency, and Network and Quality of Service (QoS) – as presented in Table 4.

Table 4. Summary of performance efficiency metrics identified in analysed papers

Performance Metric	Count. of Papers	References*
Energy measurement		
Energy consumption	**9**	R4, R10, R16, R17, R19, R24, R26, R28, R29
Energy efficiency	**2**	R3, R15
Efficiency	**1**	R14
Time and latency measurement		
Response time	**8**	R1, R5, R23, R24, R26, R27, R30, R31
Execution time	**5**	R5, R6, R27, R28, R29
Latency	**4**	R17, R23, R24, R26
End-to-end delay	**3**	R3, R4, R15
Delay	**2**	R10, R17
Modeling & analysis time	**2**	R22, R23
Task completion time	**1**	R24
Handshake time	**1**	R11
Latency overhead	**1**	R11
Packet transmission delay	**1**	R7
Network and Quality of Services measurement		
Throughput	**9**	R3, R6, R7, R8, R9, R10, R15, R23, R26
Packet delay	**2**	R8, R9
Packet delivery ratio	**2**	R8, R15
Success rate	**2**	R5, R14
Overhead ratio	**1**	R8
Load balancing	**1**	R17
Spectrum utilization	**1**	R12
System capacity	**1**	R7
Transmission rate	**1**	R2
User capacity	**1**	R12

* The full list of references is presented in the GitHub repository (see https://github.com/KSIG-VU/Baltic-DB-IS, Appendix B).

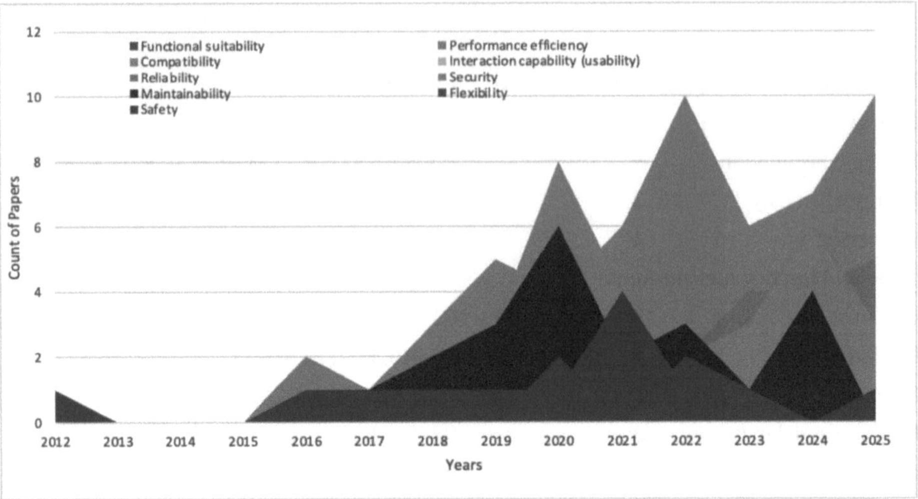

Fig. 5. Annual distribution of articles by product quality characteristic category in CPSS research (2012–2025).

The continuous dominance of performance efficiency (Fig. 5) as the most investigated characteristic throughout the analysed period, combined with the rising attention to security, reliability, and maintainability, indicates that CPSS researchers are progressively recognizing the need for a multi-characteristic approach to quality evaluation. Nevertheless, the quality characteristics (quality-in-use) addressing the social aspect of CPSS, such as user satisfaction, trustworthiness, and accuracy, do not receive sufficient attention in analysed papers and could be investigated in greater depth and constitute a critical research question for future work.

5 Conclusions

Our systematic literature review revealed that CPSS quality conceptualization and evaluation research emphasizes quality characteristics related to reliability, security, performance, robustness, and safety. This demonstrates that the field remains predominantly anchored in the dependability concerns of the cyber and physical dimensions, while the social aspect is addressed through beneficialness and acceptability characteristics that lack measurement metrics.

Quality considerations for CPSS have been consistently mentioned throughout 2012–2025, especially with performance efficiency dominating the quality characteristics. Since 2020, growing attention to security has contributed to a broader evaluation of quality characteristics in CPSS research.

While the product quality characteristics defined in ISO/IEC 25010:2023 are covered across the analysed papers, the quality-in-use characteristics specified in ISO/IEC 25019:2023 – beneficialness, freedom from risk, and acceptability – lack explicit descriptions, explanations, and measurement metrics in the current CPSS literature. Therefore, the quality assessment should be expanded to better address the quality-in-use characteristics (ISO/IEC 25019:2023), which capture the user-centred aspects of CPSS.

In terms of further research, this systematic literature review is the first step towards developing a conceptual view-based framework for specifying and modelling the quality of CPSS. It contributes to a deeper understanding of the CPSS quality phenomenon, which is necessary to ensure such quality in complex real-world systems.

Declaration. During the preparation of this work, the authors used AI tools only for grammar and spelling correction and for paraphrasing and rewording assistance. The authors take full responsibility for the content of the publication.

References

1. Yang, B., Guo, H., Cao, E.: Design of cyber-physical-social systems with forensic-awareness based on deep learning. Adv. Comput. **120**, 39–79 (2021). https://doi.org/10.1016/bs.adcom.2020.09.001
2. Sobb, T., Turnbull, B., Moustafa, N.: A Holistic review of cyber–physical–social systems: new directions and opportunities. Sensors **23**, 7391 (2023). https://doi.org/10.3390/s23177391
3. Wang, F.Y.: The emergence of intelligent enterprises: from CPS to CPSS. IEEE Intell. Syst. **25**, 85–88 (2010). https://doi.org/10.1109/MIS.2010.104
4. Panetto, H., Zdravkovic, M., Jardim-Goncalves, R., Romero, D., Cecil, J., Mezgár, I.: New perspectives for the future interoperable enterprise systems. Comput. Ind. **79**, 47–63 (2016). https://doi.org/10.1016/j.compind.2015.08.001
5. INCOSE: A World in Motion – System Engineering Vision 2025 (2014). https://www.incose.org/wp-content/uploads/legacy/se-vision-2025/se-vision-2025/incose-se-vision-2025.pdf. Accessed 27 Apr 2026
6. Boardman, J., Sauser, B.: System of systems - the meaning. In: Proceedings 2006 IEEE/SMC International Conference on System of Systems Engineering, pp. 118–123 (2006). https://doi.org/10.1109/sysose.2006.1652284
7. Patil, D.A., Shyamala, G.: A comprehensive survey on securing the social internet of things: protocols, threat mitigation, technological integrations, tools, and performance metrics. Sci. Rep. **15** (2025). https://doi.org/10.1038/s41598-025-23865-4
8. Alam, S., Zardari, S., Noor, S., Ahmed, S., Mouratidis, H.: Trust management in social internet of things (SIoT): a survey. IEEE Access **10**, 108924–108954 (2022). https://doi.org/10.1109/ACCESS.2022.3213699
9. Karkouch, A., Mousannif, H., Al Moatassime, H., Noel, T.: Data quality in internet of things: a state-of-the-art survey. J. Netw. Comput. Appl. **73**, 57–81 (2016). https://doi.org/10.1016/j.jnca.2016.08.002
10. ISO/IEC 25000 SQuaRE series: ISO 25000 SQuaRE series. https://committee.iso.org/sites/jtc1sc7/home/projects/flagship-standards/iso-25000-square-series.html. Accessed 14 Mar 2026
11. Gordieiev, O., Kharchenko, V., Fominykh, N., Sklyar, V.: Evolution of software quality models in context of the standard ISO 25010. Adv. Intell. Syst. Comput. **286**, 223–232 (2014). https://doi.org/10.1007/978-3-319-07013-1_21
12. Argotti, Y., Kenfaoui, Y., Baron, C., Abran, A., Esteban, P.: An operational quality model of embedded software aligned with ISO 25000. ACM Trans. Embedded Comput. Syst. **24**, 41 (2024). https://doi.org/10.1145/3691642
13. ISO/IEC 25019:2023 - Systems and software engineering — Systems and software Quality Requirements and Evaluation (SQuaRE) — Quality-in-use model. https://www.iso.org/standard/78177.html. Accessed 14 Mar 2026
14. Ogawa, R., Sagawa, Y., Shima, S., Takemura, T., Fukuzumi, S.I.: A case study on AI system evaluation from users' viewpoints. In: Lecture Notes in Computer Science (including subseries Lecture Notes in Artificial Intelligence and Lecture Notes in Bioinformatics). LNCS, vol. 14690, pp. 238–248 (2024). https://doi.org/10.1007/978-3-031-60114-9_17

15. Kitchenham, B., Charters, S.: Guidelines for performing systematic literature reviews in software engineering (2007). https://legacyfileshare.elsevier.com/promis_misc/525444systematicreviewsguide.pdf. Accessed 27 Apr 2026
16. Kitchenham, B., Pearl Brereton, O., Budgen, D., Turner, M., Bailey, J., Linkman, S.: Systematic literature reviews in software engineering - a systematic literature review. Inf. Softw. Technol. **51**, 7–15 (2009). https://doi.org/10.1016/j.infsof.2008.09.009
17. Carrera-Rivera, A., Ochoa, W., Larrinaga, F., Lasa, G.: How-to conduct a systematic literature review: a quick guide for computer science research. MethodsX. **9**, 101895 (2022). https://doi.org/10.1016/j.mex.2022.101895
18. Kalibatienė, D., Miliauskaitė, J.: A hybrid systematic review approach on complexity issues in data-driven fuzzy inference systems development. Informatica (Netherlands) **32**, 85–118 (2021). https://doi.org/10.15388/21-INFOR444

Man–LLM Shared Graph Workspace: Spec-First NL-To-VIS via Serialisation

Paulis Barzdins(✉) and Normunds Gruzitis

Institute of Mathematics and Computer Science, University of Latvia, Riga 1459, Latvia
paulis.barzdins@lumii.lv

Abstract. "Man–Computer Symbiosis" demands a shared workspace for cooperation, yet most modern NL-driven data systems collapse collaboration into text and execute too early on real data. We present a spec-first NL → VIS workflow that restores a shared visual workspace via serialisation: the system proposes 1–N candidate Vega-Lite "mock graphs" from the natural-language question and schema alone, LLM-populated with small plausible data for instant preview. After human edits and approval, the agreed Vega-Lite spec acts as a precise data shape contract that drives SQL generation and final rendering. The approach targets organisations like Latvia's Ministry of Economics (EKMIN) and Central Statistical Bureau (CSP), where stakeholders ask open questions but need curated, comprehensible visuals rather than wide tables. This agreement-before-execution loop (a) prevents wide, under-structured outputs that trigger downstream transformation hell, (b) shortens iterations to seconds on mock data, and (c) preserves privacy by keeping real data local. Across replications of public NL → VIS cases and EKMIN/CSP tasks over multi-table schemas, 11/13 tasks produced acceptable visuals on the first mock and 13/13 within one round of feedback, while eliminating unnecessary wide selections. We argue Vega-Lite is a practical lingua franca for shared visual work today, and we outline design principles and limits. The contribution reframes NL → VIS evaluation from one-shot automation to cooperative productivity: the fastest path to a correct, comprehensible visualisation the user actually wants.

Keywords: NL2VIS · NL2SQL · human–LLM shared visual workspace · serialisation · Vega-Lite

1 Introduction

Licklider's argument for "Man–Computer Symbiosis" presumes a shared workspace for people and machine cooperation, as opposed to automation [1]. In data work, that workspace should be visual when the goal is a visualisation. Yet today's NL → SQL and NL → VIS systems mostly converse in text and execute early on real data. The result is a common anti-pattern: a direct NL → SQL path returns a wide, under-structured table that does not line up with any specific visual intent, forcing ad hoc pivots, re-aggregations, and re-runs – transformation hell – before anything communicative emerges.

R. Matulevičius et al. (Eds.): DB&IS 2026, CCIS 3085, pp. 169–184, 2026.
https://doi.org/10.1007/978-3-032-30863-4_11

We flip the order and recover a shared visual workspace via serialisation (Fig. 1). The system first proposes candidate Vega-Lite [2] "mock graphs" from the question and schema alone. Vega-Lite is a declarative visualisation grammar in a compact JSON format. A mock graph is a fully specified Vega-Lite chart, which the LLM prompt populates with small, plausible synthetic data, providing an instant, editable preview with explicit encodings, aggregations, bins, and filters. Once a candidate is approved, we treat that spec as a contract: a data shape contract enumerating the exact fields, types, groupings, filters, and sort order the chart requires. Only then do we generate SQL whose output matches that contract precisely – agreement-before-execution.

This spec-first loop delivers three practical benefits. First, it surfaces ambiguity and overcrowding cheaply, in seconds, before touching protected data. Second, it prevents wide outputs and the downstream reshaping churn that plagues execute-first workflows. Third, it supports privacy and governance constraints by keeping the LLM stage schema-only; real data are queried once, locally, under least privilege to satisfy the approved contract.

We target EKMIN/CSP settings where stakeholders ask open questions over multi-table schemas but need a handful of curated visuals, not raw tables. In EKMIN/CSP, fragmented sources and very wide tables turned every question into weeks of wrangling and re-runs – exactly the execute-first churn we replace. Technically, we sit at the junction of NL $\rightarrow$ SQL and NL $\rightarrow$ VIS but invert the usual order: propose and agree on Vega-Lite specs first, then derive SQL to fit them. Vega-Lite is used as a lingua franca: compact, declarative, widely learned by LLMs, and reliably round-trippable between human edits and machine generation.

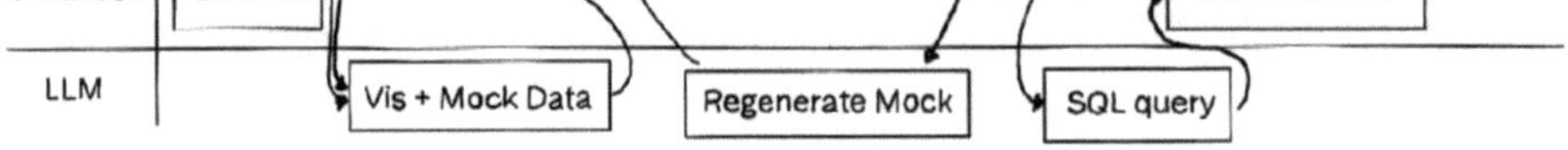

Fig. 1. System pipeline, split by roles.

Contributions:

- Spec-first NL $\rightarrow$ VIS with mock-before-execute: propose and edit candidate Vega-Lite charts from schema-only context, then lock that data shape contract and run precisely one constrained query.
- Privacy and security: ideation without data exfiltration; local execution after agreement.
- Multi-table by construction and multi-view when needed: contracts compile across joins and encourage coordinated small multiples when a single view would overload meaning.

- Evaluation lens on cooperative productivity: fastest path to an acceptable chart and avoidance of wide outputs, not brittle one-shot exactness.
- Evidence from replications and EKMIN/CSP cases: 11/13 first-mock acceptances; 13/13 within one feedback round.

2 Background and Related Work

2.1 NL → Query Over Structured Data

Natural-language interfaces to databases have matured markedly in recent years. Modern NL → SQL pipelines combine schema linking and content-aware grounding to translate free-form questions into executable SQL over multi-table schemas, often with explicit submodules for linking, generation, and debugging [3]. Parallel work extends this capability to graphs, e.g., NL → Cypher [4], framing long-term LLM memory as structured query recall. In practice, these systems are most useful to analysts who already think in relational terms and want to write queries faster; they return tables, not stakeholder-ready explanations. For non-technical users who need curated visuals, a direct NL → query path often becomes a detour: the result is a wide, under-structured table that still requires substantial shaping, cutting, and pivoting before it communicates anything.

This gap motivates integrating NL → query with visualisation intent from the start.

2.2 NL → VIS: Code-First vs Spec-First, and What Today's Systems Assume

Execute-First Code Generation on a Single Table. a large swath of recent LLM-based NL → VIS work takes an execute-first posture: given a natural-language utterance and access to a selected table, the model emits plotting code that is immediately run on the real data, and the resulting image is inspected for correctness.

- Chat2VIS [5] demonstrates that off-the-shelf LLMs (GPT-3/Codex/ChatGPT) can directly emit Python plotting scripts from free-form NL. The prompt includes column names, types, and enumerated categorical values; raw data are not sent to the LLM, but the app must still load the data to render the chart. The workflow is one-shot with light re-asking; there is no explicit spec/mock phase, no multi-view planning, and no support for multi-table join planning. Evaluation is small-N and qualitative, and they explicitly note non-determinism and fragile styling.
- VisEval [6] codifies this dominant workflow in its benchmark harness: NL + data → Matplotlib/Seaborn code → execute → chart. Their legality/readability checks show current models are far from "fire-and-forget": GPT-4 passes 75.27% of curated nvBench [7] cases, with quality/readability still leaving room for human judgment; adding two irrelevant tables drops pass rates by 7–20 percentage points. These results substantiate that (a) ambiguity is common enough to warrant a feasible-region notion of correctness, and (b) small changes in the surrounding schema meaningfully degrade reliability – both arguments for a mock-before-execute loop.

Spec-Templated NL → Vega-Lite Under Single-Table Scope. Other lines target a declarative spec instead of imperative code, typically on a single, pre-shaped table.

- NL4DV [8] parses NL into a JSON analytic spec and generates one or more Vega-Lite candidates. It requires raw data at initialisation to infer types and values. Ambiguity is surfaced for UI widgets, not resolved upfront; there is no explicit mock/spec approval loop and no multi-table or NL $\rightarrow$ SQL.
- ADVISor [9] blends BERT-based semantic parsing with rule-based visualisation templates to answer open questions over one table. It requires the raw table, supports a limited aggregation vocabulary and chart repertoire, and is primarily automatic and one-shot. On WikiSQL, classifier accuracies are ~83–85%; in a user study, 72.5% of answers were rated "reasonable," leaving ~27.5% needing rework – empirical support for human-in-the-loop refinement.
- ChartGPT [10] fine-tunes FLAN-T5-XL to assemble Vega-Lite from six templated sub-tasks (select/filter/aggregate; chart/encodings/sort), exposing intermediate outputs for inspection and re-generation. It assumes a single clean table and explicitly excludes joins; the prompt includes column names, types, and the top two rows, and the full CSV is required at render time. In comparative/user studies, it outperforms NL4DV and ncNet [11], yet still relies on edits and rephrasing: only 47% of successful charts were correct on the first attempt; the remainder required configuration or input changes. ChartGPT confirms that LLMs can reliably target Vega-Lite and that surfacing intermediate decisions helps – while underscoring that one-shot exactness is not the norm.

Collectively, these systems share assumptions that clash with EKMIN's constraints:

- Single-table bias: multi-table/join scenarios are excluded or unsupported.
- Data-first execution: most require data upload or direct DB access to render; "privacy" is addressed at most by omitting raw values from prompts, not by eliminating execution on protected data during ideation.
- Execute-first iteration: ambiguity is resolved after running code on real data; there is no spec-first mock that locks intent before any heavy query.
- Limited multi-view planning: they typically emit a single chart per utterance; coordinated views/dashboards are out of scope.
- Narrow transformation coverage: wide or under-structured outputs are not a first-class concern; pivot/melt/reshape planning is largely future work.

This paper's pipeline (Fig. 1.) addresses these gaps by proposing candidate specs with mock data from schema-only context, surfacing ambiguity early, and compiling the approved spec into SQL that returns exactly the columns and orders the visual expects.

2.3 Benchmarks and the Problem of Evaluating NL $\rightarrow$ VIS

The community has leaned on synthetic or curated datasets and exact-match metrics that fit automation-first systems but do not measure cooperative productivity.

- nvBench [7] bootstraps NL $\rightarrow$ VIS pairs from NL $\rightarrow$ SQL (Spider [12]), yielding one chart per query across seven basic types. Tables are small by enterprise standards (median $<$ 5 columns; most 5–100 rows), no multi-view answers are included, and methods often rely on data distributions and distinct counts – precluding schema-only workflows. Reported exact-match scores around 60–70% for neural baselines show that many cases still require redo loops.

- VisEval [6] advances beyond tree-exactness by checking legality and readability of executed code. Its "feasible region" labelling explicitly admits multiple acceptable mappings for an underspecified utterance, mirroring real practice. Yet the harness still presumes immediate execution on data and measures single-shot pass/fail – useful to quantify raw model behaviour, but orthogonal to the metrics that matter in EKMIN-style settings (time-to-acceptable-graph, iterations to agreement, and the rate at which wide, under-structured outputs are avoided).
- Surveys reinforce these tensions. Shen et al. [13] catalogue Visualisation-oriented Natural Language Interfaces and highlight that most systems operate over single tables, emphasise automatic mapping, and provide only ad hoc ambiguity resolution. They explicitly call multi-table support a future research hotspot and note the lack of standardised evaluation. Qin et al. [14] frame visualisation as inherently iterative and human-in-the-loop and elevate declarative grammars (Vega/Vega-Lite) as learnable, round-trippable specs – evidence that a serialised shared workspace is a pragmatic foundation today.

These benchmarks and surveys point to two conclusions. First, ambiguity and underspecification are endemic; feasible regions, top-k candidates, and human edits are the rule, not the exception. Second, existing metrics undercount what matters for stakeholder-facing analytics with expensive backends: preventing avoidable executions, minimising re-shaping churn, and converging to agreed visuals quickly.

2.4 Shared Workspaces, Serialisation, and the Limits of Vision-Only Tooling

Licklider's "Man–Computer Symbiosis" from 1960 [1] argues that progress in the long interim before full automation depends on a shared workspace where humans and machines co-operate rather than one replacing the other. Contemporary multimodal LLM demos that turn sketches into UIs (e.g., MakeReal [15], Uizard [16]) hint at that future but remain imprecise marketing tactics for visualisation: they lack explicit semantics, are brittle under small changes, and provide no guaranteed round-trip between what the human means and what the model executes.

Textual serialisation fills that gap now. Declarative specs like Vega-Lite, together with simple tabular encodings (TSV/CSV), act as a lingua franca that both humans and LLMs can co-edit deterministically and render identically. Adjacent ecosystems (Mermaid, PlantUML, Graphviz) show that text-first diagramming supports reliable round-trips; the visualisation literature [14] and systems like NL4DV and ChartGPT confirm Vega-Lite is both expressive and model-learnable. This paper's workflow operationalises Licklider's premise for data work: use serialised specs as the shared desk surface; mock with small plausible data to resolve ambiguity cheaply; the agreed spec then acts as the data shape contract that drives SQL and final rendering.

2.5 Positioning and Contributions Relative to Prior Work

Relative to NL $\rightarrow$ query and NL $\rightarrow$ VIS systems above, this paper contributes:

- Spec-first, mock-before-execute. Unlike execute-first NL → VIS (Chat2VIS; VisEval's default pipeline), ambiguity is surfaced and resolved on mock data before any heavy query runs, cutting iteration costs when backends are slow or data are sensitive.
- Schema-only ideation with a real privacy story. Where most NL → VIS methods require data upload or DB execution during ideation (NL4DV, ADVISor, ChartGPT), this paper's loop keeps sensitive data local until a spec is approved; only then is SQL generated and run.
- Multi-table by construction. Rather than excluding joins (ChartGPT) or assuming a single table (NL4DV, ADVISor, Chat2VIS), this paper's data shape contracts provide a target that the NL → SQL stage compiles to across multi-table schemas – aligning with the realities flagged as a "hotspot" by Shen et al. [13] and operationalised by modern NL → SQL pipelines [3].
- Multi-view planning up front. Single-chart biases in current NL → VIS are replaced with coordinated multi-view proposals at the mock stage when one chart would overload meaning.
- A reframed evaluation lens. Building on evidence from nvBench and VisEval that single-shot exactness is brittle, and ambiguity is pervasive, this paper's evaluation targets cooperative productivity: time-to-acceptable-graph, iterations to agreement, and avoidance of wide, under-structured outputs.

In short, prior work shows that LLMs can emit plotting code or Vega-Lite specs from NL when given a single, clean table – and that humans routinely need to intervene. This paper's contribution is to make that intervention the centrepiece: a serialised shared workspace that reaches agreement before any data leaves protected systems or long queries are run, and that treats the approved spec as a contract the database must satisfy rather than as an after-the-fact interpretation of whatever a query happened to return.

3 Requirements and Design Goals

We target stakeholder-facing analytics over relational data, where open NL questions should yield a small number of clear charts rather than wide tables. From the EKMIN/CSP context and preliminary trials, we derive the following design goals.

Cooperation over Automation. Keep the human in the loop. Front-load human/LLM alignment so the first costly step (data extraction/wrangling) happens only after intent is concrete.

Curation over Mass Production. Visualisations are for humans. The goal is communicative, comprehensible visuals, not chart spam. Prefer a small set of deliberate, edited charts that answer the question clearly, instead of mass production.

Shared Workspace via Serialisation. Licklider's requirement for man-machine cooperation. To roughly see and agree on output quickly. Available today through serialisation. Vega-Lite and tabular encodings (TSV) as a common workspace with immediate visual rendering, that both human and LLM can co-edit.

Data Shape Contracts. Mock visualisation before data query. Once mock visualisation is human approved, that Vega-Lite spec acts as data shape contract, so SQL query output matches the visualisation input requirement exactly. To completely avoid over-wide output tables that require unmanageable transformations on visualisation side.

Multi-View Planning up front. A single question is not always best served by a single visualisation. At the mock stage, the system or the user can propose and pivot to 1 to N coordinated charts, to avoid an overcrowded and confusing single output and to surface complementary perspectives early.

Minimal, Reproducible Stack. Use stable, text-based components that others can reproduce on their own schemas without heavy tooling, and that will age well as models improve:

- Vega-Lite for declarative chart specs.
- TSV/CSV for small data payloads and mock data.
- SQL for retrieval; jq for TSV → JSON quoting when embedding data into specs.
- Prompt templates for the two-step loop (spec-first, then SQL).

This avoids a brittle monolith that rots with dependencies. The pipeline runs in any environment that can render Vega-Lite (browser/notebook/CLI) and execute SQL locally. If Vega-Lite is superseded, the same pattern transfers to a successor grammar with minimal change. The emphasis is on transparency, portability, and longevity: the workflow should still be repeatable a decade from now, only better as LLMs improve.

Security and Privacy by Design. Treat the LLM and orchestration layer as untrusted with respect to production data; keep sensitive data local until after agreement:

- Schema-only ideation. During the mock/spec stage, the LLM sees the schema and comments but never raw rows. Mock data are synthetic.
- Local/controlled execution. Execute generated SQL in a controlled environment; paste or pipe only the minimal result (matching the contract) into the renderer. An offline/air-gapped path is supported.
- Least-privilege queries. The contract constrains SELECTs to only the required columns, aggregations, filters, and sort order; no wide SELECT * or unnecessary joins.
- No data exfil during iteration. Agreement-before-execution prevents "probe" queries on protected data just to see what's there.
- Auditability. Persist all artifacts – question, approved Vega-Lite spec, data shape contract, generated SQL, and checksums of outputs – for compliance and reproducibility.
- Optional local models. Where required, swap remote LLM calls for on-prem/local models without changing the workflow.

These measures match EKMIN/CSP constraints and generalise to other settings with strict data-governance or Data Loss Prevention (DLP) requirements.

4 Concept and Workflow

4.1 Mock Stage – Preview and Agree

Given a natural-language question and a relational schema (with optional comments), the system proposes one or more candidate charts as Vega-Lite specifications populated with small, plausible mock data. This establishes a serialised shared workspace the human can see and edit immediately.

- Inputs – NL question, schema, optional schema comments/quirks.
- System proposal – 1-N Vega-Lite specs with synthetic mock data sized for instant preview.
- Human-in-the-loop refinement – Accept, edit, split, or merge candidates; Iterate until the intended mappings and scope are unambiguous.
- Agreement and shape lock – The approved spec becomes the single source of truth. It is the data shape contract: the exact output fields, types, groupings/aggregations, filters, sort orders, and any required derived fields per chart/view.

This mock-before-execute loop keeps iteration times to seconds, surfaces underspecification early, and naturally supports multi-view answers when one chart would overload meaning.

4.2 Output Stage – Contract, Query, and Render

Once the spec is locked, execution becomes a constrained translation and rendering problem.

- Contract-driven SQL – The system treats the approved spec as a data shape contract and generates SQL whose output matches that contract exactly – no wide SELECT, no extra columns.
- Local, least-privilege execution – SQL is run in a controlled environment. Only the minimal result needed by the spec is exported (e.g., TSV/CSV).
- Render and finalise – The result is embedded or linked into the approved Vega-Lite spec and rendered.

4.3 Failure Modes and Recovery

The workflow is designed to surface ambiguity and risk early, before expensive execution. We distinguish conceptual catches (Sect. 4) from technical defenses (Sect. 5).

- Underspecified intent (e.g., “by age” without bins or units)

- Caught at: mock stage. Candidates must choose explicit binning/aggregation, making the choice visible.
- Human action: confirm or adjust bin edges, aggregations, and encodings.

- Overcrowded single-view answers

- Caught at: mock stage when marks or legends overwhelm the view.
- Human action: split into coordinated small multiples or facet; remove non-essential encodings.

- Wrong field or proxy choice

- Caught at: mock stage via selected fields and derived expressions.

- Human action: redirect to the appropriate column or accept a documented proxy.

- Hidden schema quirks (inconsistent enums, sentinel values, null patterns)

  - Caught at: mock stage if called out in schema comments; otherwise during first real render if distributions look off.
  - Human action: add/adjust filters or mappings in the spec; update schema comments for future runs.

- Contract/query mismatch

  - Caught at: compile or render time if returned columns/types do not match the contract.
  - Human action: adjust spec or regenerate SQL under the unchanged contract.

- Governance or privacy violations (accidental over-selection)

  - Caught at: compile time by the least-privilege contract.
  - Human action: narrow scope or redact sensitive fields before approval.

5 System and Implementation

The prototype is operator-mediated: system is executed with a clean chat API, an online Vega-Lite renderer, and per-task SQL runners.

5.1 Prompt One – Query to Mock Graph

Responsibilities: read schema, map the question to fields/derivations, propose 1–N Vega-Lite specs, include small plausible mock data.

Locked prompt (for evaluation case studies):

```
Instructions:

Below is a query and a SQL schema. Output Vega-lite code
fulfilling the query, inputting fake mock-data for now.
Once the visualisation is agreed upon, you will generate
an SQL query matching the Vega-lite visualisation
exactly.
---
Query:
{query}
---
Schema:

{schema}
```

Though the prompt was locked for the evaluation case studies, in practical use there are potential additions to achieve more tailored results:

To Avoid Full Table Data in Vega-Lite. The locked prompt allows importing full data to Vega-Lite and processing it there. If this is unwanted behaviour (say for CSP with millions of data entries) the prompt can be extended thus:

```
{Instructions ...}

mock-data is of custom sql query output, not full data
table

{Query and Schema}
```

To Specify Data Output. For the small evaluation case studies this wasn't important, but for larger runs you might want to specify the SQL query output format, to lock in a method of importing it to Vega-Lite. For EKMIN tasks I specified TSV output, then the Vega-Lite spec is extended with TSV data specifications, and data import runs without surprises.

To Supplement Poor SQL Schemas. The initial prompt can contain comments on specific schema quirks. This can also be further mediated in the back and forth before spec approval. Reasonable schemas (all evaluation case studies) need no special treatment. CSP schema has a few quirks with data coverage issues that need special treatment.

5.2 Prompt Two – Lock Data Shape and Generate SQL Query

Prompt one initiates a chat loop, which finishes upon user acceptance of the Vega-Lite spec, where acceptance is the sending of prompt two (also locked for evaluation):

```
perfect! Now output an SQL query matching the schema,
that returns data in a way that exactly matches the shape
used for the Vega-Lite visualisation.
```

This outputs the SQL query and marks the privacy line, behind which LLMs are no longer used and everything can be run locally and securely.

5.3 Query Execution and Final Rendering

Run the SQL query.

Place SQL output into Vega-Lite. For evaluation case studies this process was manual, differing from case to case. For EKMIN use this was pre-agreed to be done via.tsv, with the following command making the file placeable into the Vega-Lite spec (e.g. making white spaces explicit as text):

```
jq -Rs '.' out.tsv
```

Vega-Lite renderer will update upon receiving the real data, and the final visualisation is rendered.

6 Evaluation Design

Goal and Rationale. We evaluate the spec-first, mock-before-execute workflow on what matters for stakeholder-facing analytics: how quickly and reliably a user reaches an acceptable visual answer with zero unnecessary executions and no wide, under-structured outputs. Prior work shows why automation-centric exact-match metrics are insufficient for this setting: nvBench synthesises single-chart pairs from NL → SQL over small tables; VisEval still assumes execute-first code and scores one-shot legality/readability in a "feasible region," explicitly acknowledging multiple acceptable mappings. Our evaluation therefore centres on cooperative productivity rather than single-shot exactness.

Evaluation Questions

- EQ1: Does a spec-first mock stage reduce avoidable executions and post-query reshaping relative to execute-first NL → VIS?
- EQ2: How many iterations are typically required to reach an acceptable chart, and how long does it take?
- EQ3: Does the contract-driven handoff eliminate wide outputs and redundant columns in practice?
- EQ4: Can the approach scale to complex real-world multi-table schemas and motivate multi-view answers when a single chart would overload meaning?

Task Suites. We adopt case-study replication as in Chat2VIS and ADVISor, aiming for comparative parity while measuring the cooperative productivity of a spec-first workflow.

- Chat2VIS replication (all case studies)

- Scope: We replicate every case study reported in Chat2VIS, using the same data sources (e.g., nvBench-sourced tables; public CSVs referenced in their paper/examples).
- Purpose: Provide an apples-to-apples contrast with an execute-first, one-shot code-generation workflow over single tables.
- Expectation from related work: Chat2VIS acknowledges non-determinism, fragile styling, and a lack of explicit mock/spec phases; we test whether early agreement shortens the path to acceptable visuals.

- ADVISor replication (representative case studies until saturation)

- Scope: We reproduce the canonical ADVISor case families on their public datasets (e.g., energy production), then stop once additional cases become monotone (same semantic pattern, same single-table mapping).
- Purpose: Compare against a template-driven, one-shot NL → Vega-Lite system that assumes a single pre-shaped table.
- Expectation from related work: ADVISor's own user study found that 27.5% of results needed rework; we test whether a mock stage absorbs that rework upfront and whether multi-view proposals emerge when a single view overloads meaning.

- EKMIN real-world cases (complex and large multi-table; governance-constrained)

  - Scope: Questions sourced from Latvia's Ministry of Economics over ~40 tables in the CSP-aligned schema. We select a real batch of tasks that were done and delivered manually before the development of this system.
  - Purpose: Demonstrate the intended target: big schemas (with quirks), large tables, zero data exfil during ideation, and willingness to propose multiple coordinated views when appropriate.

Protocol

- Prompts: Use the frozen prompts from Sect. 5 for all case studies. No prompt engineering mid-run.
- Model settings: Temperature 0.1; one fixed model (OpenAI gpt-5 with reasoning).

Threats to Validity and Mitigations.

- Small-N and selection bias: We replicate all Chat2VIS cases and a saturated set from ADVISor to limit cherry-picking; EKMIN tasks are pre-listed before running.
- Single-operator bias: We freeze prompts, show all iterations.
- Non-determinism: We report one canonical run per task.

7 Results

Across 13 tasks (Fig. 2.) (replications of Chat2VIS and ADVISor cases plus EKMIN/CSP tasks over complex multi-table schemas), 11/13 (85%) were acceptable on the first mock; all 13/13 (100%) reached an acceptable visual within a single round of feedback. In 8/13 cases, the final visual was judged clearer than "gold" ("gold" is published best visualisation from reference paper), due to clearer visuals, more appropriate tick marks, extra analytics. No run emitted a wide or under-structured output: every SQL was generated from the approved spec's data shape contract and executed exactly once per task (Table 1.). Minor corrections surfaced without changing contracts (e.g., x-axis year tick formatting; preferred stack order in one EKMIN area chart).

Table 1. Results summary.

Metric	Result
Tasks (N)	13
First-mock acceptable	11/13 (85%)
Completed within 1 feedback	13/13 (100%)
"Improved over gold"	8/13
Wide outputs emitted	0/13
SQL executions per task	1

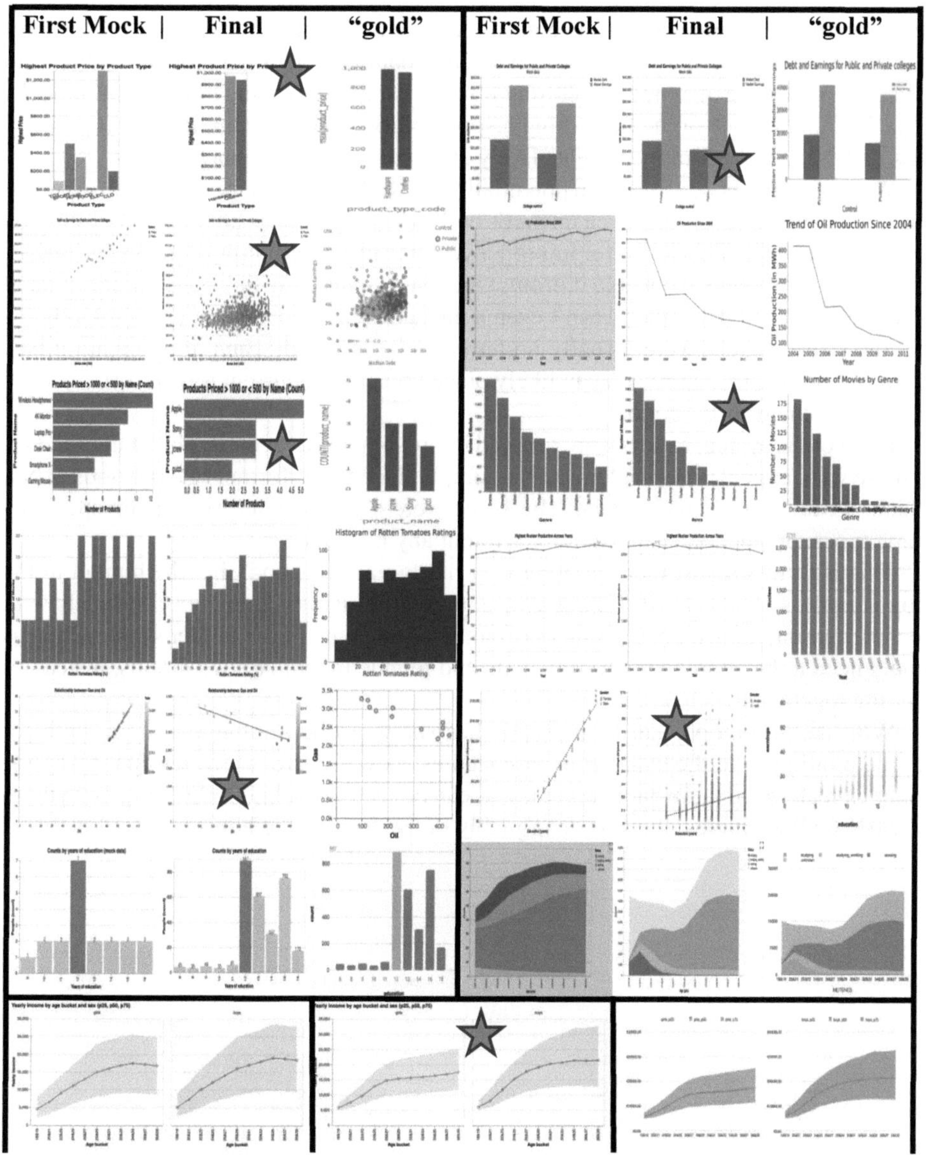

Fig. 2. First mock, final, and "gold" (published best visualisation from reference papers) for each of 13 tasks. Greyed out = accepted after one feedback; the rest = accepted at first mock; star marks cases judged clearer than the published gold.

8 Discussion

This work uses an appropriate graphing language (Vega-Lite over python plotting libraries), current best LLM models, and leaves human in the loop for cheap and rapid tweaks if needed. In practice, this explains most of the observed gains. We observed an

85% first-mock acceptance rate. The most recent and capable NL → VIS models report at most 75% perfect scores over whole evaluation datasets. Our high score is likely due to the use of Vega-Lite over python plotting libraries, and due to using newer LLM models. Vega-Lite takes some of the formatting responsibility off the system, making it easier to pass on first go. LLM improvements likely also gain some percentage points.

What is more, those 15% could potentially be avoidable if that were the goal, allowing our score to potentially push even upwards of 85% (though this is not on a full evaluation set). One needed feedback was for improper year tick mark formatting ("2,018" instead of "2018") – likely easily catchable if prompt included "make sure tick marks are formatted accordingly to…". The other wasn't even a mistake, just feedback on user preference – that the stacked areas were visually preferred to be inverted. Thus, if automation best score was a goal, this approach can likely place you among current top performers even without a human-in-the-loop.

Eight of the system results were deemed improvements over the "gold" standard. Part of these were expected, as the "gold" was simply the best performer of a previous paper, which doesn't always mean good. But some were a genuine surprise, using specialist graph types, or stacked visualisations, without any hiccups.

This isn't to suggest that the graphs on first go are so good, that the human in the loop is useless. There were still signs of non-determinism (e.g. angled tick labels with no clear reason, almost obstructing one another) and some of the bolder system choices would need to be approved (splitting male and female income to two graphs, instead of plotting together).

With the human present though, this has shown to be a reliable system, both for simple plotting as in the evaluation case studies, as well as for more serious tasks over complex real-world multi-table schemas, as can be seen in the highlight in Fig. 3. In these EKMIN/CSP examples, the system arguably outperformed the human-crafted plots.

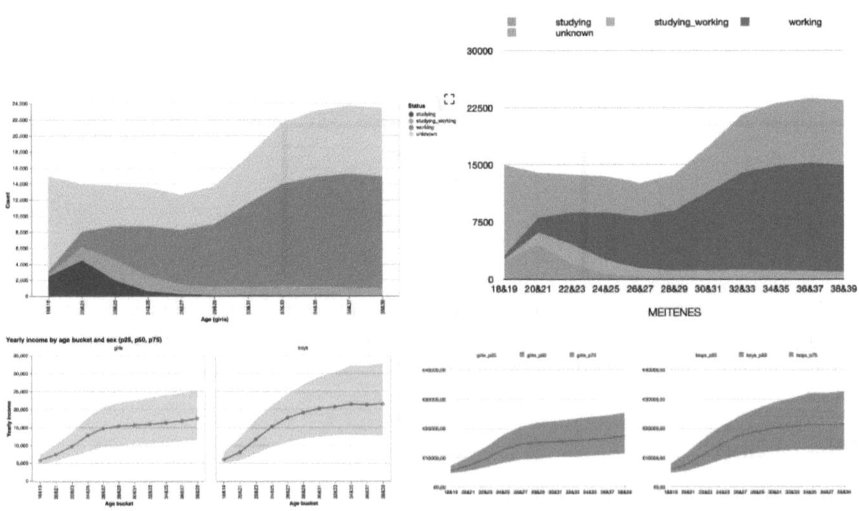

Fig. 3. System outputs (left) vs manual human-crafted (right) on real EKMIN/CSP use-cases.

9 Conclusion

We presented a spec-first, LLM-assisted NL → VIS workflow that restores a shared visual workspace via serialisation. The system proposes mock Vega-Lite charts from the question and schema alone, then treats the approved spec as a data shape contract that drives least-privilege SQL and final rendering. This agreement-before-execution reframes success from brittle one-shot exactness to cooperative productivity: the fastest path to a correct, comprehensible visual that the user actually wants. In replications and EKMIN/CSP cases, 11/13 tasks were acceptable on the first mock and 13/13 within one round, while eliminating wide, under-structured outputs.

Vega-Lite serves as a practical lingua franca today: compact, declarative, and reliably round-trippable between human edits and model generation. The approach aligns with privacy and governance constraints by keeping real data local until after agreement and by executing a single constrained query.

As multi-modal LLMs develop, their visual acumen might eventually replace the need for serialisation based shared workspaces, but as Licklider said "the {interim years} may be 10 or 500, but those years should be intellectually the most creative and exciting in the history of mankind" [1].

Acknowledgments. This study was funded by the EU Recovery and Resilience Facility's project "Language Technology Initiative" (2.3.1.1.i.0/1/22/I/CFLA/002).

Disclosure of Interests. The authors have no competing interests to declare that are relevant to the content of this article.

References

1. Licklider, J.C.R.: Man–computer symbiosis. IRE Trans. Hum. Fact. Electron. HFE-**1**, 4–11 (1960)
2. Satyanarayan, A., Moritz, D., Wongsuphasawat, K., Heer, J.: Vega-Lite: a grammar of interactive graphics. IEEE Trans. Visual Comput. Graphics **23**(1), 341–350 (2016)
3. Luo, Y., Li, G., Fan, J., Chai, C., Tang, N.: Natural language to SQL: state of the art and open problems. Proc. VLDB Endowment **18**(12), 5466–5471 (2025)
4. Barzdins, P., Gruzitis, N.: OB-GRAG: LLM-assisted graph creation and querying via domain-specific ontology (2025)
5. Maddigan, P., Susnjak, T.: Chat2Vis: generating data visualizations via natural language using ChatGPT, codex and GPT-3 large language models. IEEE Access **11**, 45181–45193 (2023)
6. Chen, N., Zhang, Y., Xu, J., Ren, K., Yang, Y.: VisEval: a benchmark for data visualization in the era of large language models. IEEE Trans. Visual Comput. Graph. **31**(1), 1301–1311 (2024)
7. Luo, Y., Tang, N., Li, G., Chai, C., Li, W., Qin, X.: Synthesizing natural language to visualization (NL2VIS) benchmarks from NL2SQL benchmarks. In: Proceedings of the 2021 International Conference on Management of Data, pp. 1235–1247 (2021)
8. Narechania, A., Srinivasan, A., Stasko, J.: NL4DV: a toolkit for generating analytic specifications for data visualization from natural language queries. IEEE Trans. Vis. Comput. Graph. **27**(2), 369–379 (2020)

9. Liu, C., Han, Y., Jiang, R., Yuan, X.: Advisor: automatic visualization answer for natural-language question on tabular data. In: 2021 IEEE 14th Pacific Visualization Symposium (PacificVis), pp. 11–20 IEEE (2021)
10. Tian, Y., et al.: ChartGPT: leveraging LLMs to generate charts from abstract natural language. IEEE Trans. Vis. Comput. Graph. **31**(3), 1731–1745 (2024)
11. Luo, Y., Tang, N., Li, G., Tang, J., Chai, C., Qin, X.: Natural language to visualization by neural machine translation. IEEE Trans. Vis. Comput. Graph. **28**(1), 217–226 (2021)
12. Yu, T., et al.: Spider: a large-scale human-labeled dataset for complex and cross-domain semantic parsing and text-to-SQL task. In: Proceedings of the 2018 Conference on Empirical Methods in Natural Language Processing, pp. 3911–3921 (2018)
13. Shen, L., et al.: Towards natural language interfaces for data visualization: a survey. IEEE Trans. Vis. Comput. Graph. **29**(6), 3121–3144 (2022)
14. Qin, X., Luo, Y., Tang, N., Li, G.: Making data visualization more efficient and effective: a survey. VLDB J. **29**(1), 93–117 (2020)
15. Make real homepage. https://makereal.tldraw.com. Accessed 14 Mar 2026
16. Uizard wireframing page. https://uizard.io/wireframing/. Accessed 14 Mar 2026

Constraint-Aware Data Collection and Observational Analysis of Digital Labor Platforms

Ayoub Frihaoui[1(✉)], Olivier Pons[1], and Léa Lima[2]

[1] Cedrid CNAM, Paris, France
{ayoub.frihaoui,olivier.pons}@lecnam.net
[2] Lise CNAM, Paris, France
lea.lima@lecnam.net

Abstract. Digital labor platforms mediate access to work through opaque interfaces, enforced filters, and internal ranking mechanisms that remain only partially visible to researchers and workers. Naive scraping strategies often reproduce these visibility constraints: pagination caps, mandatory search dimensions, and hidden parameter ranges can exclude large portions of the underlying worker population before any substantive analysis begins. Empirical studies may therefore confound platform effects with artifacts introduced by the data collection process itself. This paper presents a constraint-aware methodological framework for the study of digital labor platforms. At the collection layer, a Platform Analysis Protocol systematically identifies API constraints, enforced query dimensions, and cap behavior, while a Hierarchical Density-Reduction Algorithm (HDRA) recursively partitions oversaturated queries until retrieval falls below platform limits. Applied to Sitly in Brazil, this approach increases retrieval from the visible limit of 10,000 profiles to 231,999 unique workers, showing that naive queries may expose only a small fraction of the underlying population. The paper also includes a preliminary observational illustration on Yoopies.fr, where a more complete corpus supports exploratory analyses based on logistic regression, SHAP, and semantic clustering of profile descriptions. Taken together, these results show that data completeness is not merely a technical detail but a methodological precondition for more defensible observational analyses of digital labor platforms.

Keywords: algorithmic fairness · platform labor · computational social science · data collection · DataOps

1 Introduction

Digital labor platforms have become central intermediaries in sectors such as childcare, domestic work, and freelance services, where they shape how workers are discovered, compared, and selected [10,19,20]. They do more than host

R. Matulevičius et al. (Eds.): DB&IS 2026, CCIS 3085, pp. 185–199, 2026.
https://doi.org/10.1007/978-3-032-30863-4_12

listings: they format information, impose search hierarchies, and organize visibility through technical and interface choices that influence which workers become comparable and which remain marginal. In care work, these dynamics are especially important because selection involves not only price and availability, but also trust, emotional presentation, language, and other socially coded signals. For research, the central difficulty is that the data visible through ordinary use are not necessarily the data needed for systematic observation [4,18]. Public interfaces and internal APIs are optimized for algorithmic matching, not for reproducible inquiry, and they frequently impose pagination ceilings, mandatory location anchors, category restrictions, and hidden parameter bounds whose existence is not always signaled to the user. When researchers scrape only what is immediately exposed [5,9], they risk analyzing populations whose boundaries are determined by platform constraints rather than by the research design itself. These constraints actively produce *shadow populations*: workers who exist on the platform but remain invisible to standard queries, generating silent selection biases in empirical research [12]. That problem is methodological before it is substantive. Observed inequalities may reflect two distinct mechanisms that should not be conflated: platform-mediated stratification on the one hand, and truncation introduced by the collection process on the other. A pagination cap, in this light, is not merely a stopping point but a signal of local density that calls for recursive segmentation of the search space. A scientifically defensible design therefore requires recovering candidate sets as completely as possible, and only then move to the analysis of correlations between worker characteristics and platform-mediated outcomes [2,6,16]. This matters especially in the context of algorithmic auditing, where valid bias assessments require a credible baseline population: if the collection method silently excludes subpopulations, observed inequalities may be sampling artifacts rather than platform effects [17]. This paper addresses the collection problem first and the analytical problem second. Its main contribution is methodological: we present a Platform Analysis Protocol for identifying API constraints, enforced query dimensions, and cap behavior, together with a Hierarchical Density-Reduction Algorithm (HDRA) that recursively partitions saturated queries until retrieval falls below platform limits. This contribution is demonstrated on Sitly Brazil, where naive retrieval is strongly truncated by a hard cap. The paper also includes a preliminary observational illustration based on Yoopies.fr. Yoopies did not require HDRA because its architecture allowed iterative retrieval without a hard global cap, but it provides a useful first corpus for showing the kinds of downstream analyses that more complete platform datasets can support. We therefore treat the Yoopies results as exploratory and separate from the technical demonstration on Sitly, rather than as a direct validation of HDRA itself.

2 Related Work

2.1 Platform Data Access and the Pipeline Problem

Digital labor platforms have become central infrastructures in care work and freelance services, shaping how workers are discovered and selected through opaque algorithmic systems [10,19]. For researchers, the central difficulty is that platform interfaces are optimized for algorithmic matching, not for systematic observation [4,18]: they impose pagination ceilings, enforced filter hierarchies, and hidden parameter bounds that produce *shadow populations* of workers invisible to standard queries [5,12].

Web scraping has evolved from HTML parsing and DOM extraction toward more structured approaches leveraging API inspection and hierarchical extraction [7,11]. Yet most of that literature focuses on how to extract content reliably on the client side, not on how to reason about server-side constraints. Platform APIs expose two distinct constraint types: explicit caps, where a `totalCount` field reveals the true population size while returning only a truncated subset, and censored caps, where the count itself is hidden and truncation is only detectable when returned results reach the pagination limit. Both types produce silent selection biases that naive scraping strategies reproduce rather than overcome. Silva et al. [17] confirm this empirically, finding that only 7% of 397 empirical studies on labor platforms use platform-provided data, and that sampling strategies and API constraints are rarely documented, making completeness and replicability difficult to assess.

Overcoming this access problem is a necessary but insufficient condition for credible analysis. Complete retrieval must be followed by structured data processing and statistically sound observational methods before any claim about platform-mediated inequality can be defended. The methodological challenge is therefore not collection alone, but the construction of an end-to-end pipeline in which each layer—retrieval, processing, and analysis—is designed to avoid introducing artifacts that could be mistaken for platform effects.

2.2 Data Engineering for Reproducible Platform Analysis

Beyond collection, reproducible platform analysis requires structured data processing pipelines that enforce quality at runtime. DataOps-compliant approaches [8] provide the relevant standards: comprehensive metadata tracking, automated schema validation, and explicit uncertainty quantification. Third Normal Form normalization eliminates redundancy and ensures referential integrity across heterogeneous platform schemas, while runtime validation libraries such as Pandera enforce type, range, and uniqueness constraints that prevent silent data corruption downstream.

Multimodal data introduces additional processing challenges. Large Vision-Language Models now enable demographic attribute inference from profile images and text at scale [1], but risk reproducing the biases they aim to document [3]. Methodologically sound pipelines must therefore treat such inferences as probabilistic rather than ground truth, propagate confidence scores through downstream analyses, and present results only in aggregate.

2.3 Observational Analysis and Algorithmic Auditing

Explainable machine learning methods have emerged as standard interpretive tools for platform auditing. SHAP [13] decomposes model predictions into individual feature contributions, revealing which worker characteristics most influence platform-mediated outcomes—while making explicit that feature importance in a predictive model is not equivalent to causal determination. Semantic embedding approaches such as Sentence-BERT enable clustering of self-presentation strategies at scale, supporting analysis of how profile text relates to labor market outcomes independently of structured attributes.

Valid audits of recommendation and ranking systems require a credible candidate-set baseline [2,16]. When APIs cap results or hide part of the matching population, observed inequalities may reflect sampling artifacts rather than platform effects [6]. The most defensible analytical contribution is therefore one that explicitly connects retrieval completeness to downstream interpretive validity, distinguishing platform-mediated stratification from truncation introduced by the collection process itself.

3 Methodology

This section presents the methodological architecture developed for the systematic analysis of digital labor platforms, organized into three layers: constraint-aware data collection, DataOps-compliant processing, and observational analysis. Figure 1 summarizes how these layers relate to one another. In the present paper, however, the collection layer is the primary validated contribution, the processing layer is reported at the level necessary to document reproducibility, and the observational layer is illustrated through preliminary analyses on Yoopies.fr. Components not used in the reported results, such as multimodal attribute inference, are included only as part of the broader pipeline design and not as empirical contributions of this paper.

3.1 Constraint-Aware Data Collection

Platform Analysis Protocol. Before any automated retrieval, we systematically characterize the target platform's architecture through three phases. In the first phase, manual exploration of public and authenticated interfaces documents enforced filter hierarchies, mandatory dimensions, and the gap between UI-exposed parameter ranges and actual API capabilities. Browser developer tools expose the underlying API calls, distinguishing stateless architectures—where search parameters are fully encapsulated in each request—from stateful architectures, where prior requests modify server-side session state and must be orchestrated before each search query. In the second phase, canonical request patterns are extracted and replayed using API testing tools to empirically determine the hard retrieval limit τ: the maximum number of profiles the API returns for any single query regardless of pagination depth. Two constraint types are

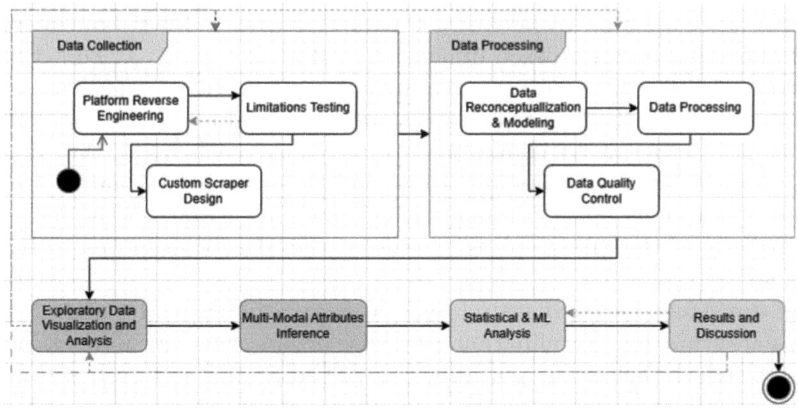

Fig. 1. Overview of the data collection, processing, and analysis pipeline.

identified: *explicit caps*, where a `totalCount` field reveals the true population size while returning only τ results, and *censored caps*, where the count itself is hidden and truncation is only detectable when $|R_q| = \tau$. In the third phase, conservative request rates are calibrated empirically by monitoring HTTP 429 responses and temporary blocks, ensuring ethical and sustainable collection. All scraped attributes are publicly visible to ordinary platform users; no authentication bypass or private data access was performed. Data is retained solely for research purposes and results are presented exclusively in aggregate.

Hierarchical Density-Reduction Algorithm. Recursive partitioning of search spaces is a well-established technique. The contribution of HDRA lies not in partitioning per se, but in the systematic protocol that precedes it: constraint discovery, architectural classification, and cap typing are prerequisites that transform an otherwise naive binary search into a platform-aware retrieval strategy. Without the Platform Analysis Protocol, neither the enforced dimension ordering nor the cap type can be determined, and the partitioning step degenerates into uninformed grid search.

Let $\mathcal{U}$ be the universe of worker profiles. The platform provides a query function $Q(S) \to (R_S, \kappa_S)$, where R_S is the set of returned profiles ($|R_S| \leq \tau$) and κ_S is the reported count. A query is *saturated* if:

$$\sigma(S) = (|R_S| = \tau) \vee (\kappa_S > \tau) \tag{1}$$

When $\sigma(S)$ is true, R_S is a truncated sample. The goal is to decompose S into disjoint subspaces $\{S_1, \ldots, S_m\}$ such that $\forall j, \neg\sigma(S_j)$, maximizing the recall ratio:

$$\text{Maximize} \frac{|\bigcup_{i=1}^{m} R_{S_i}|}{|\mathcal{U}|} \quad \text{subject to} \quad \forall i, \kappa_{S_i} \leq \tau \tag{2}$$

HDRA achieves this by treating the platform as a black-box query oracle and operating on an ordered dimension vector $\boldsymbol{D} = (D_1, \ldots, D_k)$. Enforced dimensions—those the platform requires in every query, such as city or category—appear first. Adaptive dimensions are introduced only when enforced structure is insufficient to eliminate saturation. At each node, the algorithm queries $Q(S)$; if $\neg\sigma(S)$, results are stored and the branch terminates; if $\sigma(S)$, a partition operator Ψ_i splits S along the current dimension and the recurses on each subspace. If the dimension is exhausted the algorithm moves to the next dimension.

If all dimensions are exhausted and saturation persists, the node is logged as terminal saturation. Termination otherwise occurs when all subqueries return result sets strictly below the platform cap τ. Under intersection-based filtering logic, this condition guarantees that no further truncation occurs within the query interface. In practice, this condition was verified for every terminal node of the partition tree. The total query cost is governed by:

$$C_{HDRA} \approx \mathcal{O}\left(\frac{N}{\tau} \cdot \beta \cdot \gamma\right) \tag{3}$$

where N is the total population size, $\beta \geq 1$ is a redundancy coefficient capturing overlap from non-disjoint filters, and γ represents distribution skew. Uniform distributions minimize splits ($\gamma \approx 1$); highly concentrated distributions force deep recursion. Three failure modes bound the algorithm's applicability: platforms enforcing union rather than intersection filter logic would require a modified partitioning strategy; non-orthogonal dimensions where D_1 alters the valid range of D_2 require state-aware partition operators; and collection windows spanning multiple hours introduce snapshot semantics rather than an instantaneous view of the population.

Although demonstrated here on labor platforms, the HDRA procedure is independent of platform semantics and can be applied to any API exposing capped query results with intersecting filter dimensions.

Algorithm 1 formalizes the recursive retrieval strategy implemented by HDRA. The algorithm queries the API, detects saturation conditions, and recursively partitions the search space along an ordered dimension vector until result sets fall below the platform cap.

Algorithm 1 Hierarchical Density-Reduction Algorithm (HDRA)

Require: Search Context S, Dim Index i, Vector $\boldsymbol{D}$, Cap τ

Ensure: Set of unique profiles R_{total}

```
(R_S, κ) ← QueryAPI(S)                        ▷ Fetch profiles & metadata
if ¬IsSaturated(κ, |R_S|, τ) then
    return R_S                                ▷ Base case: complete
end if
if i > length(D) then
    return R_S                                ▷ Max depth reached
end if
Subspaces ← Ψ_i.Partition(S)                  ▷ e.g., Split Age range
if Subspaces ≠ ∅ then
    R_total ← ∅
    for all S_j ∈ Subspaces do
        R_total ← R_total ∪ Harvest(S_j, i, D, τ)
    end for
    return R_total
else
    return Harvest(S, i + 1, D, τ)            ▷ Dim atomic, move to next filter
end if
```

On Sitly Brazil, location is stored in account state rather than passed as a query parameter—a stateful constraint invisible to naive scrapers. The API caps results at $\tau = 10,000$ while accepting age ranges of $[0, 160]$ beyond the $[18, 70+]$ exposed in the interface. Applying HDRA with 161 city centroids as the enforced first dimension and age as the adaptive second dimension recovered 231,999 unique profiles across Brazil. In São Paulo alone, age-based partitioning raised retrieval from the visible cap of 10,000 to 51,371 unique profiles after deduplication, with a redundancy coefficient $\beta \approx 1.20$.

3.2 Data Processing Pipeline

Retrieved profiles are processed through a DataOps-compliant pipeline [8] designed for reproducibility and runtime quality enforcement. Database schemas follow Third Normal Form normalization across all platforms 50+ tables, eliminating redundancy and ensuring referential integrity across heterogeneous platform schemas. Schema validation enforces explicit constraints on every ingested record: type enforcement (integer, float, string, boolean), range validation (age: 0–120, hourly rates: 0–500, ratings: 0–5), uniqueness constraints on primary keys, and null handling specifications. Automated quality reporting generates compliance rates, missing value patterns, duplicate detection results, and referential integrity metrics for each processing run, providing full data lineage from raw API response to analysis-ready dataset.

The pipeline additionally supports multimodal attribute inference using Large Vision-Language Models to extract demographic and visual attributes from profile images and biographical text. Every inference is assigned an explicit confidence score (0.0–1.0), and results are treated as probabilistic rather than ground truth throughout the analysis. This component is fully implemented and validated on a private annotated subset; deployment on the full corpus is pending institutional ethics committee approval and is not reported in the present results.

3.3 Observational Analysis

The observational component focuses on Yoopies.fr and treats employment as a preliminary platform-mediated outcome rather than a direct measure of labor-market success. The primary outcome variable, `has_worked`, is defined as the presence of at least one recorded worked hour on a worker's profile. This operationalization has a known limitation: the absence of worked hours may reflect either genuine non-employment or early-stage registration where no assignment has yet been completed or recorded on the platform. Results should therefore be interpreted with this measurement uncertainty in mind.

The three analytical methods are deliberately complementary. Univariate logistic regression documents marginal associations at the variable level and provides interpretable effect magnitudes for each worker characteristic considered separately. SHAP (SHapley Additive exPlanations) [13] reveals which variables jointly structure model predictions as a whole, capturing interaction patterns that univariate specifications cannot detect. Semantic clustering examines whether self-presentation strategies are associated with observed outcomes beyond structured attributes, providing a bridge between platform formatting and labor-market interpretation. Together, these methods offer a preliminary triangulation on the same outcome from different analytical angles.

Univariate logistic regression specifications are retained deliberately to document marginal associations without imposing a covariate structure that would require additional assumptions about confounding pathways. Each characteristic is therefore estimated in isolation, with odds ratios and confidence intervals enabling interpretation of effect magnitudes while remaining transparent about the absence of causal identification. SHAP (SHapley Additive exPlanations) [13] decomposes gradient boosting model predictions into individual feature contributions, revealing which characteristics most influence model predictions of platform success; SHAP values are interpreted as an indicator of predictive salience, not causal determination.

Sentence-BERT embeddings [15] convert profile descriptions into 384-dimensional semantic vectors; k-means clustering ($k = 8$) identifies distinct self-presentation strategies, and UMAP visualization enables exploration of the resulting semantic space.

All analyses are framed as observational. Observed correlations between - worker characteristics and `has_worked` may arise from multiple simultaneous mechanisms—algorithmic ranking, client preferences, reverse causality, or unobserved quality differences—and the cross-sectional design cannot distinguish between them.

4 Results

4.1 Dataset Characteristics

Table 1 summarizes the platform datasets produced during the broader collection effort. The two platforms discussed in the remainder of this paper play different roles. Sitly is the methodological demonstration case for HDRA: under a hard cap of $\tau = 10{,}000$, naive retrieval exposes only a truncated subset of the worker population, whereas recursive partitioning recovers 231,999 unique babysitter profiles across Brazil.

Table 1. Dataset overview

Platform	Profiles	Country	Cap τ	Gain via HDRA
Yoopies.fr	49,205	France	None	-
Sitly.com.br	231,999	Brazil	10,000	x23.2
Malt.fr	>66,000	France	300	x220
Care.com	8,417	USA	500	x16.8

Yoopies.fr, by contrast, did not require HDRA because its category-enforced search architecture could be enumerated through iterative requests without a hard global cap. We use Yoopies as a preliminary observational case because it was the first platform for which we obtained a sufficiently complete corpus and carried out downstream analyses, while Sitly is used to demonstrate why constraint-aware retrieval is necessary when hard caps make naive collection incomplete.

4.2 Correlational Patterns: Logistic Regression

For the Yoopies.fr analyses, workers are classified as having worked when their profile records at least one worked hour. In the Paris subsample, this represents 12.61% of profiles ($N = 393$ of 3,115). Table 2 reports descriptive statistics comparing profiles with and without recorded worked hours across the analyzed corpus. Rate bins reflect the platform's own display categories, while age and experience bins were defined prior to analysis to avoid post-hoc optimization. Workers not reporting French proficiency represent 8.3% of profiles with recorded worked hours and 12.0% of profiles without them; 6.8% of profiles with recorded worked hours are male, consistent with the feminized composition of the corpus.

Univariate logistic regression on `has_worked` identifies several systematic associations. Workers charging above the minimum wage are associated with substantially higher odds of observed platform success ($\log OR = 0.98$, $p < 0.001$), representing a 167% increase in odds relative to the minimum wage baseline. This association is consistent with multiple non-exclusive mechanisms: algorithmic ranking may privilege high-rate profiles to maximize commission revenue; clients may interpret higher rates as quality signals; or workers may raise

Table 2. Descriptive statistics and logistic regression results (Yoopies.fr)

Group	Characteristic	Worked (%)	Not worked (%)	log(OR)	p-value
Gender	% of women	93.2	88.0	–	–
	males	6.8	12	−0.62439	<0.0001
Salary	Minimum wage (11.32€)	41.5	61.5	–	–
	15 euros and more	26.0	14.5	0.98074	<0.0001
	Other	32.5	24.0	0.69833	0.00000
Age	40 years and +	23.9	29.1	–	–
	[15–25]	38.3	39.3	0.16992	0.00068
	[25–40]	37.7	31.6	0.37415	<0.0001
Language	French (native)	49.4	65.0	–	–
	French (foreign)	42.3	23.0	0.88418	<0.0001
	No proficiency in French	8.3	12.0	−0.09453	0.18614
City	Bordeaux	1.6	0.7	–	–
	Other	84.9	91.4	−0.87605	<0.0001
	Paris	13.5	7.9	−0.26001	0.12136
Experience	No experience	11.3	10.3	–	–
	Experience <1	10.3	22.4	−0.86105	<0.0001
	Experience [1–5]	51.4	44.7	0.05436	0.39356
	Experience [5–10]	16.1	10.7	0.32173	<0.0001
	Experience >10	10.9	11.9	−0.16735	0.04114

rates after accumulating worked hours, making observed success temporally prior to premium pricing rather than its consequence. The cross-sectional design cannot distinguish these mechanisms, and no causal claim about platform-imposed economic barriers is warranted from this evidence alone.

Non-native French speakers who report French proficiency show higher observed success rates than native speakers ($\log OR = 0.88$, $p < 0.001$). This association may reflect targeting of expatriate or international families, professionalism signaling through explicit language specification, or selection effects among highly motivated non-native registrants—again, the design cannot discriminate between these pathways. Male workers show lower observed success rates ($\log OR = -0.62$, $p < 0.001$), a pattern consistent with the feminized composition of the care work sector. Experience associations are more moderate, with 5–10 years showing the strongest positive association ($\log OR = 0.32$, $p < 0.001$).

4.3 Explainable ML: SHAP Analysis

Figure 2 presents SHAP values from a gradient boosting model trained on `has_worked`, decomposing predictions into individual feature contributions.

Profile creation date emerges as the dominant predictor: earlier registration dates produce the largest positive SHAP values, suggesting cumulative advantage dynamics consistent with sociological Matthew effects [14]. Early platform adopters accumulate platform experience, work hours, and potential reviews that might improve ranking, generating further opportunities in a self-reinforcing loop. Distance from Paris and maximum hourly rate follow as the next most salient features, with mid-career age (25–40) also contributing positively.

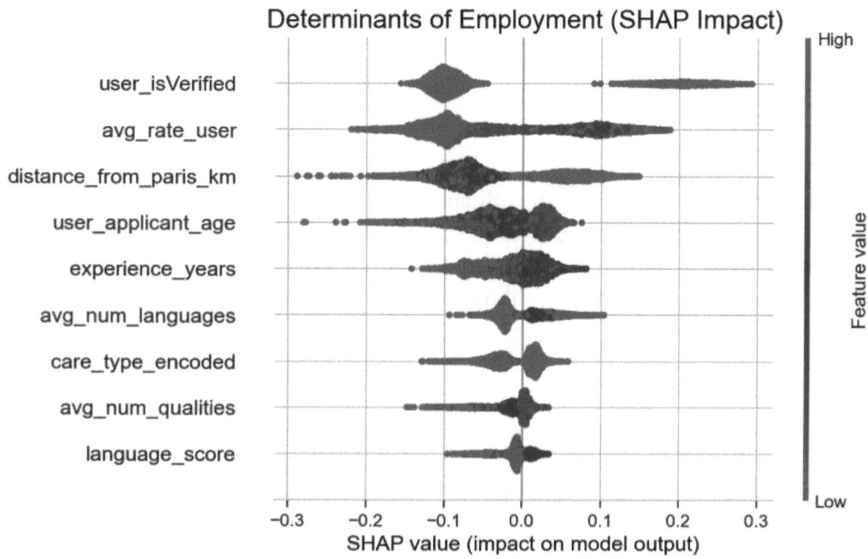

Fig. 2. SHAP summary plot for `has_worked` outcome (Yoopies.fr, N = 49,205). Features are ordered by mean absolute SHAP value. Color indicates feature value (red = high, blue = low); 0 and 1 encoded as childcare and housekeeping respectively; language_score: 0 no proficiency, 1 proficiency, 2 native.

These SHAP values indicate which features structure the model's predictions, not which features causally determine outcomes.

4.4 Semantic Analysis: The Self-Presentation Paradox

Semantic clustering of the 49,205 Yoopies profile descriptions identified eight groups with substantially different work rates, ranging from 0.70% to 10.50% (Table 3).

High-performing clusters contain professional, specific descriptions with explicit availability information and references to specialized experience. Low-performing clusters show comparable linguistic quality but lack specificity and personal detail. The most striking finding is a local paradox: a profile with 5,108 worked hours shares cosine similarity of 0.794–0.807 with five neighboring profiles that have zero worked hours. Textual quality and self-presentation strategy

Table 3. Work rates by semantic cluster (Yoopies.fr)

Cluster	Profiles	Work Rate (%)
5	6,257	10.50
4	8,270	9.69
7	5,112	9.66
0	6,697	7.90
6	6,270	7.67
2	6,201	6.06
3	6,539	4.85
1	3,859	0.70

are therefore necessary but not sufficient conditions for platform success. Pricing, timing, accumulated reputation, and platform visibility dynamics dominate over profile content alone—a result that has normative implications for workers who attempt to optimize their outcomes through description improvement.

5 Discussion

5.1 Data Completeness as a Methodological Precondition

The two platform cases serve distinct but complementary roles in the argument. Sitly demonstrates that candidate-set recovery is simultaneously a technical and epistemic problem: a naive query returns 10,000 profiles where 231,999 exist, and the gap is invisible without explicit constraint discovery. The shadow population is not a marginal residual but the majority of the actual worker population. Any analysis conducted on the naive output would not merely be incomplete—it would be systematically biased toward workers whose profiles happen to satisfy the platform's default ranking and location logic.

Yoopies demonstrates what becomes possible when retrieval is complete. The 49,205-profile corpus supports multiple complementary initial analyses—logistic regression, SHAP decomposition, semantic clustering—whose results are interpretable as platform-level observations rather than collection artifacts. The self-presentation paradox; semantically similar profiles with radically different outcomes—requires population-level coverage to identify reliably.

Together, the two cases support a general principle: data completeness is not a preliminary technical detail but a precondition for any credible audit of platform ranking or recommendation systems. When APIs cap results, observed inequalities may reflect sampling artifacts as much as platform effects, and the two sources of bias cannot be distinguished without an explicit retrieval strategy designed around constraint discovery.

5.2 Interpretive Boundaries and Multiple Mechanisms

The correlational patterns documented on Yoopies admit multiple simultaneous explanations that the cross-sectional design cannot resolve. Premium pricing correlates strongly with success, but this association is consistent with several non-exclusive mechanisms, including algorithmic privileging of high-commission profiles, client quality signaling, reverse causality from successful workers raising their rates, and unobserved quality differences. Early adopters may differ systematically in digital literacy, social networks, or service quality in ways the model cannot observe. Geographic concentration may reflect demand density, algorithmic ranking by location, or network effects linked to denser urban markets and greater opportunities for recorded work.

Maintaining these interpretive boundaries is not a limitation to be apologized for; it is a condition of scientific honesty for cross-sectional observational work. The contribution lies in establishing which associations are robust at population scale and which variables structure model predictions of success, not in resolving causal mechanisms that would require longitudinal data, randomized experiments, or direct access to ranking algorithm source code.

5.3 Pipeline Contributions and Limitations

The end-to-end pipeline introduces constraints at each layer that should be acknowledged. On the collection side, HDRA assumes that adding a filter reduces result count (intersection logic); platforms implementing union logic would require a modified partitioning strategy. The Sitly scrape covered a 16-hour window, introducing snapshot semantics rather than an instantaneous view: profiles may have appeared or disappeared during collection. On the processing side, the multimodal inference component—designed to extract 29 demographic and visual attributes per profile—is fully implemented and validated on a private annotated subset, but pending institutional ethics committee approval; results incorporating inferred attributes are therefore not reported here. On the analysis side, univariate logistic regression cannot control for confounders, and SHAP values reflect predictive salience in a gradient boosting model rather than causal effects. Coverage bias also bounds generalizability: the reverse-engineering approach inherently favors platforms with discoverable APIs, and more opaque architectures may require different strategies.

The collection of worker profile data raises ethical considerations beyond technical compliance. All scraped attributes are limited to information publicly visible to ordinary platform users; no authentication bypass, private endpoint access, or Terms of Service circumvention was performed. Request rates were calibrated conservatively (0.6–1.0 s per request) to avoid server strain. Collected data is retained solely for research purposes, stored under secure access controls, and results are presented exclusively in aggregate form. The multimodal inference component, which involves sensitive attribute extraction from profile images and biographical text, is subject to separate institutional ethics review before any deployment on the full corpus. This staged approach; implementing and validating the technical pipeline while deferring sensitive inference to formal ethics oversight; reflects the tension between the scientific value of documenting algorithmic stratification at scale and the privacy risks inherent in automated demographic classification of workers in vulnerable labor market positions [3].

These limitations define the boundary between what the current infrastructure supports and what future work must address. The pipeline is designed to be extensible: periodic re-collection on fixed query contexts would enable longitudinal monitoring of ranking stability, while controlled audits with synthetic profiles would allow disentangling of algorithmic from preference-based mechanisms. The platforms' reverse-engineering phase potentially might get automated via Agentic-AI. Multivariate regression specifications and hierarchical models accounting for geographic clustering represent natural analytical extensions once the full multimodal corpus is available.

6 Conclusion

Digital labor platforms cannot be analyzed adequately if the data collection stage simply reproduces the visibility limits imposed by their interfaces and APIs. This paper has argued that data completeness is a methodological precondition for credible observational work on platform-mediated labor markets. Its main contribution is therefore on the collection side: a Platform Analysis Protocol for identifying API constraints and enforced query dimensions, combined with the Hierarchical Density-Reduction Algorithm (HDRA) for recursively partitioning saturated queries until retrieval falls below platform caps.

The methodological contribution is demonstrated on Sitly Brazil, where retrieval increases from a visible cap of 10,000 profiles to 231,999 unique workers. The paper also includes a preliminary observational illustration on Yoopies.fr, where a more complete corpus supports exploratory analyses based on logistic regression, SHAP, and semantic clustering. These analyses should be interpreted cautiously: they document initial correlational patterns and predictive structure, not causal effects.

Taken together, the results support a narrower but stronger claim than a full platform audit. They show that constraint-aware collection can substantially reduce retrieval bias, and that more complete datasets create better conditions for downstream observational analysis. In that sense, the work provides a reproducible methodological basis for future research on platform ranking, visibility, and inequality, including longitudinal monitoring, controlled audits, and richer multivariate analyses once additional data and approvals are available.

References

1. AlNuaimi, K., et al.: Enriching datasets with demographics through large language models: what's in a name? arXiv preprint arXiv:2409.11491 (2024)

2. Bandy, J.: Problematic Mach. Behav. Syst. Lit. Rev. Algorithm Audits **5**(CSCW1), 1–34 (2021). https://doi.org/10.1145/3449148
3. Barocas, S., Hardt, M., Narayanan, A.: Fairness and machine learning: limitations and opportunities. MIT press (2023)
4. Brenning, A., Henn, S.: Web scraping: a promising tool for geographic data acquisition, (2023). arXiv preprint arXiv:2305.19893
5. Brown, M.A., et al.: Web scraping for research: legal, ethical, institutional, and scientific considerations. Big Data Soc. **12**(4), 20539517251381686 (2025). https://doi.org/10.1177/20539517251381686
6. Carraro, D., Bridge, D.: A sampling approach to debiasing the offline evaluation of recommender systems. J. Intell. Inf. Syst. **58**(2), 311–336 (2022)
7. Chasins, S.E., Mueller, M., Bodik, R.: Rousillon: scraping distributed hierarchical web data. In: Proceedings of the 31st Annual ACM Symposium on User Interface Software and Technology, pp. 963–975 (2018)
8. Ereth, J.: Dataops-towards a definition. LWDA **2191**(104–112), 106 (2018)
9. Graham, M., et al.: The risks and rewards of online gig work at the global margins. Oxford Internet Institute (2017)
10. Kalleberg, A.L., Vallas, S.P.: Probing precarious work: theory, research, and politics. In: Precarious Work. Emerald Publishing Limited (2017). https://doi.org/10.1108/S0277-283320170000031017
11. Latif, A., Wildah, S.K., Agustiani, S., Juningsih, E.H.: Implementation of a data-testid attribute-based web scraping method for accommodation data extraction from a dynamic e-commerce website (case study: Traveloka). J. Artif. Intell. Eng. Appl. (JAIEA) **5**(1) (2025). https://doi.org/10.59934/jaiea.v5i1.1256
12. Lima, L., Guimarães, N., Pons, O.: How platforms structure unequal access to employment opportunities in paid domestic work: a comparison of two online marketplaces in France and Brazil. In: Proceedings of the III International Conference "Who Cares". São Paulo (2025). https://hal.science/hal-05363870
13. Lundberg, S.M., Lee, S.I.: A unified approach to interpreting model predictions. In: Proceedings of the Advances in Neural Information Processing Systems, p. 30 (2017)
14. Merton, R.K.: The Matthew effect in science: the reward and communication systems of science are considered. Science **159**(3810), 56–63 (1968)
15. Reimers, N., Gurevych, I.: Sentence-Bert: Sentence embeddings using Siamese Bert-networks. In: Proceedings of the 2019 Conference on Empirical Methods in Natural Language Processing and the 9th International Joint Conference on Natural Language Processing (EMNLP-IJCNLP), pp. 3982–3992 (2019)
16. Selbst, A.D., Boyd, D., Friedler, S.A., Venkatasubramanian, S., Vertesi, J.: Fairness and abstraction in sociotechnical systems. In: Proceedings of the conference on fairness, accountability, and transparency, pp. 59–68 (2019)
17. Silva, V., Susha, I., Hoekman, J., Frenken, K.: How data access shapes research into labour platforms. SSRN Working Paper (2025). https://doi.org/10.2139/ssrn.5213743. https://ssrn.com/abstract=5213743
18. Trezza, D.: To scrape or not to scrape, this is dilemma. the post-API scenario and implications on digital research. Front. Sociol. **8**, 1145038 (2023)
19. Vallas, S., Schor, J.B.: What do platforms do? Understanding the gig economy. Ann. Rev. Sociol. **46**(1), 273–294 (2020)
20. Wood, A.J., Graham, M., Lehdonvirta, V., Hjorth, I.: Good gig, bad gig: Autonomy and algorithmic control in the global gig economy. Work Employ Soc. **33**(1), 56–75 (2019). https://doi.org/10.1177/0950017018785616, pMID: 30886460

Data Science and Analytics in Education

Ensuring Data Privacy and Utility in Synthetic Data Generation for Analysis of International Student Admissions Data

Diana Kalibatiene, Julius Jancevičius(✉), Kęstutis Normantas, and Algirdas Laukaitis

Vilnius Gediminas Technical University, 10223 Vilnius, Lithuania
julius.jancevicius@vilniustech.lt

Abstract. The growing availability of digital records in higher education creates new opportunities for data-driven decision-making in international student admissions (ISA). ISA datasets contain sensitive personally identifiable information whose sharing is constrained by the General Data Protection Regulation (GDPR): sharing real records risks applicant re-identification and can expose institutions to regulatory penalties. However, synthetic data must retain sufficient realism for valid analysis, while remaining abstract enough to protect privacy. This paper investigates which data synthesis approaches best balance realism, privacy, and analytical validity. A domain-specific real data pre-processing pipeline addressing high-cardinality categorical features, heterogeneous English proficiency test normalisation, and missing value handling is proposed. Four generative models – Bayesian Networks (BN), Conditional Tabular Generative Adversarial Network (GAN) (CTGAN), Differentially Private GAN (DPGAN), and Private Aggregation of Teacher Ensembles GAN (PATEGAN) are evaluated under privacy budgets $\varepsilon \in \{0.1, 1.0, 2.0, 3.0, 5.0, 10.0\}$. Evaluation covers statistical fidelity (inverse Kullback–Leibler (KL) divergence, Jensen–Shannon distance (JSD), chi-squared test), empirical privacy (k-anonymity, δ-presence), downstream utility via a Train-on-Synthetic, Test-on-Real paradigm and extended assessment of fairness and causal relationship preservation. Results show that BN achieves near-ideal fidelity, fairness and empirical privacy through distributional smoothing alone, while PATEGAN at $\varepsilon \geq 3.0$ represents a viable operating point combining formal differential privacy guarantees with acceptable utility, fairness and causal validity. In contrast, DPGAN exhibits severe empirical privacy, fairness and causal distortions, demonstrating that ε values alone are insufficient as a safety criterion. These findings offer practical guidance for institutions seeking GDPR-compliant and analytically reliable admissions data sharing.

Keywords: Synthetic Data Generation · Differential Privacy · Generative Adversarial Networks · Admission Process · Privacy-Preserving Data Sharing

R. Matulevičius et al. (Eds.): DB&IS 2026, CCIS 3085, pp. 203–218, 2026.
https://doi.org/10.1007/978-3-032-30863-4_13

1 Introduction

The increasing availability of digital records in higher education has created substantial opportunities for data-driven decision-making in international student admissions (ISA) [1–3]. ISA datasets contain rich applicant information, including demographic attributes, academic qualifications, language proficiency scores, and enrolment outcomes [4]. However, such data encompass personally identifiable information, imposing significant legal and ethical constraints on sharing and secondary use [5]. Regulations such as the General Data Protection Regulation (GDPR) strictly limit the processing of personal data, thereby restricting the ability of researchers to access and collaborate on real ISA records [6].

Synthetic data generation has emerged as a promising approach to address a tension between data utility and privacy preservation [7, 8]. Synthetic datasets replicate the statistical properties of original data without exposing individual records, enabling analysis while mitigating re-identification risks. Several generative modelling techniques have been proposed for tabular data synthesis, including Bayesian Networks (BN) [9], Conditional Tabular Generative Adversarial Networks (CTGAN) [10], and variational autoencoders (VAE) [11]. Differentially private variants, such as DPGAN [12] and PATE-GAN [13], further introduce calibrated noise during training to provide mathematically rigorous privacy bounds parameterized by a privacy budget ε (where smaller values of ε impose stricter privacy constraints) [14].

Despite these advancements, the application of synthetic data generation to admission datasets remains underexplored [15, 16]. ISA data present unique challenges due to mixed data types, high-cardinality features (e.g., citizenship, native language), substantial missing values, and inherent class imbalance in enrolment outcomes [17]. Moreover, the utility–privacy trade-off of differential privacy mechanisms in this domain has not been systematically investigated [18].

Therefore, the main research question is: to what extent do alternative synthetic data generation techniques for ISA data jointly achieve robust privacy protection while preserving statistical fidelity, downstream predictive utility, fairness, and causal relationships relevant for institutional analysis and decision-making?

To answer this question, we present a systematic analysis employing both non-private (BN, CTGAN) and differentially private (DPGAN, PATEGAN) models at varying privacy budgets ($\varepsilon \in \{0.1, 1.0, 2.0, 3.0, 5.0, 10.0\}$), evaluated through statistical fidelity metrics (inverse KL divergence, Jensen–Shannon distance, chi-squared test), privacy metrics (k-anonymity, δ-presence), and application-level utility via a Train-on-Synthetic, Test-on-Real paradigm [1, 19, 20]. The approach was applied to a real-world ISA dataset comprising 9,506 submitted applications with 15 features. The main contributions are as follows:

1. A structured data pre-processing workflow for ISA records addressing high-cardinality categorical encoding, derived feature extraction (e.g., CEFR-level mapping), and systematic missing value handling.
2. A comparative analysis of four generative models (two non-private, two differentially private) under multiple privacy budget configurations.

3. A multi-dimensional evaluation combining statistical fidelity, empirical privacy, downstream machine learning utility, and preservation of fairness and causal relationships.
4. Practical guidance for institutions seeking GDPR-compliant and analytically reliable ISA data sharing.

The remainder of this paper is organized as follows. Section 2 reviews related works. Section 3 describes the methodology. Section 4 presents the results. Section 5 discusses findings and limitations. Section 6 summarizes conclusions and future directions.

2 Related Works

2.1 Synthetic Data Generation for Privacy-Preserving Data Sharing

Unlike traditional anonymisation, which modifies original records and remains vulnerable to linkage attacks, synthetic data generation (SDG) has become a practical alternative for privacy-preserving data sharing under regulations such as the GDPR [6]. Recent surveys [8, 21] taxonomize SDG methods along a spectrum: from statistical models (BN [9], copulas [22]), through deep generative models (GANs [10], VAEs [11]), to emerging approaches based on diffusion models [23] and large language models [24]. While standard generative models can closely reproduce data distributions, they offer no formal privacy guarantees and may inadvertently memorize individual records [18]. This has motivated differentially private (DP) variants [25] that inject calibrated noise during training, bounding disclosure risk through a privacy budget ε at the cost of potential utility degradation [14, 18]. Despite extensive benchmarking in healthcare and finance [18, 21], education remains underexplored.

2.2 Non-private Generative Models for Tabular Data

Two major paradigms dominate non-private tabular data synthesis: probabilistic graphical models and deep generative adversarial models [7, 26]. Among probabilistic methods, BN have received particular attention for their interpretability. PrivBayes [9] approximates the joint distribution of a dataset by constructing a BN over low-dimensional conditional distributions, with an optional DP mechanism for structure learning. The same approach, without DP noise injection, is used in tools such as DataSynthesizer [27] and serves as a widely adopted non-private baseline [7, 21]. BN-based generators are valued for interpretability and computational efficiency; however, their scalability degrades with high-dimensional data as the number of possible network structures grows exponentially [17, 28].

CTGAN [10] extends the standard GAN framework with two tabular-specific innovations: a mode-specific normalization for continuous columns and a conditional generator addressing imbalanced categorical distributions via training-by-sampling. These design choices have made CTGAN as a de facto baseline in tabular data benchmarks [8, 21]. Xu et al. [10] also introduced a Tabular Variational Autoencoder (TVAE), a counterpart offering more stable training at the potential cost of less sharp distributions.

These two paradigms represent fundamentally different approaches to distribution learning, i.e., structure-based probabilistic modelling versus implicit adversarial training, and are therefore frequently compared [21, 29]. Therefore, we adopt one representative from each, i.e., BN and CTGAN, as non-private baselines.

2.3 Differentially Private Generative Models

While the non-private models (Sect. 2.2) can produce high-fidelity synthetic data, they offer no formal guarantees against memorization of individual records [18]. Differential privacy (DP) [25] addresses this by introducing calibrated noise during training, ensuring that the inclusion or exclusion of any single record has a bounded effect on model output, parameterized by a privacy budget ε, where lower values correspond to stronger protection at the cost of utility degradation [14]. The foundational mechanism for integrating DP into deep learning is Differentially Private Stochastic Gradient Descent (DP-SGD) [30], which clips per-sample gradients and adds Gaussian noise, with cumulative privacy expenditure tracked through the moments accountant [31].

DPGAN [12] integrates DP-SGD into the GAN framework by applying gradient perturbation to the discriminator, providing rigorous (ε, δ)-differential privacy guarantees. However, the added noise exacerbates training instability, particularly at low privacy budgets [18, 32], and because noise is added to each gradient component, its effective magnitude scales with input dimensionality [32]. Consequently, although DPGAN is theoretically attractive, its practical effectiveness depends on careful calibration of clipping thresholds, noise scales, and training duration.

PATEGAN [13] adopts an alternative architecture inspired by the Private Aggregation of Teacher Ensembles (PATE) framework. Instead of perturbing gradients directly, it partitions real data among teacher discriminators whose votes are aggregated with Laplacian noise, and a student discriminator then learns from these noisy labels. Since noise is added only to teacher outputs, whose dimension is independent of input dimensionality, this design avoids the scaling problem of gradient perturbation and yields more stable training dynamics [14].

The architectural distinction, i.e., gradient-level noise in DPGAN versus aggregation-level noise in PATEGAN, produces different sensitivity profiles across privacy budgets, making their systematic comparison at identical ε values a meaningful design choice [18]. Recent benchmarking confirms that no single DP synthesis method dominates across all evaluation dimensions [32]. Furthermore, DP mechanisms have been shown to have disparate impacts on class distributions: DP-SGD-based models tend to reduce class imbalance (a "Robin Hood" effect), while PATE-based models can amplify it (a "Matthew" effect) [33], a finding particularly relevant for ISA datasets with inherent enrolment outcome imbalance.

2.4 Synthetic Data in ISA

Synthetic data generation in education is only recently emerging as a distinct research area [1]. Early work evaluated non-private SDG methods on the Open University Learning Analytics Dataset (OULAD) [34], while subsequent studies combined synthetic generators with DP mechanisms on learning analytics datasets, showing that no single generator consistently outperformed others across all metrics [1]. Related efforts have investigated fairness–privacy interactions [35], finding that fairness-aware generators can improve demographic parity at the cost of predictive utility [36], compared CTGAN with transformer-based LLMs for synthetic student records, evaluated GAN-based generators with membership inference attacks [16], benchmarked multiple generators on European university data [15], and proposed diffusion-based frameworks jointly optimizing utility, fairness, and DP [36].

Despite this growing body of work, several limitations persist. First, many studies rely on general benchmarks rather than domain-specific institutional records [37]. Second, ISA data have not been addressed by any existing study, despite presenting unique challenges: mixed data types, high-cardinality categorical features, substantial missing values, inherent class imbalance, and direct GDPR implications [5, 6]. Third, no study has systematically compared both non-private and differentially private generators on the same educational dataset at multiple ε values using a comprehensive evaluation framework encompassing fidelity, privacy, and downstream utility.

The present study addresses these gaps by evaluating BN, CTGAN, DPGAN, and PATEGAN on a real European ISA dataset under multiple privacy budgets, assessed through statistical fidelity, empirical privacy, and Train-on-Synthetic, Test-on-Real classification.

2.5 Evaluation Methods

Evaluating synthetic tabular data requires a multidimensional framework [19]. Recent surveys converge on three core dimensions: statistical fidelity, privacy preservation, and downstream utility [21, 26], though no consensus exists on the optimal metric set for specific contexts [38].

Statistical fidelity quantifies distributional similarity between real and synthetic data using measures such as inverse KL divergence, Jensen–Shannon distance (JSD), and chi-squared tests [28]. Structural tools such as SDMetrics further assess column-level shapes and inter-column relationships [39].

Privacy preservation combines formal and empirical approaches. Formal (ε, δ)-differential privacy bounds disclosure risk at configuration time [25], while empirical metrics such as k-anonymity [40] and δ-presence [41] quantify re-identification risk from synthetic output. Critically, formal and empirical privacy can diverge, i.e., strong ε guarantees do not necessarily translate into low empirical re-identification risk [18, 32].

Downstream utility is most commonly assessed via the Train-on-Synthetic, Test-on-Real (TSTR) paradigm [1, 20, 38], where a classifier trained on synthetic data is evaluated on held-out real data and compared against a real-data-trained baseline. The performance gap quantifies utility loss, with smaller gaps indicating greater fidelity to the decision-relevant structure of the original dataset [14, 19].

Beyond these core dimensions, recent work highlights the importance of fairness and causal structure preservation [33, 35, 42]. DP mechanisms have been shown to produce disparate impacts on class distributions [33], and iterative synthetic training can amplify biases [35]. Toolkits such as Fairlearn [43] support disaggregated evaluation across protected attributes. Regarding causality, models optimized for distributional fidelity can converge on simpler causal structures than those in the real data [42], and tools such as DoWhy enable testing whether interventional relationships are preserved [44].

Despite the maturity of these evaluation dimensions, most studies in education apply only a subset and rarely incorporate fairness or causal assessments alongside fidelity–privacy–utility evaluation [5, 15, 16]. A comprehensive protocol combining all these dimensions on ISA records remains lacking.

3 Materials and Methods

This research follows a three-stage approach to investigate privacy-preserving synthetic data generation for ISA datasets (Fig. 1): (1) domain-specific pre-processing of raw ISA records, (2) synthetic data generation using non-private and differentially private models under multiple privacy budgets, and (3) evaluation of statistical fidelity, privacy, utility, fairness and causality.

3.1 Dataset Description

The experiments were conducted on a real-world ISA dataset obtained from a European university, comprising 21,198 international student applications spanning multiple admission cycles. Each record is described by 70 attributes grouped into eight categories: personal demographics (7), application metadata (9), contact and address (4), documents (3), educational background (22), language proficiency (4), employment history (5), and admission offer (16).

3.2 Data Pre-processing

A multi-step pre-processing pipeline (Fig. 1) was applied to prepare the raw dataset. 53 of the 70 attributes were removed to eliminate personally identifiable information (names, dates of birth), system identifiers, timestamps, high-cardinality free-text fields, and columns with excessive missing values, reducing the feature set to 17 attributes.

The dataset was filtered to retain only submitted applications ($n = 9{,}506$), excluding 11,692 inactive, withdrawn, and incomplete records. Scholarship and Accepted binary indicators were derived from offer fields. Value standardisation mapped education level codes and ISO 639 language codes to descriptive names and stripped country code prefixes. Feature transformation replaced the language list with a numeric count, split composite English test results into test type and CEFR level (A2–C2) and dropped the raw score column. Finally, three identifying columns were removed.

The final dataset comprised 9,506 records and 15 attributes: three demographic features (gender, citizenship, age), two education features (level, country), four language features (native language, knowledge count, English test type, CEFR level), four application features (term, course name, submission date, payment status), and two binary targets (scholarship, accepted). The dataset includes high-cardinality categorical features, with citizenship spanning 146 countries and 66 study programmes.

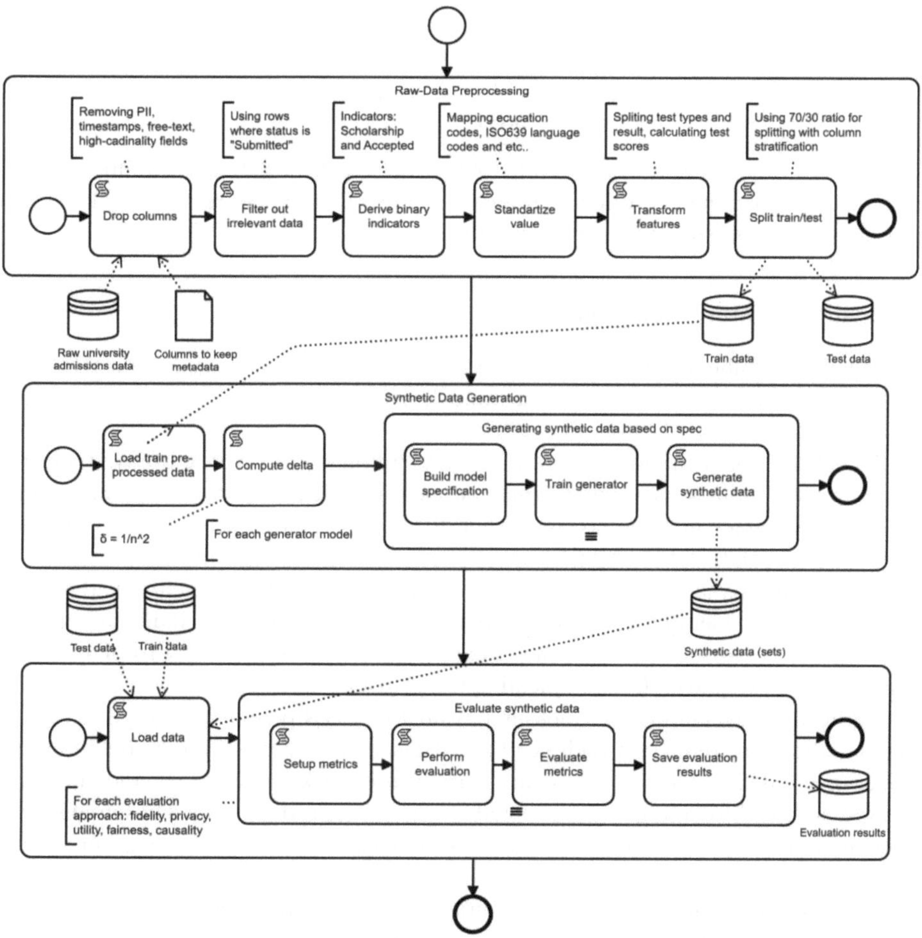

Fig. 1. The pipeline for comparing privacy-preserving synthetic data generation algorithms.

3.3 Training and Data Synthesis

All synthetic data generation experiments were conducted using the synthcity library (version 0.2.12) [45], which provides a unified interface for configuring, training, and sampling from multiple generative model families (see Fig. 1). The dataset was split into a 70% training set (n = 6,654) and a 30% held-out test set (n = 2,852), stratified by the Term attribute. Each generative model was trained exclusively on the training partition, and every synthetic dataset was sampled to contain 6,654 records, i.e., matching the training set size.

Four generative model families were employed. BN was configured with default synthcity settings, learning a directed acyclic graph via greedy hill-climbing with a BIC scoring function. CTGAN was trained for 1000 epochs with a patience parameter of 5, with remaining hyperparameters following synthcity defaults. DPGAN and PATEGAN were each configured under six privacy budgets, with δ set to the inverse square of the training set size (see Eq. 1).

$$\delta = \frac{1}{n^2} = \frac{1}{6654^2} \approx 2.26 \times 10^{-8} \quad (1)$$

Both DP models were trained for 1000 epochs with a patience parameter of 5. All other hyperparameters followed library defaults. Each model run was isolated in a separate subprocess subject to a 60-min timeout.

3.4 Synthetic Data Evaluation

The generated synthetic datasets were assessed along five dimensions: statistical fidelity, privacy preservation, downstream machine learning utility [45], fairness [43] and causality [44].

To evaluate statistical fidelity following distribution metrics were employed: inverse KL divergence (values closer to 1.0 indicate near-identical distributions), chi-squared test (higher p-values indicate no significant difference), and Jensen–Shannon distance (bounded between 0 and 1). All metrics were averaged across columns.

To evaluate privacy, two metrics were evaluated. k-Anonymity measures the minimum group size under quasi-identifier groupings, with higher values indicating greater re-identification resistance. δ-Presence quantifies re-identification risk from synthetic output, with values closer to 1.0 indicating lower disclosure.

Application-level utility was measured using the TSTR paradigm. A logistic regression classifier was trained on each synthetic dataset and evaluated on the held-out real test set (n = 2,852), performing a binary classification task to predict whether an applicant was accepted for admission (accepted: yes/no). A real-data-trained baseline served as the upper-bound reference, with utility loss defined as the difference in accuracy and weighted F1-score between classifiers.

Fairness was evaluated using Demographic Parity Difference (DPD) (maximum difference in positive outcome rates between demographic groups) across gender, citizenship, and age group. For each attribute, both the DPD value and its absolute deviation (Δ) from the training baseline were used to quantify fairness preservation.

Causal preservation was assessed using a causal inference framework by examining three relationships: English test performance – outcome, age – outcome, and language knowledge – outcome, under appropriate confounder control. Average Treatment Effects were estimated using linear regression, with causal fidelity quantified through absolute and relative deviations from real-data baseline effects.

4 Results

The real-data baseline logistic regression classifier achieved accuracy of 0.880 and weighted F1 = 0.881 on the held-out test set (n = 2,852), serving as the upper-bound reference for all utility comparisons. The comparative performance of the evaluated models across statistical similarity, privacy, and utility metrics is presented in Fig. 2.

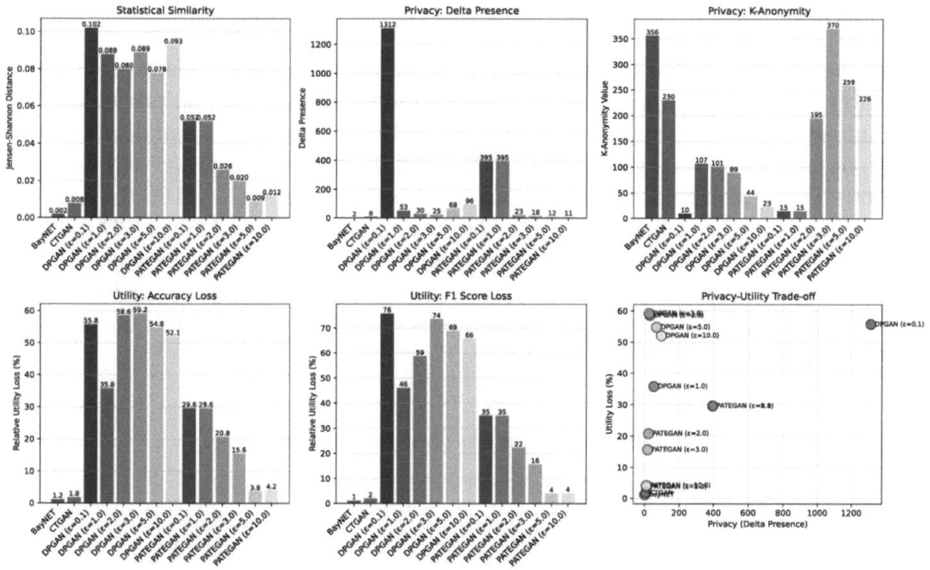

Fig. 2. Synthetic data generation: key performance metrics comparison. Colours denote models: brown – BayNET; green – CTGAN; blue shades – DPGAN and orange shades – PATEGAN where lighter shades indicate higher privacy budgets (ε = 0.1, 1, 2, 3, 5, 10).

4.1 Statistical Fidelity, Privacy Preservation, and Downstream Utility

Figure 2 summarises performance across statistical fidelity, empirical privacy, and downstream utility. The following discussion highlights key patterns.

BN achieved the strongest results across all three dimensions: near-perfect fidelity (inv. KL = 0.997, JS = 0.002), near-ideal empirical privacy (δ-presence: 1.09–1.29, k-anonymity: 294–356), and the lowest utility loss (ΔAcc. = 0.012). CTGAN performed comparably in fidelity and utility but with weaker empirical privacy and no formal guarantees.

PATEGAN exhibited a coherent, monotonic trade-off: all three dimensions improved systematically with increasing ε, approaching non-private quality at $\varepsilon \geq 3.0$. An ε-saturation effect was observed at $\varepsilon \leq 1.0$, where both budget levels produced near-identical results, indicating that aggregation noise dominates the learning signal under strict privacy budgets.

DPGAN presented the most problematic profile, with consistently poor fidelity (inv. KL: 0.233–0.490), unstable utility (accuracy: 0.347–0.610), and no monotonic relationship between ε and any metric. Most critically, it exhibited paradoxical empirical privacy failures (δ-presence exceeding 1,400 at ε = 0.1), indicating that gradient-level noise destabilises convergence before meaningful distributions are learned while still permitting partial memorisation. These results demonstrate that formal DP guarantees are necessary but not sufficient for practical privacy preservation on high-cardinality tabular data.

4.2 Fairness

The fairness results (Table 1) revealed a critical trade-off between privacy preservation and fairness maintenance in synthetic data generation. Among the non-private models, BN remains closest to the training baseline overall, with only very small deviations for age group ($\Delta = 0.011$) and gender ($\Delta = 0.013$), while citizenship is preserved exactly ($\Delta = 0.000$). The near-universal preservation of citizenship fairness ($\Delta \approx 0.000$) reflects the extreme class imbalance in this attribute: the training set already exhibits DPD = 1.000, meaning one dominant category receives nearly all positive outcomes, a pattern that most generative models replicate trivially. CTGAN also preserves citizenship exactly but introduces a larger deviation for age group ($\Delta = 0.131$) and a moderate deviation for gender ($\Delta = 0.062$).

Table 1. DPD across sensitive attributes.

Dataset	Age Group		Citizenship		Gender	
	DPD	Δ	DPD	Δ	DPD	Δ
Train	0.397	0.000	1.000	0.000	0.099	0.000
BN	0.386	0.011	1.000	0.000	0.086	0.013
CTGAN	0.528	0.131	1.000	0.000	0.036	0.062
DPGAN (ε = 0.1)	0.000	0.397	0.002	0.998	0.000	0.099
DPGAN (ε = 1.0)	0.003	0.394	1.000	0.000	0.080	0.019
DPGAN (ε = 2.0)	0.207	0.190	1.000	0.000	0.135	0.036
DPGAN (ε = 3.0)	0.285	0.112	0.500	0.500	0.040	0.059
DPGAN (ε = 5.0)	0.043	0.354	1.000	0.000	0.019	0.080
DPGAN (ε = 10.0)	0.077	0.319	1.000	0.000	0.076	0.023
PATEGAN (ε = 0.1)	0.115	0.282	1.000	0.000	0.093	0.006
PATEGAN (ε = 1.0)	0.115	0.282	1.000	0.000	0.093	0.006
PATEGAN (ε = 2.0)	0.151	0.246	1.000	0.000	0.039	0.059
PATEGAN (ε = 3.0)	0.244	0.153	1.000	0.000	0.175	0.076
PATEGAN (ε = 5.0)	0.438	0.041	1.000	0.000	0.113	0.014
PATEGAN (ε = 10.0)	0.368	0.029	1.000	0.000	0.114	0.015

In contrast, the differentially private models are less stable. DPGAN shows the strongest distortions, particularly for citizenship at $\varepsilon = 0.1$ (DPD = 0.002, $\Delta = 0.998$) and $\varepsilon = 3.0$ (DPD = 0.500, $\Delta = 0.500$), where heavy noise disrupts even trivially imbalanced distributions, and also substantial deviations for age group across several privacy budgets. PATEGAN behaves more consistently than DPGAN: it preserves citizenship exactly in most settings, while deviations for age group decrease as ε increases, reaching $\Delta = 0.041$ at $\varepsilon = 5.0$ and $\Delta = 0.029$ at $\varepsilon = 10.0$. For gender, most models remain relatively close to the baseline, although some distortion is still visible, particularly for DPGAN at $\varepsilon = 0.1$ and PATEGAN at $\varepsilon = 3.0$.

Overall, BN provides the strongest fairness preservation, PATEGAN offers a more robust differentially private alternative, and DPGAN produces the least reliable fairness behaviour.

4.3 Causality

Causality evaluation results (Fig. 3) show that preservation of the baseline causal effects varies substantially across synthetic data generators. Among the non-private models, BN remains closest to the training-data baseline overall, with small absolute differences across all three analysed relationships: 0.003 for English test → outcome, 0.001 for age → outcome, and 0.012 for language knowledge → outcome, corresponding to relative differences of 13.141%, 6.670%, and 18.658%, respectively. CTGAN also preserves the effect directions and remains reasonably close to the baseline, although its deviations are consistently larger than those of BN, with relative differences of 30.400%, 12.272%, and 20.333% across the three relationships. In contrast, DPGAN exhibits the weakest causal preservation, with several configurations showing very large relative deviations and, in some cases, reversals in effect direction; for example, at $\varepsilon = 0.1$, the English test → outcome effect changes from − 0.022 in the real/training data to 0.001, while at $\varepsilon = 10.0$, the language knowledge → outcome effect changes from 0.065 to − 0.067, with a relative difference of 203.00%. PATEGAN shows intermediate behaviour: some settings remain relatively close to the baseline, such as age → outcome at $\varepsilon = 10.0$ (CE = − 0.022, AD = 0.000, RD = 0.053%) and age → outcome at $\varepsilon = 5.0$ (AD = 0.003, RD = 14.962%), whereas other settings still show notable deviations, such as English test → outcome at $\varepsilon = 3.0$ (RD = 159.76%).

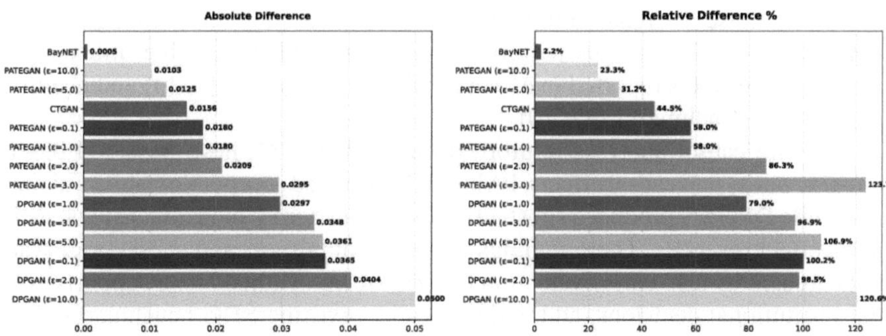

Fig. 3. Causal effect preservation score: comparison of absolute difference (left chart) with relative difference (right chart). Colours and model configurations are consistent with Fig. 1.

These findings underscore a critical limitation in the synthetic data literature: standard privacy-utility metrics (e.g., statistical similarity) poorly capture causal validity, and synthetic datasets achieving high scores on conventional benchmarks may nevertheless corrupt causal relationships essential for downstream causal discovery and effect estimation tasks. We conclude that applications requiring causal inference should prioritize non-private synthetic generation methods or accept substantial epistemic uncertainty when deploying privacy-preserving synthetic data, and advocate for causal preservation metrics to become standard evaluation criteria in synthetic data quality assessment frameworks.

5 Discussion

The results confirm that privacy-preserving synthetic data generation is applicable to ISA records, but model choice and privacy budget substantially shape the trade-off. BN's strong performance is attributable to its structure-based learning, which approximates joint distributions through probabilistic smoothing rather than memorising individual records, a property directly relevant for GDPR-aligned risk reduction [5]. CTGAN achieves comparable fidelity and utility but lacks formal privacy guarantees, limiting suitability for cross-institutional sharing.

The most significant finding concerns DPGAN's empirical failure despite strong formal guarantees. DP-SGD injects noise proportional to gradient dimensionality, which on high-cardinality tabular data destabilises adversarial convergence before the generator learns meaningful distributions, while still permitting partial memorisation. This demonstrates that formal DP guarantees are necessary but not sufficient, making empirical privacy evaluation indispensable – a conclusion corroborated by Sarmin et al. [17] and Chen et al. [31]. For policy, this implies that treating ε alone as a GDPR compliance proxy is insufficient; empirical re-identification auditing is required alongside formal certification.

PATEGAN's superior performance stems from applying noise only to teacher vote aggregation, whose dimensionality is independent of input features. Under strict budgets ($\varepsilon \leq 1.0$), aggregation noise dominates the learning signal, requiring extended training for meaningful convergence, explaining both the ε-saturation effect and epoch dependency. At $\varepsilon \geq 3.0$, the noise-to-signal ratio permits effective learning, representing the viable operating region for institutions requiring formal DP with acceptable utility, in line with practical thresholds reported in educational DP benchmarks [1, 14] and healthcare tabular synthesis benchmarks [17, 20].

Fairness and causal analyses reinforced this ranking. BN best preserved baseline demographic parity and causal effects, PATEGAN provided acceptable stability at higher ε values, while DPGAN produced substantial distortions across both dimensions, including causal effect reversals. These findings indicate that fairness and causal preservation should be treated as first-class evaluation criteria where synthetic data supports consequential institutional decisions, addressing a gap in existing SDG benchmarks [7, 20] that evaluate fidelity and utility but rarely include fairness or causal validity.

To answer the research question: BN and PATEGAN (at $\varepsilon \geq 3.0$) jointly offer the most practical path for ISA data sharing, with selection depending on whether formal DP guarantees are institutionally required. Limitations include evaluation on a single dataset from one institution, exclusive use of logistic regression in TSTR, and reliance on default hyperparameters; BN's smoothing advantage and PATEGAN's $\varepsilon \geq 3.0$ threshold may both shift on larger, more heterogeneous datasets or alternative classifier benchmarks.

Computational cost is also relevant for practical applicability. On our test machine (Intel i7-11800H, 32 GB RAM, NVIDIA T1200, CUDA 12.8), the full pipeline required approximately 200 min under the 1000-epoch configuration. These runtimes are feasible for research but may limit operational deployment at scale.

6 Conclusions and Future Works

This study evaluated four synthetic data generation approaches (BN, CTGAN, DPGAN, PATEGAN) on ISA data (9,506 records, 15 attributes) across statistical fidelity, empirical privacy, and downstream machine learning utility, fairness, and causal relationship preservation under multiple privacy budgets.

The findings confirm that synthetic data generation is feasible for this domain, though the trade-off is strongly model-dependent. BN yielded high utility and favourable empirical privacy, and the most consistent preservation of fairness and causal structure through distributional smoothing. PATEGAN achieved the most robust DP profile, approaching non-private quality at $\varepsilon \geq 3.0$ while providing a more stable fairness profile than DPGAN. In contrast, DPGAN exhibited elevated δ-presence despite stringent budgets, alongside substantial fairness distortions and weak causal preservation, confirming that formal guarantees alone are insufficient for practical privacy-preserving data release. The ε-saturation regime at low budgets further implies that training duration is critical for PATE-based methods.

Future work should validate the framework on multi-institutional ISA datasets, extend privacy assessment with membership inference attacks, and broaden the comparison set to include RTVAE, RadialGAN, and diffusion-based generators. It should also further investigate fairness-aware and causality-preserving synthesis strategies, as well as expand downstream evaluation beyond logistic regression to better reflect the requirements of consequential institutional analysis. Further research is needed to identify methods for explicitly controlling fairness and causal structure during synthetic data generation, rather than assessing these properties only after data have been produced.

Acknowledgments. These results are part of the project "Artificial intelligence and multimodal data fusion system for assessing and detecting fraud in applicants' videos" (FAIR-VID), which is funded by the Research Council of Lithuania (LMTLT), agreement No. S-ITP-25-14.

Disclosure of Interests. The authors declare no conflicts of interest.

References

1. Liu, Q., Shakya, R., Jovanovic, J., Khalil, M., de la Hoz-Ruiz, J.: Ensuring privacy through synthetic data generation in education. Br. J. Edu. Technol. **56**, 1053–1073 (2025). https://doi.org/10.1111/bjet.13576
2. Bilal, M., Omar, M., Anwar, W., Bokhari, R.H., Choi, G.S.: Bridging the gap: from traditional admissions to data-driven insights for predicting and supporting undergraduate performance. Educ. Inf. Technol. **30**, 27085–27110 (2025). https://doi.org/10.1007/s10639-025-13820-1
3. Laukaitis, A., et al.: FAIR-VID: a multimodal pre-processing pipeline for student application analysis. Appl. Sci. **15**(24), 13127 (2025). https://doi.org/10.3390/APP152413127

4. Jin, X., Ruegg, R., Coxhead, A.: From entry to excellence: exploring relationships between admission pathways, disciplinary areas of study, and EAL international undergraduate students' academic success in New Zealand. J. Engl. Acad. Purp. **75**, 101517 (2025). https://doi.org/10.1016/j.jeap.2025.101517
5. Liu, Q., Khalil, M.: Understanding privacy and data protection issues in learning analytics using a systematic review. Br. J. Edu. Technol. **54**, 1715–1747 (2023). https://doi.org/10.1111/bjet.13388
6. Beduschi, A.: Synthetic data protection: towards a paradigm change in data regulation? Big Data Soc. **11**(1) (2024), https://doi.org/10.1177/20539517241231277
7. Koubeissy, H., Amine, A., Kamradt, M., Makhoul, A.: Survey on tabular data privacy and synthetic data generation in industry 4.0. Appl. Intell. **55**(13), 935 (2025). https://doi.org/10.1007/s10489-025-06823-5
8. Shi, R., Wang, Y., Du, M., Shen, X., Chang, Y., Wang, X.: A comprehensive survey of synthetic tabular data generation. arXiv:2504.16506 (2025). https://doi.org/10.48550/arXiv.2504.16506
9. Zhang, J., Cormode, G., Procopiuc, C.M., Srivastava, D., Xiao, X.: PrivBayes: private data release via bayesian networks. ACM Trans. Database Syst. (TODS) **42** (2017). https://doi.org/10.1145/3134428
10. Xu, L., Skoularidou, M., Cuesta-Infante, A., Veeramachaneni, K.: Modeling tabular data using conditional GAN. In: 33rd Conference on Neural Information Processing Systems Proceedings (NeurIPS 2019), pp. 1–11, Vancouver, Canada (2019)
11. Kingma, D.P., Welling, M.: Auto-Encoding Variational Bayes. arXiv preprint arXiv:1312.6114 (2013)
12. Xie, L., Lin, K., Wang, S., Wang, F., Zhou, J.: Differentially private generative adversarial network. arXiv:1802.06739 (2018)
13. Jordon, J., Yoon, J., Van Der Schaar, M.: PATE-GAN: generating synthetic data with differential privacy guarantees. In: International Conference on Learning Representations. ICLR, pp. 1–21 (2019)
14. Pereira, M., Kshirsagar, M., Mukherjee, S., Dodhia, R., Ferres, J.L., de Sousa, R.: Assessment of differentially private synthetic data for utility and fairness in end-to-end machine learning pipelines for tabular data. PLoS ONE **19**(2), e0297271 (2024). https://doi.org/10.1371/journal.pone.0297271
15. Kostopoulos, G., Tsiakmaki, M., Kotsiantis, S.: Benchmarking statistical and deep generative models for privacy-preserving synthetic student data in educational data mining. Algorithms **19**(1), 39 (2026). https://doi.org/10.3390/a19010039
16. Iloh, D., Temitope Olayinka, O., Iyere, F., Chilakala, S.: Generative private synthetic student data for learning analytics: an empirical study. IEEE Access **13**, 177345–177351 (2025). https://doi.org/10.1109/ACCESS.2025.3619091
17. Wang, A.X., Chukova, S.S., Simpson, C.R., Nguyen, B.P.: Challenges and opportunities of generative models on tabular data. Appl. Soft Comput. **166**, 112223 (2024). https://doi.org/10.1016/j.asoc.2024.112223
18. Sarmin, F.J., Sarkar, A.R., Wang, Y., Mohammed, N.: Synthetic data: revisiting the privacy-utility trade-off. Int. J. Inf. Secur. **24**(4), 156 (2025). https://doi.org/10.1007/s10207-025-01072-6
19. Hernandez, M., Epelde, G., Alberdi, A., Cilla, R., Rankin, D.: Synthetic tabular data evaluation in the health domain covering resemblance, utility, and privacy dimensions. Methods Inf. Med. **62**(S 01), e19-e38 (2023). https://doi.org/10.1055/s-0042-1760247
20. Qian, Z., Callender, T., Cebere, B., Janes, S.M., Navani, N., van der Schaar, M.: Synthetic data for privacy-preserving clinical risk prediction. Sci. Rep. **14**(1), 25676 (2024). https://doi.org/10.1038/s41598-024-72894-y

21. Lautrup, A.D., Hyrup, T., Zimek, A., Schneider-Kamp, P.: Systematic review of generative modelling tools and utility metrics for fully synthetic tabular data. ACM Comput. Surv. **57**(4), 1–38 (2024). https://doi.org/10.1145/3704437
22. Restrepo, J.P., Rivera, J.C., Laniado, H., Osorio, P., Becerra, O.A.: Nonparametric generation of synthetic data using copulas. Electronics **12**(7), 1601 (2023). https://doi.org/10.3390/electronics12071601
23. Kotelnikov, A., Baranchuk, D., Rubachev, I., Babenko, A.: TabDDPM: modelling tabular data with diffusion models. In: the 40th International Conference on Machine Learning, PMLR 202, pp. 17564–17579. MLResearchPress (2023). https://doi.org/10.5555/3618408.3619133
24. Borisov, V., Seßler, K., Leemann, T., Pawelczyk, M., Kasneci, G.: Language Models Are Realistic Tabular Data Generators. arXiv:2210.06280 (2023)
25. Dwork, C., Roth, A.: The algorithmic foundations of differential privacy. Found. Trends® Theor. Comput. Sci. **9**(3–4), 211–487 (2014). https://doi.org/10.1561/0400000042
26. Restrepo, M.F.D., Wollmer, B., Panse, F., Wingerath, W.: Benchmarking tabular data synthesis: evaluating tools, metrics, and datasets on prosumer hardware for end-users. Data Sci. J. **24** (2025). https://doi.org/10.5334/dsj-2025-037
27. Ping, H., Stoyanovich, J., Howe, B.: DataSynthesizer: privacy-preserving synthetic datasets. In: the 29th International Conference on Scientific and Statistical Database Management Proceedings, New York, NY, USA, pp. 1–5 (2017). https://doi.org/10.1145/3085504.3091117
28. Hyrup, T., Lautrup, A.D., Zimek, A., Schneider-Kamp, P.: A systematic review of privacy-preserving techniques for synthetic tabular health data. Discov. Data **3**, 5 (2025). https://doi.org/10.1007/s44248-025-00022-w
29. Drechsler, J.. Haensch, A.C.: 30 years of synthetic data **39**, 221–242 (2024). https://doi.org/10.1214/24-STS927
30. Abadi, M., et al.: Deep learning with differential privacy. In: the 2016 ACM SIGSAC Conference on Computer and Communications Security Proceedings, pp. 308–318. ACM, New York, USA (2016)
31. Mohammadi, M., et al..: Differential privacy for medical deep learning: methods, tradeoffs, and deployment implications. npj Digit. Med. **9**, 93 (2026). https://doi.org/10.1038/s41746-025-02280-z
32. Chen, K., Li, X., Gong, C., Mckenna, R., Wang, T.: Benchmarking differentially private tabular data synthesis: [experiments & analysis]. ACM Manag. Data **3**(6), 1–25 (2025). https://doi.org/10.1145/3769764
33. Ganev, G., Oprisanu, B., De Cristofaro, E.: Robin hood and Matthew effects: differential privacy has disparate impact on synthetic data. In: the 39th International Conference on Machine Learning Proceedings (PMLR), vol. 162, pp. 6944–6959 (2022)
34. Liu, Q., Khalil, M., Jovanovic, J., Shakya, R.: Scaling while privacy preserving: a comprehensive synthetic tabular data generation and evaluation in learning analytics. In: the 14th Learning Analytics and Knowledge Conference Proceedings, pp. 620–631. ACM, New York, USA (2024)
35. Wyllie, S., Shumailov, I., Papernot, N.: Fairness feedback loops: training on synthetic data amplifies bias. In: The 2024 ACM Conference on Fairness, Accountability, and Transparency (FAccT '24) Proceedings, pp. 2113–2147. ACM, New York, USA (2024)
36. Kesgin, K.: FairSYN-Edu a diffusion-based model for fair and private educational data synthesis. Discov. Educ. **4**, 336 (2025). https://doi.org/10.1007/s44217-025-00743-9
37. Švábenský, V., Flanagan, B., López Zapata, E.D., Shimada, A.: Open datasets in learning analytics: trends, challenges, and best PRACTICE. ACM Trans. Knowl. Discov. Data **20**(4), 1–56 (2026). https://doi.org/10.1145/3798096
38. Hernandez, M., Osorio-Marulanda, P.A., Catalina, M., Loinaz, L., Epelde, G., Aginako, N.: Comprehensive evaluation framework for synthetic tabular data in health: fidelity, utility and

privacy analysis of generative models with and without privacy guarantees. Front. Digit. Health **7**, 1576290 (2025). https://doi.org/10.3389/fdgth.2025.1576290
39. Patki, N., Wedge, R., Veeramachaneni, K.: The synthetic data vault. In: IEEE International Conference on Data Science and Advanced Analytics (DSAA 2016) Proceedings, pp. 399–410. IEEE, Montreal, QC, Canada (2016), https://doi.org/10.1109/DSAA.2016.49
40. Sweeney, L.: K-anonymity: a model for protecting privacy. Int. J. Uncertain. Fuzziness Knowl.-Based Syst. **10**(05), 557–570 (2002)
41. Nergiz, M.E., Atzori, M., Clifton, C.: Hiding the presence of individuals from shared databases. In Proceedings of the Proceedings of the 2007 ACM SIGMOD International Conference on Management of Data, 11 June 2007, pp. 665–676. ACM, New York, NY, USA (2007)
42. Bauwelinckx, Y.C., Dhaene, J., van den Heuvel, M., Verdonck, T.: On the causality-preservation capabilities of generative modelling. J. Comput. Appl. Math. **457**, 116312 (2025). https://doi.org/10.1016/j.cam.2024.116312
43. Bird, S., et al.: Fairlearn: a toolkit for assessing and improving fairness in AI, https://www.microsoft.com/en-us/research/wp-content/uploads/2020/05/Fairlearn_WhitePaper-2020-09-22.pdf. Accessed 8 May 2026
44. Sharma, A., Kiciman, E.: DoWhy: an end-to-end library for causal inference. arXiv preprint arXiv:2011.04216 (2020)
45. Vanderschaarlab/Synthcity, A Library for Generating and Evaluating Synthetic Tabular Data for Privacy, Fairness and Data Augmentation. https://github.com/vanderschaarlab/synthcity. Accessed 27 Feb 2026

Integrating Data Science into K–12 Education: A Spiral Curriculum Model

Kairi Osula(✉) and Mart Laanpere

Tallinn University, Tallinn, Estonia
{kairi.osula,mart.laanpere}@tlu.ee

Abstract. Current approaches to teaching introductory data science in schools are often fragmented across subjects and grade levels. This paper proposes a spiral curriculum model for integrating data science elements into existing STEM courses in primary and secondary education. We discuss curriculum design principles and pedagogical conditions for effective implementation, including a concepts - first instructional design, differentiated task design, and collaborative interpretation of results. Drawing on interviews with teachers, we identify practical constraints and professional development needs. The proposed framework contributes a curriculum-level perspective to ongoing discussions on early data science education, bridging the gap between isolated classroom or extracurricular initiatives and a coherent K–12 learning architecture.

Keywords: Data Science Education · K–12 Curriculum · Data Literacy · Spiral Curriculum · Computational Thinking

1 Introduction

The growing role of data and artificial intelligence in contemporary society has fundamentally reshaped what it means to be an informed participant in social, economic, and civic life. As data-driven analyses, algorithmic models, and automated decision-making systems increasingly underpin public and private decisions, it is no longer sufficient to consume information passively. Individuals must understand how data are generated, collected, analyzed, and interpreted - and must be able to critically evaluate data-driven claims encountered in everyday life. In this context, data literacy has emerged as a core competency for twenty-first century citizenship [1]. Despite this growing recognition, the integration of data science into K–12 education remains inconsistent. In many educational systems, data-related learning occurs through isolated projects, short-term initiatives, or elective courses that introduce important ideas but do not support the gradual, cumulative development of data literacy across school years. Without a coherent developmental structure, students may repeatedly encounter introductory activities without progressing toward deeper analytical understanding or more sophisticated practices.

R. Matulevičius et al. (Eds.): DB&IS 2026, CCIS 3085, pp. 219–233, 2026.
https://doi.org/10.1007/978-3-032-30863-4_14

This challenge is particularly visible in the Estonian context. While national strategies emphasize digital competence and data literacy as policy priorities, practical implementation within school curricula remains limited. In the mathematics curriculum, data-related topics are largely addressed through traditional descriptive statistics and probability theory. Where data analysis does appear more prominently - such as in upper secondary research projects - the emphasis often shifts toward formal aspects of research reporting rather than toward authentic engagement with datasets, pattern discovery, or computational tools. Students may thus develop skills in presenting findings while having fewer opportunities to explore data, test models, or reason computationally. The core challenge, therefore, is not simply the absence of data-related content in school curricula, but the lack of a coherent developmental model that connects such content into a structured learning pathway across grade levels and subjects.

This article addresses that challenge by proposing a spiral curriculum model for integrating data science elements into K–12 education within existing subjects, particularly mathematics and computer science, without introducing a new mandatory discipline. The model is grounded in three structural principles: spiral revisiting of core data science concepts with increasing analytical depth; the reciprocal development of statistical reasoning and computational thinking; and the use of the data science investigative process as an organizing structure for learning activities.

The central research question guiding this study is: how can data science elements be systematically integrated into the K–12 curriculum in a way that creates a coherent developmental pathway between and within mathematics and computer science, supports the reciprocal development of statistical and computational thinking, and operates within existing school subjects without introducing a new mandatory discipline?

This paper contributes a theory-informed curriculum framework that integrates these elements into a coherent K–12 progression.

2 Data Science Education in the K–12 Context

2.1 Data Literacy and Statistical Thinking in School Education

Research on students' development of statistical reasoning has a substantial history in mathematics education. Studies consistently demonstrate that statistical thinking cannot be reduced to computational proficiency alone - it involves the ability to formulate meaningful questions, reason under uncertainty, and draw conclusions from data in context [2]. A central insight from this body of work is that understanding develops through repeated engagement with data investigations rather than through procedural instruction alone.

The GAISE II framework [3] reflects this perspective at the curriculum level, conceptualizing statistical thinking as a progressive learning process that begins in early schooling. Rather than emphasizing mechanical calculation, GAISE II foregrounds data exploration, question formulation, and interpretation - an inquiry orientation that has since become widely influential in statistics education research and curriculum design.

In parallel, the concept of statistical literacy has expanded toward the broader notion of data literacy. Beyond traditional statistical skills, data literacy encompasses the ability to assess the provenance and quality of data, understand the contexts in which data are generated, and critically evaluate data-driven claims in media and public discourse [4, 5]. This broader framing positions data literacy not only as an academic competency but as a civic skill increasingly necessary for informed participation in contemporary society.

The emergence of data science as a field has further extended these discussions. Data science is typically characterized as an interdisciplinary domain integrating statistics, computer science, and domain knowledge to identify meaningful patterns and support evidence-based decision-making [1, 6]. Crucially, data science is not a collection of isolated techniques but a holistic investigative process - one that moves iteratively through stages of question formulation, data collection and preparation, exploratory analysis, modeling, visualization, and interpretation [7].

From an educational perspective, this process orientation has important implications. Learning data science elements requires students to develop not only statistical reasoning but also computational thinking, facility with digital tools, and the capacity to critically evaluate data-driven conclusions. Contemporary research increasingly emphasizes that these competencies develop most effectively in combination - through authentic data investigations where statistical and computational perspectives reinforce one another [1].

2.2 Data Science Education Initiatives

Over the past decade, a growing number of educational initiatives have sought to bring data science elements into school education. While they differ in scope and approach, several are particularly instructive for curriculum design.

Data 8: Foundations of Data Science [8], developed at UC Berkeley, introduced key data science practices - visualization, statistical inference, and predictive modeling - through authentic datasets and computational tools. Though originally designed for higher education, it has influenced secondary curriculum design considerably [9].

Bootstrap: Data Science takes a complementary approach, integrating programming and data analysis within a unified learning environment. Research on Bootstrap has demonstrated that, with appropriate scaffolding, foundational data science ideas are accessible even in elementary school contexts [10].

Other initiatives have foregrounded the civic dimensions of data science. The DataScEd4CiEn project [11], for instance, engages students in using data analysis to investigate environmental and public health issues, developing both analytical skills and critical awareness of data-driven claims in public debate. In the European context, the ProDaBi project [12] has developed competency models and teaching materials that connect data literacy with critical reflection on the social and economic contexts in which data are produced and used.

The Introduction to Data Science (IDS) project [13], aimed at high school education, provides another model for integrating data-driven inquiry into STEM subjects. Students in IDS engage with spatial, temporal, and textual datasets - often collected through digital sensors or mobile technologies - while simultaneously developing competencies in data representation, algorithmic problem-solving, and statistical modeling.

The above-mentioned initiatives demonstrate both the feasibility and the value of introducing data science elements into school education. At the same time, most remain focused on specific courses, tools, or pilot contexts. The broader question of how to develop data science learning systematically across the entire K–12 trajectory - as a coherent and developmental curriculum architecture - remains largely unaddressed.

2.3 Research Gaps and the Need for a Curriculum-Level Perspective

Recent reviews have noted that research on data science education is distributed across several academic fields, including statistics education, computer science education, and the learning sciences, with limited integration across these communities [14]. This fragmentation reflects the interdisciplinary nature of the field but also means that insights remain siloed and that broader curriculum-level questions are rarely addressed.

Existing initiatives provide valuable evidence of what is possible in individual classrooms and specific courses. What is missing, however, is a conceptual model that explains how statistical reasoning, computational thinking, and data-driven inquiry can be developed together across the full span of K–12 education. In particular, the literature offers limited guidance on how to structure a curriculum that is both developmentally coherent - building progressively on prior learning - and practically sustainable within the constraints of existing school subjects and timetables.

This gap forms the starting point of the present study. The following section introduces a spiral curriculum model designed to address it, proposing a framework for integrating data science elements into existing subjects in a manner that supports continuous and progressive development of data literacy from early primary through to upper secondary education.

3 Framework for Introducing Data Science in K–12 Education

The research gap identified in the previous section points to a need that goes beyond the design of individual lessons or courses. What is required is a curriculum-level framework - one that organizes data science learning progressively across school years while remaining compatible with existing subjects and instructional practices. Next, we introduce such a framework, built around three structural principles that together provide the conceptual foundation for the spiral curriculum model proposed in Sect. 4. Rather than introducing data science as a separate subject, the model conceptualizes it as a cross-disciplinary topic that develops gradually within mathematics and computer science education. This integration strategy reflects both practical realities (school curricula tend to change once in a decade) and a substantive educational argument: data science competencies are most meaningfully developed when statistical and computational thinking are learned together, in the context of real problems, rather than in disciplinary isolation.

The first principle of our framework - spiral progression of conceptual development - draws on Bruner's concept of the spiral curriculum [15], in which central ideas are revisited across multiple stages of schooling with increasing levels of conceptual depth and abstraction. Applied to data science education, this means that a small set of foundational concepts recurs throughout the K–12 pathway, each time approached with more sophisticated analytical tools and representations. Four conceptual categories provide the organizing spine of this progression:

- patterns - recognizing regularities and anomalies in data
- relationships - understanding how variables interact and covary
- classification - grouping observations according to shared properties
- models - constructing simplified representations that capture important features of data

These categories are not arbitrary. They represent ideas that recur across nearly every domain of data science practice, from exploratory data analysis to machine learning, and they are tractable at every level of schooling - from sorting objects in Grade 1 to building predictive models in Grade 12. In early grades, students encounter these ideas through concrete, intuitive activities: sorting objects into categories, organizing classroom survey results, or identifying visible patterns in simple charts. At later stages, the same conceptual ideas reemerge in more formal analytical contexts. Patterns and relationships may be explored through correlation analysis or regression; classification through clustering or introductory machine learning tasks; models through formal predictive frameworks. This spiral structure allows learners to build on prior knowledge while progressively deepening their understanding of how data can be analyzed and interpreted.

The second principle - reciprocal development of statistical and computational thinking - concerns the relationship between the two disciplines most central to data science education: mathematics and computer science. Traditionally, statistical thinking has been located within mathematics education, while algorithmic thinking and programming have belonged to computer science. In practice, however, contemporary data science requires these competencies to work together - statistical questions are explored through computational tools, and computational processes are evaluated using statistical reasoning. The framework therefore proposes that data science thinking develops most effectively when statistical and computational perspectives are deliberately coordinated within the curriculum, rather than developed separately and left for students to integrate on their own. Within this structure, mathematics education primarily contributes to the development of statistical reasoning, understanding of variability and uncertainty, interpretation of relationships in data, and model-based thinking. Computer science education, in turn, supports the development of algorithmic thinking, understanding of data structures, data processing techniques, and computational modeling. When these two strands are intentionally connected in curriculum design - for example, when students use tools such as CODAP or Jupyter Notebooks to explore datasets whose patterns they then interpret using statistical concepts - the result is a more integrated and durable understanding than either discipline could support alone.

The third principle - focus on Data Science process - concerns how learning activities are organized. Rather than structuring instruction around isolated techniques or procedures, the framework proposes using the data science investigative process itself as a pedagogical organizing structure. This process, described consistently across major frameworks in the field [1, 7], comprises the following stages:

1. formulating a research question
2. collecting or locating relevant data
3. cleaning and preparing data for analysis
4. exploratory analysis, pattern discovery, and visualization
5. modeling and interpreting results

6. communicating and reflecting on findings

Importantly, this process is iterative rather than linear: question formulation shapes what data are needed; exploratory analysis may refine the original question; modeling outcomes prompt reconsideration of data preparation choices. Structuring learning activities around this cycle encourages students to approach data analysis as a coherent investigative practice rather than a sequence of disconnected computational steps.

A framework for curriculum integration must also account for how new knowledge areas realistically enter educational systems. Research on educational innovation suggests that this process is rarely driven by a single curriculum reform. Instead, new topics typically spread through multiple overlapping channels before becoming formally embedded in national curricula [16]. Table 1, adapted from Laanpere [16], summarizes the levels of intervention on which a new competence may be introduced into school practice. The top levels in this taxonomy have wide impact but require significant time and other resources, while the latter are increasingly easy, cheap, and fast to implement, yet have only limited impact among small groups of innovators.

Table 1. Levels of integrating the new content into school education [16]

Form of Integration	Description
New required course	Changing the national curriculum
Elective course or module	Teaching a new topic as an elective
A new topic within an existing course	Adding new content to textbooks
Key competence or horizontal theme	Recurring topic in multiple subjects
Multidisciplinary project	Project-based learning in 2–3 subjects
Extracurricular education	Non-formal learning in hobby groups
Competitions and contests	Problem-solving oriented events
Campaigns and theme days	Raising awareness through events
Teaching materials & teacher training	Resources for teacher training

This taxonomy is directly relevant to the integration of data science. A new mandatory subject is neither realistic nor necessarily desirable in the short-term, the proposed model combines the middle level interventions in this table: embedding data science elements within existing subjects, supporting cross-curricular connections, and providing teachers with accessible materials and professional development opportunities.

For curriculum integration to be coherent rather than ad hoc, a data science competence framework is needed. The development of digital competence frameworks in Estonia provides a useful precedent. Such frameworks define specific skill areas and describe expected learning outcomes at different stages of schooling, helping schools align competencies with subjects and assessment practices [17, 18]. A comparable framework for data science competencies would describe the progression of skills related to data collection, analysis, modeling, visualization, and critical interpretation across K–12 education.

Within the Estonian context, upper secondary research projects offer a particularly promising site for both enacting and assessing such competencies. The research process - formulating questions, collecting and analyzing data, interpreting results, and communicating findings - closely parallels the stages of the data science investigative process described in Sect. 3. A competency framework would clarify which data-related skills students are expected to demonstrate in these projects, and provide a basis for more systematic assessment of data literacy development at the end of compulsory schooling.

Research on data science education has developed at the intersection of statistics education, computer science education, and the learning sciences, resulting in valuable but often fragmented approaches. The model proposed in this paper addresses this gap by framing data science education as a curriculum-level design problem and by introducing a developmental structure that connects learning across mathematics and computer science. It integrates statistical thinking, computational thinking, and the data science investigative process into a coherent framework, while applying a spiral progression of core concepts-patterns, relationships, classification, and models-with increasing analytical sophistication. The model also reflects practical constraints by conceptualizing implementation as a gradual process grounded in existing subjects, cross-curricular connections, and teacher professional development. Its contribution lies in systematically integrating these elements into a coherent and progressive curriculum-level framework that bridges classroom-level practices and system-level curriculum design.

4 A Spiral Data Science Curriculum for K–12 Education

Building on the three structural principles introduced in Sect. 3, this section presents the proposed developmental model in concrete terms - describing how data science competencies can be organized progressively across grade levels within existing school subjects. The goal is not to prescribe a fixed syllabus but to articulate a coherent learning progression that schools and curriculum designers can adapt to their own contexts.

The progression is organized into four broad developmental stages, each characterized by a distinct analytical focus, a set of primary subjects, and a corresponding range of learning activities and tools. Across all stages, the four core conceptual categories - patterns, relationships, classification, and models - recur with increasing analytical sophistication, enacting the spiral structure described in Sect. 3. Figure 1 below illustrates the overall structure of this progression.

Stage 1: Observing and Describing Data (Grades 1–3).

In the earliest grades, the primary aim is to establish that data are representations of the world - that observations can be recorded, organized, and used to answer questions about everyday phenomena. Students begin to recognize that organizing information makes patterns visible, and that different ways of representing the same data can reveal different aspects of them. Typical learning activities at this stage include classroom surveys, sorting objects into categories, and constructing simple pictograms or bar charts. Many of these activities can be implemented through unplugged exploration - card-based classification games, physical sorting tasks, or collaborative data collection within the classroom - without requiring digital tools. The primary curricular home for this work is mathematics, supported by science and general studies where authentic data contexts arise naturally.

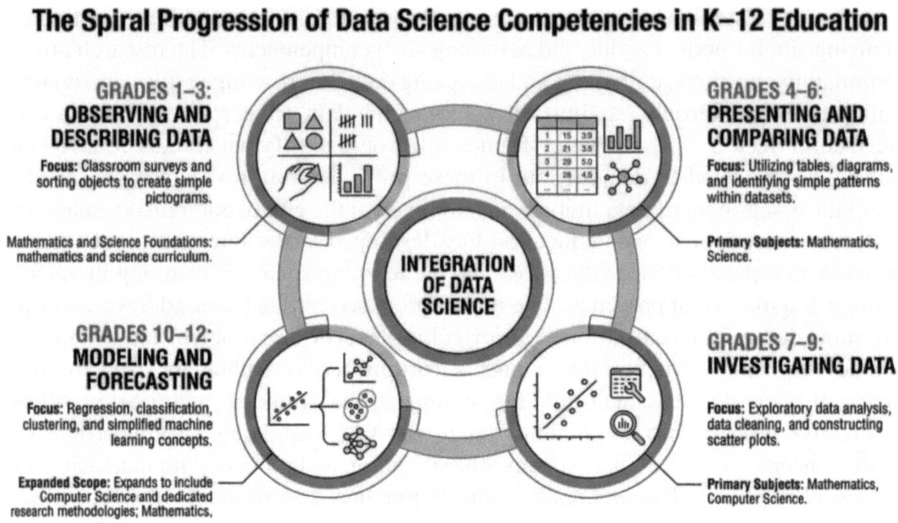

Fig. 1. Spiral Development of Data Science Competencies in K–12 Education

The conceptual emphasis at this stage is on patterns and classification at an intuitive level: students learn to group observations, identify simple regularities, and describe what they notice in organized data.

Stage 2: Presenting and Comparing Data (Grades 4–6).

In the middle elementary grades, students move from describing individual observations toward comparing data across categories and identifying patterns within datasets. They learn to construct and interpret tables, diagrams, and basic statistical representations, and are introduced to foundational concepts such as frequency, averages, and simple distributions. Learning activities at this stage emphasize pattern discovery and the interpretation of data representations. Students may explore datasets related to environmental observations, school surveys, or publicly available sources. Digital tools such as spreadsheet software or introductory data exploration environments like CODAP can support these investigations, allowing students to manipulate and visualize data interactively. The primary subjects supporting this stage are mathematics and science. The conceptual focus shifts toward relationships - students begin to ask not only what the data show, but how different variables relate to one another and what comparisons reveal.

Stage 3: Investigating Data (Grades 7–9).

In upper elementary and lower secondary grades, the focus shifts toward exploratory data analysis. Students begin to investigate relationships between variables using scatterplots and more advanced visualization techniques, and encounter the practical realities of working with data - including the need to clean, organize, and critically evaluate datasets before analysis can begin. At this stage, computational tools become more central. Environments such as CODAP or introductory programming tools allow students to work with larger datasets, perform more complex visualizations, and experiment with different analytical approaches. Mathematics continues to provide the conceptual foundation for statistical reasoning, while computer science education increasingly contributes algorithmic thinking and data processing skills. The conceptual emphasis here is on relationships and early modeling: students begin to move from describing patterns to constructing explanations and simple predictions of what the data show.

Stage 4: Modeling and Forecasting (Grades 10–12).

In upper secondary education, students engage with the full scope of the data science investigative process - from formulating research questions through to constructing, evaluating, and communicating data-driven models. Topics such as regression, classification, clustering, and forecasting are introduced as ways of building and critically assessing models that generalize beyond observed data. Students may also encounter introductory forms of machine learning through accessible tools such as Teachable Machine, or conduct more sophisticated data analysis workflows using Jupyter Notebooks. The emphasis at this stage is not on mathematical formalization for its own sake, but on understanding how models are constructed, what assumptions they involve, and how their outputs should be interpreted and communicated responsibly [6].

This stage spans both mathematics and computer science, and connects naturally with upper secondary research projects, where students already engage in question formulation, data collection, analysis, and presentation of findings. Such projects provide an authentic context for enacting the full data science process and for assessing the data literacy competencies students have developed across their schooling.

An important feature of this model is that data science learning is not confined to any single subject. While mathematics and computer science carry the primary responsibility for developing statistical and computational thinking respectively, other subjects provide essential contexts for authentic data investigation.

Science and natural studies offer real-world datasets and research problems - from environmental monitoring to biological observations - in which data analysis can be applied meaningfully. Social studies and geography provide opportunities for working with demographic, economic, and spatial data. Even language and humanities subjects can contribute, for instance through the analysis of textual or historical datasets.

This cross-curricular dimension serves two purposes. First, it reinforces the idea that data science is a method of inquiry applicable across domains, not merely a technical skill belonging to mathematics or computing. Second, it distributes the responsibility for data literacy development across the curriculum, making the model more sustainable and less dependent on any single teacher or subject area.

The progression described above demonstrates that integrating data science elements into K–12 education does not require major structural changes to existing curricula. By reorganizing and reframing existing learning opportunities - statistics in mathematics, algorithmic thinking in computer science, data collection in science - within a coherent developmental framework, schools can create a continuous learning pathway in which data literacy grows progressively across all years of schooling.

What distinguishes this model from a collection of isolated activities is precisely its coherence: the same core concepts recur across all four stages, tools and methods grow in sophistication in step with students' cognitive development, and the data science investigative process provides a consistent organizing structure for learning at every level.

5 Pedagogical Heuristics for Teaching Data Science Elements

The curriculum architecture described in Sect. 4 defines what data science learning looks like across grade levels. However, curriculum structure alone does not determine learning outcomes - how data science is taught matters as much as what is taught. This section articulates a set of pedagogical principles that support effective implementation of the proposed model. These principles draw on research in statistics and data science education, as well as on insights from teacher interviews conducted in the context of earlier research on designing data science learning materials for upper secondary schools [19].

These insights are informed by a design-based research study conducted in the Estonian upper secondary education context. As part of the study, qualitative data were collected through semi-structured group interviews with three stakeholder groups: informatics teachers, mathematics teachers, and university-level didactics experts involved in teacher education. The collected data were analyzed thematically, focusing on recurring patterns related to instructional design, tool use, and classroom implementation. Across groups, consistent themes emerged, including the importance of authentic datasets, modular and non-linear learning structures, differentiated tasks, and the need for clear pedagogical guidance. While these insights do not constitute a formal empirical validation of the proposed curriculum model, they serve to ground a set of pedagogical heuristics that are meaningful for teachers and relevant in authentic classroom contexts.

A consistent finding from those interviews was that successful implementation depends less on sophisticated technological infrastructure than on the quality of learning activity design and the availability of a coherent pedagogical framework. The heuristics described below reflect both the research literature and these practical perspectives.

The first heuristic: Hands-on Inquiry with Authentic Data. A central feature of effective data science education is the use of authentic datasets - data drawn from real phenomena rather than constructed for instructional convenience. Research in statistics education consistently demonstrates that students develop deeper understanding when they work with meaningful real-world contexts, because such contexts make the purpose of analysis visible and motivate genuine inquiry [2, 3]. In classroom practice, authentic datasets may originate from environmental observations, social phenomena, or topics connected to students' everyday lives - climate data, school survey results, or publicly available open datasets. In earlier grades, students can generate their own data through classroom measurements or small experiments, helping them understand that data represent real observations and that analyzing them provides a way of answering meaningful questions. In later grades, engagement with larger and messier datasets introduces students to the practical realities of data work, including the need to evaluate data quality and make deliberate choices about analytical approach. The exploratory tasks based on authentic data support the full data science process described in Sect. 3 - from question formulation through to interpretation and communication of results - rather than reducing learning to isolated analytical procedures.

The second heuristic: Conceptual Understanding Before Technical Procedures. Traditional statistics instruction has often emphasized computational procedures - performing calculations, applying formulas - while interpretation and meaning-making receive comparatively less attention. A central pedagogical principle of the proposed model is to reverse this priority: instruction should begin with helping students understand the patterns, relationships, and structures present in data, before introducing formal analytical techniques. This conceptual-first orientation serves several purposes. It reduces the risk that students focus on mechanical execution without understanding what their results mean. It supports the development of genuine statistical reasoning - the ability to interpret findings, evaluate alternative explanations, and recognize the limitations of an analysis. And it makes data science learning more accessible to students who may be intimidated by formal mathematics, by establishing meaning before formalism. Digital tools play an important supporting role in this approach, but are best understood as instruments for thinking rather than ends in themselves. Teacher interviews suggest that relatively simple and widely accessible tools are often sufficient for meaningful data analysis in school contexts. Interactive visualization environments such as CODAP allow students to explore datasets and discover patterns without requiring programming knowledge. For older students, Jupyter Notebooks support more sophisticated computational workflows, while introductory machine learning environments such as Teachable Machine allow experimentation with classification models in an accessible way.

The third heuristic: Open and Differentiated Task Design. Data science tasks are characteristically open-ended: they often have multiple plausible solution strategies and may lead to different, equally defensible interpretations of results. This property, which can feel uncomfortable in contexts where instruction emphasizes correct answers, is in fact a pedagogical resource - it encourages active participation, supports differentiation, and reflects authentic data science practice. Effective task design for data science learning can apply the principle of "low threshold - high ceiling" [20] tasks are designed to be accessible to all learners while still offering sufficient depth to challenge more advanced students.

The fourth heuristic: The Evolving Role of the Teacher. The pedagogical approaches described above require a corresponding shift in the role of the teacher. In traditional mathematics instruction, teachers typically demonstrate solution procedures and students practice applying them to well-defined problems with unambiguous answers. In data science learning environments, problems are frequently open-ended, results are uncertain, and multiple interpretations may be simultaneously defensible.

This does not mean that the teacher's role diminishes; rather, it changes. Rather than being the source of correct answers, the teacher becomes a facilitator of inquiry: supporting students in formulating productive questions, selecting appropriate analytical strategies, interpreting results in context, and reflecting on the limitations and assumptions of their analyses.

The fifth heuristic: Communication, Reflection, and Critical Awareness. An essential and often underemphasized component of data science learning is the communication and critical reflection of results. Students should learn not only to produce analytical outputs but to present findings using appropriate visualizations, explain how conclusions relate to original research questions, and acknowledge the limitations and uncertainties inherent in their analyses. Such communication may take the form of presentations, written reports, concept maps, or structured group discussions.

Reflective activities of this kind serve a deeper educational purpose beyond developing communication skills. They help students understand that data-driven conclusions are always conditional - dependent on the analytical choices made, the quality of the data used, and the assumptions built into any model. This understanding becomes particularly important in the context of artificial intelligence and automated data analysis, where algorithmic outputs can appear authoritative while resting on contestable assumptions. Developing critical awareness of these dynamics is an essential component of data literacy for responsible citizenship in a data-rich society.

An additional heuristic concerns the relationship between data science and artificial intelligence (AI). The rapid development of AI is reshaping how data are analyzed, interpreted, and used across domains, with direct implications for data science education. In contemporary contexts, many aspects of data analysis, including pattern detection, classification, and predictive modeling, can be performed automatically by AI-based systems. This shift changes not only the tools available to learners, but also the nature of the competencies that education should prioritize. On the one hand, AI lowers the technical barriers to engaging with complex data analysis. Tools that embed machine learning capabilities allow students to work with classification and modeling tasks without requiring advanced programming or mathematical formalization. Environments such as CODAP increasingly incorporate features that support interactive data exploration and, in some cases, simplified forms of automated analysis. As a result, students can engage earlier with meaningful data investigations that would previously have required more advanced technical preparation.

The increasing use of AI in data analysis introduces important epistemic challenges, particularly related to the opacity of models and the risk of overtrust in automated outputs. In this context, the ability to interpret results critically and understand model limitations becomes more important than performing computations.

This reinforces the relevance of the proposed framework, which emphasizes conceptual understanding, interpretation, and reasoning about data-driven claims. As analytical tools become more powerful, data science education plays a crucial role in helping learners evaluate when and how such tools can be used responsibly, supported by the spiral progression from intuitive data engagement to advanced reflection on modeling and inference.

6 Conclusions

The central argument of this article is straightforward: data science competencies are too important to leave to isolated classroom initiatives, and too complex to develop without a coherent developmental structure. The spiral curriculum model proposed here addresses both concerns simultaneously - by embedding data science learning within existing subjects, it avoids the political and practical obstacles of introducing a new mandatory discipline; by organizing that learning around recurring core concepts, a shared investigative process, and the reciprocal development of statistical and computational thinking, it creates the conditions for genuine and cumulative growth in data literacy across the full span of K–12 education.

Three contributions stand out. First, the model offers a curriculum-level response to a problem that existing research has largely addressed at the classroom level. While numerous studies demonstrate that data science learning is feasible and valuable in individual courses or projects, the question of how to connect these experiences into a coherent developmental pathway has received comparatively little attention. The proposed framework - grounded in spiral conceptual progression, cross-disciplinary integration, and the data science process as a pedagogical organizing structure - provides a principled answer to that question.

Second, the article situates curriculum design within a realistic theory of educational change. Drawing on Laanpere's [16] multi-level curriculum intervention model, it argues that sustainable implementation does not require immediate curriculum reform. Combining teacher-led integration of data science topics, elective modules, interdisciplinary projects, and targeted professional development can collectively build the conditions under which more formal integration becomes feasible. This approach is not a concession to conservatism - it is a recognition that durable educational change accumulates through multiple connected interventions rather than through single large-scale reform.

Third, the discussion of pedagogical principles and implementation challenges makes explicit what curriculum frameworks often leave implicit: that structural design is necessary but not sufficient. The shift toward inquiry-based, open-ended, collaborative data investigation requires corresponding changes in classroom culture, teacher professional identity, assessment practice, and the availability of accessible teaching materials. Identifying these conditions clearly is itself a contribution, because it translates an abstract curriculum vision into a concrete agenda for development.

An important aspect of this work is its positioning as a theory-informed design framework rather than a validated instructional model. The aim is not to present a finalized solution, but to articulate a coherent structure that can guide both curriculum design and subsequent empirical investigation. In this sense, the model represents a necessary intermediate step between fragmented instructional innovations and systematic, evidence-based curriculum development.

Several limitations of the present study should be acknowledged. The proposed model remains conceptual and has not yet been systematically tested across grade levels or classroom contexts. As such, the competency progression it outlines requires empirical validation in relation to how students' data literacy develops in practice.

This limitation reflects a deliberate scope choice, as curriculum-level design necessarily precedes large-scale empirical testing. Without an articulated developmental structure, research risks focusing on isolated interventions rather than cumulative learning trajectories.

In addition, the teacher interview data informing the pedagogical heuristics derive from a single prior study and do not constitute a comprehensive empirical base. Further research is therefore needed to examine how the proposed principles function across diverse educational contexts.

Future work should focus on pilot implementations, longitudinal studies of competency development, and the design of assessment approaches that capture interpretation, reasoning, and critical reflection in data science learning.

More broadly, the model proposed here reflects a particular vision of what data science education is for. Its goal is not to produce miniature data scientists, nor to equip students with a set of technical tools that will quickly become obsolete. It is to develop learners who can ask meaningful questions of data, reason carefully about what evidence does and does not support, recognize the assumptions and limitations embedded in analytical models, and participate critically and responsibly in a society in which data-driven claims are ubiquitous and consequential. That is, ultimately, an argument not just about curriculum design but about the kind of thinking that democratic citizenship in the twenty-first century requires.

References

1. National Academies of Sciences, Engineering, and Medicine: Data Science for Undergraduates: Opportunities and Options. National Academies Press (2018). https://doi.org/10.17226/25104
2. Ben-Zvi, D., Makar, K., Garfield, J. (eds.): The International Handbook of Research in Statistics Education. Springer, Cham (2018). https://doi.org/10.1007/978-3-319-66195-7
3. Bargagliotti, A., et al.: Pre-K–12 Guidelines for Assessment and Instruction in Statistics Education II (GAISE II). American Statistical Association (2020). https://www.amstat.org/asa/files/pdfs/GAISE/GAISEIIPreK-12_Full.pdf. Accessed 10 Mar 2026
4. Engel, J.: Statistical literacy for active citizenship: a call for data science education. Stat. Educ. Res. J. **16**(1), 44–49 (2017). https://doi.org/10.52041/serj.v16i1.213
5. Wise, A.F.: Educating data scientists and data literate citizens for a new generation of data. J. Learn. Sci. **29**(1), 165–181 (2020). https://doi.org/10.1080/10508406.2019.1705678
6. Cao, L.: Data science: a comprehensive overview. ACM Comput. Surv. **50**(3), 1–42 (2017). https://doi.org/10.1145/3076253
7. Keller, S.A., Shipp, S.S., Schroeder, A.D., Korkmaz, G.: Doing data science: a framework and case study. Harvard Data Sci. Rev. **2**(1) (2020). https://doi.org/10.1162/99608f92.2d83f7f5
8. Data 8: Foundations of Data Science. UC Berkeley (2017). https://data8.org. Accessed 10 Mar 2026
9. De Veaux, R., et al.: Curriculum guidelines for undergraduate programs in data science. Annu. Rev. Stat. Appl. **4**, 15–30 (2017). https://doi.org/10.1146/annurev-statistics-060116-053930
10. Schanzer, E., Krishnamurthi, S., Fisler, K., Politz, J.G.: Bootstrap: Data Science. Brown University, BootstrapWorld (2026). https://www.bootstrapworld.org/materials/data-science/
11. DataScEd4CiEn: Data Science Education for Citizenship (2024). https://datasc4ed.euc.ac.cy/welcome-to-datasced4cien/. Accessed 12 Mar 2026
12. ProDaBi: Promoting Data Literacy in Schools (2023). https://prodabi.de. Accessed 12 Mar 2026
13. Introduction to Data Science (IDS). UCLA (2019). https://www.idsucla.org/. Accessed 12 Mar 2026
14. Rosenberg, J.M., Jones, R.S.: Data science learning in grades K–12: synthesizing research across divides. Harvard Data Sci. Rev. **6**(3) (2024). https://doi.org/10.1162/99608f92.b1233596
15. Bruner, J.: The Process of Education. Harvard University Press, Cambridge (1960)
16. Laanpere, M.: Integrating emerging competencies into school curricula (2025, Unpublished manuscript)
17. Laanpere, M., Sillat, L.H., Luik, P., Lehiste, P., Požogina, K.: National policies and services for digital competence advancement in Estonia. In: Keane, T., Lewin, C., Brinda, T., Bottino, R. (eds.) Towards a Collaborative Society Through Creative Learning. WCCE 2022. IFIP AICT, vol. 685, pp. 675–686. Springer, Cham (2023). https://doi.org/10.1007/978-3-031-43393-1_60
18. Haridus- ja Noorteamet [Education and Youth Board]: Õppija digipädevusmudel [Learner's Digital Competence Model] (2020). https://digipadevus.ee/oppija-digipadevusmudel/. Accessed 10 Mar 2026

19. Osula, K., Laanpere, M.: Designing an interactive e-textbook on project-based learning in data science for high schools. In: ICERI2025 Proceedings, pp. 4160–4166. IATED, Valencia (2025). https://doi.org/10.21125/iceri.2025.1225
20. Boaler, J.: Mathematical Mindsets: Unleashing Students' Potential Through Creative Mathematics, Inspiring Messages and Innovative Teaching. Jossey-Bass (2016)

Hybrid Vision-Language Extraction for Inclusive and Accessible Educational Content

Mohamed Amine Lasheb[1](✉), Olivier Pons[1], Isabelle Barbet[1], and Caroline Huron[2]

[1] Cedric, CNAM, Paris, France
{mohamed-amine.lasheb,olivier.pons,isabelle.barbet}@lecnam.net
[2] SEED, Inserm, University Paris Cité, Paris, France
caroline.huron@cri-paris.org

Abstract. Inclusive education aims to ensure that every learner, regardless of ability, can access knowledge on equal terms. Yet for many children with developmental coordination disorder (DCD), a condition affecting the planning of fine motor tasks, the classroom remains a daily challenge. These students struggle to work with traditional printed textbooks. Completing exercises requires additional effort due to handwriting difficulties, while oculomotor disorders further hinder access because of visually dense layouts. To support them, educational materials must be adapted into interactive digital formats. However, manual adaptation of a single textbook can take three months, making large-scale inclusion logistically difficult. We present a hybrid vision-language pipeline that automates the extraction and structuring of multimodal exercise content from primary school textbooks. Our system integrates YOLOv11x for detecting exercise-related illustrations (96.9% mAP@0.5, F1 = 0.93) with a vision-language model (e.g., Gemini or local open-weight alternatives) for interpreting and organizing textual and visual information. The pipeline relies on a multimodal prompting process where annotated page images are paired with native PDF text enriched with styling cues. This design aligns text and visuals while avoiding OCR distortions. The extracted content is organized into JSON files, providing a unified representation where each exercise is categorized by its pedagogical type (e.g., identification, classification) to map directly to accessible interface templates. Experiments on textbooks with complex layouts show the system achieves near-perfect structural accuracy (JSON Structure = 0.998) and reproduces educational content with high character-level fidelity (Content Text F1 = 0.897). This work illustrates a method to reduce the cost of digital adaptation, helping to provide accessible materials for children with learning differences.

Keywords: Inclusive Education · Multimodal Document Understanding · Vision-Language Models · Information Extraction · Assistive Technology

R. Matulevičius et al. (Eds.): DB&IS 2026, CCIS 3085, pp. 234–248, 2026.
https://doi.org/10.1007/978-3-032-30863-4_15

1 Introduction

In France, the right to inclusive education is established by national legislation, most notably the *Law No. 2005–102 of February 11, 2005* on equality of rights and opportunities for persons with disabilities. This law amended the French Education Code to guarantee access to education for children, adolescents, and adults with disabilities [1]. It defines inclusion not as a compensatory measure but as a structural principle of the educational system, requiring that teaching materials, learning environments, and pedagogical tools be adapted to each learner's specific needs. This commitment to inclusion is further echoed at the international level.

At the global scale, inclusive education is recognized as a fundamental human right by the *United Nations Convention on the Rights of Persons with Disabilities (CRPD)*, which France ratified in 2010 [2]. The CRPD explicitly encourages the use of assistive and digital technologies to remove barriers to learning and participation. Yet despite this legal and moral framework, the practical realization of inclusion, particularly the adaptation of printed educational resources, remains limited and uneven across institutions.

These legal instruments highlight the necessity of providing equitable access to educational resources for all students, especially those with specific learning or motor difficulties. Among these, *dyspraxia* is one of the most frequently under-recognized developmental coordination disorders. It affects the planning and execution of fine motor tasks such as handwriting, page organization, or manipulating school materials. As described by Huron et al. [9], dyspraxic children often experience high cognitive load on mechanical actions, which interferes with comprehension and problem-solving. Without adapted interfaces, the cognitive overload caused by handwriting or spatial disorganization results in fatigue, frustration, and a gradual decline in confidence. Similarly, learners with visual impairments encounter static, visually dense textbooks that are incompatible with assistive readers and do not meet accessibility standards defined by the WHO and ISO guidelines [26].

The transcription of educational materials for visually impaired students remains a complex and highly manual process, involving multiple experts and delays [19]. Such adaptations enable children to access identical academic content through alternative modalities (tactile, auditory, or visual) depending on the learner's profile (Fig. 1). However, the manual adaptation of textbooks continues to represent a major bottleneck. Transforming printed textbooks into accessible digital formats is a time-consuming and resource-intensive process. At the international level, UNICEF reports that "the production of an Accessible Digital Textbook (ADT) typically takes six to nine months and costs between $20,000 and $50,000 for a single textbook" [24]. This estimate highlights the human and financial investment required even in well-resourced contexts. In France, similar challenges are documented in the ANRâĂŞMALIN project (MAnuels scoLaires INclusifs)[1], which seeks to automate the adaptation of textbooks for students

[1] https://anr.fr/Projet-ANR-21-CE38-0014.

with disabilities, particularly those with dyspraxia, thereby underscoring the persistent delays and labor demands of current manual workflows [3]. Together, these findings confirm that large-scale inclusion remains economically and logistically unattainable without automation.

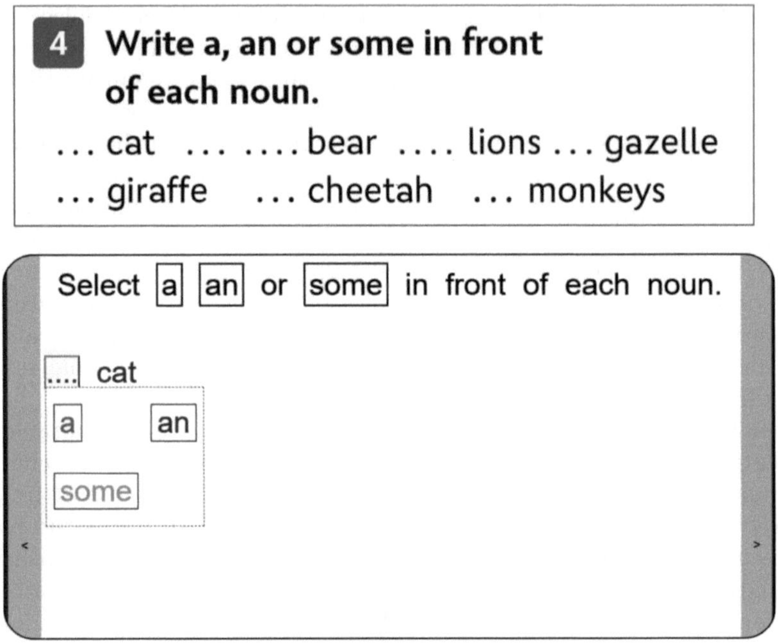

Fig. 1. Example of a web adaptation from structured content.

To address this, associations specializing in inclusive education, often in collaboration with academic laboratories, have proposed semi-automated textbook adaptation pipelines (Fig. 2). These systems follow a structured workflow: data acquisition from educational publishers, multimodal content extraction (text, layout, and images), exercise classification based on pedagogical functions, and final transformation into interactive web or tactile formats. Yet the extraction stage remains the most labor-intensive and technically complex, particularly when handling heterogeneous layouts typical of primary-school textbooks.

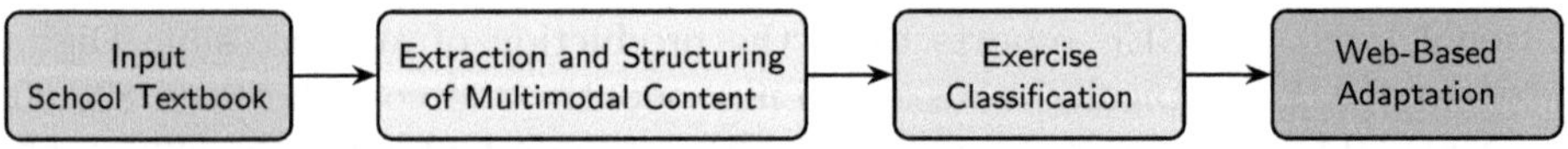

Fig. 2. Global adaptation pipeline.

Our study focuses on this pivotal stage: the automated extraction and structuring of multimodal exercise content. We introduce a hybrid vision-language pipeline that integrates the spatial localization of computer vision for detecting exercise-related illustrations with the semantic capabilities of large language models. The system jointly processes a detailed native text extraction (retaining layout and typographic features) together with the annotated page image to produce a coherent, structured output. This integration ensures both visual alignment and pedagogical coherence, enabling downstream adaptation systems to directly map exercises onto inclusive interface templates. The dataset comprises French primary-school textbooks characterized by dense layouts, abundant illustrations, and multilingual annotations spanning multiple subjects such as reading, mathematics, grammar, and science. The material originates from official educational publishers (e.g., https://www.magnard.fr), and is therefore protected by copyright. Although these restrictions prevent the public release of the original pages, Fig. 3 presents a representative annotated example illustrating the visual and semantic diversity of the multimodal elements to be extracted, including exercises, illustrations, instructions, labels, statements, numbers, titles, indicators, lessons, examples, and tips.

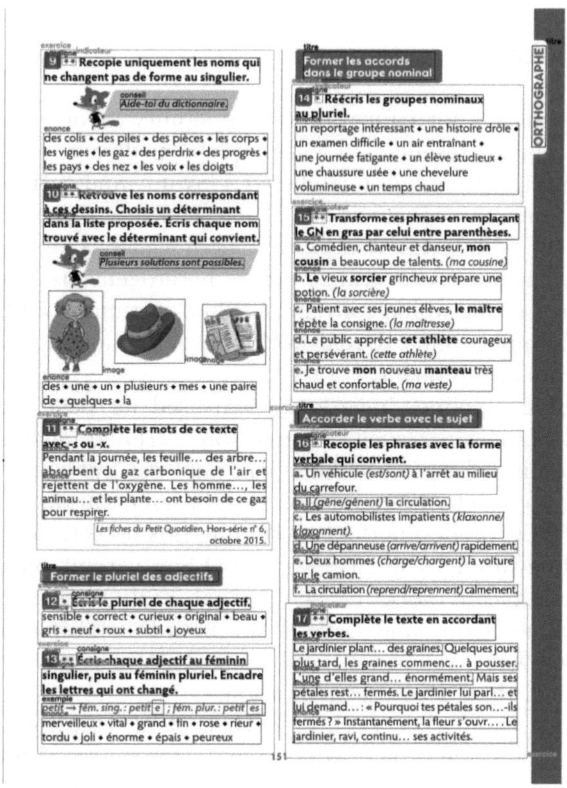
9 ** Recopie uniquement les noms qui ne changent pas de forme au singulier.
conseil Aide-toi du dictionnaire.
des colis • des piles • des pièces • les corps • les vignes • les gaz • des perdrix • des progrès • les pays • des nez • les voix • les doigts
10 ** Retrouve les noms correspondant à ces dessins. Choisis un déterminant dans la liste proposée. Écris chaque nom trouvé avec le déterminant qui convient.
conseil Plusieurs solutions sont possibles.
des • une • un • plusieurs • mes • une paire de • quelques • la
11 ** Complète les mots de ce texte avec -s ou -x.
Pendant la journée, les feuille... des arbre... absorbent du gaz carbonique de l'air et rejettent de l'oxygène. Les homme..., les animau... et les plante... ont besoin de ce gaz pour respirer.
Les fiches du Petit Quotidien, Hors-série n° 6, octobre 2015.
Former le pluriel des adjectifs
12 * Écris le pluriel de chaque adjectif.
sensible • correct • curieux • original • beau • gris • neuf • roux • subtil • joyeux
13 ** Écris chaque adjectif au féminin singulier, puis au féminin pluriel. Encadre les lettres qui ont changé.
exemple petit → fém. sing. : petite ; fém. plur. : petites
merveilleux • vital • grand • fin • rose • rieur • tordu • joli • énorme • épais • peureux
Former les accords dans le groupe nominal
14 * Réécris les groupes nominaux au pluriel.
un reportage intéressant • une histoire drôle • un examen difficile • un air entraînant • une journée fatigante • un élève studieux • une chaussure usée • une chevelure volumineuse • un temps chaud
15 ** Transforme ces phrases en remplaçant le GN en gras par celui entre parenthèses.
a. Comédien, chanteur et danseur, mon cousin a beaucoup de talents. (ma cousine)
b. Le vieux sorcier grincheux prépare une potion. (la sorcière)
c. Patient avec ses jeunes élèves, le maître répète la consigne. (la maîtresse)
d. Le public apprécie cet athlète courageux et persévérant. (cette athlète)
e. Je trouve mon nouveau manteau très chaud et confortable. (ma veste)
Accorder le verbe avec le sujet
16 * Recopie les phrases avec la forme verbale qui convient.
a. Un véhicule (est/sont) à l'arrêt au milieu du carrefour.
b. Il (gêne/gênent) la circulation.
c. Les automobilistes impatients (klaxonne/klaxonnent).
d. Une dépanneuse (arrive/arrivent) rapidement.
e. Deux hommes (charge/chargent) la voiture sur le camion.
f. La circulation (reprend/reprennent) calmement.
17 ** Complète le texte en accordant les verbes.
Le jardinier plant... des graines. Quelques jours plus tard, les graines commenc... à pousser. L'une d'elles grand... énormément. Mais ses pétales rest... fermés. Le jardinier lui parl... et lui demand... : « Pourquoi tes pétales son...-ils fermés ? » Instantanément, la fleur s'ouvr.... Le jardinier, ravi, continu... ses activités.
ORTHOGRAPHE
151

Fig. 3. Sample annotated textbook page showing exercise zones, instructions, and visual elements.

Despite advances in document AI, automating the extraction of structured pedagogical content from textbooks remains an open challenge. Existing models often fail to maintain reliable mappings between text and illustrations across complex layouts, particularly in visually rich educational materials.

Our goal is to reduce the time and cost required to adapt these textbooks into interactive formats for learners with motor or visual challenges. In our proposed workflow, automation shifts the expert's effort from manual data entry to content review. The pipeline enforces strict image-text consistency checks through explicit identifier validation to prevent multimodal mismatches. By combining bounding box detection with language modeling, the system handles complex layout motifs and provides a stable foundation for human-in-the-loop validation, ultimately accelerating the creation of accessible learning environments.

In summary, our main contributions are: (1) a hybrid pipeline combining YOLOv11x and LLMs to extract and structure educational content, (2) a style-aware text extraction method that preserves typographic cues for better segmentation, and (3) a decoding step that explicitly aligns text references with image crops.

2 Related Work

Textbook understanding for educational accessibility involves document layout analysis, multimodal representation learning, and pedagogical content structuring. Early work by Lincker et al. introduced a layout- and activity-based extraction framework aimed at generating TEI or DocBook representations of educational PDFs [16]. While effective within homogeneous textbook collections, their approach struggles to generalize across heterogeneous publishers, diverse layouts, and varied typographic conventions, and it remains restricted to native PDFs, limiting its applicability to real-world inclusive education workflows where scanned documents are frequent.

Computer-vision pipelines have long been used for page segmentation and layout detection. Frameworks such as Detectron2 [27] and LayoutParser [21] provide standard baselines for generic document analysis, particularly because they natively support both detection and pixel-level segmentation. In contrast, standard one-stage YOLO models perform bounding-box detection only, and segmentation requires fine-tuning a dedicated YOLO-Seg variant on mask-annotated data. Nevertheless, recent work has shown that YOLO-based detectors [20,25] still outperform Detectron2 and LayoutParser on fine-grained pedagogical elements under heterogeneous and class-imbalanced settings, where object localization is more critical than dense segmentation.

In this context, the earlier work of Lasheb et al. [12] applied a computer-vision pipeline to the same type of educational documents. While this approach demonstrated reliable visual detection capabilities, it remained limited by its lack of semantic reasoning. The system could detect visual regions such as exercise boxes or layout components, but it could not reconstruct the internal pedagogical structure of exercises, distinguish between roles (instruction, statement, example, hint), or interpret textual dependencies. As a result, CV-only pipelines cannot produce the semantic, pedagogically meaningful structures required for accessible textbook adaptation.

Multimodal transformer architectures integrate textual, visual, and spatial cues, improving general document understanding. Representative approaches include LayoutLMv2/v3 [8,28], DocFormer [4], VILA [15], which perform joint reasoning over OCR tokens and image features. Meanwhile, models such as Donut (ECCV 2022) [11] and Pix2Struct (ICML 2023) [13] propose end-to-end, OCR-free image-to-text modeling for visually rich documents.

Despite their established performance on benchmarks such as PubLayNet [29] and DocBank [14], these unified architectures remain limited when applied to educational textbooks. Their training corpora primarily emphasize typographic patterns rather than pedagogical roles, making them poorly aligned with the functional structures found in exercises, examples, and instructional sequences. Moreover, the long-tailed and domain-specific categories characteristic of textbooks (icons, cues, labels, boxed statements, multimodal prompts) are largely absent from public datasets, resulting in inconsistent behavior across publishers. Consequently, these models often fail to maintain reliable alignment between textual content and visual elements, particularly in dense, heterogeneous page layouts where pedagogical meaning depends on precise relationships between text, style, and illustrations.

Modern LLMs, including multimodal variants such as Gemini [23] and the GPT family [18], provide semantic reasoning capabilities and can extract structured information from textbook pages. Nonetheless, they cannot retrieve or reference the actual visual crops; at best, they note the presence of an image without providing its grounded location. Furthermore, LLMs often lose spatial fidelity when pages are densely structured, making them insufficient for tasks requiring precise alignment between text, layout, and visual elements, a requirement central to accessible exercise adaptation.

Hybrid pipelines that combine explicit vision modules with language-based reasoning provide an alternative. However, existing systems typically rely on OCR outputs and heuristic segmentation, lacking mechanisms for robust multimodal grounding, style-aware text interpretation, or consistent crop referencing.

Our work advances this direction by proposing a hybrid vision-language pipeline that integrates YOLOv11x for detecting exercise-related illustrations, PDFMiner-based extraction of text and typographic metadata [22], a multimodal LLM capable of semantically structuring content using the annotated page image and style-aware text map, and a consistency-constrained decoding mechanism ensuring exact alignment between textual references and visual crops. This design overcomes the limitations of vision-only, language-only, and unified VLM approaches by enabling precise crop-level grounding, pedagogical role identification, and stylistically informed segmentation.

3 Proposed Approach

Our approach combines computer vision for exercise-related image detection with large language models (LLMs) for the semantic extraction and structuring of multimodal content. The overall workflow is illustrated in Fig. 4.

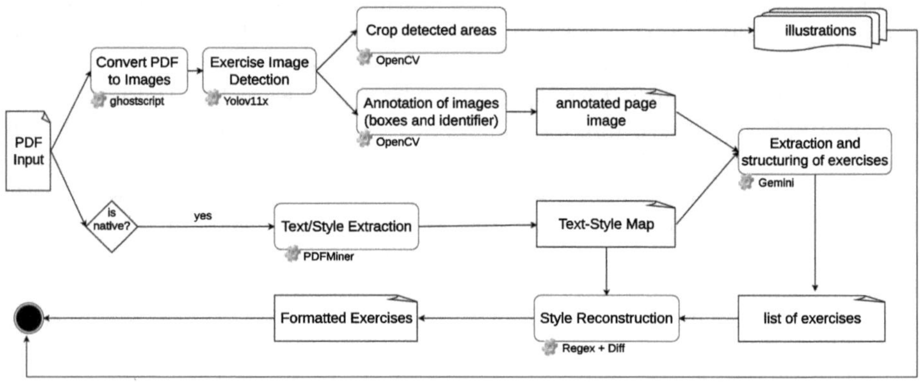

Fig. 4. Overview of the proposed hybrid pipeline combining YOLOv11x-based image detection with Gemini-based semantic structuring.

Each PDF page is processed through two complementary branches that operate in parallel: a **text-style extraction branch** for native PDF content and an **image-based branch** for visual analysis. If the input PDF page is *native* (i.e., contains an embedded text layer), we employ **PDFMiner** to extract both textual content and detailed typographic attributes. Each extracted sentence w_i is represented as a tuple:

$$w_i = (\texttt{text}, \texttt{font\_family}, \texttt{size}, \texttt{color\_hex}, \texttt{style\_tag}, \texttt{overrides})$$

where the `style_tag` captures the dominant appearance of the phrase (e.g., `bold`, `medium`, `light`), and the optional field `overrides` lists local deviations in style for one or more words within the phrase (for instance, when a word is underlined, highlighted, or printed in a different color). This representation enables fine-grained modeling of stylistic contrasts such as **bold keywords** or colored emphasis appearing within medium-weight statements. Each text segment thus preserves both its overall visual style and any embedded variations that carry semantic meaning at the word level. The resulting structured CSV, generated by our PDFMiner parser, provides line-level entries with global style attributes and local overrides that indicate deviations in font or color within each sentence. These cues later serve as soft constraints for the LLM to improve semantic segmentation between instructional, example, and statement zones during multimodal parsing. However, the LLM outputs a simplified text structure without explicit typographic tags. To recover the exact formatting, a post-processing step based on Regex and text alignment is applied.

The structured set $T = \{w_i\}_{i=1}^{N_p}$, where N_p denotes the total number of extracted text segments on page p, preserves layout, visual hierarchy, and stylistic emphasis, which is key for distinguishing textual zones such as *"title"*, *"instruction"*, or *"example"*. When a page is *scanned* and lacks a text layer, this branch is skipped ($T = \varnothing$), and processing relies exclusively on the image branch with OCR-based text extraction. This fallback does not preserve style information and yields lower accuracy, but it is rarely required since most educational textbooks are distributed as native PDFs.

In parallel, Ghostscript [5] is used to rasterize each page into a high-resolution image. The resulting image X_{img} is passed to the trained YOLOv11x detector [10], which identifies and localizes exercise-related illustrations, such as diagrams, figures, or pictorial elements explicitly associated with pedagogical tasks. While large language models can infer that an illustration is present, they cannot retrieve or represent the actual visual content; the vision branch therefore provides this missing modality explicitly.

$$(B, I) = P_\phi(X_{\text{img}}),$$

where B denotes the bounding boxes and $I = \{(id_k, b_k, s_k)\}$ is the set of detected crops with unique identifiers (`pXXcY`) and confidence scores. All detected crops are stored in a structured directory (`crops/pXX/`) for reproducibility and visualization, and red bounding boxes are overlaid on the original page image to create an annotated representation. Both branches operate independently and can be executed modularly, allowing easy reproducibility across new textbook collections.

The LLM receives synchronized multimodal inputs: the annotated page image containing visual detections with crop identifiers, the textual content and style metadata T from PDFMiner (when available), and the symbolic identifiers $\{pXXcY\}$, which are used as referential anchors to maintain a consistent multimodal structure.

The prompting strategy depends on the deployed model's capacity. For the Gemini API, the system uses a single-step multimodal prompt that simultaneously extracts the text, classifies the pedagogical roles, and maps the visual identifiers within a unified JSON schema. Conversely, local open-weight models (such as Llama [7,17] or Qwen [6]) often encounter context limitations when resolving both dense text structuring and spatial image mapping simultaneously. For these local deployments, we implemented a sequential two-step prompting strategy. The first request focuses exclusively on textual extraction, JSON structuring, and pedagogical classification. A second request isolates the visual detection task, identifying which image crops belong to which exercise. Finally, a deterministic Python post-processing script sequentially merges the outputs of these two requests.

If the page is scanned, the LLM operates only on the annotated image, using OCR to extract text and leveraging the spatial arrangement and bounding boxes to reconstruct the semantic hierarchy (Fig. 5).

Fig. 5. Example of annotated textbook pages with bounding boxes and structured JSON output referencing cropped images.

Formally, let X_{img} denote the rasterized page image and T the set of text–style tuples (possibly empty). The multimodal input U given to the extractor is:

$$U = \begin{cases} \{\, X_{\text{img}}, B^*, I^*, T \,\}, & \text{if the PDF is native,} \\ \{\, X_{\text{img}}, B^*, I^* \,\}, & \text{otherwise.} \end{cases} \tag{1}$$

The structured prediction $\hat{Y}$ is obtained by:

$$\hat{Y} = \arg\max_{Y \in \mathcal{S}} \left[\log P_\theta(Y \mid U) - \lambda\, \Omega_{\text{consistency}}(Y, I^*) \right]. \tag{2}$$

where:

- $\mathcal{S}$ is the space of admissible structured outputs (JSON/TSV);
- (B^*, I^*) are the bounding boxes and crop identifiers predicted by the detector P_ϕ (YOLOv11x) from X_{img};
- P_θ is the vision–language extraction model (Gemini 2.5 flash in our experiments);
- T is the text-style map extracted from native PDFs (empty for scanned PDFs);
- λ is a hyperparameter controlling the weight of the consistency penalty;
- $\Omega_{\text{consistency}}(Y, I^*)$ penalizes structural inconsistencies, notably when Y references crop identifiers not present in I^*.

Equation (2) represents the decoding stage of the hybrid pipeline. The two models are trained independently, and the consistency term Ω is enforced at inference time. In practice, this penalty is operationalized as a post-processing validation step: any JSON output referencing an unmapped crop identifier triggers a formatting error. To handle the majority of formatting edge cases encountered during development, we augmented this validation with specific Regular Expressions (Regex) adapted to correct common output anomalies before the final JSON is generated.

Each extracted exercise $e \in Y$ is represented using a unified notation:

$$e = \big(\mathrm{id}(e), n_e, \mathrm{textmap}(e), \mathrm{img}(e), \gamma(e), s_e\big) \tag{3}$$

where:

- $\mathrm{id}(e)$ is a persistent identifier for the exercise;
- n_e is the exercise number;
- $\mathrm{textmap}(e)$ contains the keys: {**instruction**, **labels**, **statement**, **hint**, **example**, **references**};
- $\mathrm{img}(e)$ indicates whether the exercise references visual content;
- $\gamma(e)$ is the set of referenced crop identifiers;
- s_e contains the recovered typographic metadata (font, size, emphasis) integrated by the Style Reconstruction engine.

To ensure multimodal consistency, every crop identifier referenced in Y must map to an existing crop file. Let $\mathcal{F}$ denote the set of all available crop images extracted from the page. Then:

$$\forall k \in \gamma(Y): \quad \pi(k) \in \mathcal{F}. \tag{4}$$

To produce the final Formatted Exercises, the unstyled structured output Y is passed through a Style Reconstruction engine. This text transformation module employs regular expressions (Regex) combined with a sequence matching algorithm (e.g., Python's SequenceMatcher) to compute the differences between the LLM-generated JSON text and the original Text-Style Map (T). By aligning the two representations, the engine automatically re-injects the missing typographic metadata (such as bold styling or color overrides) directly into the final structure. This decoupling ensures that the LLM focuses solely on semantic structuring, while the deterministic Regex and Diff engine guarantees the high-fidelity preservation of the original layout's stylistic emphasis.

The YOLOv11x model was trained on 228 annotated pages from four textbook collections, totaling approximately 500 instances. Training used 100 epochs, batch size 9, input size 736×736, AdamW optimizer (1×10^{-4}), cosine learning scheduler, and standard data augmentation. A pretrained YOLOv11x checkpoint served as initialization to ensure stable convergence across heterogeneous layouts.

This hybrid strategy leverages both the semantic content of native PDF text and the spatial localization of computer vision. When PDFMiner style metadata is available, it improves the discrimination between exercise components (titles, instructions, examples) and supports more accurate structuring. When only images are available, the system switches to a vision-only mode, ensuring wide applicability across both digital and scanned educational resources. The framework scales to hundreds of textbook pages, as both the YOLO inference and PDFMiner extraction are linear in page count and fully parallelizable.

The complete implementation, including YOLO model weights, configuration files, and LLM prompts, will be released if the paper is accepted.

4 Results and Discussion

We first evaluated the YOLOv11x detector independently on a held-out test set to verify its ability to locate exercise-related visual elements. It achieved an average precision of 0.969 (mAP@0.5) and an F1-score of 0.93 at a 0.47 confidence threshold. The 93% correct classification rate confirms that this stage provides accurately cropped image regions. This ensures the subsequent language models operate on clean multimodal inputs rather than cluttered full pages.

To assess the complete pipeline, we expanded the evaluation to 100 textbook pages from 5 different publishers, representing a variety of layouts and pedagogical formats. This provided a test set of 791 manually annotated exercises. We compared the system's output against a gold-standard JSON schema based on four criteria: ID Recall (detecting the exercise), Structural accuracy (schema validity and categorization), Textual fidelity (content F1-score sensitive to syntax), and Image Recall (bounding box alignment for spatial traceability). Table 1 details the metrics across four Vision-Language architectures. Gemini 2.5 Flash provided the most consistent results across all categories.

Table 1. Evaluation metrics for the multimodal extraction pipeline across 791 exercises.

Metric	Gemini 2.5 Flash (API)	Llama 4 (128 × 17B)	Qwen 2.5VL (72B)	Llama 3.2-V (90B)
ID Recall	0.980	0.910	0.960	0.380
JSON Structure	0.998	0.996	0.970	0.917
Labels Score	0.978	0.855	0.826	0.762
Content Text (F1)	0.897	0.767	0.725	0.612
Image Recall	0.978	0.894	0.746	0.148
Global Score*	0.931	0.785	0.773	0.235

* Calculated as: ID Recall × (Content Text × 0.40 + JSON × 0.25 + Image × 0.20 + Labels × 0.15)

The Labels Score in Table 1 evaluates the accuracy of assigning the correct pedagogical tags (e.g., instruction, statement, hint) to the extracted text segments. The weights for the composite Global Score were heuristically assigned based on downstream requirements for accessible web adaptation, prioritizing strict textual fidelity (0.40) and structural validity (0.25) over auxiliary labels.

These results indicate that combining explicit object detection with semantic reasoning provides a more stable strategy than relying solely on end-to-end transformers. Vision-only models lack semantic understanding, while generative models often lose spatial precision. Our hybrid pipeline bridges this gap. YOLOv11x was chosen due to its observed accuracy over alternatives like LayoutParser or Detectron2. Furthermore, this modular design allows independent fine-tuning of either the vision or language component without restructuring the entire application.

The performance difference between Gemini and the local models highlights that scaling up parameter counts does not automatically resolve spatial reasoning deficits. For example, Llama 3.2-Vision [7] demonstrated limitations with image identification (14.8% Image Recall). However, open-weight solutions like Qwen 2.5VL-72B [6] and Llama 4 [17] remain practical for local execution, which is an important consideration for student data privacy and API costs. When tested on a high-end local workstation[2], these local models achieved global scores around 77–78%.

The primary trade-off is inference latency: processing a single page took an average of 123.02 s for Qwen 2.5VL (72B), 127.61 s for Llama 3.2-Vision (90B), and 464.46 s for Llama 4 (128×17B). It is important to note that this latency is hardware-dependent; upgrading the server configuration would reduce these processing times. Furthermore, to benefit from the cost-free nature of open-weight models while preserving student data privacy (avoiding external cloud APIs), real-time processing is not necessary. In such scenarios, the system is practical for offline, overnight batch-processing workflows. Specifically, the models can autonomously process textbooks during the night, generating structured outputs that human experts then validate and adapt during their regular daytime working hours. This operational workflow resolves the latency issue and aligns with the standard schedules of accessibility organizations.

Finally, the 97.8% Image Recall achieved by the leading configuration is critical for adapting materials for students with dyspraxia. To effectively relieve the cognitive and motor load associated with traditional textbooks, the structured output must include properly cropped visual elements. By generating accurate bounding boxes, the architecture ensures that the extracted text is consistently paired with its corresponding diagrams or figures in the final interactive web interface. Ultimately, the system relies on combining computer vision for spatial precision with language models for semantic structure, offering a reliable foundation for inclusive document digitization.

Real-World Application and Future Work: It is important to note that the accessible digital formats and pedagogical templates targeted by our pipeline have already been extensively studied, designed, tested, and validated by special education experts to effectively support children with dyspraxia. Therefore, the

[2] Hardware configuration: Dual NVIDIA RTX Ada Generation 6000 GPUs (48 GB VRAM each).

primary objective of this study was not to re-evaluate and test the clinical or cognitive efficacy of these adaptations, but rather to solve the technical bottleneck of producing them at scale. By evaluating our system's output against manually and expertly crafted "gold standard" adaptations, we demonstrated that the automated extraction achieves the strict structural and textual fidelity required for production. Future work will focus on integrating this pipeline into the daily workflow of accessibility associations (such as within the ANR-MALIN project) to formally quantify the reduction in manual labor time and assess the human-in-the-loop validation dynamics in a real-world production environment. Furthermore, we plan to extend our framework to mathematics textbooks, which present unique multimodal challenges such as extracting geometric diagrams, shapes, and complex spatial arrangements like vertical mathematical operations.

5 Conclusion

This work introduced a hybrid vision-language pipeline that combines spatial detection and semantic reasoning to automate the structuring of educational documents. By integrating YOLOv11x with large language models, the system addresses the limitations of both vision-only and language-only approaches. It achieved near-perfect structural validity (JSON Structure = 0.998) and a 0.931 Global Score (using Gemini 2.5 Flash) under a strict evaluation protocol on dense textbook layouts. The inclusion of typographic metadata was necessary for distinguishing pedagogical roles, and the crop identifier mechanism maintained alignment between text and images. These results indicate that effective document understanding relies heavily on combining complementary architectures rather than simply increasing model size.

The framework provides a working foundation for scaling the adaptation of printed educational materials. Its modular design allows it to be applied to different languages and layouts, and the viability of open-weight models (like Qwen 2.5VL) shows that local, privacy-preserving processing is achievable. By automating the extraction phase, this approach reduces the manual workload required to create interactive exercises, offering a technical solution to help support inclusive learning and equitable access to education.

While these results are promising, the study has specific contextual boundaries. The primary evaluation dataset was restricted to French curricula, as this was the explicit requirement of the underlying national inclusion project. However, preliminary tests conducted on English-language textbooks yielded positive results, indicating consistent cross-lingual generalizability. Furthermore, the pipeline already supports scanned documents by bypassing the PDFMiner text-style extraction and relying directly on the VLM for OCR and structuring; however, integrating a dedicated, optimized OCR module remains a viable path to further improve robustness.

Acknowledgments. This work was supported by the ANR-21-CE38-0014 MALIN project.

References

1. Law no. 2005-102 of february 11, 2005, for equality of rights and opportunities, participation and citizenship of persons with disabilities. Légifrance (2005), accessed online via Legifrance
2. Convention on the rights of persons with disabilities (crpd). United Nations (2006), ratified by France in 2010
3. Agence Nationale de la Recherche (ANR): Projet malin – manuels scolaires inclusifs. https://anr.fr/Projet-ANR-21-CE38-0014 (2021), describes the objective of automating textbook adaptation for learners with disabilities (focus on dyspraxia) to reduce the lengthy manual processes in France
4. Appalaraju, S., Jasani, B., Kota, B.U., et al.: Docformer: End-to-end transformer for document understanding. In: 2021 IEEE/CVF International Conference on Computer Vision (ICCV), pp. 973–983 (2021). https://doi.org/10.1109/ICCV48922.2021.00103
5. Artifex Software, Inc.: Ghostscript 10.03.0 (2024). https://www.ghostscript.com, interpreter for the PostScript language and PDF. Accessed 12 Mar 2026
6. Bai, S., Chen, K., Liu, X., et al.: Qwen2.5-vl technical report (02 2025). https://doi.org/10.48550/arXiv.2502.13923
7. Grattafiori, A., Dubey, A., Jauhri, A., et al.: The llama 3 herd of models (2024). https://arxiv.org/abs/2407.21783
8. Huang, Y., Lv, T., Cui, L., et al.: Layoutlmv3: pre-training for document ai with unified text and image masking. In: Proceedings of the 30th ACM International Conference on Multimedia, pp. 4083–4091. MM '22, Association for Computing Machinery, New York, NY, USA (2022). https://doi.org/10.1145/3503161.3548112
9. Huron, C.: Aider l'enfant dyspraxique à l'école. Approche Neuropsychologique des Apprentissages chez l'Enfant **25**, 197–201 (2013). II
10. Khanam, R., Hussain, M.: Yolov11: An overview of the key architectural enhancements (2024). https://arxiv.org/abs/2410.17725
11. Kim, G., Hong, T., Yim, M., et al.: OCR-free document understanding transformer. In: Computer Vision – ECCV 2022: 17th European Conference, October 23–27, 2022, Proceedings, Part XXVIII, pp. 498–517. Springer-Verlag, Berlin, Heidelberg (2022). https://doi.org/10.1007/978-3-031-19815-1_29, https://doi.org/10.1007/978-3-031-19815-1_29
12. Lasheb, M.A., Pons, O., Bekkouche, M., et al.: Extracting and structuring textbooks for inclusive education: a computer vision approach. In: 2025 IEEE International Conference on Advanced Learning Technologies (ICALT), pp. 199–203 (2025). https://doi.org/10.1109/ICALT64023.2025.00062
13. Lee, K., Joshi, M., Turc, I.: Pix2struct: screenshot parsing as pretraining for visual language understanding. In: Proceedings of the 40th International Conference on Machine Learning. ICML'23, JMLR.org (2023)
14. Li, M., Xu, Y., Cui, L., et al.: DocBank: A benchmark dataset for document layout analysis. In: Scott, D., Bel, N., Zong, C. (eds.) Proceedings of the 28th International Conference on Computational Linguistics, pp. 949–960. International Committee on Computational Linguistics, Barcelona, Spain (Online) (Dec 2020). https://doi.org/10.18653/v1/2020.coling-main.82, https://aclanthology.org/2020.coling-main.82/
15. Lin, J., Yin, H., Ping, W., et al.: VILA: On pre-training for visual language models . In: 2024 IEEE/CVF Conference on Computer Vision and Pattern Recognition (CVPR), pp. 26679–26689. IEEE Computer Society, Los Alamitos, CA,

USA (Jun 2024). https://doi.org/10.1109/CVPR52733.2024.02520, https://doi.ieeecomputersociety.org/10.1109/CVPR52733.2024.02520
16. Lincker, E., Pons, O., Guinaudeau, C., et al.: Layout- and Activity-based Textbook Modeling for Automatic PDF Textbook Extraction. In: Sosnovsky, S., Brusilovsky, P., Lan, A. (eds.) Proceedings of the 5h International Workshop on Intelligent Textbooks (iTextbooks 2023) co-located with the 24th International Conference on Artificial Intelligence in Education (AIED 2023). vol. 3444, pp. 37–53. CEUR-WS, Tokyo, Japan (Jul 2023), https://hal.science/hal-04184895
17. Meta AI: The llama 4 herd: The beginning of a new era of natively multimodal ai innovation. https://ai.meta.com/blog/llama-4-multimodal-intelligence/ (Apr 2025), meta AI Blog
18. OpenAI, Achiam, J., Adler, S., et al.: Gpt-4 technical report (2024). https://arxiv.org/abs/2303.08774
19. Pacini, L., Dupire, J., Barbet, I., et al.: Modeling transcription process of educational documents for visually impaired students. In: AAATE2025. Nicosia, Cyprus (Sep 2025). https://hal.science/hal-05042750
20. Redmon, J., Divvala, S., Girshick, R., et al.: You only look once: Unified, real-time object detection. In: 2016 IEEE Conference on Computer Vision and Pattern Recognition (CVPR), pp. 779–788 (2016). https://doi.org/10.1109/CVPR.2016.91
21. Shen, Z., Zhang, R., Dell, M., et al.: Layoutparser: a unified toolkit for deep learning based document image analysis. In: Document Analysis and Recognition – ICDAR 2021: 16th International Conference, Lausanne, Switzerland, September 5–10, 2021, Proceedings, Part I, pp. 131–146. Springer-Verlag, Berlin, Heidelberg (2021). https://doi.org/10.1007/978-3-030-86549-8_9
22. Shinyama, Y.: Pdfminer: Python pdf parser and analyzer. https://github.com/pdfminer/pdfminer.six (2016). Accessed 20 Mar 2026
23. Team, G., Anil, R., Borgeaud, S., et al.: Gemini: A family of highly capable multimodal models (2025). https://arxiv.org/abs/2312.11805
24. UNICEF: Openai and unicef accelerate digital textbook access. https://www.unicefusa.org/about-unicef-usa/partnerships/companies/openai (2024). Accessed 20 Mar 2026
25. Wang, A., Chen, H., Liu, L.: Yolov10: real-time end-to-end object detection. In: Proceedings of the 38th International Conference on Neural Information Processing Systems. NIPS '24, Curran Associates Inc, Red Hook, NY, USA (2024)
26. World Health Organization: World Report on Vision. World Health Organization, Geneva (2019), see also ISO 9241-171: Ergonomics of Human-System Interaction — Guidance on Software Accessibility, ISO, 2008
27. Wu, Y., Kirillov, A., Massa, F., et al.: Detectron2. https://github.com/facebookresearch/detectron2 (2019)
28. Xu, Y., Xu, Y., Lv, T., et al.: LayoutLMv2: Multi-modal pre-training for visually-rich document understanding. In: Zong, C., Xia, F., Li, W., et al. (eds.) Proceedings of the 59th Annual Meeting of the Association for Computational Linguistics and the 11th International Joint Conference on Natural Language Processing (Volume 1: Long Papers), pp. 2579–2591. Association for Computational Linguistics, Online (Aug 2021). https://doi.org/10.18653/v1/2021.acl-long.201, https://aclanthology.org/2021.acl-long.201/
29. Zhong, X., Tang, J., Jimeno-Yepes, A.: Publaynet: Largest dataset ever for document layout analysis (09 2019). https://doi.org/10.1109/ICDAR.2019.00166

Quantifying Success: Establishing Benchmark Retention Rates in Undergraduate CS Programs

Darja Solodovnikova(✉), Laila Niedrite, and Juris Borzovs

Faculty of Science and Technology, University of Latvia, Riga 1586, Latvia
{darja.solodovnikova,laila.niedrite,juris.borzovs}@lu.lv

Abstract. The high dropout rate of students in higher education institutions in many countries, especially in engineering and computer science study programs, has a long history, and this problem is still observed and relevant today. A particularly high dropout rate is observed in the first year of studies. This study analyzes retention rates in European countries. We examine statistics on students enrolled in Computer Science bachelor's degree programs obtained from the Informatics Europe Higher Education Data Portal. Data on student retention rates are not directly available in the analyzed dataset. Therefore, we estimate retention using the available indicators by applying a stockâĂŞflow (population balancing) approach. Data analysis reveals significant variation in retention rates and shows the average retention rate 84.89% across European countries. We compared these rates with our declared benchmark from the ACM performed retention study in USA, and these rates are above the typical ranges in ACM study. We also conducted a literature study to find out what interventions have been implemented and evaluated to improve retention in specific universities. Five studies that demonstrate some effective strategies are described in more detail.

Keywords: Retention rate · Computer science studies · Interventions

1 Introduction

The high dropout rate of students in higher education institutions in many countries, especially in engineering and computer science study programs, has a long history, and this problem is still observed and relevant today. A particularly high dropout rate is observed in the first year of studies. A similar trend is also observed in the undergraduate computer science programs of the University of Latvia. 10 years have passed since our first study [2,3] on student dropout in order to create a method for identifying students who are likely to drop out in the first year of studies. This problem was and still is relevant in various external evaluations and accreditation of study programs and raises questions such as what is being done to improve the situation. Unfortunately, the trend

R. Matulevičius et al. (Eds.): DB&IS 2026, CCIS 3085, pp. 249–265, 2026.
https://doi.org/10.1007/978-3-032-30863-4_16

has persisted, and this encourages us to look at the latest research in this field and analyze the latest results and recommendations.

In our first study, we focused on the problem of student dropout, but this concept of dropout is also closely related to the problem of retention. The concept of retention is not unambiguously defined according to [19] and tends to vary depending on what is or is not taken into account in the analysis of this indicator. For example, if students starting their studies in a bachelor's program in computer science change study program within the same university after the first year of study, the university may consider such students as continuing their studies [19]. Accordingly, universities may only be interested in maximizing the number of graduates, without being interested in what happens within each individual study program, for example, in computer science studies.

In connection with retention, one can study both factors that increase student retention and, on the other hand, factors that influence the so-called dropout, as a result of which students leave computer science study programs. There are many questions that can be analyzed in connection with retention as well as with dropout: how do students' previous experience with computer science or its absence affect student results, what is the students' perception of what awaits them in computer science studies, what is the layout and content of the study program, especially the first study courses. For example, it is important to understand whether the first-year subjects are designed to attract students, to equalize different levels of knowledge, or to select the most capable students. Even these few example questions usually cannot be answered from the available data. If there is a need to compare data on computer science programs at higher education institutions on a larger scale, one should take into account the limited possibilities of discovering the true reasons for the retention rate values. Accordingly, when comparing retention indicators by country, if only quantitative data is available, they can only be considered a reference point for comparison. The results of a single study, regardless of the authority of the organization that initiated the study, cannot be considered a global benchmark.

Many studies [6,9,12,23] on student dropout create a model of "dropouts" with the idea of identifying students with problems early in order to provide individual support. We have mentioned here only a few articles found in our literature research covering the period 2020–2026, but there are many more similar studies. The solutions mentioned in these articles are often at the level of recommendations and there is no concrete evidence (quantified) that the recommended measures have actually improved the indicators. Often these are review articles that give an idea of the reasons for dropout, as well as examine possible measures (interventions) to improve the situation. As our research showed, there are very few specific articles that describe specific experiences in improving retention at a university in a computer science program.

Two research questions were formulated for our study: RQ1: What are the retention rates in computer science undergraduate programs in different countries? RQ2: What interventions have been implemented to improve retention in specific universities and has their impact been evaluated?

2 Previous Work and Our Motivation for Study

The University of Latvia offers a bachelor‘study program in computer science and each year 260 new students are admitted. For many years, before we began our first series of studies in 2015, it was observed that up to 50% of newly enrolled computer science students drop out during their first year of study at the Faculty of Computing. This trend motivated us to investigate the causes of dropout. We analyzed data about students enrolled in 2013 to uncover the characteristics of potential dropouts [3]. We examined high school grades, midterm exam scores in some core university courses, and prior programming knowledge of enrolled students. The conclusions of the study [3] were that none of the studied factors nor a combination of them could be used to predict the dropout. Our second study [2] was devoted to investigation of existing studies on how to determine the programming aptitude of the prospective students, but in neither of the studied publications an acceptable solution was found. Unfortunately, beyond the study, no further actions were taken to try to improve the indicators. Time has passed, and the question of whether the issue is still relevant has arose. Looking at student data on enrollment in the 1st semester of the 2023/2024 academic year in our computer science programs, a total of 256 students were enrolled. It should be noted that almost all applicants are accepted, and that these are studies financed by the state budget. The dropout rate after the 1st semester was 34%, but after the 1st year of study the dropout rate increased to 42%. As can be seen from these figures, the problem persists and the rates are close to those of 10 years ago. The question arises: is that a lot or a little?

Our new study was motivated by [21] that cited our previous study. This prompted us to explore the latest lessons in the field of student dropout. The time period for articles was from 2020 to 2026. We examined articles that cited [21] and articles found by Google Scholar using the keywords "Computer Science", "Undergraduate student", "Dropout". We selected for closer investigation those studies that described specific interventions aimed at improving student retention and that included evaluations before and after the interventions.

3 Can We Find a Benchmark for Comparison?

When we started our research, we wanted to find a published benchmark against which we could compare retention rates at other universities for undergraduate computer science studies. One of the sources that was found and evaluated was the review provided by [19]. The authors represent the Association for Computing Machinery (ACM), more specifically the ACM Education Board and its Retention Committee, which conducted a study to evaluate retention in undergraduate computer science programs at US universities.

The main problem that initiated the study by the Retention Committee members was the relatively low number of women and various other groups, such as different ethnicities, in computer science field in the United States, and the goal was to understand how retention among undergraduate computer science students can be increased, specifically in these groups. The primary focus of this study was on introductory-level courses (referred to in the study as CS1 and CS2), rather than on the total number of graduates in computer science programs, as understanding what happens in the first courses enables the implementation of measures to improve retention. The authors in their study defined retention as the number of students who began their studies in CS1 and continued their studies in CS2 computer science study programs, regardless of the institution at which the student began or continues his studies.

The authors examined data from The National Center for Women and Information Technology (NCWIT), where about 200 computer science or other related departments had submitted data in 2017. They used statistics submitted by universities on the number of students by dimensions relevant to the study (gender, ethnic groups) and created an overview of many US universities for a 4-year period. The results of Stephenson et al.'s study show that retention in undergraduate computer science programs in the United States from the first to the second year of study typically ranges from about 60% to 70%, but in some cases it can be lower than 50%, or higher than 80% if targeted interventions are implemented.

[19] also emphasizes that the study's results are applicable only to the USA, taking into account various external factors (e.g., economic, social, etc.) that may affect retention. However, since the authors represent the ACM, which unites computer science professionals from all over the world as members, and we found no other alternatives that would be better, we consider the results of the Stephenson et al. study as a benchmark for comparison, at least for the purposes of this article. However, this should be interpreted with caution, as their study focuses on early-stage courses, whereas our analysis covers the entire study period.

4 Literature Review: Interventions

According to [16], the goal of intervention programs is to prevent students leaving the studies by supporting students at risk. Stephenson et al. in their article [19] mention several interventions, for example, giving students a better understanding of computer science, holding informative sessions, offering attractive study programs and courses to potential students. It should also ensure that the program meets the different backgrounds of students, for example, by offering different paths through introductory courses, both for the more experienced students and those who are just starting to learn computer science [11]. In order for studies to be successful, helpful collaboration should also be provided, where pair programming [14] can be mentioned as an example, as well as a sense of belonging and a supportive study environment should be promoted. The last point is actually the most important to improve retention, for example, mutual communication between students and teachers should be encouraged [7].

In search of answers to the RQ2, various examples of interventions were identified in different sources of literature. These articles usually describe various intervention practices without experimentally evaluating the impact of the implemented measures on retention.

Interesting evolution of pair programming as an intervention method is found in [13], where LLMs are used to implement a human-AI pair programming solution. The similar idea implemented by using AI agent as a pair is described in [18], where the results were promising in supporting learning as well as improving student retention.

[5] article investigates how gamification techniques influence study results in first-year computer science studies, improving student engagement and problem-solving skills. The article offers both a broad review of gamification articles for the period from 2020 to 2023, showing frequently used gamification techniques such as points, badges, leader boards, virtual goods, etc. The authors also conducted a student survey, which showed that students preferred immediate rewards, such as extended deadlines for submissions, additional attempt to retake the test, nomination for VIP student for one day, etc. The authors concluded that this choice of students reduces pressure, thus improving the overall learning experience.

[4] studied how growth mind-set intervention was used for computer science students to shift their belief from seeing the abilities as fixed to the belief that domain specific abilities can be developed through effort. The authors conclude that this intervention stimulates career interest, but its impact on academic success is indirect and may not make it the most effective choice.

The article [22] describes a software system developed to support instructors of large classes in identifying students who need help, selecting appropriate interventions, and monitoring the results. Two types of interventions were used: emails were sent to at-risk students and additional training sessions were offered. The system also allowed regular post-intervention assessments. It turned out that targeted emails were even more effective (participation improved), compared to additional tutorials. Although this study does not contain comparative figures for retention rates, the use of the system demonstrates the technical feasibility of implementing interventions and tracking outcomes in the case of a large number of students.

5 Implemented and Evaluated Interventions: Case Studies

To find the answers to our RQ2, we will shortly describe the findings of our literature review, including only publications that contain practical experiments that impact student retention and provide numbers that measure the situation before and after the implemented actions.

5.1 Effects of Adding a CS0 Course to a Computer Science Curriculum

The authors of the article [20] are from Indiana University South Bend, USA. They describe the typical dropout rate of students in the first programming course (CS1) as ranging from 30% to almost 50%. To improve the situation, an introductory course CS0 was created more than 10 years ago, which was focused on problem solving and simple algorithms rather than learning the syntax of the programming language used in CS1. This was done with the hope of engaging students and increasing their interest in their studies.

Fourteen years later, all collected results were analyzed. The results showed that the CS0 pass rate was 67.2% compared to the historical CS1 pass rate of less than 60%. After the introduction of CS0 into the curriculum, it was not mandatory, so the authors also compared CS1 pass rates for students with and without prior CS0. Students without CS0 had a CS1 pass rate of 65.9%, and those with CS0 had a better success rate: 70.2%. The authors also emphasize that the implementation of this introductory course required additional resources, so it is also important to evaluate the effectiveness of such activities and whether the increase in student retention is worth the investment.

5.2 Change of Programming Language

The research [15] investigates how changing the programming language from Octave to Python in Spanish university Artificial Intelligence course affects student outcomes. The Artificial Intelligence course is a compulsory subject in the last study year, and in previous study years students have learned different programming languages.

The research consists of four experiments analyzing 3 academic years before and 2 years after the programming language change. The dataset contains five parameters: four exams (Practical and Theoretical midterm, Practical and Theoretical final), as well as the academic year.

The data analysis showed that, for student academic outcomes, the most important factor associated with the failed course with Octave programming language was the practical midterm exam, whereas for Python it was the theoretical final exam.

Although this is not a typical dropout study as it studies final-year students, it is distinguished by a series of experiments over a long period, studying the situation both before and after the implementation of the changes, which is why it was included in this description of practical experiments.

5.3 Compulsory Attendance and a Learning Methodology Course

[21] in their study analyze the academic results of undergraduate computer science students from 2010 to 2018 using the Rasch-model.

In 2016, an intervention consisting of 2 activities was applied: attendance at all theoretical lectures became mandatory and an introductory course in studies was introduced for all 1st-year students.

The introductory course "Preparation course for university studies and developing learning skills", like the other courses, was mandatory for all newly admitted students. The course consisted of a training program and a mentor program. The training program was conducted by psychologists together with peer counselors. Each course group was kept small, consisting of approximately 20 students. Psychologists taught different general learning and time management techniques, provided information about the study process and course grading, and helped students understand how to build close ties in the student group. Since peer counselors also participated in the training, a positive role model and links with students of other courses were also formed in this way. Peer counselors also organized separate classes for effective learning of math and programming subjects. It should be noted that most of the course (18 lectures) was organized before the first study semester, while some lectures were also held later during the semester.

The study showed that, after the intervention, the results in study subjects improved, students with lower success during the semester also tried to take the exams, whereas before the intervention they would most likely have dropped out. When evaluated numerically, the authors conclude that as a result of the intervention, student retention increased by 28%.

5.4 Reduction of Curricular Complexity

The authors of the paper [8] investigate the impact of structural complexity in Computer Science curricula on student attrition. The curriculum is modeled as a graph where nodes represent courses and edges represent prerequisite relationships. Based on this graph, several complexity metrics are calculated, including the delay factor (the longest prerequisite path containing the course), the blocking factor (the number of courses dependent on it), and centrality (the sum of delays across all paths involving the course). An overall program complexity measure is then obtained by aggregating a linear combination of the delay and blocking factors across courses.

The interventions applied in the study were aimed at reducing program complexity and included the removal of unnecessary prerequisites to allow more pathways through which students could complete the program, as well as greater flexibility in choosing when courses are taken. As a result, the updated curriculum had 60% lower structural complexity. In addition, the new optional CS0 course was offered to students who prefer a more introductory entry into their studies and for those who have insufficient math knowledge to take CS1 course.

To evaluate the impact of curriculum changes, the authors analyzed data from 40,869 students over six years. Students were divided into two groups: those enrolled before the curriculum change introduced in Fall 2021 and those who began their studies afterward. The results indicate a substantial improvement in retention, increasing from 67% to 98%.

5.5 Modularization for Mastery Learning

The study [1] examines improvements in student success in an introductory CS1 course following changes in course design over a four-year period. The interventions implemented during the study were aimed at supporting mastery learning.

The course content was organized into four modules, with each module requiring the successful completion of the preceding one as a prerequisite. At the same time, the course allowed students to progress at their own pace: beginning with the second module, several modules were offered in parallel, and earlier modules were repeated. This structure enabled students to retake modules in which they encountered difficulties without penalty.

As a result of the introduced interventions, student attrition in the course decreased significantly, from 25% to 3.8%. In addition, the average time required to complete the course was reduced from 23.2 to 14.9 weeks. Although the results of this approach are promising, the authors also note several challenges, including increased complexity of the course content and assessment, student procrastination, and the need to coordinate the work of multiple instructors.

6 Data Analysis

To analyze retention rates, we examined statistics on students enrolled in Computer Science bachelor's degree programs from the Informatics Europe Higher Education Data Portal [10]. The data include the total number of students, the number of first-year students, and the number of degrees awarded per country and year, with corresponding figures also available for female students. As of February 2026, the dataset covers the study years 2010/2011 through 2023/2024 and includes 22 European countries: Austria, Bulgaria, the Czech Republic, Estonia, Finland, France, Germany, Greece, Ireland, Italy, Latvia, Lithuania, the Netherlands, Norway, Poland, Portugal, Romania, Spain, Sweden, Switzerland, Turkey, and the United Kingdom. The data are collected from state education authorities or statistics agencies. To ensure comprehensive coverage of all institutions awarding bachelor's degrees in the analyzed countries, we used the statistics from both Research Universities and Universities of Applied Sciences.

6.1 Retention Rate Calculation

Data on student retention rates are not directly available in the analyzed dataset. Therefore, we estimate retention using the available indicators by applying a stockâĂŞflow (population balancing) approach [17] widely used in cohort-component population accounting. According to the population balancing equation, the population at time t equals the population at time $t-1$ plus entries minus exits. We adapt this framework to the student population by treating first-year students as entries and graduates and dropouts as exits. As a result, the population balance equation in our context is the following:

$$T_N = T_{N-1} + F_N - G_{N-1} - D_{N-1} \tag{1}$$

where

- T_N is the total number of students in year N
- T_{N-1} is the total number of students in year $N-1$

- F_N is the number of first-year students in year N
- G_{N-1} is the number of degrees awarded in year $N-1$
- D_{N-1} is the number of students who dropped out in year $N-1$

We calculate the number of students who remained enrolled (i.e., retained students) R_{N-1} from year $N-1$ to year N as follows:

$$R_{N-1} = T_{N-1} - G_{N-1} - D_{N-1} \tag{2}$$

After rearranging the first equation, substituting D_{N-1} in the second equation and simplifying, we obtain the number of retained students in year $N-1$ as the total enrollment in year N minus the number of first-year students in that year:

$$R_{N-1} = T_N - F_N \tag{3}$$

Finally, we calculate the student retention rate (proportion of students who continue their studies) as follows:

$$Retention\ Rate_{N-1} = \frac{T_N - F_N}{T_{N-1} - G_{N-1}} \tag{4}$$

6.2 Limitations and Assumptions

Several factors may affect the accuracy of the calculated retention rates. One such factor is the timing of student count measurements. Our assumptions regarding this timing are based on the reporting practice in Latvia. In Latvia, the total number of students and the number of first-year students are measured at the beginning of the academic year on 1 October, while the number of graduates includes all students who receive their degrees during the entire academic year.

Besides, the total number of students and the number of graduates may include not only those who entered the university in the first year of study, but also students who transferred from other institutions or study programs and entered directly into the second or later years.

Even though, the literature more commonly focuses on the analysis of retention among first-year students, we could calculate retention rates only for students across all study years combined due to the nature of the available data. Although direct validation of our calculated rates is not possible, consistent results across years suggest that the method provides a reasonable approximation.

6.3 Data Availability

Although the dataset includes data beginning with the 2010/2011 academic year, we limited our analysis to the most recent ten years available.

Data availability varies across countries, and some indicators are only partially available. In several cases, information on total enrollment, first-year students, or graduates is missing for parts of the dataset, which prevented the calculation of retention rates for all countries and years. Due to these data limitations, Denmark, Belgium, and Iceland were excluded from the analysis.

According to the data interpretation notes provided in the Informatics Europe Higher Education Data Portal, total enrollment figures for Sweden include not only students pursuing first-cycle degrees but also students taking individual courses within first-cycle degree programs. As a result, retention rates cannot be calculated reliably for Sweden, since the total enrollment includes students who are not counted among first-year entrants and graduates.

For France, the reported number of students is underestimated due to the structure of the national higher education system. The statistics exclude students in preparatory and technical programs who may later transfer directly into the third year of university Computer Science programs.

Due to this inconsistency between the stock and flow measures, we excluded Sweden and France from our analysis. For the remaining countries, retention rates were calculated only for the academic years with sufficient data.

6.4 Findings

Retention rates were analyzed in two ways. First, we compared retention levels across countries and examined their dynamics over time to identify trends and patterns of change. Second, we conducted a gender-based comparison of retention rates to assess whether female or male students are more likely to remain enrolled in the university.

Average Retention Rate. Figure 1 shows average retention rates by country (overall average: 84.89%). Turkey has the highest average retention rate (97.81%) followed by the Netherlands (93.13%). A group of countries including Romania, Portugal, Greece, Finland, Switzerland, and Norway also have retention rate above the overall average ranging from 88.58% to 92.25%. Lithuania, Germany, the United Kingdom, Italy, Bulgaria, and Ireland are close to the overall average and have retention rate between 85.11% and 85.92%.

In contrast, the lowest retention rates are observed in the Czech Republic (64.32%), Latvia (70.88%), and Poland (76.33%). Estonia, Austria, and Spain with retention rate ranging from 79.90% to 83.55% also fall below the overall average. Overall, the chart reveals substantial difference exceeding 33% between the highest and lowest average retention rates across different countries.

Retention Rate Dynamics. For comparative analysis, countries were grouped into five regional clusters: the Baltic states, Western Europe, Nordic countries, Southern European countries, and Central and Eastern European countries.

Figure 2 illustrates retention rate dynamics for the Baltic States alongside the overall average across all analyzed countries. The overall average retention rate shows a slight upward trend until the 2020/2021 academic year, when a decline of approximately is observed. This drop is very likely associated with the effects of the COVID-19 pandemic.

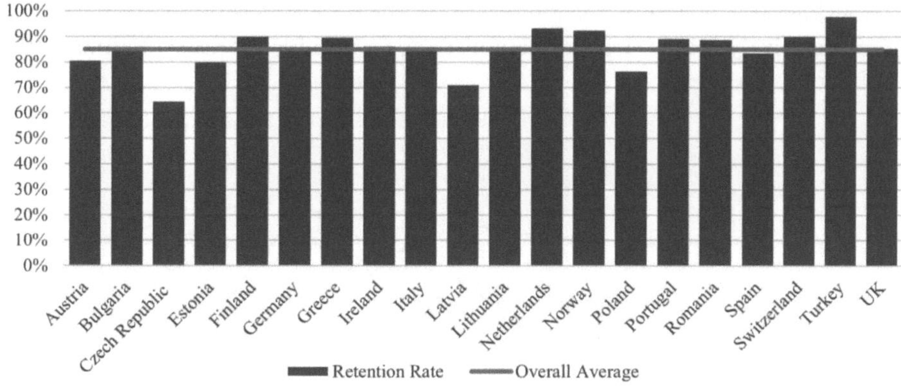

Fig. 1. Average retention rate for all countries.

Lithuania shows the highest retention among the Baltic States, although recent data are incomplete. Estonia's retention rate is the second highest while Latvia reports the lowest values throughout the whole analyzed period. Starting from 2015/2016, Latvia and Estonia have similar fluctuation patterns reaching the minimal value in 2016/2017 and increasing subsequently. The drop in retention in 2020/2021 is more pronounced compared to all countries average. In the most recent year, Estonia shows an increase in retention rate whereas Latvia has a decline.

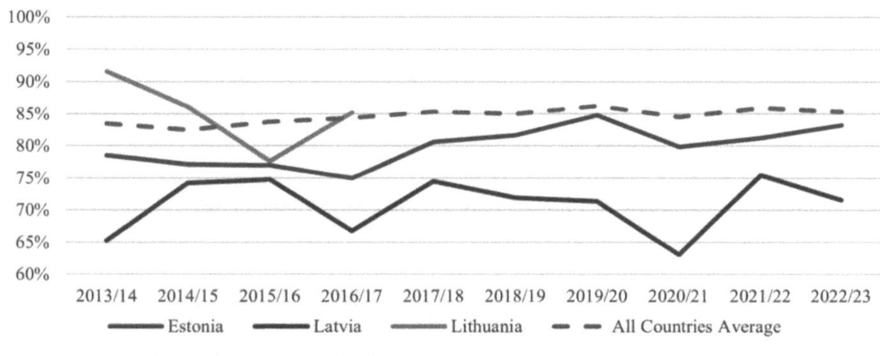

Fig. 2. Retention rate in the Baltic States.

Figure 3 presents retention rate dynamics in Western Europe. Retention rates in most countries are close to or above the overall average, with the exception of Austria. However, Austria shows a gradual increase in retention and approaches the overall average in the later years of the observed period. A decline in retention following the COVID-19 pandemic is also observed in several Western European countries. At the same time, Germany and Austria demonstrate a slight increase in retention rates just after the pandemic. While retention rates in most countries remain relatively stable, Ireland demonstrates a notable increase of almost 10%.

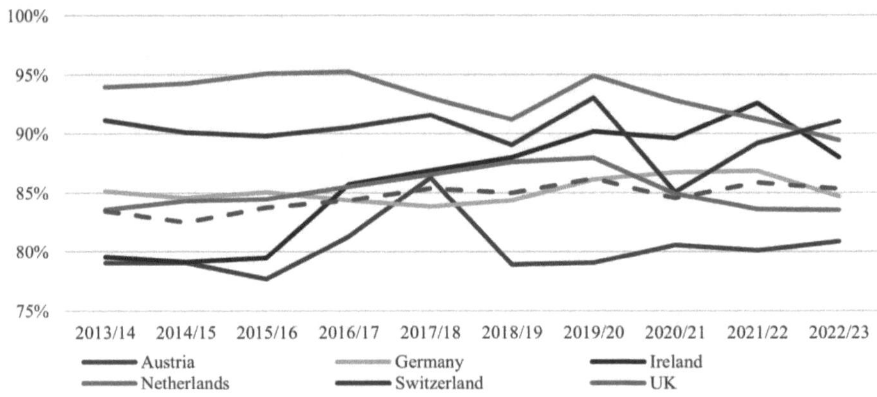

Fig. 3. Retention rate in the Western European countries.

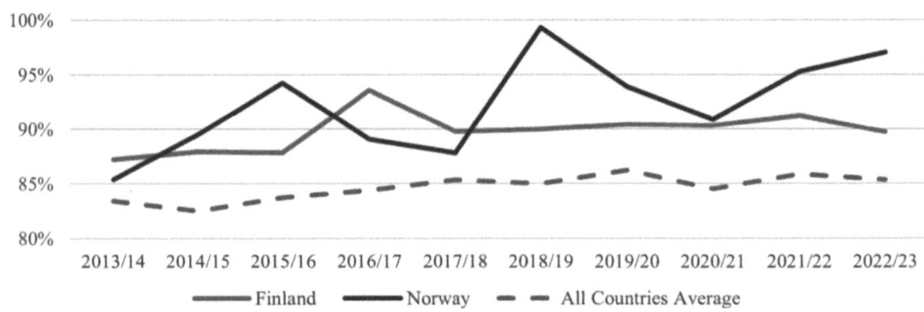

Fig. 4. Retention rate in the Nordic countries.

Figure 4 shows the retention trends in Nordic countries. Overall, retention rates in both countries are very high and remain well above the average for all analyzed European countries. In Finland, student retention is relatively stable (around 90%) in recent years. In contrast, the retention rate in Norway is more volatile with a peak in the 2018/2019 academic year (99.33%). A decline following the COVID-19 pandemic is observed in Norway, however, the pandemic does not appear to have a noticeable impact on retention rates in Finland.

Figure 5 illustrates retention trends in Southern Europe for the academic years for which the necessary student data are available. Trends vary across countries. Spain shows a generally increasing retention rate throughout the analyzed period. In contrast, Italy and Portugal exhibit a decline beginning in the 2019/2020 academic year, followed by a slight increase in the most recent year.

Overall, retention in this region remains consistently above the overall European average, indicating relatively high student persistence in Computer Science bachelor's programs.

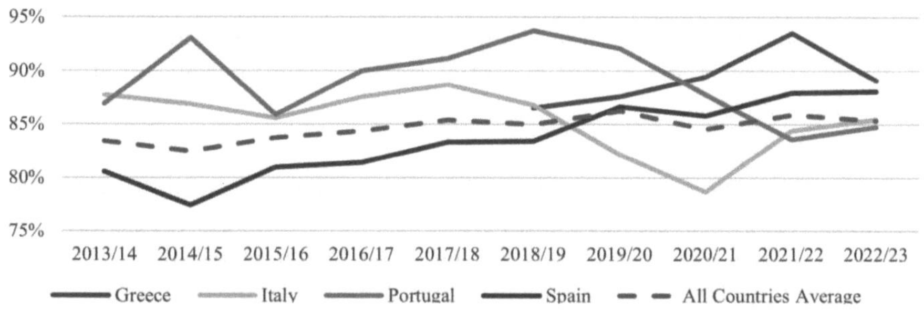

Fig. 5. Retention rate in the Southern European countries.

Figure 6 presents retention rate trends in Central and Eastern Europe. In general, this region shows greater variability in retention rates than others with larger fluctuations over time. Turkey consistently exhibits the highest retention (>95%) throughout the whole analyzed period not only among Central and Eastern European countries but also among all other European countries. Romania and Bulgaria are near or slightly above average, while Poland and the Czech Republic remain below. Moreover, Czech Republic has the lowest retention rate among all European countries.

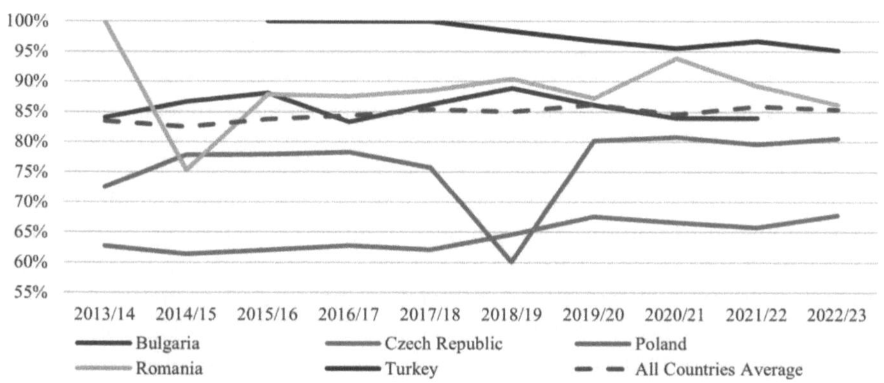

Fig. 6. Retention rate in Central and Eastern Europe.

Across the analyzed regions, retention rates show clear regional differences but in general remain relatively stable over time. Nordic countries, Western European countries and Turkey demonstrate the highest retention levels, while

Baltic states and Eastern European countries have considerably lower retention rates. Overall, the observed regional differences in retention rates may be caused by variations in educational system structures, admission policies, curriculum design, and the level of institutional support provided to students. These factors should be examined in more detail in future research. On the whole, the results suggest that although retention in Computer Science study programs is relatively high across Europe, there is still potential for targeted interventions to further improve this indicator.

Retention Rate by Gender. Our second objective was to examine differences in retention rates between male and female students. Retention rates for female and male students were calculated by the same formula described in Sect. 6.1 using the number of female students available in the Informatics Europe dataset. Data on the number of female students are not available for Italy and Poland, therefore, these countries were excluded from the gender-based analysis.

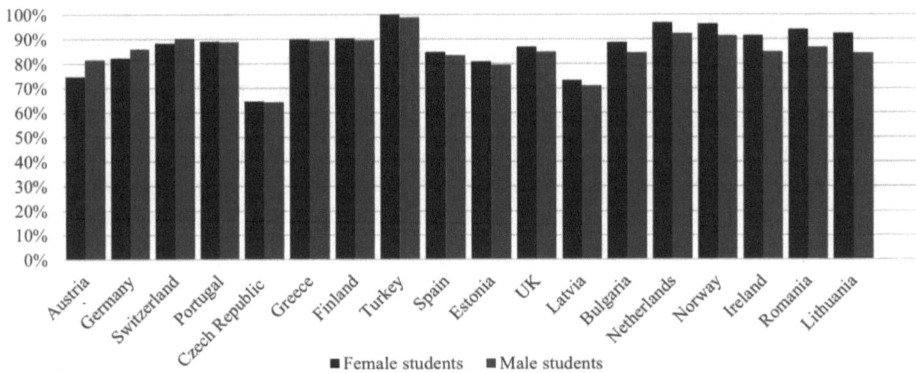

Fig. 7. Average retention rate of male and female students.

Figure 7 compares average retention rate of male and female students across countries. Overall, retention rates for both genders are relatively close in most countries, with differences within a few percent. The highest gap between retention rates of males and females is observed in Lithuania and makes 7.92%. In several countries such as Lithuania, Romania, Ireland and others, female students have higher retention rates than male students. On the other hand, there are countries, such as Austria, Germany, and Switzerland where male students demonstrate higher retention. It can be concluded that across the analyzed countries gender differences in retention exist but are generally not large.

7 Conclusions

The ACM study that we declared as a potential benchmark to compare, shows retention in early study courses in a range from 60% to 70%, with some programs achieving over 80% through targeted interventions. The ACM study focuses on early courses, not for the whole study period, but due to the fact that a particularly high dropout rate is observed in the first year of studies, the evaluations can be compared.

Our European data analysis reveals significant variation in retention rates. The average retention rate across countries is 84.89%. Regional trends in different years show stability in Nordic countries, variability in Central and Eastern Europe. Latvia consistently reports the lowest retention among Baltic states. Retention rates for male and female students are generally similar across countries, with minor differences. Overall, European retention rates vary widely, with some countries approaching 98% and others below 65%. Comparing these rates with our declared benchmark we can see that mostly these rates are above the typical ranges in ACM study.

Regarding the state of the art with interventions, our research shows that there are many studies that describe methods how potential dropouts can be identified, and recommend possible interventions. Some studies highlight new types of interventions that look promising, for example, AI-assisted pair programming and gamification methods. However, the number of studies that actually implement interventions and provide some numeric evaluation of success is much smaller. We found only 5 studies and they demonstrate some effective strategies, for example, adding introductory courses, changing programming language, introducing mandatory attendance, reducing curricular complexity by removing prerequisites, and providing modular mastery.

The study indicates that while retention in European computer science programs is relatively high, there is room for improvement through targeted strategies.

References

1. Álvarez, C., Samary, M.M., Wise, A.F.: Modularization for mastery learning in cs1: A 4-year action research study. J. Comput. High. Educ. **36**(2), 546–589 (2024)
2. Borzovs, J., Niedrīte, L., Solodovnikova, D.: Computer programming aptitude test as a tool for reducing student attrition. In: Proceedings of the VTR Conference, pp. 29–35. Rēzekne, Latvia (2015)
3. Borzovs, J., Niedrīte, L., Solodovnikova, D.: Factors affecting attrition among first year computer science students: The case of university of latvia. In: Proceedings of the VTR Conference, pp. 36–42. Rēzekne, Latvia (2015)
4. Burnette, J.L., Hoyt, C.L., Russell, V.M., Lawson, B., Dweck, C.S., Finkel, E.: A growth mind-set intervention improves interest but not academic performance in the field of computer science. Social Psychol. Person. Sci. **11**(1), 107–116 (2020)

5. Chong, M.M., Subramanian, P., Ting, M., Ying, L.J.: An investigation into the perception of gen z students in higher education towards gamification techniques in learning computing subjects. In: 2024 International Visualization, Informatics and Technology Conference (IVIT), pp. 165–170 (2024)
6. Dirzyte, A., et al.: Factors contributing to dropping out of adults' programming e-learning. Heliyon **9**(12), e22113 (2023)
7. Frieze, C., Quesenberry, J.: Kicking Butt in Computer Science: Women in Computing at Carnegie Mellon University. Dog Ear Publishing, Indianapolis, IN, USA (2015)
8. Ganesan, S., Lionelle, A., Gill, C., Brodley, C.: Does reducing curricular complexity impact student success in computer science? In: Proceedings of the 56th ACM Technical Symposium on Computer Science Education V. 1., p. 360–366. SIGCSETS 2025, Association for Computing Machinery, New York, NY, USA (2025)
9. Garcia, G.P., Holanda, M., Mandelli, M., Moreira, J.R., Da Silva, D.: Predictive analysis of student dropout in the computer science program at the university of Brasilia. In: IEEE Frontiers in Education Conference (FIE), pp. 1–8 (2025)
10. Informatics Europe: Higher education data portal.https://www.informatics-europe.org/data-portal/?page=index.html
11. Lewis, C.M., Yasuhara, K., Anderson, R.E.: Deciding to major in computer science: a grounded theory of students' self-assessment of ability. In: 7th International Workshop on Computing Education Research, pp. 3–10. ICER '11, Association for Computing Machinery, New York, NY, USA (2011)
12. Luciano, R.G., Olipas, C.N.P., Dela Cruz, A.P.: Factors affecting the dropout rate among information technology students: a basis for an intervention plan. Online Submission **8**(4), 2013–2017 (2022)
13. Ma, Q., Wu, T., Koedinger, K.: Is AI the better programming partner? human-human pair programming vs. human-ai pair programming (2023). https://arxiv.org/abs/2306.05153
14. McDowell, C., Werner, L., Bullock, H.E., Fernald, J.: Pair programming improves student retention, confidence, and program quality. Commun. ACM **49**(8), 90–95 (2006)
15. Melgar-García, L., Troncoso-García, Á., Gutiérrez-Avilés, D., Torres, J.F., Troncoso, A.: Explainable artificial intelligence for education: A real case of a university subject switched to python. In: 16th International Conference on Computational Intelligence in Security for Information Systems, 14th Int. Conference on European Transnational Education, pp. 358–367. Springer Nature Switzerland (2023)
16. Pellegrini, M., Pannone, C., Fadda, D., Scalas, L.F., Vivanet, G., Neitzel, A.: Protocol: prevention, intervention, and compensation programs to tackle school dropout: an evidence and gap map. Campbell Syst. Rev. **21**(1), e70032 (2025)
17. Preston, S.H., Heuveline, P., Guillot, M.: Demography: Measuring and Modeling Population Processes. Blackwell Publishers, Oxford, UK (2001)
18. Robe, P., Kuttal, S.K.: Designing pairbuddy—a conversational agent for pair programming. ACM Trans. Comput.-Hum. Interact. **29**(4) (May 2022)
19. Stephenson, C., Miller, A.D., Alvarado, C., Barker, L., Barr, V., Camp, T., et al.: Retention in Computer Science Undergraduate Programs in the US: Data Challenges and Promising Interventions. Tech. rep, Association for Computing Machinery, New York, NY, USA (2018)
20. Surma, D.R., Surma, Z.E.: Understanding the effects of adding a cs0 course to a computer science curriculum: a long-term study. J. Comput. Sci. Coll. **40**(4), 108–117 (2024)

21. Takács, R., Kárász, J.T., Takács, S., Horváth, Z., Oláh, A.: Applying the rasch model to analyze the effectiveness of education reform in order to decrease computer science students' dropout. Human. Social Sci. Commun. **8**, 44 (2021)
22. Utamachant, P., Anutariya, C., Pongnumkul, S.: i-ntervene: applying an evidence-based learning analytics intervention to support computer programming instruction. Smart Learn. Environ. **10**, 37 (2023)
23. Vera, A.A., Martinez, J., Espinoza, A.P.: Determinants of university dropout and educational quality improvement. In: Computational Science and Its Applications – ICCSA 2025 Workshops, pp. 337–354. Springer Nature Switzerland (2026)

Digitalization and Intelligent Systems for Organisations

Governing AI Agents in Organizations: Toward an Opportunity - and Risk-Based Framework

Johannes Schneider[1(✉)] and Dimitrios Symeonidis[2]

[1] University of Liechtenstein, Vaduz, Liechtenstein
johannes.schneider@uni.li
[2] Institute of Computer Science, University of Tartu, Tartu, Estonia
dimitrios.symeonidis@ut.ee

Abstract. The impact of AI agents on companies might be more disruptive than that of Generative AI. Instead of producing digital artifacts, AI agents execute (business) processes autonomously, performing actions that change our world. This shift challenges prevailing AI governance for organizations, centered on governing static, passive artifacts (like data and models) and human roles around them. Therefore, we ask whether existing AI governance approaches are sufficient for organizations adopting agentic AI to leverage opportunities while mitigating risks, and if not, how governance could change. Our conceptual work synthesizes (i) established governance frameworks, (ii) work contrasting Generative and Agentic AI, and (iii) literature on agentic AI governance. We follow prior work and analyze governance through three lenses: scope (what is governed), mechanisms (who/what enforces governance), and targets (what governance aims at). We argue that AI agents share many commonalities from a governance lens with a human workforce but also exhibit important differences. Human skill sets and governance of well-studied artifacts such as data and models may need to be extended. This typology is a conceptual foundation whose practical utility should be evaluated through future empirical studies of AI-agent governance in organizational settings.

Keywords: AI Agents · Governance · Framework · Conceptual

1 Introduction

Generative AI (GenAI) achieved unprecedented adoption within a few weeks after the launch of ChatGPT [40]. While agents are adopted more slowly, AI agents are likely leading to the next, possibly bigger disruption. Early GenAI successfully generates digital artifacts but performs poorly on tasks essential to AI agents such as tool calling. AI agents execute complex tasks through reasoning and tool use, thereby affecting organizational processes directly. An illustrative example are agents offered by major corporations like OpenAI and Anthropic

R. Matulevičius et al. (Eds.): DB&IS 2026, CCIS 3085, pp. 269–284, 2026.
https://doi.org/10.1007/978-3-032-30863-4_17

that can control a computer [1,24] by analyzing screenshots and controlling the mouse and the keyboard to potentially perform organizational tasks performed by office workers. Media articles argue that such AI agents have sent stock prices of traditional SaaS software plummeting albeit concerns of a "SaaSpocalypse" [21]. In short, AI agents present tremendous opportunities but also risks for corporations. Thus, seizing their opportunities and mitigating their risks âĂŞ essential goals of AI governance âĂŞ becomes a necessity. A Microsoft report suggests that already 80% of Fortune 500 companies employ AI agents and almost one third of employees have turned to unsanctioned AI agents for work tasks [23]. At the same time, the current discourse on AI is marked by considerable hype, making greater conceptual clarity necessary. These developments immediately give rise to the question:

Are existing AI governance approaches sufficient? If not, what should Agentic AI governance look like?

This question is also motivated by the fact that prior literature has discussed frameworks for AI governance prior to AI agents [26,31,32]. The literature on AI agents is rapidly emerging, but often targeted toward policymakers [19,20], risk-focused [16,18,27,43], or emphasizing technical aspects touching on specific governance aspects often related to governance implementation [36]. The literature on AI agents focusing on governance for businesses is fragmented and only emerging, and a variety of different perspectives given the potential impact of AI agents are needed.

We develop a first framework of agentic AI governance by contrasting prior AI governance with emerging agentic AI literature with respect to: *Does the what (scope), who (mechanisms), targets (what for) change for AI agents?* Thus, our governance framework is naturally incomplete as it does not repeat many classical concerns for governance that also apply to agents in a very similar manner, but emphasizes novel aspects and aspects that have changed strongly in relevance. We focus on organizations adopting AI (rather than organizations building foundation models and agent frameworks from scratch like OpenAI, Google or Anthropic) as the latter are more commonly discussed in the context of policy. Furthermore, we aim at balancing deep technical insights and high-level governance aspects of organizations by adopting a socio-technical lens as such a perspective is also absent.

In turn, our framework provides a broad view that is both valuable for practitioners and academics as it treats technical, economic, and human aspects jointly though we acknowledge that our work is conceptual and empirical validation is outstanding.

2 Background: Evolution from GenAI to Agentic AI

We provide a brief comparison of GenAI and agentic AI discussing technical aspects and fundamental characteristics enabled by technology. We also discuss related governance frameworks aimed at pre-GenAI and GenAI.

2.1 Technical and Capability Evolution

We build on recent comprehensive conceptualizations, i.e., [30]. Early GenAI, e.g. (Chat)GPT 1 to 3.5 consisted of a large neural network trained up to internet scale data. These models tend to reply "instantly" to user requests.

Early models quickly evolved along two dimensions: Their reasoning and their interaction capabilities. Reasoning capabilities were originally latent in the model, rudimentary, and had to be elicited, e.g., using prompt additions such as "Think step-by-step". Current reasoning models implement complex reasoning processes, which lead to slow response times as models might reply to a sequence of (self-generated) prompts being part of the reasoning process or elicit long "chain-of-thoughts" traces. The management and implementation of this process are often handled by an orchestrator, which interacts with the LLM and keeps track of intermediate results and states. An LLM might first be queried to generate a plan, which is assessed and executed in a step-wise manner. Intermediate steps might be checked for their correctness and potential to reach a (good) solution. In turn, plans might be altered.

Rudimentary interaction capability was already added to precursors of Chat-GPT 3.5, e.g., the ability to interact with external databases to retrieve and add information to existing prompts (RAG). Also, already GPT-4 possessed the ability to use tools, e.g., call a calculator to perform simple calculations and generate and execute Python code as an intermediate step to solve tasks. However, prior to Agentic AI these tools rarely performed actions that changed the environment. Tools become increasingly broad. They can be digital (e.g., APIs for function calls) and physical (e.g., robots) and differ strongly in complexity (e.g., a simple calculator vs. another agent). Thus, an essential trait of interaction of AI agents was missing: Actions impacting the real world.

Furthermore, AI agents also accumulate large amounts of information, when solving long, complex tasks (episodic memory) [15]. This information might stem from the current execution of a task involving data from humans, tool usage, but also internal reasoning and execution of prior tasks. Memory might be shared directly with other agents as a deliberate design decision. That is, in principle, the experiences of one agent might directly affect the behavior of another agent reasoning using the shared memory. The addition of data of one agent might lead to the deletion of data generated by another agent, e.g., if it seems to be outdated or incorrect in light of the new data.

In GenAI, a prompt is typically a (short) textual instruction potentially accompanied by data. A so-called system prompt can define more generic model behavior and roles across multiple prompts, such as "You are a helpful assistant". In contrast, an AI agent's definition is often more comprehensive, involving a profile, goals, workflow instructions, constraints (such as guardrails to obey or process steps to follow) and potentially permissions covering, e.g., tool and data access.

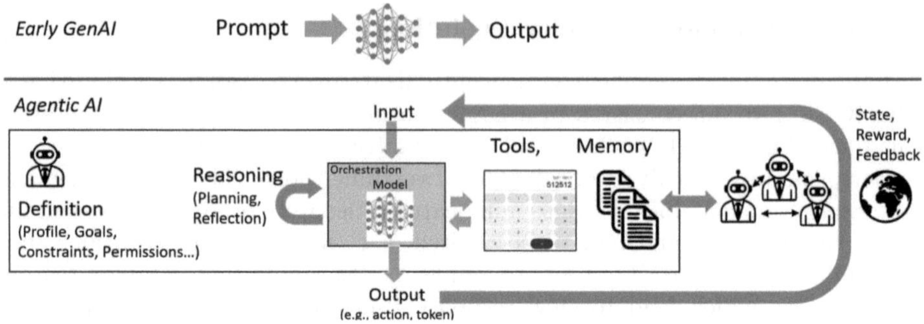

Fig. 1. Evolution from (early) GenAI to Agentic AI. Both rely on a foundation model. But Agentic AI is much more complex due to models that reason (plan and reflect), perform actions using tools and leverage (shared) experiences. Extended from [30].

2.2 Earlier AI Governance for Businesses

In pre-GenAI, a model typically addressed only one narrow task like cancer recognition on MRI scans or credit scoring. A model was typically trained on company-internal data producing simple outputs, such as single numbers, categories, and rankings. However, many concerns of the pre-GenAI governance era (see e.g., [26,31]) transfer to AI agents, e.g., data quality, bias, security, and model correctness, efficiency, robustness, and explainability. Also system level concerns related to safety and security, ethics and societal impact and human-AI collaboration are still important [22]. Generative AI governance [32] introduced novel concerns such as prompt injection, harmlessness of generated content, and novel types of failures such as hallucinations, which required careful assessment of generated content by people. In addition, employees can access GenAI easily without explicit deployments, making governance related to people more relevant.

3 Methodology

We performed an integrative literature review aiming to integrate diverse, emerging literature [38,42]. Thus, the included literature is not exhaustive. We started from search terms such as "AI agents governance for corporations" on Google Scholar and Google, combining forward and backward search. That is, we also included grey literature, i.e., non-peer reviewed governance literature from reputable sources namely major consulting companies, AI companies, government bodies, or independent research institutions. At the same time we excluded articles from journals and publishers not appearing in common rankings and providing no clear insights. This selection approach aims at a timely and impactful treatment of the topic, as many development guidelines are developed within companies, and publication of journal articles often takes years, i.e., publications happen after organizations have already addressed governance. This approach allows us to expose emerging governance aspects. We build upon governance frameworks that adopt a similar lens to our framework but do not account for AI agents. That is, we build on a line of frameworks for GenAI [32] and AI [31] rooted ultimately in IT governance [37]. Our analysis is interpretative. We reassess dimensions in light of the evolution from GenAI to AI agents. We base our discussion on this evolution (see background) and literature on AI. We match the concepts identified in each article to those already present in prior frameworks leading to the following outcomes: i) the concept is already present and fully covered, and ii) the concept is either partially present or differs strongly in relevance, and iii) the concept is novel. As we focus on differences, we only discuss concepts falling under (ii) and (iii).

4 Agentic AI Governance Framework

4.1 Agentic AI Governance: A Fundamental Shift

Governance shifts toward **operational actors (agents) rather than static IT artifacts** [19]. AI agents fundamentally change how organizations work as they create a **joint workforce of AI agents and people**. Even if AI agents execute the same tasks as humans, they differ in many aspects, e.g., they evolve quickly, can be replicated, but lack intentions and are non-social. Their action spaces and resource needs also differ as illustrated in Fig. 2 which is only an incomplete snapshot but aims to list key dimensions. Because AI behavior is statistical, guarantees of predictability and reliability are generally weaker. Error sources also differ: AI agents suffer from hallucinations, brittleness while humans can suffer from fatigue and inattention. Whereas human performance depends on time, attention, and motivation, agent performance depends on compute, model capabilities, and tool access. Some actions require human oversight due to regulation, e.g., high-risk decisions having a strong impact on other humans. Actions like large scale data processing by examining and reasoning on individual data items, executing workflows, cannot be done by humans, as humans are physically bounded, i.e., they cannot read millions of tokens/words in a short time.

Governance mechanisms partly overlap, but they also diverge because of these characteristics. AI agents are machines without rights and can therefore be inspected and modified arbitrarily. However, in contrast to conventional, simple machines, AI agents can be assigned objectives and act autonomously, while also being subject to role definitions, hierarchy, and oversight. However, providing incentives (such as a bonus) can make people work harder or trade personal goals in favor of company goals. AI Agents do not have personal goals rather they are programmable through direct prompts, and different data and training regimes to an extent that exceeds those of humans. They can be monitored at a very detailed level, e.g., their reasoning process can be introspected and individual steps can be assessed though with some caution as fidelity is not warranted [30].

	Scope	Human	AI Agent	Both Human + AI Agent
Opportunity	Capacity & Evolution	Physically bounded, slow to scale	Scalable, replicable, 24/7	Resource-dependent, teachable
	Behavior	Intentional, social, common-sense	Statistical, programmable, inspectable	Follow instructions & goals, adaptive
	Actions	High-stakes, special cases, judgments	High volume, repeatable workflow runs	Delegate, Access/Modify/Execute
	Resources	Time, motivation	Compute, foundation models	Data, tools, budget, other agents
	Legal & Accountability	Rights-bearing, accountable	No legal rights, only attributable	Regulated, subject to oversight
	Error causes	Inattention, fatigue	Hallucinations, brittleness	Incapable, poor instructions/data, bias
Risk	Vulnerability	Social engineering, coercion	Prompt injection, protocol/tool exploits	Manipulation
	Governance			
	Structural	Incentives, Accountability	Autonomy boundaries	Roles, hierarchy, decision rights, oversight
	Procedures	Conflict-of-interest, fitness-for-duty	Reasoning control, rollback	Policies, approvals, processes
	Relational	Social norms, reputation	Inter-agent coordination	Training, communication
	Technical	Co-signing	Design (e.g., Kill-switch, sandboxes)	Access-control

Fig. 2. Joint Workforce: Humans and AI Agents jointly form the workforce with many similar characteristics and governance mechanisms, but also profound differences.

4.2 Framework Outline

The outline of our framework (Fig. 3) follows earlier work dating back to [37]. We maintain foundational dimensions, i.e., scope(objects of governance) and targets (goals captured by measurable properties) and governance mechanisms controlling the scope so that targets are reached.

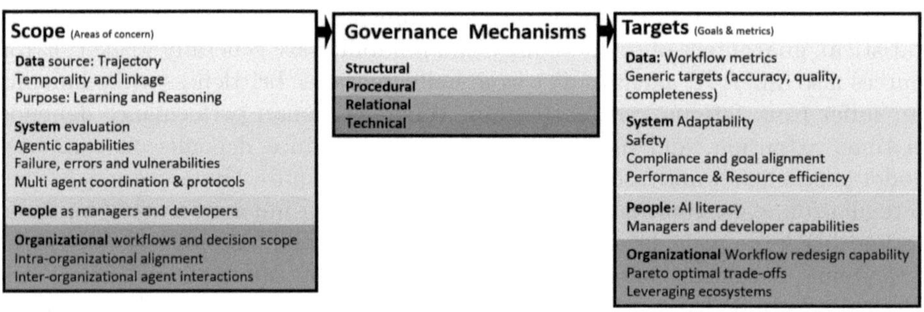

Fig. 3. Framework outline with detailed sub-dimensions in text.

4.3 Scope and Targets

4.4 Data Scope and Targets

Scope: Data Source: When agents run they generate a wealth of "operational data" stemming from agents directly or tools. Agents also obtain and process a wealth of "contextual data from the environment". We call data in connection with agents executing tasks "trajectory data" comprising observation data from the environment, deliberation data (e.g., plans), action related data (tool calls), outcome data (e.g., tool responses, environment changes), and oversight data (e.g., approvals, interventions) [35]. Aside from data generated directly by agents as part of solving the task, data might also be generated from monitoring tools observing the agent (e.g., a toxicity API monitoring a guardrail) or the environment [9].

Data Temporality and Linkage emerges as a central concern for trajectory data as agents operate in a dynamic environment and old data might become superseded by newer data. Correct ordering can be crucial, as often newest data is given preference. Furthermore, in complex settings involving many agents in dynamic environments, linking data to actors and events is more challenging [35].

Data Purpose: *Learning and reasoning* are essential for an agent's ability to operate in dynamic environments and to solve complex tasks, where solutions and the detailed solution process might be unknown (even to humans). Thus, agents might collect information to improve their "world model" (including anticipated tool behavior) either by "trial and error" or by retrieving information on past environment interactions [15]. Data might also be used for monitoring agents with respect to specific dimensions such as safety, security etc., or to improve and understand specific capabilities (such as planning, tool usage). Learning can be implemented by changing the underlying foundation model's parameters, which occurs typically in well-planned intervals. But data can also be leveraged instantly by agents by inclusion into its context and through reasoning. The importance of step-by-step reasoning (and the underlying data containing reasoning steps) is arguably growing for agentic AI as executing workflows is an essential use case. Demonstrations in different modalities (e.g., a video rather than textual instructions or a screen recording of a workflow) might further grow in relevance as they might be the basis to instruct agents or train underlying models.

Targets: *Generic data targets* like accuracy, quality and completeness (Is all data of agents, tools, etc. logged?) are still valid for agents – in particular for their trajectory accumulated as agent memory. But the interpretation of data targets might change. For workflows, accuracy might be seen as "fidelity", i.e., does the description match the real process, while completeness might include concerns such as process description granularity (Are sub-steps described in detail?) and coverage might account for the inclusion of process variants. Data lineage and metadata become important targets to identify actors and impact of actions, in particular, also the correct ordering, which is one prerequisite for causality and accountability often termed as system rather than data targets [35]. Novel metrics are related to *workflows* and could be executability and parallelizability, i.e., is the described workflow executable by agents (in parallel)? Somewhat more stringent is the goal of *reproducibility*, allowing exact reproduction of prior outcomes.

4.5 System Scope and Targets

A company might operate multiple agentic AI systems. An agentic AI system is complex (Fig. 1) with potentially many agents [43]. Each agent has a number of components. Thus, concerns listed below often apply at different levels: agent components(tools, foundation model), a single agent, entire system consisting of multiple agents.

Agentic Capabilities refer to the functional capabilities of AI Agents. Agents can *select, create, and use tools* to execute actions with significant real world impact [30]. In contrast to GenAI, where tool choice was often limited and usage had mostly little real world implications. That is, agents can potentially select among a large number of diverse tools with different properties or unique, proprietary tools. Both tool selection and usage can be challenging. For example, an agent might have to operate a company specific ERP system with little available documentation. As tools might not be static, e.g., new tools in the form of services might emerge or existing ones might be updated, tool related capabilities must be dynamic. *Reasoning* capabilities are often more critical and pronounced than for GenAI [30]. Agents must produce complex plans and reflect on outcomes. These capabilities can considerably impact overall system performance. *Learning* increasingly occurs online through retrieval of past experiences, appending them to context allowing to reason about failed attempts, as well as through imitating given demonstrations. Imitation learning aims at mimicking (human) demonstrations illustrating how to solve a task using multiple steps. Efficient skill acquisition is well-studied in the field of robotics [2]. Agent (self-)improvement is subject to the *exploration-exploitation trade-off*. Agents can exploit existing knowledge to derive solutions that are typically associated with little risk or they can explore novel solutions, where no knowledge is available, which could be both significantly worse or better than prior solutions [3]. For instance, if a new tool promising better outcomes emerges for a specific task, an agent might try such a tool despite lacking experience in its usage potentially leading to initial failures or discovering fundamental flaws in the tool making it unsuitable. But potentially the tool might lead to long-term improvements. Thus, in a corporation the trade-off translates to the risk-appetite and the loss of predictability originating from exploration and the ability to invest in innovations.

Evaluation of agents is complex as each component on its own can be demanding to evaluate – most notably the underlying foundation model. Agent evaluation is brittle, difficult, and costly – in particular, for AI agents [36]. That is, while relatively fast and cheap automatic evaluations (e.g. using LLM-as-a-judge) are possible and frequently employed, current evaluations are often not aligned with real world demands and not sufficiently comprehensive [36]. One reason why evaluation is brittle is that agents often exhibit poor *predictability*, e.g., an agent's behavior cannot be anticipated well [43]. For example, similar inputs should lead to similar outputs. In practice, this might be violated due to concerns such as prompt sensitivity: Minor changes to a prompt can have a profound impact on model outputs [33].

Failure, Errors, and Vulnerabilities might be more or less problematic depending on whether actions are reversible or alter the environment, e.g., appending a record to a database might be undone by deletion. Many errors originate from model limitations such as hallucinations and specific tasks such as planning, tool use, and execution [36]. For example, reordering sentences disrupting logical flows of text has led to performance drops of more than 10% of state-of-the-art models [8]. Low model performance can amplify in long-running workflows as success probability reduces exponentially, e.g., the probability that 10 independent steps are correct is 90% given an individual step success probability of 99% and just $0.9^{10} \approx 34\%$ if a step succeeds with 90%. Agent failures, which often originate from one or multiple errors, differ in their impact compared to failures of GenAI in multiple dimensions: As agents require more computational resources and longer time to compute often leading to idle time of workers (waiting for their results), an agent failure tends to lead to higher costs. Also real world impact can be more profound as agents perform actions, for example, a hallucinated "delete" or "send by E-Mail" action in a computer control agent can lead to severe data loss and leakage due to compromised agents.

Agentic AI systems are subject to correlated failures [34,36], e.g., there is a high risk that multiple agents fail if one fails. One reason is that the underlying foundation model might be identical or at least behave similarly as it is being trained on similar data and model architecture. Failures might also easily cascade through hierarchies, e.g., if an agent performing low-level tasks fails, higher level agents might fail, e.g., an agent miscounting the inventory could trigger a reorder by another agent [16]. Vulnerabilities such as prompt injection, e.g., inserting instructions into data in the hope that they are followed despite being part of the data, pose security threats [11]. Furthermore, as infrastructure and protocols (such as MCP and agent-agent protocols) are emerging and have not yet proven long-term robustness, vulnerability risks remain high leading to a large threat landscape [25]. For example, (early versions of) the model context protocol (MCP) introduced in 2024 suffered from a number of severe security flaws allowing attackers to steal data and execute remote code [4,14]. They also allow for attacks such as malicious skill plugins [11], where malicious activity is shadowed by legitimate functions making it hard to identify.

Multi-agent: Coordination, Protocols. When multiple agents interact, typically, each agent takes on a different role and addresses a different sub-task. Agents can be organized in specific structures, e.g., hierarchical involving a manager and several worker agents. Agent structures might be static or dynamic involving tools and agents dynamically discovered on MCP servers based on capabilities exposed by these servers. Agent structures can be pre-defined or agents can be self-organizing. Large scale agent groups could lead to emergent behavior that cannot be observed on smaller agent groups [39]. For instance, a single agent might not cause a denial-of-service DoS attack but if (for some reason) thousands of agents (self-)coordinate to perform an attack a distributed DoS (DDoS), it might be successful. As agents increasingly interact with other agents, possibly outside company perimeters, the risk of unpredictable dynamics [16] and also attacks increases, i.e., neither what one might call "agent group" dynamics nor security risks are well-understood.

Targets: Adaptability *Learning efficiency:* Agents should self-improve and leverage data efficiency, but also the organization should learn. For example, evaluations potentially relying on agent tailored benchmarks should be leveraged to define safeguards and accountability [43]. Self-improvement and learning are also key concerns as agents generate and collect data. When solving a task, an agent should leverage data gained from attempts at the micro-level from the immediate past. For instance, an agent should try only few times to determine the right parameter for tool usage. An agent should learn from collective experiences from multiple agents at a strategy-level, e.g., that a tool is generally unreliable for a task type and another tool should be used. Technically both might be implemented very differently (e.g., through leveraging context on a model level vs. data consolidation followed by fine-tuning of models) and, thus, there might be metrics for "on-task, immediate learning" and "long-term learning". *Update-ability* refers to how quickly and easily an agentic AI system can be altered, especially, without operational disruptions and incurring large costs. Newer models are cheaper to use and provide superior output quality. Existing agent instructions might have to be re-evaluated and, potentially, require adjustments. Tools, potentially being ordinary software, should be easy to update with automatic tests. Knowledge used by agents (e.g., RAG relying on vector-databases) might become outdated and should be kept consistent and up-to-date. As such, update-ability can be a competitive advantage. Furthermore, updates can be the only way to improve on model weaknesses beyond easy-to-use techniques such as prompt engineering including in-context learning (providing examples in the prompt to teach the model during inference [5]).

Safety implies operation without causing harm and unsafe outcomes. Its relevance is high for agents as failures can have severe impact. Measuring unsafe, risky behavior is difficult as it often requires predicting agent behavior. Metrics such as (human) approval or intervention ratios, guardrail obedience might serve as valuable proxies. *Harm mitigation and resilience:* Harm mitigation aims at damage control and minimizing impacts of manifested risks. A potential (sub-)target can be model interruptibility, i.e., the ability to intervene and steer ongoing executions [41] and, specifically, to halt the operation of one or multiple agents with a "kill-switch" in a graceful manner [34]. This has both a technical and organizational component. Technically the question is: Can an agent be gracefully stopped or altered? For example, a malfunctioning self-driving car should slowly stop on the side of the road rather than crash. Furthermore, other interlinked AI agents should remain operational. Organizationally, the question is: Can the organization function without (specific) agents?

Compliance and Goal Alignment: According to [17] key dimensions for alignment (and governance) of AI agents are: Autonomy, efficacy, goal complexity, and generality. Metrics could be human approval rates and detected guardrail violations.

Performance of agents integrates a number of aspects. One key concern is *task performance* captured, e.g., by successful executions of a task [43]. Performance measures might also be accompanied by complementary measures such as *per-*

formance variance capturing agent predictability. For example, an agent might perform well in most cases, but take substantial risks leading to a significant number of failures. *Latency & task completion time* can both be relevant. The latter refers to the time until an agent completes a task. Latency refers to the time for an agent to start generating the output and it is, thus, a measure of responsiveness. For knowledge tasks, once generation of the response starts, tokens are often generated faster than humans can consume them. Thus, latency and task completion time are essential metrics, as they directly impact labor costs (due to waiting) and user satisfaction.
Resource Needs and Efficiency: *Human resource needs* refers to the efficient usage of human resources during agent development and operation. It incorporates the capability to follow prompts, e.g., helpfulness measures for GenAI, but it also includes effort to verify outputs and the frequency of human engagement. That is, a model providing faithful, easy to understand reasoning traces might require less effort to audit than a model whose reasoning traces are hard to understand and not faithful [29]. Also, potentially, models might choose to perform actions that require human approval such as access to company internal data. Clearly, such accesses should be minimized as approval might delay agents and cause labor costs. *Tool efficiency* refers to how well an agent uses tools. An agent should select the right tool [16] and use it correctly, where tools themselves might be characterized by a number of metrics such as reliability, costs, tool response time, etc. *Computational efficiency* is often more concerned with employing the right model or tool for a task rather than optimizing models or tasks themselves.

4.6 People Scope and Targets

Scope: Employees as managers and developers AI Agents turn employees into *managers*, which potentially instruct (specify tasks), supervise (monitor and approve), and ideally also support continuous improvements of AI agents. This is a considerable change compared to GenAI, which provided humans with a "simple" assistant similar to an intern for simple knowledge tasks. AI agents might soon become well-trained, general-purpose workers executing complex tasks with limited supervision.

Furthermore, workflows might change fundamentally from executing sequential detailed tasks with support of GenAI to a more managerial workflow, involving specifying and monitoring multiple tasks executing in parallel by diverse agents. In software engineering, one agent might review code for readability, another might identify bugs, and another might work on integrating separate features. While these agents work for minutes or hours on their own or with limited developer intervention, a developer might at the same time interactively work with an agent, e.g., for brainstorming architectures, review short but critical code passages, etc. Furthermore, supervision and control become increasingly more difficult as agents perform more complex tasks. At the same time, the *attitude* towards AI might become more extreme in multiple ways, e.g., trust might

increase as agents become more capable and err less but at the same time fear of job loss might grow.
Targets: AI Literacy of stakeholders within and outside the organization should be ensured covering understanding both limitations and capabilities of AI agents or systems relying on them [16]. To seize opportunities and innovate on a broad scale, an *AI Developer mindset* might be helpful covering skills such as specification to instruct and define agents. More broadly, employees might benefit from a basic engineering mindset aiming at ideation, creating, evaluation, and improvement. For AI agents, this translates to skills such as identify, define, or alter workflows (to improve or enable agents), evaluating agents (identify security flaws, performance issues, etc.), In turn, to leverage existing agentic AI systems *manager capabilities* such as advanced planning, task switching, supervision gain in importance.

4.7 Organizational Scope and Targets

Scope: Intra-Organizational alignment is highly relevant, comprising, e.g., policy compliance [16] as a key goal. Also agents might employ thousands of different agents that must all be managed.

As AI agents constitute a flexible workforce more **inter-organizational** interaction across companies is possible, e.g., by offering services using MCP servers that can be automatically discovered and consumed [7]. This comes with opportunities for scaling services but also risks as such AI agents might undergo attacks [14]. The wider ecosystem becomes more important [20].
Workflows and Decision Scope become central objects of governance, i.e., what type of workflows and decisions can be executed by agents and with what degree of autonomy, e.g., what actions require approvals, or what agent plans must be reviewed prior to execution [16]. The need also arises as human-AI delegation might undergo considerable dynamics over time in organizational routines [13].
Targets: Workflow redesign capability to account for the effective use of AI agents, human needs accounting for their characteristics (see Fig. 2), and mitigating risks due to inter-organizational interactions in less protected environments and other factors becomes vital.
Pareto-Optimal Tradeoffs aim at configurations that cannot be improved in one dimension without substantial sacrifices in another dimension. For example, if companies rely on older models, they are not pareto-optimal as these models can be more expensive and perform worse (e.g., GPT-4 compared to GPT-5). So, both can be improved jointly.
Leveraging ecosystems: Organizations should benefit from ecosystems such as APIs and MCP servers while limiting risk such as security breaches.

4.8 Governance Mechanisms

Mechanisms can be structural, procedural, relational [37], and also technical. **Structural Mechanisms** cover roles and distribution of decision making authority. High level responsibilities for key decision makers, product and cybersecurity teams, and users have been set forth in [16]. As proposed they appear similar to "classical" mechanisms but agent specific responsibilities such as more comprehensive control mechanisms covering aspects such as guardrails to constrain agents play a more profound role.

"Classical" human governance roles can also be enhanced, in some cases, also be performed by agents, e.g., agent governance by agents [16,20]. Agents can perform automatic real-time audits and failure detection using trajectory data [34,36]. Agents can be instructed to be managers to which others might report and ask for approval. It has been shown that a setup of two LLMs, where one takes the role of supervisor and editor, potentially also to leverage an untrusted, deceptive LLM [12]. Suggestions for meaningful human oversight to define checkpoints or boundaries requiring human approval, complementing human and automated monitoring have also been made [16,41].

Procedures aim to shape the way decisions are made, and actions are taken. Critical human assessment capabilities must be trained and audited regularly [16]. Agents can be instructed similarly to humans with adequate processes and policies, e.g., related to incident reporting [7] and agent escalation paths, basic behavioral policies, etc. For instance, tool selection policies can provide guidance to minimize tool risks (e.g., prefer tools with strict input formats [16]). Similarly to humans, agents must also be instructed (through prompting) or trained (changes to underlying model parameters) to obey these processes, which falls under implementation. Transparency, e.g., agents revealing their thought process [34] has also been proposed. Also agent actions should be attributable to an agent – in particular, in multi-agent settings with agents from different stakeholders [34]. This requires as a pre-requisite that agents have unique IDs [6,7]. The trust-utility framework for Human-AI Governance [10] aims at ensuring trust taking into account its utility which differs from risk- or principle-focused approaches. It advocates critical, use-case, and time-dependent thresholds along the authority, autonomy, and accountability dimension, which necessitate governance adaptation. For example, the process to outcome trust threshold hypothesizes that over time trust might no longer be obtained by (partially) understanding internal AI processes detailing how decisions are reached to validated outcomes. Gradual rollout of agents in production has been recommended [16]. Thresholds have also been proposed as a practical mechanism to trigger human intervention during (automatic) monitoring, e.g., number of failed attempts, degree of deviation from normal behavior, etc. [16].

Relational Mechanisms improve collaboration targeting communication, training, and coordination of decision-making. As tasks get more complex, evaluating agent behavior or plans, in particular identifying failure modes and suspicious anomalies, requires human training [16].

Technical Mechanisms: Technology is often seen as a means to implement governance mechanisms, e.g., facilitate approval processes. If used as such it is not a governance mechanism in its purest sense. However, if technology allows to impact targets directly, it can also constitute a mechanism in its own right. Furthermore, some implementation mechanisms come with fundamental trade-offs, e.g., regarding costs and governance targets so that they are more than simple implementation choices. Furthermore, as of now the infrastructure supporting governance of AI agents is only emerging with many open challenges [7]. (Technical) recommendations on how to build agents have been made by academics [11] and large organizations [28,41]. Concrete technical recommendations include minimum privileges for agents (similar to role hardening in classical IT) [16], and real-time conformance monitoring [41], setting reasonable default agent behavior, constraining the action space of agents has been advocated [34]. Monitoring planning and intervening at the planning have also been proposed [41]. An agent rollback option can support the goal of recovery [7], while allowing humans to take over agent behavior or steer it in real-time can also serve as a mitigation [16]. To ensure that AI remains controllable (by humans), avoid resource abuse, and reduce risk of large scale harms, rate-control limiting the amount of actions allowed to be taken by agents could be implemented [41].

5 Conclusions

We have discussed governance of AI agents focused on businesses aiming to highlight novel aspects that emerge due to AI agents. AI agents and humans form a joint workforce, where AI agents perform increasingly complex tasks autonomously using tools impacting the real world in potentially severe ways. Thus, governance must adapt an actor-oriented perspective rather than viewing agents as static artifacts. Governance should leverage AI-specific mechanisms like rollback, kill-switches, while also acknowledging similarities between humans and agents that might manifest in similar principles like definition of roles, hierarchies. Our conceptual work unifies and emphasizes current technological realities and longer lasting governance principles. This should be helpful for both practitioners and academics alike.

References

1. Anthropic: Introducing computer use. https://www.anthropic.com/news/3-5-models-and-computer-use (2024)
2. Argall, B.D., Chernova, S., Veloso, M., Browning, B.: A survey of robot learning from demonstration. Robotics and Autonomous Systems (2009)
3. Arumugam, D., Griffiths, T.L.: Toward efficient exploration by large language model agents. arXiv:2504.20997 (2025)
4. Bitdefender: Security risks of agentic ai: A model context protocol (MCP) introduction. Bitdefender Business Insights Blog (2025)
5. Brown, T., et al.: Language models are few-shot learners. In: Advances in Neural Information Processing Systems (NeurIPS) (2020)
6. Chan, A., et al.: Ids for ai systems. arXiv:2406.12137 (2024)
7. Chan, A., et al.: Infrastructure for ai agents. arXiv:2501.10114 (2025)
8. Chen, X., Chi, R.A., Wang, X., Zhou, D.: Premise order matters in reasoning with large language models. arXiv:2402.08939 (2024)

9. Dong, L., Lu, Q., Zhu, L.: Agentops: Enabling observability of LLM agents. arXiv:2411.05285 (2024)
10. Engin, Z.: Human-ai governance (haig): A trust-utility approach. arXiv:2505.01651 (2025)
11. Ge, Y.: Governance architecture for autonomous agent systems: Threats, framework, and engineering practice. arXiv preprint arXiv:2603.07191 (2026)
12. Greenblatt, R., Shlegeris, B., Sachan, K., Roger, F.: Ai control: Improving safety despite intentional subversion. arXiv:2312.06942 (2023)
13. Grisold, T., Schneider, J.: Dynamics of human-ai delegation in organizational routines. In: Proceedings of the International Conference on Information Systems (2023)
14. Hou, X., Zhao, Y., Wang, S., Wang, H.: Model context protocol (MCP): Landscape, security threats, and future research directions. arXiv:2503.23278 (2025)
15. Hu, Y., et al.: Memory in the age of ai agents. arXiv:2512.13564 (2025)
16. Infocomm Media Development Authority (IMDA): Model ai governance framework for agentic ai. Tech. rep., Infocomm Media Development Authority, Singapore (2026), https://www.imda.gov.sg/-/media/imda/files/about/emerging-tech-and-research/artificial-intelligence/mgf-for-agentic-ai.pdf
17. Kasirzadeh, A., Gabriel, I.: Characterizing ai agents for alignment and governance. arXiv:2504.21848 (2025)
18. Khan, R., Joyce, D., Habiba, M.: Agentsafe: A unified framework for ethical assurance and governance in agentic AI. arXiv:2512.03180 (2025)
19. Kolt, N.: Governing ai agents. arXiv:2501.07913 (2025)
20. Kraprayoon, J., Williams, Z., Fayyaz, R.: Ai agent governance: A field guide. arXiv:2505.21808 (2025)
21. Langley, H.: Marc benioff downplays software apocalypse fears: It may be eaten by the saas-quatch. https://www.businessinsider.com/marc-benioff-saas-quatch-apocalypse-salesforce-earnings-2026-2 (Feb 2026)
22. Lutz, C., Newlands, G., Jarrahi, M.H.: Hybrid intelligence. In: Xu, W. (ed.) Handbook of Human-Centered Artificial Intelligence (2025)
23. Microsoft Security Experts: Cyber pulse: An AI security report. https://www.microsoft.com/en-us/security/security-insider/emerging-trends/cyber-pulse-ai-security-report (2026)
24. OpenAI: Computer-using agent. https://openai.com/index/computer-using-agent (2024)
25. OWASP GenAI Security Project, Agentic Security Initiative: Multi-agentic system threat modelling guide (2025). https://genai.owasp.org/resource/multi-agentic-system-threat-modeling-guide-v1-0/
26. Papagiannidis, E., Enholm, I.M., Dremel, C., Mikalef, P., Krogstie, J.: Toward ai governance: Identifying best practices and potential barriers and outcomes. Inform. Syst. Front. (2023)
27. Raza, S., Sapkota, R., Karkee, M., Emmanouilidis, C.: Trism for agentic AI: a review of trust, risk, and security management in LLM-based agentic multi-agent systems. AI Open (2026)
28. Schluntz, E., Zhang, B.: Building effective agents (2024)
29. Schneider, J.: Explainable generative ai (genxai): a survey, conceptualization, and research agenda. Artificial Intelligence Review (2024)
30. Schneider, J.: Generative to agentic ai: Survey, conceptualization, and challenges. arXiv:2504.18875 (2025)
31. Schneider, J., Abraham, R., Meske, C., vom Brocke, J.: Artificial intelligence governance for businesses. Inform. Syst. Manage. (2023)

32. Schneider, J., Kuss, P., Abraham, R., Meske, C.: Governance of generative artificial intelligence for companies. arXiv:2403.08802 (2024)
33. Schneider, J., Meske, C., Kuss, P.: Foundation models. Business & Information Systems Engineering (2024)
34. Shavit, Y., et al.: Practices for Governing Agentic AI Systems. Research Paper, OpenAI (2023)
35. Souza, R., : Prov-agent: unified provenance for tracking AI agent interactions in agentic workflows. In: IEEE International Conference on eScience (2025)
36. Srikumar, M., et al.: Prioritizing real-time failure detection in ai agents. Partnership on AI (2025)
37. Tiwana, A., Konsynski, B., Venkatraman, N.: Information technology and organizational governance: The it governance cube. J. Manage. Inform. Syst. (2013)
38. Torraco, R.J.: Writing integrative literature reviews: Guidelines and examples. Human Resource Development Review (2005)
39. Tran, K.T., Dao, D., Nguyen, M.D., Pham, Q.V., O'Sullivan, B., Nguyen, H.D.: Multi-agent collaboration mechanisms: a survey of LLMs. arXiv:2501.06322 (2025)
40. Vincent, J.: Openai's chatgpt now has 100 million weekly active users. The Verge (November 2023). https://www.theverge.com/2023/11/6/23949190/openai-chatgpt-100-million-weekly-active-users
41. Wang, C.L., Singhal, T., Kelkar, A., Tuo, J.: Mi9: An integrated runtime governance framework for agentic AI. arXiv preprint arXiv:2508.03858 (2025)
42. Webster, J., Watson, R.T.: Analyzing the past to prepare for the future: Writing a literature review. MIS Quarterly (2002)
43. World Economic Forum, Capgemini: Ai agents in action: Foundations for evaluation and governance. Tech. rep., World Economic Forum (2025). https://reports.weforum.org/docs/WEF_AI_Agents_in_Action_Foundations_for_Evaluation_and_Governance_2025.pdf

From Process Model to Fractal Enterprise Model: Practical Generation and Lessons Learned

Toomas Saarsen[1(✉)] and Ilia Bider[2]

[1] University of Tartu, Tartu, Estonia
toomas.saarsen@ut.ee
[2] DSV - Stockholm University, Stockholm, Sweden
ilia@dsv.su.se

Abstract. The authors' previous study focused on the applicability of the fractal enterprise model (FEM) in risk analysis, in which the FEM was compiled from operational-level process diagrams. While the process diagrams describe a detailed timeline and asset use at the operational level, the FEM model allows a similar (but more general) structure to be viewed 2–3 levels higher in the process hierarchy, i.e., at a generalized strategic level. In the case of medium-sized organizations, deriving the FEM model from the process model proved effective: aggregating operational-level elements at the strategic level provided a sufficiently precise structure for risk analysis of the infrastructure's timeline and asset use at the general level. The present study expands the sample to larger organizations, where process models are more voluminous, and the number of assets and relationships is significantly higher. The study aims to clarify whether aggregating the operational-level process model into a single FEM model map enables the creation of a comprehensive, readable structure for the strategic analysis of more complex systems. Unlike the previous research phase, which focused solely on risk analysis, this work does not limit the model's application areas, reflecting all possible uses that emerged during the research. In addition, feedback from the model creators is analyzed, focusing on the complexity of creating the model and its practical value in use in an organization.

Keywords: Business Process Model · Fractal Enterprise Model

1 Introduction

Process models are used to understand and analyze organizational operations and to plan improvement actions at the system level [1, 2]. They typically constitute an important part of an organization's knowledge base by offering employees detailed descriptions of data flows and workflows. Consequently, the readers of process model are not only technical specialists who conduct process analysis or manage information processes. Many diagrams included in process model are also intended for non technical audiences (such as managers or regular employees) who rely on them to make sense of organizational activities [3, 4].

R. Matulevičius et al. (Eds.): DB&IS 2026, CCIS 3085, pp. 285–298, 2026.
https://doi.org/10.1007/978-3-032-30863-4_18

The main challenge in using diagrams lies in ensuring their cognitive comprehensibility for human readers [5]. At the operational level, a process model (levels 4–5 in the process hierarchy, following SAP hierarchy classification [6]) may contain up to one million factual elements - for example, tasks, actors, or data units [7, 8]. In diagrams, the number of visually perceived elements is even higher, as each factual element is accompanied by at least one relational link. This effectively doubles the number of items the reader must process and significantly increases the diagram's cognitive load.

Factual and relational information together provide both a temporal dimension (the sequence of activities over time) and a contextual dimension (such as the assets used in each activity). Due to this high level of complexity, readers are typically able to concentrate on only one or two business processes at a time. In the context of a large organization, this accounts for less than 1% of the description of the entire system. In conclusion, although operational-level process models provide an exhaustive overview of a system's details, their large size and complexity limit a person's ability to understand larger units (e.g., a single process) within the model.

To gain a holistic understanding of an organization, it is necessary to move several levels higher in the process hierarchy, where the number of elements is substantially smaller. At these higher levels, temporal information is typically presented in a simplified form. For example, detailed activities are aggregated into generalized value chains [9]. Although such generalization and simplification improve readability, their key limitation lies in their one dimensionality - the reader is exposed to only a single view at a time, namely the overarching temporal sequence of processes. While this provides a useful structural framework for organizing process model content, it does not, on its own, offer a meaningful high level representation of the organization without complementary contextual information.

At higher levels of abstraction, asset usage is represented by the Fractal Enterprise Model (FEM), which captures an organization's general infrastructure [10] and focuses on asset utilization in a generalized form. Similar to the value chain, the FEM presents processes along an abstracted timeline, but it adds contextual information by showing which key assets are employed during the execution of each process. The primary distinction from operational level diagrams lies in the level of abstraction: in the FEM, activities correspond to significantly higher levels of the process hierarchy (i.e., they are more general), and assets are represented as larger, aggregated units.

The FEM model is often presented through multiple diagrams in which the organization's infrastructure is distributed across several views. Such decomposition reduces the number of elements and relationships within each individual diagram, making them easier for readers to interpret. In our study, however, this simplicity was intentionally set aside: instead of decomposing, the entire organizational infrastructure was consolidated into a single comprehensive diagram. To maintain the diagram's graspability and readability, the number of processes was limited to approximately ten, while assets were generalized and grouped into about thirty strategic assets.

In summary, our focus is on a diagram that presents all organizational processes within a single visual map, achieving compactness through the generalization of elements. Ensuring the accuracy and correctness of relationships across different levels of detail remains essential. However, the precise temporal sequencing and detailed representation of asset usage (characteristic of BPMN based operational models [1]) cannot be fully retained in a general FEM diagram. This loss of detail is, in effect, the price we pay for achieving visibility into the entire organization within a single, unified representation.

2 Context of the Study

In the previous study [11], we consolidated the entire organizational infrastructure into a single comprehensive FEM diagram. To ensure the model's human graspability and readability, the number of processes was limited to approximately ten, and assets were aggregated into roughly thirty strategic units through generalization.

Using the organization's existing process model as input (where tasks and asset usage were already structured at the operational level) proved effective for constructing a comprehensive infrastructure view via a bottom up approach. During the analysis, it became evident that the first level of the value chain was often too abstract, whereas the second level was excessively detailed: the number of second level processes typically far exceeded the imposed limit of ten. Accordingly, an intermediate representation, referred to as value chain level 1.5, was employed in constructing the FEM model. In this step, first level processes were only partially decomposed, with only the more complex processes being divided into two or three more specific sub processes.

Asset mapping followed a bottom up strategy, in which hundreds of detailed operational level assets were grouped according to their areas of use and generalized into approximately thirty strategic assets. This approach allowed the model to remain compact while still preserving sufficient informational depth for both readers and for substantive structural analysis.

A previous study examining the application of the FEM model in strategic-level risk analysis confirmed the effectiveness of the chosen structure. The model enabled the visualization of adverse cascading effects resulting from risk realization along the organization's strategic timeline and supported the identification of infrastructure components affected through inter-process relationships.

The study compared the implementation of risk analysis at the operational and strategic levels. At the operational level, the FMEA (Failure Mode and Effects Analysis) method was applied, in which risk parameters (threat, probability, and impact) were assessed within detailed business process diagrams [12]. These diagrams provide an accurate temporal sequence of tasks and a comprehensive representation of the infrastructure required to execute processes. At the strategic level, we analyzed risks using the FEM model. A Fractal Enterprise Model (FEM) model [13] provides us with such a high-level structure of asset usage. The FEM model brings together various types of assets at a general level and shows the relations that arise through the use of these assets in general processes.

In the FEM model (see Fig. 1), assets are shown with rectangles and processes with ovals. The relations are shown in the FEM model with a line between processes and assets. A solid-line arrow pointing into a process indicates the process's use of the asset; a dashed-line arrow pointing out of the process indicates the asset's change by the process (the asset the outgoing arrow points to). By adding a name to a relationship, we can specify the type of relationship - the role of the asset in the process (solid-line) or the way the asset is affected by the process (dashed-line).

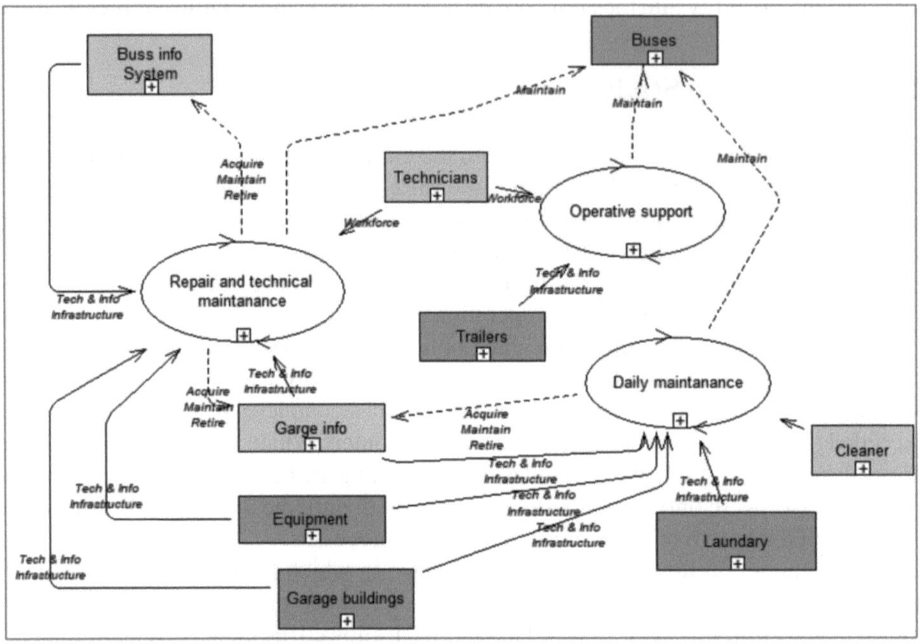

Fig. 1. Description of a bus company support unit using FEM.

Color does not have a direct semantic meaning in the FEM model. In the model presented in our previous study (Fig. 1), we emphasized actor-assets in green, data-assets in red and other type of assets (devices, buildings or materials) in blue.

Although a single FEM diagram covering the entire organization is highly abstract, it enables the identification of critical process sequences and strategic asset use across the organization.

In the medium sized organizations that participated in the previous study, the elements of the process models and FEM models were relatively similar. Strategic value chains were familiar to employees, and the assets incorporated into the FEM model largely overlapped. When elevating assets to the strategic level, the focus was typically on larger data sets that were already well known to readers, making the abstraction intuitive. It was also unnecessary to consolidate core process performers into larger units, as the number of distinct roles within core processes was limited and clearly defined.

In this study, we deliberately included larger institutions whose process models are more extensive and contain significantly higher numbers of assets. Our aim was to maintain the number of elements in the FEM model at the same level as in the previous study (approximately ten processes and around thirty assets) which required a considerably higher degree of generalization.

Whereas in the earlier study the process hierarchy was elevated from the operational to the strategic level by two levels, in this study we moved up by three to four levels. In the present study, at the operational level, a process model (levels 4–5 in the process hierarchy) can contain up to a million factual elements (such as tasks, actors, or data items). In asset consolidation, this meant combining several dozen operational level assets into a single generalized strategic asset.

This approach allowed us to examine whether such a high degree of abstraction can still provide sufficient readability and informativeness for understanding strategic issues and supporting the analysis of information.

The previous study focused primarily on technical aspects: generating a FEM model based on an existing process model and evaluating its applicability in risk analysis. At that stage, attention was directed toward the technical performance of the structure rather than the subjective experiences or judgments of the analysts.

The present study expands this perspective in two new directions:

- **Assessment of modeling complexity by experienced analysts.** Analysts participating in the study were asked to evaluate the complexity of creating FEM model. In addition to measuring the time spent on modeling, we examined the substantive challenges and obstacles encountered during model development.
- **Broader exploration of potential application areas.** Unlike the previous study, which concentrated narrowly on strategic risk analysis, the present study did not impose restrictions on the model's use. The aim was to identify additional potential application areas and gather innovative ideas for the practical use of the FEM model across different organizational contexts.

3 Methodology Description

We included two organizations representing different yet equally complex sectors in the study sample:

- **Telecommunications company (Elisa Estonia).** This company provides fixed and mobile communication services across a wide range of domains and bases its operations on the eTOM framework [14]. Its complexity stems from the large number of processes involved (the eTOM model already contains 15 core processes at a high level) as well as from the heterogeneity of infrastructure components and the substantial volumes of data they generate and manage.
- **Public sector institution (Estonian Rescue Services Agency).** This organization oversees a large, multilayered national domain. Its extensive infrastructure, combined with the resulting multitude of processes and services, contributes to the system's overall complexity.

The study was carried out in three stages to evaluate the applicability of the FEM model and to collect qualitative feedback from analysts:

- **Analysis and preparation of the existing process model.** Both organizations had previously used operational level process model, which served as the basis for building the FEM model. Analysts identified general processes (value chains) from the existing process structures and aggregated operational level assets into higher level entities.

- **FEM model development.** Organizational analysts constructed a strategic FEM model using the institution's process model as input.
- **Collection of analyst feedback.** Feedback from analysts focused on the technical and substantive complexity of the modeling process, as well as the challenges encountered during development. Analysts also provided assessments of how well the structures in the process model supported the creation of the FEM model. In addition, the analyst highlighted the purposes for which the FEM model could be used.
- **FEM model quality control.** We checked the model's syntactic correctness and removed common semantic errors. Since the companies used their everyday tools to build the model rather than specialized FEM software, they lacked automatic constraints to ensure the model's technical compliance.

We used a qualitative research approach to collect and analyze data. Semi-structured interviews with analysts were organized around different focus areas, each guiding the interview through targeted questions:

1. **Integrating processes into the FEM model:** What challenges arose when using the existing value chain as the structural basis for the FEM model?
2. **Systematizing and generalizing assets:** What difficulties appeared when consolidating operational level assets into strategic level entities?
3. **Creating and visualizing the FEM structure:** Which steps turned out to be the most challenging in the construction and visualization of the FEM model?
4. **Time required to develop the FEM model:** How much time did analysts spend on generalizing processes and assets and on designing the diagram?
5. **Application areas of the FEM model:** In which analysis or other activities is the application of the FEM model most useful?
6. **Strategic value of the FEM model:** What is the principal strategic benefit the FEM model provides?

We recorded all interviews and transcribed them, after which a qualitative text analysis was conducted.

4 Research

In both organizations participating in the study, analysts developed an FEM model that consisted of approximately ten generalized processes and around thirty assets (see Fig. 2).

Since asset aggregation introduced new, higher level abstraction objects into the model, an asset aggregation table was added to the FEM model in both cases. This auxiliary material ensures transparency and traceability by providing readers with a clear overview of which operational level assets were consolidated into each strategic level entity. This approach preserves the link between the detailed infrastructure and the generalized management view. An additional color code was used to more clearly distinguish between different types of assets: actor-assets in green, data-assets in red, and other types of assets in blue.

To keep the diagram readable, we omitted the names of the two most common relationship types: "Workforce" (relationship between a process and an asset "actor") and "Tech & Info Infrastructure" (relationship between a process data element)). These

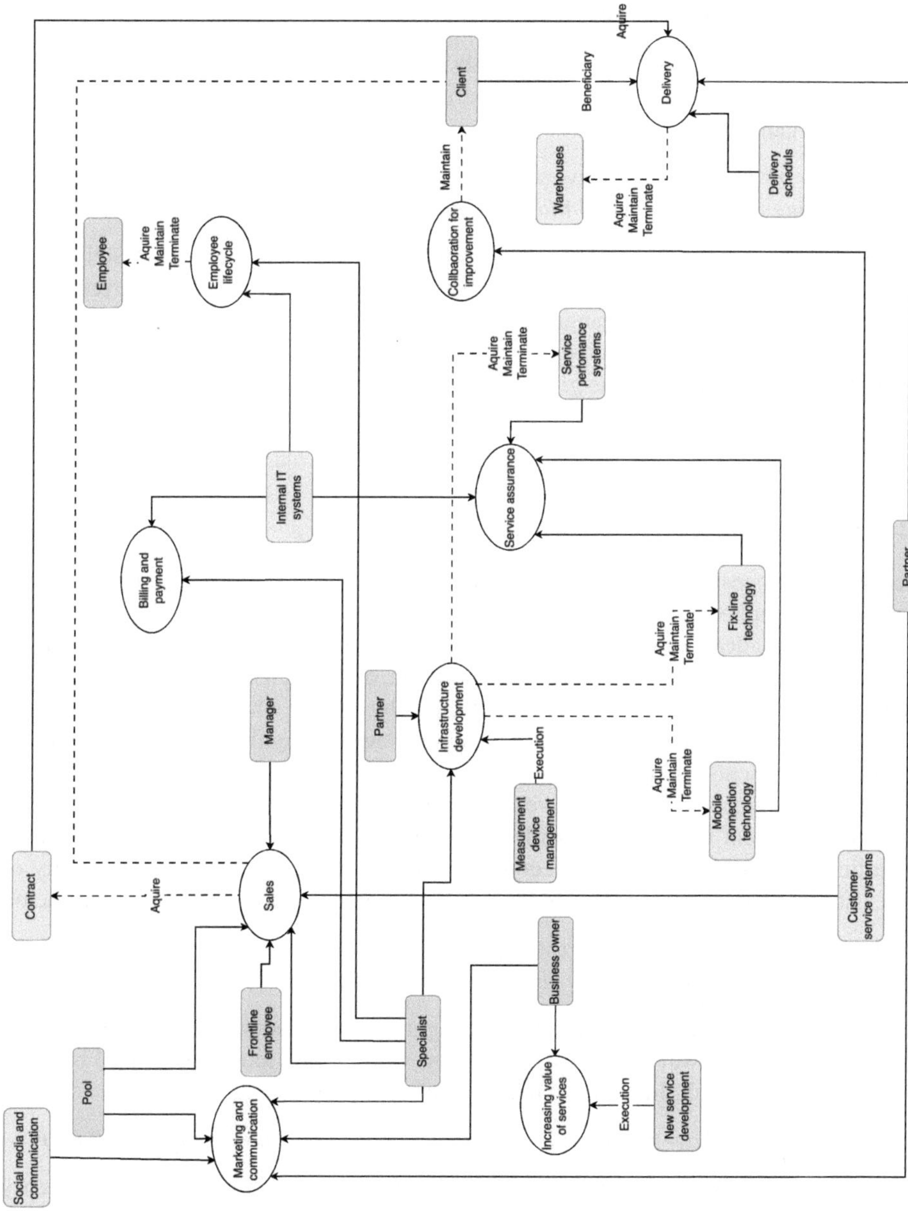

Fig. 2. FEM model - all processes on one map.

are easily inferred from the context and would otherwise clutter the view. A relationship name is shown only if its type differs from these two defaults - for example, when the link between an actor and a process is specifically defined as a "Beneficiary".

4.1 Integrating Processes into the FEM Model

According to the analysts, one of the easiest stages in creating the FEM model was integrating the value chain, as it relied on structures that were already well established within the organization.

- *"Well, for me personally, it was easy because we have had it in place for a long time, highlighting those [processes] that have direct value to the customer." (I1)*

The estimated time spent on this stage was relatively small - approximately 0.5 h. Although some minor structural adjustments were made during the model development process, the placement and arrangement of processes in the diagram largely mirrored the institution's existing value chain.

A similar time estimate was given by the Rescue Services Agency analyst, whose main processes had been previously generalized - a large number of services grouped into logical units.

4.2 Systematizing and Generalizing Assets

In contrast to processes, the extraction and systematization of assets were considered one of the most complex steps in developing the FEM model. The main challenge involved making strategic decisions about which assets (for example, actors or IT systems) have a critical impact in the context under consideration, and which could be omitted for the sake of higher-level generalization. Unlike the value chain, which remained relatively stable throughout the modeling process, the asset view was highly dynamic and required repeated adjustments and additions.

Analysts emphasized that effective asset aggregation requires thorough prior systematization to prevent information overload. The modeling of IT systems was described as particularly challenging in a telecommunications company, and the availability of pre-existing architectural diagrams or system views emerged as a critical success factor.

- *"In the case of IT systems, it was tough in general, fortunately, such a picture existed and I was able to use it... Such views are extremely useful." (I1)*

The estimated time required for the asset aggregation phase was approximately four hours on average. However, analysts noted that without previously structured baseline data, this process would likely have taken significantly longer.

- *"I think it would have taken me a week to get the same picture [of assets]." (I1)*

The Rescue Service Agency has 10 central information systems, and so it was easy to present them on the diagram. It was more difficult to generalize and reflect the actors, which had not been generalized in this form before:

- *"... we have too many of them, and they [names] are not informative enough. There was a lot of thinking here to pick out the important things." (I2)*

4.3 Creating and Visualizing the FEM Structure

Based on the study results, the third stage (the final construction of the FEM structure) proved to be the most challenging for analysts. The central difficulty lay in determining the optimal level of abstraction for assets and the appropriate degree of representativeness for the relationships included in the model.

The decision-making process regarding which relationships to display at the strategic level required the greatest effort. Analysts emphasized that they must filter out lower-level details that are irrelevant for strategic decision-making and retain only those high-level dependencies that are critical for understanding organizational functioning.

– *"It's not difficult to draw this arrow, but where do we draw it, what do we show at a high level?" (I1)*

Unlike operational-level process diagrams, which specify relationships based on detailed factual interactions, the FEM model requires establishing relationships between generalized process groups and aggregated assets. Analysts noted that graphical visualization can quickly become unreadable when the number of connections grows too large.

– *"In principle, it is not difficult to put these puzzle pieces together, but too many connections can complicate the picture." (I1)*

During the discussions, analysts emphasized the importance of accurately naming the assets and relations (arrows). The labels must communicate the strategic nature of the relationship between two generalized elements; they should not function merely as graphical links but must convey meaningful information about value creation.

– *"The scheme will be very anonymous. It could describe any large company.... Making a correspondence table [which shows what the asset consists of] during the generalization is a good idea." (I2)*

In summary, analysts noted that building FEM model poses a fundamentally different challenge compared to process modeling. They described the strategic generalization and synthesis required during FEM construction as cognitively far more demanding than the technical mapping of detailed operational-level processes. Whereas detailed modeling primarily relies on the documentation of factual interactions, creating an FEM structure requires the analyst to identify strategically critical components and define complex relationships among them, while simultaneously avoiding information overload. The complexity of the FEM model thus lies in filtering information and visualizing the filtered content clearly, transforming the organization's complex infrastructure into a representation that is comprehensible for managers.

Compared with other stages, the time spent on this phase was considerably greater, approximately one full working day. Analysts noted that the cognitive load was substantial, which is why they divided the work across several days, completing the modeling in shorter, concentrated sessions.

4.4 Application Areas of the FEM Model

When moving from model development to practical implementation, a detailed list of use cases was compiled, outlining the situations in which analysts believed the FEM model provides strong decision-making support for management. Based on the feedback, the main value-creation areas can be grouped into four categories:

- **Strategic planning and goal setting.** The FEM model serves as a structural framework that helps map the infrastructure required to achieve strategic objectives. This enables managers to see the broader landscape of assets on which the strategic ambitions of their respective areas rely.
- **Change management and impact analysis.** When organizational changes are planned, the model offers a visual overview of interdependencies. This helps identify which units or stakeholders will be affected by the change and which external factors may influence the manager's area of responsibility.
- **Comprehensive risk management and identification of cascading effects.** One of the model's most significant benefits is its ability to support systematic risk analysis. Since risks rarely affect a single component in isolation, the FEM framework makes it possible to visualize the "ripple" or cascading effects that propagate across the value chain and infrastructure elements, ultimately influencing multiple parts of the organization.
- **Optimizing asset utilization and reducing duplication.** The model helps uncover inefficiencies and duplicated activities across the organization. Its generalized perspective enables managers to assess whether similar assets are being used in parallel without meaningful synergy and to anticipate the cumulative impact of optimization decisions.

In summary, the FEM model's most significant value lies in creating organizational visibility - a shared information space in which complex relationships become understandable. This visibility enhances managerial capabilities to analyze, decide, and plan more effectively and predictably.

– *"It is in this model that this value will be in the future, when visibility is created." (I1)*

4.5 Strategic Value of the FEM Structure

The analysts' overall assessment of the FEM structure was positive, particularly highlighting the model's ability to bridge the gap between the high-level value chain and the overly detailed operational model. Compared with the standard value chain, the FEM model provides an additional layer of strategic-level information by incorporating assets and the relationships that arise from them within the value chain.

– *"We simply have a value chain, but here [in the FEM model] there are already assets - the picture is more meaningful and concrete." (I1)*

The Rescue Service Agency highlighted the strategic dimension of the FEM model, which opens up broader perspectives and shows connections that extend beyond the institution.

– *"The boundaries of our organization are not clear. We have a good example to follow - we have volunteer rescuers who do a very important part of the processes, but they are not [part of] our organization." (I2)*

The main negative aspect concerned the rapid increase in the complexity of the graphical representation. Analysts pointed out that the diagram can quickly turn into a maze of relationships that are difficult to visually trace and interpret unambiguously.

To mitigate this issue, analysts emphasized two critical factors:

- **Semantic clarity:** Assets and each relationship must be clearly defined and named so that readers can understand the substantive meaning of the connection.
- **Interactive decomposition:** The ability to navigate between hierarchical levels is essential for managing complexity. The solution used by the telecommunication company was effective and easy to use: a list of assets (with a more detailed view) was presented when users clicked on an asset in the diagram.

4.6 FEM Model Quality Control

After the interview phase, we entered the initial FEM model into a special editing tool. The modeling constraints and automation of the software allowed the elimination of two main shortcomings:

- Automation of connection types: All arrows in the model received the correct type, as the FEM tool automatically determines the type of the arrow according to the elements.
- Detailed specification of connections: For each arrow, the specific way of using or influencing the assets was specified. Sections highlighted in the FEM model that need improvement.

During the refinement of the model, important details emerged that had previously remained unnoticed due to the incomplete definition of the types of relationships:

- Details of core vs. support processes: This deficiency did not result from the transformation of the model, but from the uneven detail of the original process model. Core processes were described in detail, covering the asset's complete life cycle (acquire, maintain, terminate). Support processes were described in a more general way, focusing on influencing assets only at critical points, leaving gaps in the life-cycle treatment.
- Treatment of undescribed activities: The parts of the undescribed main process (e.g., an outsourced service) were treated as process extensions, with the use of the assets in them left undefined.

The supplemented diagram (see Fig. 3) highlights in blue the assets that are not treated in detail in the process model and were therefore not reflected correctly in the FEM model. The yellow color highlights assets with the incomplete life-cycle treatment. The diagram is prepared with FEM model editing tools.

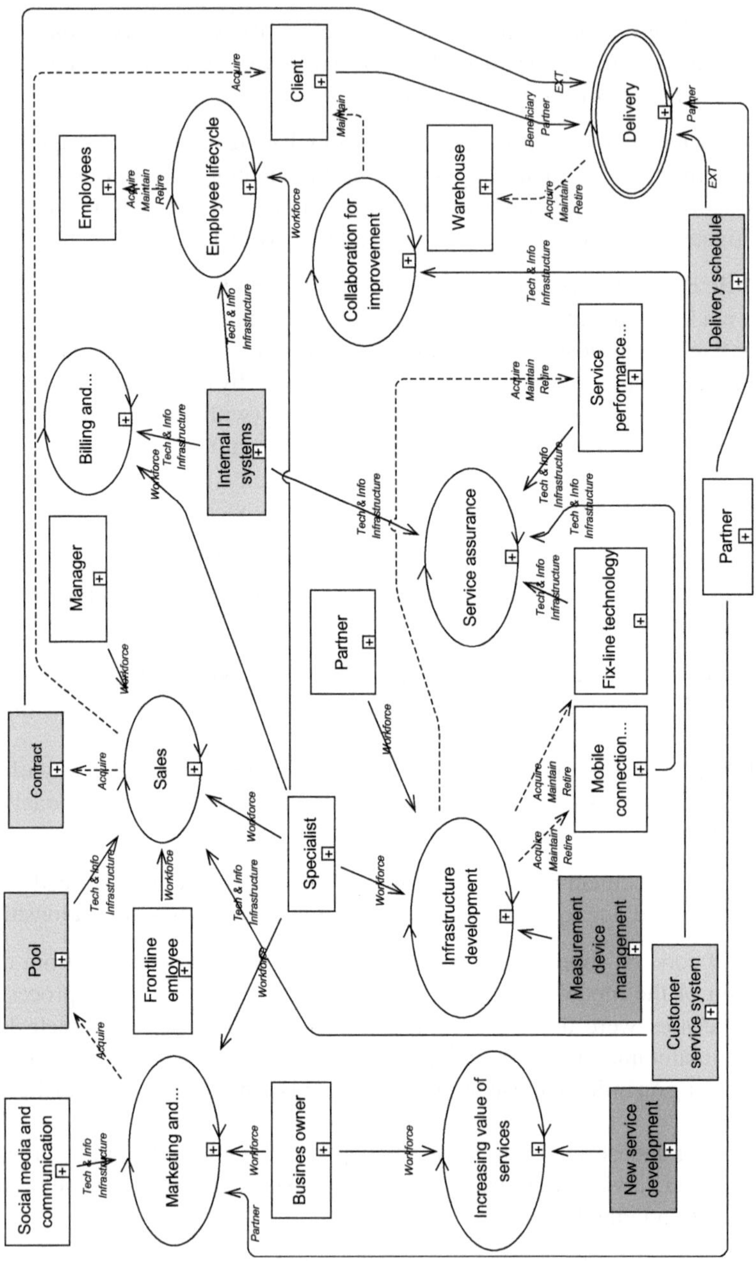

Fig. 3. FEM model with elements that need to be improved.

5 Analysis and Discussion of Results

The authors emphasize that the applicability of the FEM structure should not be limited to risk analysis, as was the case in our initial study. The FEM model is a universal tool for strategic reasoning, **providing visibility** that enables readers to look beyond the boundaries of individual units or information systems and recognize indirect relationships across the organization that would otherwise remain hidden.

At the strategic level, inaccuracies in the timeline or asset usage that arise from generalization are not viewed as disadvantages but rather as necessary prerequisites for ensuring the model's comprehensibility. In large organizations, overly detailed diagrams make it impossible to obtain a holistic overview of the infrastructure without overwhelming the reader. The generalized view offered by the FEM model supports the **identification of indirect relationships and strategic dependencies**, which can later be specified at the operational level if needed. Thus, a deliberate increase in abstraction is essential for revealing strategic relationships.

Given the higher level of abstraction used in this study and the larger volume of operational data aggregated into each element, the **correspondence table** proved critical for maintaining model readability. This tool enables readers to **trace the decomposition** and understand which operational-level sub-elements make up each strategic aggregate. In the case of the telecommunications company, an interactive solution was particularly effective: by clicking on an element in the diagram, the user could immediately view the corresponding list of sub-elements. The correspondence table links the model's general structure to a specific organization. The **institution-specific terminology** used refines the model and emphasizes the institution's strategic uniqueness.

The results of this study confirm that the **time required** to create an FEM model is comparable to that observed in the first study - **approximately 1–2 working days**. It is important to note, however, that such efficiency can be achieved with large process models only when the organization's assets have already been systematically structured at the operational level (e.g., grouped into logical sector-based units or organized in distinct diagrams such as a map of IT systems). Without this preparatory work, an additional asset-structuring phase becomes necessary, and in a large organization, the time required for this stage may range from days to several weeks.

Quality control confirmed that human **errors occur when manually converting** a process model to an FEM model, which is largely due to the uneven depth and quality of the description of the process model: the details of the relationships remain incompletely defined, and undescribed processes are depicted in an overly simplified manner.

References

1. Dumas, M., La Rosa, M., Mendling, J., Reijers, H.A.: Fundamentals of Business Process Management, vol. 1, p. 2. Springer, Heidelberg (2013)
2. Freeman, R.K.: The theory, practice, and future of process improvement in general thoracic surgery. In: Seminars in Thoracic and Cardiovascular Surgery, vol. 26, no. 4, pp. 310–316. WB Saunders, December 2014
3. Jošt, G., Huber, J., Heričko, M., Polančič, G.: An empirical investigation of intuitive understandability of process diagrams. Comput. Stand. Interfaces **48**, 90–111 (2016)

4. Rodrigues, R.D.A., Barros, M.D.O., Revoredo, K., Azevedo, L.G., Leopold, H.: An experiment on process model understandability using textual work instructions and BPMN models. In: 2015 29th Brazilian Symposium on Software Engineering, pp. 41–50. IEEE, September, 2015
5. Huckin, T.N.: A cognitive approach to readability. In: New Essays in Technical and Scientific Communication, pp. 90–108. Routledge (2019)
6. Davis, R.: Modelling variety: variants in hierarchical modelling. In: Business Process Modelling with ARIS: A Practical Guide, pp. 311–323. Springer, London (2001)
7. Kudryavtsev, D., Grigoriev, L.: Systemic approach towards enterprise functional decomposition. In: 2011 IEEE 13th Conference on Commerce and Enterprise Computing, pp. 310–317. IEEE, September 2011
8. Kholod, M., Lyandau, Y., Maslennikov, V., Kalinina, I., Mrochkovskiy, N.: Upper level processes and projects model building. In: Intelligent Decision Technologies 2019: Proceedings of the 11th KES International Conference on Intelligent Decision Technologies (KES-IDT 2019), vol. 2, pp. 267–276. Springer, Singapore, Singapore, June 2019
9. Simatupang, T.M., Piboonrungroj, P., Williams, S.J.: The emergence of value chain thinking. Int. J. Value Chain Manag. **8**(1), 40–57 (2017)
10. Bider, I., Perjons, E., Johanneson, P.: Using ontologies for comparing modeling techniques: experience report. In: International Conference on Conceptual Modeling, pp. 180–190. Springer International Publishing, Cham, November 2019
11. Saarsen, T., Bider, I.: How to use a FEM model as a basis for strategic-level risk analysis. In: International Conference on Research Challenges in Information Science, pp. 120–129. Springer Nature, Cham, Switzerland, May 2025
12. Lipol, L.S., Haq, J.: Risk analysis method: FMEA/FMECA in the organizations. Int. J. Basic Appl. Sci. **11**(5), 74–82 (2011)
13. Bider, I., Perjons, E., Elias, M., Johannesson, P.: A fractal enterprise model and its application for business development. Softw. Syst. Model. **16**(3), 663–689 (2017)
14. Shangguan, Z., Gao, Z., Zhu, K.: Ontology-based process modeling using eTOM and ITIL. In: Research and Practical Issues of Enterprise Information Systems II: Volume 2 IFIP TC 8 WG 8.9 International Conference on Research and Practical Issues of Enterprise Information Systems (CONFENIS 2007) October 14–16, 2007, Beijing, China, pp. 1001–1010. Springer, Boston, MA, US (2008)

Digital Twin-Driven Supply Chain Resilience with Predictive and Optimization Techniques

Vimal Dwivedi[1](✉), Sabah Suhail[2], and Mubashar Iqbal[3]

[1] Ulster University, Belfast, UK
v.dwivedi@ulster.ac.uk
[2] Munster Technological University, Cork, Ireland
sabah.suhail@mtu.ie
[3] University of Tartu, Tartu, Estonia
mubashar.iqbal@ut.ee

Abstract. Supply chain enabled by digital integration and real-time coordination is highly efficient but increasingly vulnerable to operational and cyber disruptions that create a ripple effect across suppliers and manufacturers, undermining supply chain resilience. Existing approaches often address resilience requirements in isolation or treat prediction and optimization separately, limiting actionable, integrated decision support. To address this gap, we propose a digital twin (DT)-driven supply chain resilience framework that integrates five critical resilience requirements, including flexible sourcing, visibility, demand-based management, collaboration, and risk management, within a unified DT framework. The framework combines predictive and optimization algorithms to enable real-time monitoring, disruption simulation, and data-driven decision support. Simulations demonstrate that the approach effectively anticipates and mitigates disruptions, yielding a composite resilience score of 0.91, reflecting high predictive and operational performance. The proposed framework enhances resilience in complex supply chain environments, providing actionable insights for researchers and practitioners.

Keywords: Digital Twin (DT) · Supply Chain Resilience · Prediction and Optimization Algorithms · Digital Business · Intelligent Systems

1 Introduction

Supply chain enabled by advanced digital technologies associated with Industry 4.0 to create a highly connected, data-driven, and intelligent supply network for improving operational efficiency [27]. While this structure increases the responsiveness, productivity, and cost efficiency of the supply chain system, it also creates strong interdependencies among suppliers, manufacturers, and distributors. In recent years, cyber-induced disruptions have emerged as a significant threat to

R. Matulevičius et al. (Eds.): DB&IS 2026, CCIS 3085, pp. 299–315, 2026.
https://doi.org/10.1007/978-3-032-30863-4_19

such digitally connected supply chains. For example, Jaguar Land Rover experienced production disruptions following a cyberattack at a key supplier [4]. This incident demonstrates how a cyberattack on a single supplier can affect downstream manufacturing operations. Similarly, when a supplier becomes unavailable due to ransomware or system compromise, production schedules, material flows, and demand fulfillment processes can be interrupted. Therefore, a critical concern arises: how resilient are supply chains when digital disruptions, rather than physical breakdowns, become the primary source of risk?

Supply chain resilience is defined as the ability of a supply network to prepare for, respond to, and recover from disruptions while maintaining operational continuity [12]. To achieve supply chain resilience, a system should include defined resilience requirements such as flexible sourcing, supply chain visibility, demand-based management, supply chain collaboration, and risk management [8]. However, existing studies frequently focus on individual resilience requirements and often treat them as conceptual objectives rather than measurable, optimizable constructs. Also, many existing approaches utilize prediction and optimization as separate tasks. For example, predictive models in the supply chain can estimate risks or disruptions, while optimization models can independently adjust operational decisions [9]. This separation limits the ability to systematically enhance resilience in an integrated and data-driven manner. To address these research gaps, we operationalize supply chain resilience by proposing a DT-driven supply chain (Fig. 1). DT creates a virtual representation of the physical supply chain that mirrors its time- and state-dependent behavior for real-time monitoring, simulation, and scenario analysis [13]. This enables decision-makers to test disruption scenarios and evaluate response strategies. A feedback loop generates objective-specific insights, which are fed back into the supply chain for informed decision-making and performance improvement.

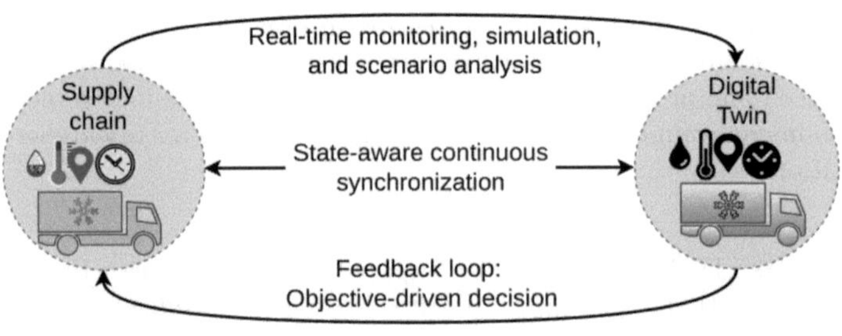

Fig. 1. Illustrating the concept of DT-driven supply chain.

Additionally, by integrating predictive and optimization techniques within a unified DT-driven supply chain system, the study seeks to move beyond descriptive resilience analysis toward actionable, computational decision support. The research question guiding this work is: *How can DT operationalize supply chain resilience as measurable and optimizable constructs and integrate prediction and optimization algorithms?* The main contributions are:

- DT-driven supply chain resilience framework systematically integrating resilience requirements, prediction, and optimization algorithms.
- Empirical evaluation of multiple predictive and optimization algorithms for DT-driven supply chain resilience enhancement.
- Composite resilience score to quantitatively assess supply chain resilience.

The paper is structured as follows. Section 2 overviews the related work. Section 3 introduces the DT-driven supply chain resilience framework. Section 4 evaluates the proposed framework, and Sect. 5 concludes the paper.

2 Related Work

Several studies have examined the application of DTs for improving supply chain resilience and operational decision support (Table 1). Ivanov and Dolgui [9] introduced the digital supply chain twin to analyze the propagation of disruptions and support risk monitoring. Zhang et al. [28] proposed DTs for improving supply chain visibility and system integration. Ivanov [10] further extended this line of research by introducing an intelligent DT capable of stress-testing supply chains under disruption scenarios. In addition, Zaidi et al. [27] provided a systematic review of DT applications in supply chains, highlighting their role in improving transparency and data-driven decision support. Singh et al. [24] examined how DT technologies can support resilient and sustainable manufacturing supply chains by emphasizing flexibility and visibility. Similarly, Kim et al. [13] proposed a DT–based framework closely related to our work that integrates simulation and optimization techniques to improve dynamic supply chain decision-making. While these studies demonstrate the potential of DTs for enhancing supply chain resilience, they typically address only a subset of resilience requirements or focus on specific predictive or optimization capabilities.

Table 1. Comparative overview of DT–driven supply chains.

Ref.	Resilience reqs.	Simulation	Prediction	Optimization	Quantification
[9]	◐	●	●	○	○
[28]	◐	○	○	●	○
[10]	◐	●	●	●	○
[27]	◐	○	○	○	○
[24]	◐	◐	●	○	○
[13]	◐	●	●	◐	○
Ours	●	●	●	●	●

Legend: ● Covered; ○ Not covered; ◐ Partially Covered.

Table 1 presents a comparative overview of DT–drive supply chain studies, highlighting the resilience requirements addressed. The comparison indicates that existing approaches concentrate partially on resilience requirements. In addition, the integration of simulation, prediction, optimization, and resilience quantification within a unified DT system remains limited. This work addresses these limitations by integrating these capabilities within a unified DT system while explicitly incorporating supply chain resilience requirements.

3 DT-Driven Supply Chain Resilience Framework

The framework (Fig. 2) is structured around the interaction between the physical supply chain and its DT counterpart. The physical process consists of suppliers, manufacturers, and customers, representing the flow of materials and products across the network. The operational data generated at each stage, such as shipment information, production status, and customer transactions, is continuously transmitted to a centralized database. This database stores both historical and real-time monitoring data, which serve as the foundation for the DT environment. The framework is designed as a closed-loop system, where data from the physical layer is mirrored in the digital layer, and optimized decisions are fed back to improve operational performance.

The DT process, which replicates the supplier–manufacturer–customer structure in a virtual environment for continuous monitoring, modeling, and testing of supply chain conditions without interrupting physical operations. The DT operates through iterative stages, including design and development, operations and maintenance, testing, and business analytics [7]. These stages ensure that the virtual model remains aligned with real-world dynamics while enabling performance evaluation and scenario analysis. The framework integrates supply chain resilience requirements, such as flexibility sourcing, supply chain visibility, demand-based management, supply chain collaboration, and risk management [21], discussed in Sect. 3.1. Furthermore, another key component of the framework is the integration of anticipation and adaptation techniques, specifically prediction and optimization algorithms, discussed in Sect. 3.2.

3.1 Supply Chain Resilience Requirements Mapping for DT-Driven Supply Chain Solution

This section examines the supply chain's resilience requirements and maps to the DT-driven supply chain solution. These requirements minimize the consequences of disruptions and support timely responses. The resilience requirements are operationalized through measurable indicators derived from [5,9] (Table 2).

Flexibility sourcing represents the ability of the supply chain to adjust sourcing, production, and logistics decisions when disruptions occur [24]. The aftermath of Hurricane Mitch in 1998 highlighted the dangers of relying on a single supplier, as seen in the banana trade [19]. For instance, Dole, which relied entirely on a single vendor, took a significant hit when the hurricane destroyed 70% of its global production. The scenario emphasizes the importance of a flexible sourcing strategy. DT contributes to flexibility by simulating alternative operational

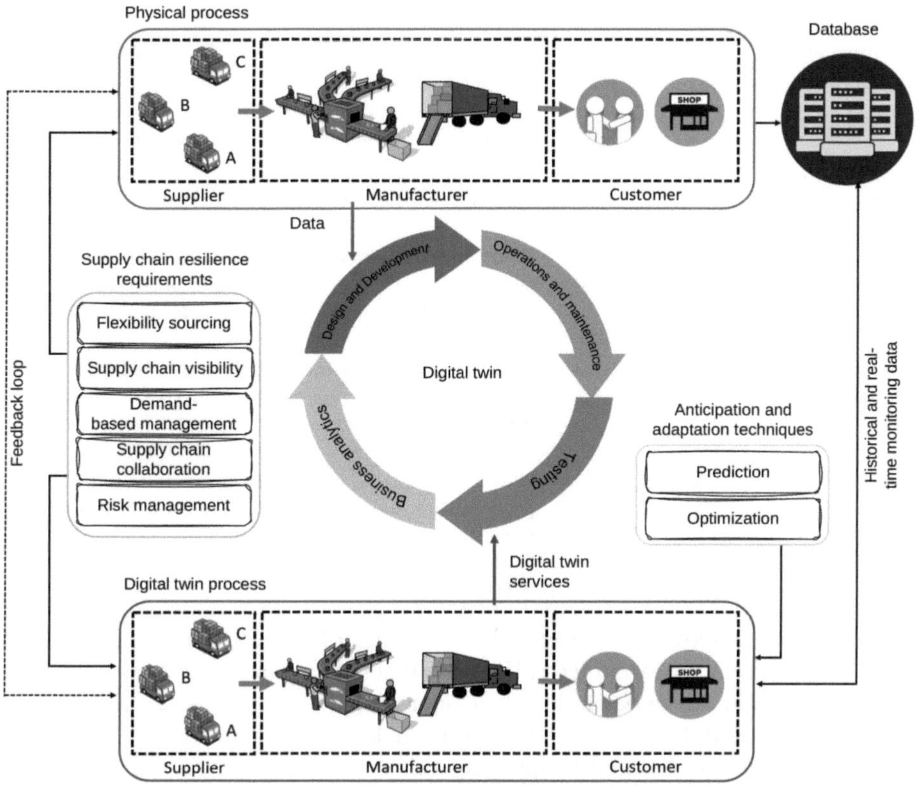

Fig. 2. DT-driven supply chain resilience framework.

configurations before implementation [6]. For instance, DT-based supply chain solutions can simulate flexibility sourcing scenarios and recommend a suitable strategy, such as offshore vendors or local suppliers, or a combination of both. Through such DT-based scenario analysis, decision-makers can evaluate the feasibility, cost, and performance impact of different recovery strategies. Indicators such as reconfiguration time, the number of feasible alternative plans, and switching costs serve as measurable proxies for flexibility, as they directly reflect the system's ability to adapt to disruptions.

Supply chain visibility refers to the ability of the supply chain to access timely, accurate, and integrated information across multiple tiers, including suppliers, production facilities, inventory locations, and logistics networks [1]. Supply chains are vulnerable to uncertainties and risks in today's volatile digital business environment, including supplier disruptions, natural disasters, geopolitical events, and market shifts [18]. Therefore, companies must analyze historical data to anticipate future risks and maintain real-time visibility. DT enhances visibility by synchronizing real-time operational data from physical systems into

Table 2. Supply chain resilience requirements and DT integration.

Requirement	Category	DT role	Measurable indicators
Flexibility sourcing	Reactive	Simulates sourcing, production, and routing plans.	Reconfiguration time, alternative plans, switching cost
Supply chain visibility	Proactive	Synchronizes real-time data into a virtual model.	Data latency, detection time, tier-level transparency
Demand-based management	Adaptive	Real-time, data-driven environment where demand patterns are analyzed.	Demand reallocation time, revenue preservation, back-order stabilization time
Supply chain collaboration	Proactive/Reactive	Digital environment for coordinated decision-making and multi-tier visibility.	Information sharing frequency, coordination delay, joint recovery planning rate
Risk Management	Proactive/Adaptive	Checks disruption probabilities and impact scenarios.	Risk exposure index, disruption probability, loss

a virtual model, allowing continuous monitoring of material flows, production status, and system performance [21]. In such settings, the DT can also support early identification of cyber-induced or operational disruptions [2]. Measurable indicators such as data latency, detection time, tier-level transparency, and information accuracy can be used to quantify this requirement.

Demand-based management refers to dynamically adjusting demand-related decisions in response to customer demand, supply disruptions, or system constraints [16]. For example, when seismic activity in Taiwan halted the production of computer parts and semiconductors for a fortnight in 1999, Dell redirected its customers to readily available alternative products [23]. They guided consumer choices by offering promotions and discounts, which increased their profits, while competitors saw their profits decrease. DT can provide a real-time, data-driven environment in which supply constraints and demand patterns are continuously synchronized and analyzed [2]. In disruption scenarios, such as supply shortages or production halts, the DT mirrors the current state of inventory levels, supplier availability, production capacity, and order backlog. This real-time representation allows decision-makers to identify mismatches between supply availability and incoming demand. Indicators such as demand reallocation time, revenue preservation, and backorder stabilization time are used to represent the responsiveness and effectiveness of demand adaptation strategies.

Supply chain collaboration involves coordinated planning, information sharing, and joint decision-making among supply chain partners [29]. Building a resilient supply chain requires close collaboration with suppliers, manufacturers, and logistics providers because no organization has complete control over its supply chain in today's interconnected world, and disruptions can occur at any stage. Thus, a collaborative approach can ensure real-time information sharing, detect potential cybersecurity risks, and allow shipment rerouting, capacity adjustments, or production plan revisions as needed to manage risks and respond to unexpected events. DT serves as a shared digital platform that integrates data from multiple stakeholders and can support real-time, synchronized decision-making [26]. For instance, by providing common visibility and scenario evaluation, the DT enhances collective response during disruptions. Collaboration is quantified using indicators such as frequency of information sharing, coordination delays, and the rate of joint recovery planning, which reflect the efficiency and effectiveness of inter-organizational coordination.

Risk management is the systematic identification, assessment, and mitigation of operational and cybersecurity risks across the supply chain [20]. Traditional risk management approaches often rely on static assessments and qualitative evaluation. DT enhances risk management by integrating predictive models that estimate disruption probabilities and simulate their potential impact [17]. Scenario-based evaluation enables proactive mitigation planning and vulnerability prioritization. Risk exposure indices, disruption probabilities, and expected loss metrics can be used to quantify this requirement.

3.2 Prediction and Optimization Algorithms for DT-Driven Supply Chain Resilience

We investigate and implement the ML-based prediction and optimization techniques by applying them to the dataset discussed in Appendix A. This supports anticipation and adaptation functionalities for the DT-driven supply chain resilience, consistent with the supply chain resilience requirements outlined in Sect. 3.1. We use Python with Scikit-learn and associated libraries, including Pandas, NumPy, DEAP, PySwarm, SimAnneal, and SciPy. The implementation code is available on Zenodo (https://zenodo.org/records/18834758).

Table 3 presents the integration of *predictive algorithms*, such as random forest (RF) regression, linear regression, RF classifier, and decision tree classifier that generate anticipatory insights within the DT–driven supply chain. We split the dataset into 80%–20% train–test samples to train models for predicting target variable values on the held-out evaluation set. The table links resilience requirements to specific operational features, identifies the best-performing algorithm for each feature, and reports the corresponding evaluation metric. We assess the trained model's performance using task-appropriate evaluation metrics. For instance, we evaluate regression tasks using the coefficient of determination (R^2) and binary classification tasks using accuracy.

RF is applied consistently across features; near-perfect performance in some cases reflects deterministic relationships in the data. The resilience score Φ is computed via weighted aggregation, with weights optimized using Monte Carlo sampling, selecting the configuration that maximizes Φ under balanced contribution constraints. The DT acts as an integration layer, continuously updating predictions and feeding optimized decisions for real-time adaptation.

Table 3. Integration of predictive models for DT-driven supply chain resilience.

Requirement	Feature	Algorithm	Metric
Flexibility sourcing	Real shipping days	RF regression	0.600 (R^2)
	Scheduled shipping days	RF regression	1.000 (R^2)
Supply chain visibility	Order item discount	RF regression	0.999 (R^2)
	Order item discount rate	Linear regression	1.000 (R^2)
	Product price	RF regression	1.000 (R^2)
Demand management	Sales per customer	RF regression	0.999 (R^2)
	Benefit per order	RF regression	0.971 (R^2)
	Sales	RF regression	0.999 (R^2)
Collaboration	Shipping mode	RF regression	1.000 (R^2)
	Order profit per order	RF regression	0.971 (R^2)
Risk management	Late delivery	RF classifier	73.6% (accuracy)
	Fraud	Decision tree classifier	100% (accuracy)

The implemented approach demonstrates how different predictive models contribute to the DT's anticipation capability across DT-driven supply chain resilience requirements. For instance, under the flexibility requirement, real shipping days achieved the R^2 of 0.600 using RF regression, indicating moderate predictive performance and reflecting the inherent variability in actual delivery times. In contrast, scheduled shipping days achieved the R^2 of 1.000, suggesting that this variable is largely deterministic and can be perfectly reconstructed from related planning data. For visibility and demand management, several financial and pricing-related features, such as order item discount, product price, sales, and sales per customer, achieved very high R^2 values (close to or equal to 1.000), indicating strong predictability from upstream transactional variables. These results suggest that structured pricing and sales patterns can be reliably forecasted within the digital twin environment. In the risk management requirement, classification models were applied to predict late delivery and fraud. The RF classifier achieved an accuracy of 73.6% for late delivery, indicating that delivery delays are partially predictable but still subject to operational uncertainty. The fraud detection model achieved 100% accuracy using a decision tree classifier. While this indicates strong separability in the dataset, such performance may suggest deterministic patterns or highly distinguishable features within the data.

This study evaluates four metaheuristic *optimization algorithms*, such as genetic algorithm (GA), particle swarm optimization (PSO), simulated annealing (SA), and differential evolution (DE), to support resource allocation, inventory control, routing, and cost-minimization decisions (Table 4). We select these algorithms based on their suitability for solving complex, nonlinear optimization problems commonly encountered in supply chain systems [3]. For example, the GA is well-suited for discrete decision variables and is often applied to routing and combinatorial problems [22]. PSO is known for its efficiency in handling multi-objective optimization problems [11], while SA provides a robust search mechanism that can escape local optimization [14]. DE is effective for continuous-parameter optimization and, therefore, appropriate for inventory-related decisions [25]. Together, these methods allow a comparative evaluation of different optimization strategies within a unified DT-driven supply chain, yet their effectiveness depends heavily on the accuracy and timeliness of the input data.

Table 4. Settings and performance comparison of optimization algorithms.

Algo.	Implementation settings	Optimal order quantity	Lead time (days)	Holding cost per unit	Forecast horizon (days)	Minimized total inventory cost
GA	Population = 100; Generations = 40; Mutation = 0.2; Crossover = 0.8	45	4	$1.8	6	$1,200
PSO	Search bounds: [1, 100]	50	2	$1.5	7	$1,150
SA	Dual_annealing (scipy.optimize); Bounds: [1, 100]	48	3	$1.6	5	$1,180
DE	Bounds: [1, 100]; Same cost function	44	5	$1.7	6	$1,190

For implementation, we apply these algorithms to the dataset discussed in Appendix A. The objective function was defined as the total inventory cost, consisting of holding and ordering costs, which reflects standard supply chain performance criteria. The GA was configured with a population size of 100 and executed for 40 generations, with mutation and crossover probabilities set to 0.2 and 0.8, respectively. PSO, SA (using `dual_annealing`), and DE were executed within a bounded search space between 1 and 100 to ensure consistency across experiments. The algorithms optimized key decision variables, including order quantity, lead time, holding cost per unit, and forecast horizon.

The comparative results indicate that PSO achieved the lowest total inventory cost (approximately $1,150), followed by SA and DE, while GA produced a slightly higher cost of approximately $1,200. In terms of individual performance metrics, PSO was most effective in reducing holding costs, GA and DE provided relatively favorable lead times, and SA maintained stable service levels. These findings suggest that no single algorithm dominates across different supply chain objectives. Instead, each technique offers advantages depending on the specific performance measure being optimized. This supports the potential benefit of hybrid or integrated optimization strategies within a DT-driven supply chain solution for comprehensive supply chain resilience.

4 Evaluating DT-Driven Supply Chain Resilience

This section simulates the disruption scenarios (Sect. 4.1) and quantifies the resilience (Sect. 4.2) to demonstrate the practicality of integrating DT, prediction, and optimization algorithms to support supply chain resilience.

4.1 Simulating Disruption Scenarios

We simulate real and scheduled shipping-day disruption scenarios illustrated in Fig. 3, introducing supplier- and manufacturing-level disturbances. The simulations assume that one or more suppliers become unavailable or experience a manufacturing process fault, which directly affects the time required to receive materials (T_1), complete manufacturing (T_2), and deliver the final product to the customer (T_3). The DT mirrors these disruptions in real time and captures how deviations between scheduled and actual shipping days propagate across the supply chain. The data-simulation graphs in Fig. 3 illustrate the operational impact of these disruptions across three key performance dimensions. For instance, demand fulfillment, represented in red, reflects the system's ability to meet customer demand under constrained supply conditions. When a supplier is down, unmet demand increases and order completion rates decline unless corrective measures are applied. Delivery performance, shown in blue, captures the deviation between scheduled and actual delivery times. Disruptions at supplier or manufacturing levels increase lead times and increase the likelihood of late delivery. Inventory stability, depicted in gray, reflects fluctuations in stock levels and replenishment cycles. Supplier delays and production faults create inventory position variability, which may lead to stockouts or excess holding costs.

From these simulations, the prediction algorithm predicted one in which the product delivery is delayed by Supplier C and by a manufacturing process fault. Under normal circumstances, the product is expected to be received from suppliers A, B, and C within the defined time T_1. However, an unexpected delay at Supplier C extends this to $T_1 + x$. Concurrently, the manufacturing process typically takes T_2, but is protracted to $T_2 + y$ due to a machinery fault. As a result, the customer's expected delivery time is displaced from T_3 to $T_3 + x + y$. This situation is simulated within the DT, which employs prediction algorithms to anticipate potential delays based on current and historical data and optimization algorithms to identify solutions to these delays. This structured experimentation allows the evaluation of optimization algorithms within the DT-driven supply chain. We select the PSO algorithm based on its minimized total inventory cost (as shown in Table 4) to showcase how adaptive decisions can stabilize performance despite disturbances. For instance, the optimization algorithm suggests substituting Supplier C with Supplier D, who can deliver the product within the original T_1. In the manufacturing process, the optimization algorithm proposes an alternative machine that completes the process within the standard time T_2, ensuring the customer receives their order at the expected time T_3.

Similarly, we can instantiate and visualize other scenarios from the selected features discussed in Sect. 3.2.

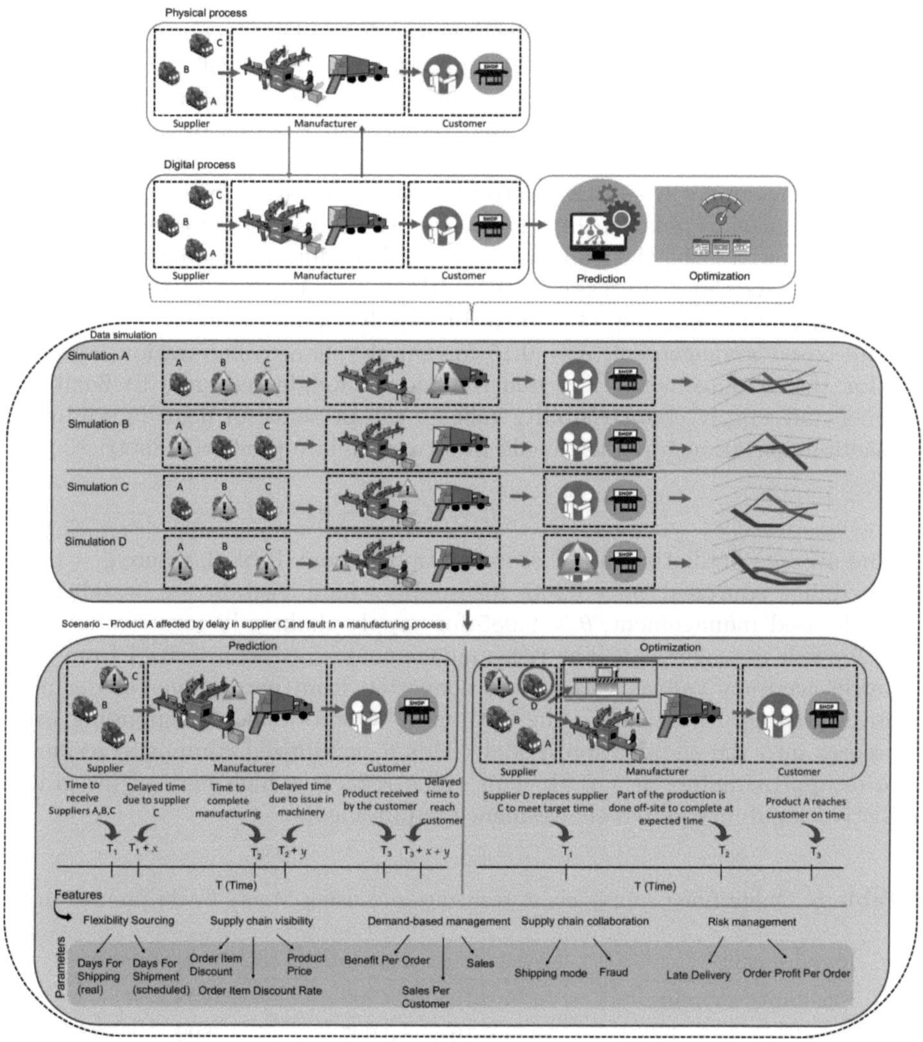

Fig. 3. Disruption scenarios within DT-driven supply chain.

4.2 Quantifying DT-Driven Supply Chain Resilience

We adopt a multi-feature aggregation approach to quantify resilience within the proposed DT-driven supply chain framework rather than relying on a single monolithic metric. Supply chain resilience is inherently multidimensional and must therefore be assessed through several operational and managerial indicators. Therefore, we adopt the five core resilience requirements discussed in Sect. 3.1. Each requirement is represented by multiple operational features, for which predictive models are trained in Sect. 3.2. The average predictive performance of each requirement is denoted by ξ, η, ζ, θ, and ι, respectively. These performance values capture how effectively each resilience requirement can be anticipated and supported within the digital twin environment.

The supply chain resilience score is computed using a weighted linear aggregation model (Eq. 1) where α, γ, δ, and ϵ represent the relative importance of each resilience requirement. We determine the weights using a Monte Carlo simulation process under a leakage-controlled setting to avoid bias introduced by deterministic feature relationships [15]. The process searched for weight combinations that maximized the resilience score while maintaining realistic predictive performance. As shown in Table 5, the optimal weights were identified as $\alpha = 0.10$ for flexibility sourcing, $\beta = 0.10$ for supply chain visibility, $\gamma = 0.40$ for demand-based management, $\delta = 0.15$ for supply chain collaboration, and $\epsilon = 0.25$ for risk management. The relatively lower weight assigned to flexibility sourcing and supply chain visibility reflects the presence of near-deterministic transactional relationships that could otherwise inflate predictive metrics.

$$\Phi = \alpha\xi + \beta\eta + \gamma\zeta + \delta\theta + \epsilon\iota \tag{1}$$

The average predictive model scores obtained from Table 3, where $\xi = 0.800$ for flexibility sourcing, $\eta = 0.997$ for supply chain visibility, $\zeta = 0.989$ for demand-based management, $\theta = 0.985$ for supply chain collaboration, and $\iota = 0.868$ for risk management. The risk management score was derived from classification accuracy values, which were converted from percentages to decimals before averaging. Substituting the optimized weights and corresponding average scores into the aggregation model yields a maximized composite resilience score of approximately $\phi = 0.91$. This value reflects a high level of integrated predictive capability across the resilience requirements.

Table 5. Quantifying supply chain resilience (Φ) using Monte Carlo simulation.

Requirement	Weight	Average model score	Feature score
Flexibility sourcing	$\alpha = 0.10$	$\xi = 0.800$	0.08
Supply chain visibility	$\beta = 0.10$	$\eta = 0.997$	0.09
Demand-based management	$\gamma = 0.40$	$\zeta = 0.989$	0.39
Supply chain collaboration	$\delta = 0.15$	$\theta = 0.985$	0.14
Risk management	$\epsilon = 0.25$	$\iota = 0.868$	0.21
Composite resilience score (Φ)			0.91

The composite score represents resilience performance under realistic predictive conditions rather than deterministic reconstruction effects. The results indicate that demand-based management and risk management contribute most significantly to overall resilience performance, as shown by both their strong predictive scores and higher optimized weights. Flexibility sourcing and supply chain visibility provide a moderate but stable contribution, while supply chain collaboration remains sensitive to data characteristics such as class imbalance in shipping mode and order profit per order-related indicators. This quantification demonstrates how predictive performance across multiple resilience requirements can be systematically integrated into a single, interpretable resilience index within a digital twin environment.

The reported results are dependent on the characteristics of the dataset used in this study (Appendix A). The distribution of transactional variables, the structure of supplier–customer interactions, and the level of operational variability directly influence both the predictive model performance and the resulting resilience weights. In alternative supply chain environments, such as different industries, network topologies, or disruption patterns, the relative importance of resilience requirements may differ. Consequently, the computed feature scores and optimized weight allocations should not be interpreted as universally applicable benchmarks. Instead, the proposed approach should be viewed as a structured and adaptable methodology that can be recalibrated for different operational settings using context-specific data. We also perform 10,000 Monte Carlo iterations to ensure statistical stability during weight optimization, reduce sampling variability, and support convergence toward stable weight distributions. Furthermore, sensitivity analysis was conducted to assess the robustness of the optimized weights under small perturbations in the average model scores. This step evaluates how variations in predictive accuracy, such as those arising from data updates or retraining, affect the overall resilience score.

5 Discussion and Conclusion

We propose a DT-driven framework to operationalize supply chain resilience by integrating predictive and optimization algorithms with five resilience requirements, including flexibility sourcing, supply chain visibility, demand-based management, supply chain collaboration, and risk management. The proposed approach enables real-time monitoring, scenario simulation, and data-driven decision support, allowing supply chain operators to anticipate disruptions and adapt effectively. Through simulations and quantitative evaluation, we demonstrated the framework's ability to generate actionable insights and support decision-making under both supplier- and manufacturing-level disturbances. The resulting composite resilience score of $\Phi = 0.91$ indicates high integrated predictive capability across the resilience requirements.

5.1 Theoretical and Practical Implications

This study contributes to the supply chain resilience literature by operationalizing resilience as a measurable, optimizable construct within a DT framework. Moreover, rather than treating resilience as a conceptual capability, the proposed framework links clearly defined resilience requirements, such as flexibility sourcing, demand-based management, collaboration, and risk management, to quantifiable predictive performance and optimization outcomes. By integrating anticipation (prediction) and adaptation (optimization) within a unified DT framework, the work bridges the gap between descriptive resilience theory and computational decision models. The introduction of a composite resilience score further advances theoretical development by providing a structured method for aggregating multidimensional resilience indicators into a single, interpretable metric. This framework supports a more systematic and data-driven understanding of resilience in digitally enabled supply chains.

From a practical perspective, the proposed framework supports more proactive, data-driven, and adaptive decision-making in complex and digitally interconnected supply chain environments. For example, the framework provides supply chain managers with a structured approach to monitor, evaluate, and improve resilience in real time. The integration of predictive analytics enables early detection of potential disruptions, while optimization techniques support informed corrective actions such as sourcing adjustments, demand shaping, and inventory reallocation. The composite resilience score provides a performance indicator to guide operational prioritization across resilience dimensions. Moreover, the simulation-based environment allows organizations to test alternative recovery strategies without disrupting physical operations.

5.2 Limitations

We use a single dataset, which may not fully represent the structural complexity and disruption dynamics of large-scale industrial supply chains. The predictive performance and optimized weight distributions are therefore dependent on the characteristics of the DataCo case and may differ in other operational contexts. Also, the composite resilience score relies on selected features and model accuracy as proxies for resilience capability, which may not capture all qualitative or organizational aspects of resilience, such as governance maturity or cultural factors. Lastly, the framework focuses primarily on cost-related objectives and does not explicitly incorporate sustainability or multi-echelon network constraints. These limitations suggest that while the framework provides a structured and adaptable approach, further work across diverse datasets and real-world industrial settings is required to strengthen generalizability.

5.3 Future Work

The proposed framework should be validated using diverse industrial datasets from sectors such as automotive, healthcare, and semiconductor supply chains to assess its generalizability across varying network structures and disruption profiles. Incorporating multi-tier supplier networks and more complex interdependencies would provide a more realistic evaluation of resilience dynamics. Future studies may also integrate additional performance dimensions such as sustainability, carbon footprint, and social risk to broaden the resilience assessment beyond cost and service metrics. This would support alignment with emerging supply chain 4.0 and sustainable operations objectives. Another promising direction is to enhance the DT architecture with advanced learning mechanisms, such as reinforcement learning and adaptive control models, to enable continuous self-improvement in the face of evolving disruption patterns.

A Appendix: DataCo Supply Chain Dataset

We utilize the publicly available DataCo Supply Chain Dataset (https://data.mendeley.com/datasets/8gx2fvg2k6/5) to train the prediction and optimization models described in Sect. 3.2. The dataset contains 2.5 years of transactional records from a global superstore and includes operational, financial, and logistics attributes. From this dataset, we select 12 resilience-related features (Table 3) to support the modeling of shipping performance, demand patterns, profitability, and disruption indicators such as late deliveries and fraud. Prior to analysis, we preprocess the data by handling missing values, encoding categorical variables, generating derived variables (e.g., total price), converting date fields for time-series analysis, and creating binary indicators for fraud and late delivery to ensure suitability for predictive modeling and optimization.

References

1. Agrawal, T.K., Kalaiarasan, R., Olhager, J., Wiktorsson, M.: Supply chain visibility: a Delphi study on managerial perspectives and priorities. Int. J. Prod. Res. **62**(8), 2927–2942 (2024). https://doi.org/10.1080/00207543.2022.2098873
2. Benhamou, L., Giard, V., Lamouri, S.: Digital twins in supply chain management: scope and methodological issues. Int. J. Prod. Econ. **291**, 109842 (2026). https://doi.org/10.1016/j.ijpe.2025.109842
3. Blum, C., Roli, A.: Metaheuristics in combinatorial optimization: overview and conceptual comparison. ACM Comput. Surv. **35**(3), 268–308 (2003). https://doi.org/10.1145/937503.937505
4. Choudhary, N., Ramkumar, M., Schoenherr, T., Rana, N., Dwivedi, Y.: Does reshoring affect the resilience and sustainability of supply chain networks? The cases of apple and jaguar land rover. Br. J. Manag. **34**, 1138–1156 (2023). https://doi.org/10.1111/1467-8551.12614
5. Christopher, M., Peck, H.: Building the resilient supply chain. Int. J. Logist. Manag. **15**(2), 1–14 (2004). https://doi.org/10.1108/09574090410700275
6. Guo, D., Mantravadi, S.: The role of digital twins in lean supply chain management: review and research directions. Int. J. Prod. Res. **63**(5), 1851–1872 (2025). https://doi.org/10.1080/00207543.2024.2372655
7. Iqbal, M., Suhail, S., Matulevičius, R., Shah, F.A., Malik, S.U.R., McLaughlin, K.: IoV-TwinChain: predictive maintenance of vehicles in internet of vehicles through digital twin and blockchain. Internet Things **30**, 101514 (2025). https://doi.org/10.1016/j.iot.2025.101514
8. Ivanov, D., Dolgui, A.: Viability of intertwined supply networks: extending the supply chain resilience angles towards survivability. A position paper motivated by COVID-19 outbreak. Int. J. Prod. Res. **58**(10), 2904–2915 (2020). https://doi.org/10.1080/00207543.2020.1750727

9. Ivanov, D., Dolgui, A.: A digital supply chain twin for managing the disruption risks and resilience in the era of industry 4.0. Prod. Plan. Control **32**(9), 775–788 (2021). https://doi.org/10.1080/09537287.2020.1768450
10. Ivanov, D.: Intelligent digital twin (IDT) for supply chain stress-testing, resilience, and viability. Int. J. Prod. Econ. **263**, 108938 (2023). https://doi.org/10.1016/j.ijpe.2023.108938
11. Kennedy, J., Eberhart, R.: Particle swarm optimization. In: Proceedings of ICNN 1995 - International Conference on Neural Networks, vol. 4, pp. 1942–1948 (1995). https://doi.org/10.1109/ICNN.1995.488968
12. Khan, A.S., Seger, C.: Enhancing supply chain resilience: a digital twin conceptual model of supplier selection factors impacting supply chain resilience. Master's thesis, KTH Royal Institute of Technology (2024). https://urn.kb.se/resolve?urn=urn:nbn:se:kth:diva-348382
13. Kim, D.H., Kim, G.Y., Noh, S.: Digital twin-based prediction and optimization for dynamic supply chain management. Machines **13**(2), 109 (2025). https://doi.org/10.3390/machines13020109
14. Kirkpatrick, S., Gelatt, C.D., Vecchi, M.P.: Optimization by simulated annealing. Science **220**(4598), 671–680 (1983). https://doi.org/10.1126/science.220.4598.671
15. Kroese, D., Taimre, T., Botev, Z.: Handbook of Monte Carlo Methods. Wiley (2013)
16. Landeghem, H.V., Vanmaele, H.: Robust planning: a new paradigm for demand chain planning. J. Oper. Manag. **20**(6), 769–783 (2002). https://doi.org/10.1016/S0272-6963(02)00039-6
17. Luo, Q., Sun, C., Li, Y., Qi, Z., Zhang, G.: Applications of digital twin technology in construction safety risk management: a literature review. Eng. Constr. Archit. Manag. **32**(6), 3587–3607 (2025). https://doi.org/10.1108/ECAM-11-2023-1095
18. Maheshwari, S., Jaggi, C.K.: Enhancing supply chain resilience through industry-specific approaches to mitigating disruptions. Opsearch **62**(4), 1687–1720 (2025). https://doi.org/10.1007/s12597-024-00872-z
19. Nagurney, A., Qiang, Q.: Quantifying supply chain network synergy for humanitarian organisations. IBM J. Res. Dev. **64**(1/2), 12:1–12:16 (2020). https://doi.org/10.1147/JRD.2019.2940430
20. Rashid, A., et al.: Role of information processing and digital supply chain in supply chain resilience through supply chain risk management. J. Glob. Oper. Strateg. Sourc. **17**(2), 429–447 (2024)
21. Roman, E.A., et al.: State of the art of digital twins in improving supply chain resilience. Logistics **9**(1), 22 (2025). https://doi.org/10.3390/logistics9010022
22. Sastry, K., Goldberg, D., Kendall, G.: Genetic algorithms. In: Search Methodologies. Springer (2014). https://doi.org/10.1007/978-1-4614-6940-7_4
23. Sheffi, Y.: The Resilient Enterprise: Overcoming Vulnerability for Competitive Advantage. MIT Press (2007)
24. Singh, G., Rajesh, R., Misra, S.C., Singh, S.: Analyzing the role of digital twins in developing a resilient sustainable manufacturing supply chain: a grey influence analysis (gina) approach. Technol. Forecast. Soc. Chang. **209**, 123763 (2024). https://doi.org/10.1016/j.techfore.2024.123763
25. Storn, R., Price, K.: Differential evolution – a simple and efficient heuristic for global optimization over continuous spaces. J. Global Optim. **11**, 341–359 (1997). https://doi.org/10.1023/A:1008202821328
26. Suhail, S., Iqbal, M., Hussain, R., Malik, S.U.R., Jurdak, R.: Triple: a blockchain-based digital twin framework for cyber–physical systems security. J. Ind. Inf. Integr. **42**, 100706 (2024)

27. Zaidi, S.A.H., Khan, S.A., Chaabane, A.: Unlocking the potential of digital twins in supply chains: a systematic review. Supply Chain Analyt. **7**, 100075 (2024). https://doi.org/10.1016/j.sca.2024.100075
28. Zhang, J., Brintrup, A., Calinescu, A., Kosasih, E., Sharma, A.: Supply chain digital twin framework design: an approach of supply chain operations reference model and system of systems, arXiv preprint arXiv:2107.09485 (2021)
29. Zhou, J., et al.: Impacts of it capability and supply chain collaboration on supply chain resilience: empirical evidence from China in COVID-19 pandemic. J. Enterp. Inf. Manag. **37**(2), 777–803 (2024)

Understanding Generative AI Adoption in Development Work: The Role of Developer Experience

Md Gulam Mashud Jaman, Abdul Mouhit, and Georgios Koutsopoulos(✉)

Department of Computer and Systems Sciences, Stockholm University, Borgarfjordsgatan 12, Kista, 16407 Stockholm, Sweden
Mashud.lu.cse@gmail.com, abdulmouhit@gmail.com, georgios@dsv.su.se

Abstract. Generative AI tools are now common in software development, reshaping how coding work is organized, performed, and learned in organizations. Thus, it is important to understand how developers at different experience levels adopt and use them. Guided by the Technology Acceptance Model (TAM), this study reports qualitative interviews with twelve Sweden-based developers (junior, mid, senior) to explore perceived usefulness, perceived ease of use, and day-to-day challenges. Experience clearly shapes interpretation. Juniors treat AI as learning support and a source of confidence, mid-level developers emphasize removal of routine friction and sustained focus, and senior developers apply selective use with strong emphasis on review and code quality. All groups acknowledge productivity benefits, but systematic validation and trust calibration remain essential. The study contributes experience-specific adoption guidelines and uses TAM as a lens to examine experience as a moderating factor that influences how usefulness and ease are framed in practice.

Keywords: Generative AI · Software development · Technology Acceptance Model · Developer experience · AI adoption

1 Introduction

Generative artificial intelligence (GenAI) is transforming contemporary digital development environments, reshaping how developers interact with information systems, tools, and knowledge resources during software development. The emergence of large language models (LLMs), most notably OpenAI's ChatGPT and GitHub Copilot, is reshaping how developers approach coding, learning, and collaboration. With the rise of GenAI assistants, developers are increasingly co-creating code with machines. This fact is changing task division, skill exercising, and responsibility in development teams. These GenAI-powered assistants have moved beyond novelty and now sit at the heart of mainstream development environments, offering real-time suggestions, automating routine elements of programming, and supporting faster problem-solving and skill acquisition [1–3]. Where developers once relied on static, community-driven platforms such

R. Matulevičius et al. (Eds.): DB&IS 2026, CCIS 3085, pp. 316–332, 2026.
https://doi.org/10.1007/978-3-032-30863-4_20

as Stack Overflow, they are increasingly turning to interactive and conversational GenAI tools for dynamic coding support.

While the adoption of GenAI assistants is accelerating, the tools that are used and the factors that support or limit their effective integration remain unclear. Research focuses on overall perceptions or aggregate productivity benefits, rather than nuanced patterns that may arise from differences in developer background, especially in experience and expertise [4, 5]. As GenAI adoption becomes ubiquitous, questions emerge. Are senior developers and novices equally able to benefit from GenAI? How does developer expertise mediate both the advantages and pitfalls of GenAI-assisted coding?

These questions are increasingly pressing, as organizations seek to standardize GenAI tool use and educators introduce these technologies into curricula. Early evidence points to both significant efficiency gains and critical challenges, including over-reliance on GenAI, verification burden, and potential erosion of programming fundamentals [3, 6, 7]. Some research further notes that skills such as prompt engineering and domain expertise have become central [1]. However, little is known about the lived realities of developers at different stages of their careers, nor about the specific practices, successes, and struggles that arise as they integrate GenAI into their workflow.

The aim of this paper[1] is to explore how seniority and expertise shape GenAI tool adoption and effective use in software developer work, and how developer experience configures both the benefits and risks of GenAI in the workplace. Our work interrogates the following key questions: (i) How do developers at various experience levels perceive and realize the usefulness and ease of use of GenAI-assisted coding tools? (ii) What are the differentiated impacts on productivity, learning, and confidence? (iii) Which strategies and practices enable responsible and optimal use for professionals?

To ensure contextual clarity, this research focuses on active software practitioners working in Sweden, with roles covering backend, mobile, embedded development, and DevOps, and delimits its attention strictly to the development phase of the software lifecycle. This intentional focus excludes managerial and planning activities, centring instead on the direct effects of GenAI on practical coding and technical collaboration.

The rest of the paper is structured as follows. Section 2 provides a brief overview of AI-Assisted Software Development gathered by studying relevant papers. Section 3 explains methodological decisions, Sect. 4 presents the findings of the study, Sect. 5 introduces a set of guidelines for optimal and responsible usage derived from the results, and Sects. 6 and 7 provide discussion and conclusion, respectively.

2 Background

2.1 AI-Assisted Software Development and Industry Adoption

AI has initiated a shift in how software work is performed, directly affecting patterns of learning, coding, and collaboration across the developer career spectrum. Contemporary AI-powered assistants, particularly have transformed traditionally static, search-driven tasks into dynamic, conversational interactions [1, 2]. The result is a new era in software

[1] A longer, earlier version of this study was written as a master's thesis at the authors' institution. The thesis is not publicly available.

engineering, in which code is not only written by hand but also authored, reviewed, and refined in partnership with intelligent tools.

Automatic code generation (ACG) eliminates much of the repetitive or boilerplate effort from everyday development, while still placing oversight and adaptation firmly in the hands of practitioners [8]. Importantly, the degree to which AI support is integrated, trusted, and leveraged is strongly conditioned by developer experience.

Industry studies indicate that adoption is now broad-based, crossing from high-tech companies into mainstream software organizations and diverse sectors [5, 9]. This proliferation is often motivated by evidence of substantial time savings, effective distribution of developer effort, and reduction in minor but costly errors [6, 10].

2.2 Impacts, Benefits, and Ongoing Challenges

Empirical studies demonstrate measurable boosts to individual and team productivity, including faster onboarding, streamlined testing, and improved focus on creative or architectural challenges [11, 12]. For example, software practitioners report not only a reduction in routine coding effort but also the ability to explore more alternative solutions within fixed timeframes [7]. Developers often describe AI assistants as 'pair programmers' that supply feedback, code explanations, and cross-language scaffolds.

However, the trajectory of AI-assisted development remains shaped by several risks and limitations. Output accuracy is a persistent concern as suggestions may include fabricated, outdated, or context-incoherent elements [7, 13]. Novice developers, in particular, may be prone to over-trust, risking propagation of errors, while experienced professionals highlight the verification burden and necessity of comprehensive testing before adopting AI-generated code in critical systems.

There is also skepticism regarding long-term impacts on skills development, learning, and maintenance. Some researchers caution that excessive dependence may result in shallow understanding, reduced debugging expertise, or an erosion of consensus-driven knowledge that is historically nurtured through community platforms [5, 14].

2.3 Outlook

Despite these challenges, the consensus in both literature and recent qualitative studies is that AI-assisted tools are becoming ubiquitous and will continue to reshape development practice [15, 16]. The evolving role of prompt engineering, the integration of human-centric review processes, and deliberate design for responsible adoption are all active areas for further research [4, 17]. Future developments may focus on tighter integration into the software delivery pipeline, improvements to contextual awareness, and systems that support both rapid iteration and sustained learning for developers at all levels of expertise. Overall, while AI-assisted software development delivers promising gains in efficiency, quality, and creative freedom, realising its full potential depends on balanced, evidence-based practices that combine technical innovation with professional judgment and continuous skill development. Furthermore, as organisations and individuals refine integration strategies, future research must address how to pair intelligent automation with inclusive, experience-aware practices, ensuring that developers at every stage can leverage AI for growth, efficiency, and responsible innovation.

3 Methodology

This study adopts a qualitative research approach in order to explore how developer experience and expertise influence the adoption and effective use of GenAI-assisted software development tools. The methodology is designed to capture nuanced, context-rich accounts that quantitative surveys alone are unlikely to reveal.

3.1 Research Strategy

A case study approach [18] was chosen as it allows for an in-depth investigation of developer perceptions and behaviors within their real-world contexts. This strategy is particularly suitable for studying emergent phenomena, such as the use of LLM-based code assistants, in environments where the boundaries between technology and workflow are fluid. By focusing on the lived experiences of developers at different career stages, the study seeks to understand not just patterns of tool adoption, but the underlying meanings and practices that inform them.

3.2 Participant Selection

Purposive sampling was used to ensure that participants would be relevant and information-rich for addressing the central research questions [19]. Developers were selected based on (i) their current involvement in code development using GenAI-assisted tools, (ii) representation across junior, mid-level, and senior experience level, and (iii) active employment in software development roles within Sweden. Experience levels were defined primarily by years of professional practice and role responsibilities, reflecting common industry distinctions. The sample comprised 12 participants (Table 1). Recruitment combined outreach to professional networks, online communities, and direct contacts, ensuring feasibility while prioritizing relevance to the study aims.

Table 1. The list of participants.

Anonymized code	Developer role	Years of experience	Experience group
P1	Software Engineer (AI Agents)	2	Junior
P2	Backend Developer (.NET C#)	4	Junior
P3	Mobile Developer (Android/iOS KMM)	3	Junior
P4	C Developer (IoT, Embedded)	16	Senior
P5	C Developer (IoT, Embedded)	19	Senior
P6	Mobile App Developer	5	Mid-level
P7	Senior Software Engineer (Java)	8	Mid-level

(continued)

Table 1. (*continued*)

Anonymized code	Developer role	Years of experience	Experience group
P8	Backend Developer (AWS Cloud)	6	Mid-level
P9	Engineering Manager (Android, iOS)	9	Senior
P10	Mobile Developer (Android)	7	Mid-level
P11	Mobile Developer	4	Junior
P12	Senior Firmware Developer (C, Embedded)	11	Senior

3.3 Data Collection

Semi-structured interviews were employed as the primary data collection method. This format offers both consistency via a core set of guiding questions and flexibility, allowing follow-up questions on topics of particular relevance to each participant [20]. Interviews lasted about 30 min and were conducted via MS Teams, enabling remote participation and maintaining convenience for respondents. All interviews were recorded, transcribed verbatim, and pseudonymized to protect participant anonymity.

3.4 Data Analysis

Thematic analysis was used to interpret the interview data, following the well-known steps described by Braun and Clarke [21]. The coding was mainly deductive, guided by the TAM concepts of perceived usefulness and perceived ease of use. The process stayed open to new patterns that appeared in the data, including themes around trust, the effort required to verify GenAI outputs, and the effects on learning and productivity.

Coding was conducted line-by-line to ensure detailed engagement with the transcripts, with codes systematically grouped into broader categories and themes. Attention was paid to variations and similarities across different experience levels, enabling meaningful comparison. Coding and category development were supported by the open-source qualitative analysis tool Taguette.

3.5 Artefact Development

An additional artefact: the guideline for best practices of GenAI tool adoption by experience level, was produced through systematic semantic mapping of interview statements. Advice, reflections, and practical tips that arose spontaneously during interviews were collated, synthesized, and structured as prescriptive Do's and Don'ts for junior, mid-level, and senior developers.

3.6 Research Quality

Credibility was supported by methodological transparency and participant diversity. Reliability was enhanced by consistent interview protocols and systematic analytic procedures. The focus on Swedish professionals provides contextual coherence but may limit transferability to other cultural or organizational settings. Objectivity and reflexivity were upheld by documenting analytic decisions and maintaining critical awareness of researcher assumptions.

4 Results

The TAM constructs of perceived usefulness and perceived ease of use provide the primary framework for interpreting developers' attitudes. We also examine related themes of productivity, trust and reliability of GenAI outputs, and the role of experience by comparing junior, mid-level and senior developer perspectives, highlighting how seniority shapes each theme.

4.1 Thematic Analysis Process

This study followed Braun and Clarke's six steps: familiarization, line-by-line semantic coding, grouping codes into categories, review and refinement, naming themes, and reporting with experience contrasts. Initial coding was deductive, guided by TAM constructs, while additional elements emerged inductively. Themes were constructed through iterative grouping of codes based on their primary analytical role. While some codes (e.g., faster coding) may conceptually relate to multiple constructs, each was assigned to a dominant theme to preserve clarity of interpretation.

Table 2 depicts the three-layer code system: concise codes distilled from quotes, categories formed by clustering similar codes, and themes mapping those categories into the five analytical lenses. Codes were assigned to a single dominant theme for analytical clarity, although conceptual overlaps between constructs are acknowledged.

Table 2. The results of the thematic analysis.

Codes (Frequency)	Category	Theme
language learning (12) reach code clarity (7) exploring solutions (3)	Learning Support	Perceived Usefulness
natural/easy to use (11) straightforward (8) integrated tools "very easy" (3)	Cognitive Simplicity	Perceived Ease of Use
automated repetitive/boilerplate tasks (12) faster coding (9) shortens task duration (14)	Increased Efficiency	Impact on Productivity & Learning

(continued)

Table 2. (*continued*)

Codes (Frequency)	Category	Theme
fabricated code (9) accuracy issues (9) hidden mistakes (4)	Accuracy & Reliability Issues	Trust, Reliability & Limitations
issues of context awareness (11) not suitable for complex scenario (8) insecure code (4)	Technical Constraints	
over-relying on GenAI (8) unable to judge code (5) AI could "hinder learning" (3)	Novice	Influence of Experience
superior ability to validate (4) better prompts (2) strategic use beyond direct coding (2)	Experienced	

4.2 Perceived Usefulness

Perceived usefulness is the developer judgment that using the GenAI-assisted development tool will improve task outcomes (e.g., speed, quality, clarity, or efficiency) compared to not using it. Simply, "Does this help me get my work done better or faster?".

Across the entire sample, developers agreed that GenAI-assisted tools offer tangible benefits, yet their definitions of value are shaped by where they stand in their professional journey. For juniors, usefulness is closely tied to GenAI's ability to act as a support system, something that helps level the playing field for those with less experience. Many described situations where instead of waiting for a colleague or supervisor, they quickly unblocked themselves by querying a GenAI assistant for coding examples, error explanations, or strategies to break down a task. This ability to access "always-on" support led juniors to feel both more independent and more confident in tackling novel aspects of their jobs. They reported that such tools bolstered their initiative, allowing them to move from confusion to action at a pace not previously possible.

Mid-level developers went further, noting how GenAI changed their entire approach to routine development tasks. They leaned on AI to generate or summarize routine material (e.g. documentation drafts), to produce starting points for refactoring, and to surface other ways of structuring logic. By outsourcing low-value steps, they could stay in flow longer and reserve attention for design trade-offs, debugging complex behaviour, and polishing quality. Usefulness meant compression of setup time and expansion of option space: get three or four plausible approaches in minutes, choose the best fit, refine, and move on. They also noted that GenAI sometimes nudged them toward cleaner or more concise formulations they might not have produced first on their own.

Senior developers offered a more conditional view. They saw GenAI as helpful in clearly bounded, low-risk contexts: quick prototyping scripts for early-stage exploration, proof-of-concept spikes, configuration snippets, data parsing, or accelerating juniors' progress. It was a practical accelerator for exploratory or repetitive edges of their workload, not a blanket solution. The value, in their assessment, depended on how easily they could verify and adapt what was produced. If oversight cost outweighed the saved minutes, they set the tool aside. They framed GenAI output as draft material, raw clay to shape, not trustworthy for architectural decisions, intricate performance paths, or domain-heavy logic. Additional value was indirect: by helping less experienced teammates move faster, AI freed senior time for design, review, and mentoring.

Across all levels, the tool's value rises when tasks are well scoped, outputs are easy to test, and human evaluation remains active; it declines when context is broad, ambiguity is high, or verification overhead grows.

4.3 Perceived Ease of Use

Perceived Ease of Use is the belief that interacting with the GenAI-assisted development tool requires little effort: i.e., it is simple to learn, operate, and integrate into existing workflow without causing friction. In plain terms: "Is this straightforward to use without it getting in my way?".

All participants pointed out that starting with GenAI tools was rarely a challenge; integration into popular integrated development environments (IDEs) and straightforward account setup made first use accessible. Yet, real ease of use: the ability to get genuinely valuable, relevant results, was not distributed evenly. For juniors, the first hurdle was learning how to interact with GenAI: prompt-crafting became an ongoing experiment. Many described extended periods of trial and error, gradually learning which queries yielded productive responses and which resulted in confusion or irrelevance. Some noted frustration, reflecting that early outputs often missed the mark, pushing them to tweak and rephrase questions, sometimes until simply asking a more senior engineer.

With more experience, mid-level developers found that their ability to collaborate with GenAI improved markedly. They appreciated features like context awareness or history within modern AI chat interfaces, using them for interactive refinement rather than "one-shot" queries. Their prior experience let them intuit what "good prompts" looked like, reducing wasted cycles and enabling the AI to act effectively as a co-pilot.

Senior developers tend to define ease of use in terms of efficiency at minimal oversight cost. The mechanics were trivial; what mattered was whether the tool produces something close enough for quick review and adaptation. They kept usage scoped to tasks where that condition held (e.g. utility scripts, boilerplate scaffolds, syntax reminders, exploratory spikes). For larger or architecture-sensitive problems they often skipped GenAI entirely, not because they could not prompt well, but because the expected verification overhead outweighed any drafting speed. This selective pattern meant their subjective ease stayed high; they rarely engaged in long iterative prompt loops to avoid problem types that would trigger them. They also framed a second layer of ease: deciding rapidly "AI or manual?", as part of professional judgement.

All groups agreed that real ease depends on investing in two skills: clear problem articulation and rapid plausibility checking. Without these, users either accept weak output or burn time iterating. With them, even imperfect answers become useful drafts.

4.4 Impact on Productivity and Learning

All interviewees agreed that GenAI tools speed up work, but the nature of the gains and the trade-offs shift with seniority. Juniors linked productivity gains tightly to learning efficiency. By interacting with AI, they could master concepts and code idioms faster than self-study. Tasks that previously stalled on missing knowledge (understanding an unfamiliar API, translating a pattern from one platform to another, writing a first test) now moved forward in the same session. They linked this acceleration directly to learning: immediate explanations and small runnable examples reduced frustration and encouraged experimentation. Yet, the same shortcut sometimes reduced deliberate practice; if they accepted a workable snippet too quickly, they spent less time reasoning through the underlying logic. With GenAI, they could try more tasks and make more mistakes in a "safe" environment, benefitting from immediate, personalized feedback.

Mid-level developers leveraged GenAI for backlog reduction. Daily bottlenecks like documentation, boilerplate, migration scripts, or code review prep became less burdensome. GenAI's potential to offer plausible approaches to problems in minutes allowed mid-levels to compare, choose, or hybridise solutions, promoting a deeper understanding of alternatives. This experimentation was especially valued when learning new APIs, frameworks, or working on unfamiliar codebases. They also reported incidental learning: seeing alternate patterns or concise formulations nudged them toward cleaner code. Overhead appeared when outputs were "almost right", needing edits for naming, edge cases, or integration which they accepted as a manageable cost for overall throughput gains. In some cases, mid-levels reported revitalised enthusiasm for their roles, as GenAI "cut the tedium" and allowed for more creative or rewarding coding work.

Seniors, by contrast, found their productivity increased in early-phase and low-risk activities. For example, spinning up quick proof-of-concept scripts or generating a suite of baseline tests via AI reduced hours to minutes. However, the enhanced pace of generation led to a new kind of work: validation, integration, and "sense-checking" outputs. Seniors described new routines for reviewing GenAI-generated code, adapting it for team standards, and often spending as much time correcting or contextualising as they would coding manually. Productivity thus improved on one front while the overall complexity of quality assurance and architectural stewardship increased.

On learning, the groups diverged. While juniors overwhelmingly credited AI with accelerating skill acquisition, seniors were apprehensive that excessive GenAI reliance could undermine the deeper habits of systems thinking, debugging, and peer learning that keep software maintainable and teams agile.

4.5 Trust, Reliability, and Limitations

However, trust and accuracy concerns tempered the participants' assessments. No group was immune to the issues of trust and reliability regarding outputs. A persistent theme was the need for careful review. Juniors were prone to "over-trusting" GenAI. They are grateful for it, but sometimes unaware of subtle errors, misuse of undocumented APIs, or suggestions that didn't fit. This occasionally resulted in wasted time on bug-hunting or, in one case, a major regression that was only caught in production.

Mid-level developers, with more practical experience, looked more carefully at GenAI suggestions to see if they were correct and matched the project. Some developed lightweight screening habits: skim for naming mismatches, run quick tests, compare against docs, ask for a simplified explanation to reveal hidden assumptions.

Seniors, responsible for overall code quality, treated every GenAI suggestion with professional skepticism. Verification was not considered optional, every proposed change was reviewed, tested, and cross-checked with system-level requirements and security considerations. Seniors often used AI for exploratory or "throwaway" work. For core code, the tools were seen as an assistant or muse, but never as the final arbiter.

All groups agreed on core limitations; the tool doesn't see full project context; sometimes hallucinates APIs or details; can mismatch documentation; and it cannot truly reason about business rules or architectural trade-offs. To mitigate these limitations, developers have built layered safeguards. They write clearer prompts, start with small testable snippets, compare answers with official docs, use peer review for any GenAI-origin code, and discard outputs that need too much fixing. Senior developers go further by enforcing rules like never merging GenAI code without review and marking generated sections for later checks. In practice, trust is granted per task, not granted globally. The tools were treated as rapid draft generators whose reliability rested on human validation, not autonomous authors whose output could bypass scrutiny.

4.6 Influence of Experience

Experience acted as moderator across all themes, shaping prompting quality, screening speed, selective restraint, and mentoring behavior. Juniors leveraged GenAI to compensate for undeveloped mental models: the assistant helped break large tasks into manageable steps and provided explanation that accelerated comprehension. The main vulnerability was over-reliance before acquiring evaluative skills, which leads to accepting code that worked superficially but introduced hidden maintenance or logic issues. When juniors were guided, the tool shifted from shortcut to structured learning aid.

Mid-level developers sat at a balance point. They had enough domain and pattern knowledge to ask targeted questions and discard weak outputs quickly, yet still gained materially from efficiency boosts in scaffolding and exploration. Experience at this stage sharpened task selection: choosing GenAI for repetitive or combinatorial tasks (e.g. generate variants) while manually handling nuanced design decisions. Their growth trajectory benefited when treating GenAI suggestions as comparative material, exploring "why version A is cleaner than B", rather than pure copy sources.

Seniors not only shaped their own AI usage, but actively set the tone for responsible adoption in their teams; they modelled habits for reviewing, questioning, and refining AI outputs, passing down critical skills that AI alone cannot confer.

Senior developers applied professional judgement to constrain use deliberately. Rather than maximising the volume of AI interaction, they optimised return on oversight. They avoided contexts where ambiguity, architectural coupling, or domain rules would trigger long iterative loops. Experience made them sensitive to subtle misfits and positioned them as gatekeepers for quality. Seniors also extended impact beyond their own workflows: modelling verification discipline, defining team norms for tagging or reviewing AI-derived code, and coaching juniors on when manual reasoning matters. Their selective use surfaced a strategic pattern: GenAI as an accelerator for low-risk tasks and a leverage point for team enablement, not a replacement for deep expertise.

Furthermore, experience influenced ethical attitudes. Juniors and mid-levels spoke less about data privacy or intellectual property, while seniors placed strong emphasis on not sharing confidential data with external AIs or relying on opaque black-box outputs for production code. These perspectives highlight that responsible, sustainable GenAI augmentation in development depends as much on maturity and mentorship as on technological proficiency. Table 3 summarizes key findings by experience level.

Table 3. Theme summaries per experience level.

Theme	Junior	Mid-level	Senior
Perceived Usefulness	On-demand help for learning Breaks tasks into smaller steps Boosts confidence; reduces "stuck" time	Removes routine friction Generates alternative implementations Supports refactoring ideas; improves focus	Speeds scripting, POCs, config, lookups Mainly useful in bounded, low-risk areas Indirectly useful by freeing time for higher-level design/review
Perceived Ease of Use	Easy to start; real ease limited by trial-and-error prompting Struggles judging correctness; many early iterations	Smooth IDE integration Clearer prompts reduce cycles Moderate refinement still needed	Interface trivial; ease defined by low verification overhead Rapid "AI vs manual" decision Avoids complex tasks that trigger long review loops
Impact on Productivity and Learning	Faster onboarding Quick concept/API clarification Progress without waiting Risk of shallow understanding if over-used	Compresses setup time; sustains focus; cumulative small gains Incidental learning from cleaner patterns and variants	Faster low-risk drafts (scripts, spikes); Overall gain tempered by review/adaptation workload; Shifts effort to curation

(*continued*)

Table 3. (*continued*)

Theme	Junior	Mid-level	Senior
Trust, Reliability, and Limitations	Hard to spot subtle errors Higher chance of accepting flawed code Verification habits still forming Exposed to hallucinated or misfit suggestions	Employs lightweight screening (naming, quick tests, docs) Adapts near-fit outputs Manages lack of full project context; Handles partial correctness	Systematic scepticism; trusts only narrow, bounded tasks Limits use where oversight cost high; Enforces tagging/review of GenAI-origin code
Influence of Experience	AI compensates for limited internal models Dependence risk without guidance Benefits from learning to verify and manual attempts before using GenAI	Balanced use Enough domain knowledge to prompt/evaluate Still refining follow-ups and adaptation Strategically delegates routine tasks	Selective, strategic adoption Filters tasks to maximize value vs oversight Mentors others; sets norms Reframes role as curator, integrator, coach

5 Guidelines for Optimal and Responsible GenAI Use in Software Development Work

Drawing from the range of perspectives and lessons learned from developers of all levels, this chapter provides a practice-oriented artifact derived from empirical patterns observed across experience levels. Rather than reiterating general guidance, the contribution shows how practices differ across junior, mid-level, and senior developers.

5.1 Universal Best Practices

1. **Always Validate Outputs:** Regardless of the developer's experience level, GenAI-generated code should never be added to production without thorough review and adaptation. This includes understanding, testing, and (where necessary) modifying suggestions to align with team standards and security policies.
2. **Craft Clear, Precise Prompts:** Invest time in requirements. Ambiguous or context-poor prompts often yield irrelevant or inaccurate responses. Include project constraints, language preferences, input/output examples, or underlying rationale.
3. **Iterate for Improvement:** Don't settle for the first result. Try several formulations, compare answers, and ask follow-up questions to triage, elaborate, or refine outputs.
4. **Balance Automation with Oversight:** Leverage GenAI to speed up routine and exploratory work, but never as a shortcut for the deliberate professional thinking that underpins sustainable software quality.

5. **Respect Data Privacy and Compliance:** Avoid exposing sensitive, proprietary, or protected information to public GenAI tools and always check licensing when integrating third-party code snippets.

5.2 Tailored Guidelines for Different Experience Levels

For Junior Developers

1. **Use AI as a Learning Aid, Not a Crutch:** Treat suggestions as starting points for deeper investigation and self-directed practice.
2. **Test and Compare with Multiple Sources:** Verify proposed solutions against official documentation and community resources.
3. **Seek Mentorship and Peer Review:** When unsure, consult with more experienced colleagues, to validate GenAI results and learn better assessment techniques.
4. **Document Learning:** Maintain notes of successful interactions and discovered pitfalls, improving future prompting and review.

For Mid-Level Developers

1. **Automate, but Customise:** Use GenAI for repetitive tasks, "scaffolding" code, and cross-platform adaptation, but always refactor outputs for fit and style.
2. **Explore Alternatives:** Request multiple solution variants and use them to broaden design considerations.
3. **Integrate with Team Workflows:** Ensure that AI-enabled efficiency does not bypass vital team practices such as code review, pair programming, or design critique.
4. **Share Practices:** As confidence grows, help onboard junior developers to effective AI use, passing along lessons about validation and ethical risk.

For Senior Developers

1. **Deploy AI Where Reliable Value is Clear:** Focus use on non-critical, low-risk, or exploratory code. For strategic or foundational parts, privilege manual development and human oversight.
2. **Mentor Responsible AI Use:** Model best practices for review and code quality, encourage open discussion of AI pitfalls, and institutionalize guidelines in onboarding/training.
3. **Champion Transparent Practices:** Cultivate team habits around documenting GenAI-generated contributions, flagging automatically produced code, and tracking rationale for changes.
4. **Proactively Address Legal/Ethical Risks:** Stay informed on intellectual property, bias, and compliance issues arising from GenAI-generated contributions.

6 Discussion

How Experience Shapes Use. The study demonstrates that experience not only shapes GenAI adoption, but also fundamentally remixes what constitutes productive, responsible development in teams. For juniors, GenAI is an opportunity to learn at speed, but they need supportive scaffolding to avoid setting poor habits or missing foundational skills.

Mid-level developers lean on GenAI to cut down repetitive tasks and free time for deeper design or problem analysis, often using suggestions to refine an initial solution. Seniors employ GenAI more selectively, reserving it for scripting, prototyping, broad exploration and summarizing information while relying on their own judgement for architectural and performance-critical work. Across these groups GenAI shifts roles: first a learning aid, then a productivity lever, and later a selective assistant. This progression shows adoption is tied as much to developmental stage as to tool capability.

Changing Developer Skills. Findings indicate that GenAI assistance is shifting core developer work from writing every line to framing, judging and refining generated suggestions. The central skill change is prompt clarity; being able to specify intent, constraints, and context produces more relevant answers and reduces trial-and-error cycles. Alongside this, rapid plausibility screening is becoming routine; experienced developers skim GenAI output for hidden logic errors, misuse of APIs, performance traps or missing edge handling before investing further time. Selective usages also emerged as senior participants deliberately avoid GenAI for domain-critical algorithms, security-sensitive flows or architectural decisions to protect deep understanding and prevent embedding brittle code. Adaptation remains a human task: raw suggestions typically need renaming, decomposition, test coverage and alignment with project idioms to avoid style drift and future maintenance cost. Because models lack full repository and business context, context stitching: connecting implications across modules, legacy constraints and non-functional requirements, still relies on human judgement. A mentoring dimension is strengthening: mid-level and senior developers increasingly narrate review steps and verification heuristics to juniors to reduce over-trust and turn assistance into genuine learning rather than passive copying. Finally, participants highlighted the need to preserve foundational reasoning by periodically solving problems without AI; unchecked reliance risks shallow mental models. The evolving skill profile emphasises clear problem articulation, fast critical evaluation, disciplined task selection, careful adaptation and active coaching.

Theoretical Implications and Model Expansion. The TAM helps frame adoption: perceived usefulness and perceived ease of use remain central. However, other additional factors surfaced repeatedly. Trust influences whether a developer accepts output after a brief check or feels compelled to perform deep validation. Perceived impact on skill development shapes ongoing usage choices; developers weigh short-term acceleration against the risk of weakening core problem-solving habits. Oversight cost which means time spent reviewing, adapting and testing GenAI code, can erode net benefit, especially for senior engineers accountable for quality. Rather than proposing a formal model, this study offers a conceptual extension of TAM, where experience acts as a moderating layer shaping perceived usefulness, ease of use, and trust calibration in GenAI-assisted development contexts.

Organizational Lessons and Implementation. Practically, the results suggest a need for deliberate, differentiated guidance in organizations, in terms of (i) Training and Onboarding: Introduce GenAI-focused modules in both onboarding and ongoing education, emphasizing critical review and prompt engineering, (ii) Workflow Integration: Mandate code review standards for GenAI-produced suggestions, and introduce version control tags to flag auto-generated code, (iii) Team Norms and Documentation:

Encourage developers to document both successes and failures with GenAI. Gather "what works" guidance and feed this back into training, and (iv) Mentorship: Encourage seniors to share their expertise, helping others recognize when and how to question outputs, and to model sceptical engagement as much as rapid throughput.

Ethics and Fairness. Ethical and fairness concerns include the risk that juniors may unknowingly insert flawed logic, that sensitive data could leak through incautious prompts, and that heavy reliance might narrow the breadth of communal learning if private GenAI chats replace public discussions. Uneven access to training or premium tooling could widen productivity gaps across teams or regions. Maintaining human oversight (e.g. mandatory tests, peer review and explicit verification routines) reduces these risks. Clear internal guidelines on data handling, licensing awareness and transparent documentation of GenAI involvement support responsible use.

Limitations. The findings should be interpreted as analytical generalizations rather than statistically generalizable results. They rest on a small, purposive sample of twelve Sweden-based developers; cultural and organizational conditions elsewhere may produce different patterns. Evidence comes from self-reported interviews, which introduces potential perception and recall bias, particularly in reported productivity and learning outcomes.. Furthermore, the study reflects a single point in time while these tools are rapidly evolving; forthcoming model versions and feature upgrades may materially alter observed adoption patterns. Finally, the experience-tiered guideline artefact emerged as a synthesis of coded data and has not been empirically tested for effectiveness; it should be treated as a provisional, practice-informed prompt for further evaluation rather than a validated intervention.

Future Research Directions. Future work should convert the interpretive interview insights into longitudinal, multi-method evidence. Tracking developers over time can show if heavy early reliance on AI affects deeper problem-solving, debugging resilience, architectural thinking, or retention of fundamental syntax compared to moderated use. Comparative studies of newer tool features can examine how evolving capabilities reshape trust calibration, task selection, and verification routines. Deliberate "AI-off" periods can test preservation of problem-solving capacity. The experience-tiered guideline offered here is a provisional synthesis; validating and iterating it in real team settings would help refine industry best practices for responsible, optimal GenAI use.

Contributions. This study contributes in three main ways. First, it provides a fine-grained empirical comparison of GenAI-supported work practices across junior, mid-level and senior developers, showing that adoption is not uniform but structurally shaped by experience. Second, it extends the application of TAM by identifying experience-mediated constructs such as trust calibration, perceived skill impact, and oversight cost that influence sustained use in GenAI-assisted development. Third, it operationalizes these insights into an experience-tiered guideline artefact, linking empirical findings to actionable practices for organizations.

7 Conclusions

AI is redrawing the boundaries of software development work, offering unmatched speed and breadth but demanding careful navigation of quality, trust, and team learning. This study provides detailed, experience-tiered guidance to maximize responsible adoption and fosters a vision of GenAI as a partner, one that amplifies, rather than replaces, human ingenuity, rigor, and judgement.

This study shows that the benefits, risks, and effective use of GenAI in development work are not uniform, but strongly shaped by developer experience. By linking TAM constructs with experience-mediated factors such as trust calibration and oversight cost, the findings provide a more nuanced account of GenAI adoption in practice. The results suggest that responsible use depends less on tool capability and more on how developers evaluate, adapt, and integrate AI-generated outputs within professional workflows.

Disclosure of Interests. The authors have no competing interests to declare that are relevant to the content of this article.

References

1. Yang, J., et al.: Harnessing the power of LLMs in practice: a survey on ChatGPT and beyond. ACM Trans. Knowl. Discov. Data **18**, 1–32 (2024). https://doi.org/10.1145/3649506
2. Da Silva, L., Samhi, J., Khomh, F.: LLMs and Stack Overflow Discussions: Reliability, Impact, and Challenges. https://arxiv.org/abs/2402.08801 (2024)
3. Ebert, C., Louridas, P.: Generative AI for software practitioners. IEEE Softw. **40**, 30–38 (2023)
4. Sergeyuk, A., Golubev, Y., Bryksin, T., Ahmed, I.: Using AI-based coding assistants in practice: State of affairs, perceptions, and ways forward. IST **178**, 107610 (2025)
5. Simaremare, M., Edison, H.: The state of generative AI adoption from software practitioners' perspective: an empirical study. In: 2024 50th Euromicro Conference on Software Engineering and Advanced Applications (SEAA), pp. 106–113. IEEE, Paris, France (2024)
6. Cui, Z., Demirer, M., Jaffe, S., Musolff, L., Peng, S., Salz, T.: The effects of generative AI on high skilled work: evidence from three field experiments with software developers, https://www.ssrn.com/abstract=4945566 (2024). https://doi.org/10.2139/ssrn.4945566
7. Barke, S., James, M.B., Polikarpova, N.: Grounded Copilot: how programmers interact with code-generating models. Proc. ACM Program. Lang. **7**, 85–111 (2023)
8. Raji, E., Ijomah, T.I., Eyieyien, O.G.: Data-driven decision making in agriculture and business: the role of advanced analytics. Comput. Sci. IT Res. J. **5**, 1565–1575 (2024)
9. Alenezi, M., Akour, M.: AI-driven innovations in software engineering: a review of current practices and future directions. Appl. Sci. **15**, 1344 (2025)
10. Bader, J., Seohyun Kim, S., Sifei Luan, F., Chandra, S., Meijer, E.: AI in software engineering at Facebook. IEEE Softw. **38**, 52–61 (2021)
11. Peng, S., Kalliamvakou, E., Cihon, P., Demirer, M.: The impact of AI on developer productivity: evidence from GitHub Copilot. https://arxiv.org/abs/2302.06590 (2023)
12. Rahmaniar, W.: ChatGPT for software development: opportunities and challenges (2023). https://doi.org/10.36227/techrxiv.23993583.v1
13. Siddiq, M.L., Roney, L., Zhang, J., Santos, J.C.S.: Quality assessment of ChatGPT generated code and their use by developers. In: 2024 IEEE/ACM 21st International Conference on Mining Software Repositories (MSR), pp. 152–156 (2024)
14. Storey, M.-A., Singer, L., Cleary, B., Figueira Filho, F., Zagalsky, A.: The (R) Evolution of social media in software engineering. In: Future of Software Engineering Proceedings, pp. 100–116. ACM, Hyderabad, India (2014). https://doi.org/10.1145/2593882.2593887
15. Terragni, V., Roop, P., Blincoe, K.: The Future of Software Engineering in an AI-Driven World. https://arxiv.org/abs/2406.07737 (2024)
16. Şimşek, T., Gülşeni, A.Ç., Arkali Olcay, G.: The future of software development with GenAI: evolving roles of software personas. IEEE Eng. Manag. Rev. **53**, 34–39 (2025)

17. Nguyen-Duc, A., et al.: Generative Artificial Intelligence for Software Engineering -- A Research Agenda. http://arxiv.org/abs/2310.18648 (2023)
18. Yin, R.K.: Case Study Research and Applications: Design and Methods. SAGE, Los Angeles (2018)
19. Bryman, A.: Social Research Methods. Oxford University Press, Oxford; New York (2016)
20. Gubrium, J., Holstein, J., Marvasti, A., McKinney, K.: The SAGE Handbook of Interview Research: The Complexity of the Craft. SAGE Publications, Inc., Oaks, California, United States (2012). https://doi.org/10.4135/9781452218403
21. Braun, V., Clarke, V.: Using thematic analysis in psychology. Qual. Res. Psychol. **3**, 77–101 (2006). https://doi.org/10.1191/1478088706qp063oa

Author Index

R. Matulevičius et al. (Eds.): DB&IS 2026, CCIS 3085, pp. 333–334, 2026.
https://doi.org/10.1007/978-3-032-30863-4

MIX
Papier aus verantwortungsvollen Quellen
Paper from responsible sources
FSC® C105338
www.fsc.org

If you have any concerns about our products,
you can contact us on
ProductSafety@springernature.com

In case Publisher is established outside the EU,
the EU authorized representative is:
Springer Nature Customer Service Center GmbH
Europaplatz 3, 69115 Heidelberg, Germany

Printed by Libri Plureos GmbH
in Hamburg, Germany